CIVIL INTERVIEWING AND INVESTIGATION FOR PARALEGALS

The West Legal Studies Series

Your options keep growing with West Legal Studies

Each year our list continues to offer you more options for every area of the law to meet your course or on-the-job reference requirements. We now have over 140 titles from which to choose in the following areas:

Administrative Law	Family Law
Alternative Dispute Resolution	Federal Taxation
Bankruptcy	Intellectual Property
Business Organizations/Corporations	Introduction to Law
Civil Litigation and Procedure	Introduction to Paralegalism
CLA Exam Preparation	Law Office Management
Client Accounting	Law Office Procedures
Computer in the Law Office	Legal Research, Writing, and Analysis
Constitutional Law	Legal Terminology
Contract Law	Paralegal Employment
Criminal Law and Procedure	Real Estate Law
Document Preparation	Reference Materials
Environmental Law	Torts and Personal Injury Law
Ethics	Will, Trusts, and Estate Administration

You will find unparalleled, practical support

Each text is augmented by instructor and student supplements to ensure the best learning experience possible. We also offer custom publishing and other benefits such as West's Student Achievement Award. In addition, our sales representatives are ready to provide you with dependable service.

We want to hear from you

Our best contributions for improving the quality of our books and instructional materials is feedback from the people who use them. If you have a question, concern, or observation about any of our materials, or you have a product proposal or manuscript, we want to hear from you. Please contact your local representative or write us at the following address:

West Legal Studies, 3 Columbia Circle, P.O. Box 15015, Albany, NY 12212-5015

For additional information point your browser at
www.westlegalstudies.com

West Legal Studies
an imprint of Delmar Publishers

an International Thomson Publishing company I$\widehat{T}$P®

CIVIL INTERVIEWING AND INVESTIGATION

FOR PARALEGALS

Cynthia Bandars Schroeder

WEST LEGAL STUDIES

an International Thomson Publishing company I(T)P®

Albany • Bonn • Boston • Cincinnati • Detroit • London • Madrid
Melbourne • Mexico City • Minneapolis/St. Paul • New York • Pacific Grove
Paris • San Francisco • Singapore • Tokyo • Toronto • Washington

NOTICE TO THE READER

Delmar Staff:

Publisher: Susan Simpfenderfer
Acquisitions Editor: Joan Gill
Developmental Editor: Rhonda Dearborn
Editorial Assistant: Lisa H. Flatley

Marketing Manager: Katherine M.S. Hans
Production Manager: Wendy Troeger
Production Editor: Laurie A. Boyce

COPYRIGHT © 1999
By West Publishing
an imprint of Delmar Publishers
a division of International Thomson Publishing

The ITP logo is a trademark under license.

Printed in the United States of America

For more information, contact:

Delmar Publishers
3 Columbia Circle, Box 15015
Albany, New York 12212-5015

International Thomson Publishing Europe
Berkshire House
168-173 High Holborn
London WC1V 7AA
United Kingdom

Nelson ITP, Australia
102 Dodds Street
South Melbourne
Victoria, 3205 Australia

Nelson Canada
1120 Birchmont Road
Scarborough, Ontario
M1K 5G4, Canada

International Thomson Publishing France
Tour Maine-Montparnasse
33 Avenue du Maine
75755 Paris Cedex 15, France

International Thomson Editores
Seneca 53
Colonia Polanco
11560 Mexico D. F. Mexico

International Thomson Publishing GmbH
Königswinterer Strasse 418
53227 Bonn
Germany

International Thomson Publishing Asia
60 Albert Street
#15-01 Albert Complex
Singapore 189969

International Thomson Publishing Japan
Hirakawa-cho Kyowa Building, 3F
2-2-1 Hirakawa-cho, Chiyoda-ku,
Tokyo 102, Japan

ITE Spain/Paraninfo
Calle Magallanes, 25
28015-Madrid, Espana

1 2 3 4 5 6 7 8 9 10 XXX 03 02 01 00 99 98

Library of Congress Cataloging-in-Publication Data

Schroeder, Cynthia B.
    Civil interviewing and investigation for paralegals / Cynthia B. Schroeder
        p.   cm.
    Includes bibliographical references and index.
    ISBN 0-7668-0244-2
    1. Attorney and client—United States.   2. Interviewing in law
practice—United States.   3. Legal assistants—United States—
Handbooks, manuals, etc.   I. Title.
KF311.Z9S37   1999
317.73'604   do21   98-54453
                                                          CIP

DEDICATION

To my grandmothers,
Anna Bandars and Florence Shanks;

and in loving memory of my grandfathers,
Valdemars Bandars and Howard Shanks

Who taught me the value of hard work
and dedication and who always
made time to encourage me.

SUMMARY CONTENTS

DETAILED CONTENTS

PART II
INVESTIGATION

PREFACE

The goal of this text is to fill the large gap in paralegal education concerning civil investigation and its ties to interviewing. Although several texts are currently available that address interviewing and investigation in a limited capacity, none addresses these topics as they relate to one another, nor do they stand alone. *Civil Interviewing and Investigation for Paralegals* is a comprehensive guide to understanding witnesses and witness interviews, and the practical investigative techniques used for uncovering evidence.

It is the intent of this text to describe how experienced paralegals manage interviewing and investigative tasks. *Civil Interviewing and Investigation for Paralegals* focuses on practical skills while applying the rules that govern civil procedure. The text reviews applicable rules from the Federal Rules of Civil Procedure, the Federal Rules of Evidence, the Freedom of Information Act, and the Fair Debt Collection Practices Act.

ABOUT THE TEXTBOOK

The objective of *Civil Interviewing and Investigation for Paralegals* is to provide students with practical applications and strategies, which are enhanced by actual case studies that enable the student to apply the techniques discussed. In addition, the text provides challenging activities at the conclusion of each chapter.

The book is divided into two sections. The first covers interviewing skills, techniques, and strategies; the second is dedicated to the mechanics of investigation, public and private records, and organization, which are the backbone of every case.

The material in the appendices supports the material in the text and is designed as a desk reference tool for later use. The appendices include a listing of state offices and sample forms referred to throughout the text; and material on basic anatomy, which provides a brief and general look at common medical applications in civil litigation.

This book references many Internet and Web sites. Please be aware that, because of the nature of the Internet, these addresses and sites may have changed since the publication of this book.

CHAPTER FORMAT

The chapters in this text have the following features, which are set apart and used both to instruct and to stimulate the interest of paralegal students.

Chapter Objectives

Every chapter opens with chapter objectives. Students will know what is expected of them as they read each chapter.

Key Terms

Key terms are boldfaced and defined on first use and are collected in the glossary at the end of the book.

Examples

Numerous examples are included in the text, to illustrate concepts and provide practical application of theoretical ideas.

Practical Tips

Specially highlighted practical tips provide students with useful insight and expert advice for practical application of concepts, they relate the discussion to real-world considerations and situations.

Concept Summaries

Each chapter ends with a concept summary that emphasizes the major points in that chapter. These summaries can be a useful tool for students to test their knowledge of the concepts discussed in the chapter.

Activities

Every chapter has activities that challenge the student to immediately apply the concepts found in that chapter. These "real-world" activities allow students to develop the skills necessary to be successful in the workplace.

Case Studies

Each case study provides case excerpts and assigns the students tasks that relate to the chapter material. Students can immediately see how the respective chapter concepts can be applied to a real case, and can begin to sharpen interviewing and investigation skills.

Appendices

The appendices offer basic anatomy material, public office data, and a catalog of forms for use in the workplace as a desk reference.

SUPPORT MATERIAL

Instructor's Manual

This supplement is designed for the instructor who may be unfamiliar with the many concepts of civil investigation and interviewing from a paralegal perspective. The Instructor's Manual provides an outline of the educational objectives and a suggested lecture structure for each chapter. It also contains a chapter-by-chapter listing of vocabulary terms and a list of additional discussion topics and activities. Three separate test banks are furnished as well: the first covers Chapters 1 through 6, the second Chapters 7 through 15, and the third test bank is comprehensive.

Computerized Testing

The test banks found in the Instructor's Manual are also offered in a computerized format on CD-ROM. The platforms supported include Windows™ 3.1 and 95, Windows™NT, and Macintosh. Features include:

- Supporting fill-in-the-blank, matching, multiple-choice, and true/false questions
- Multiple methods of question selection
- Multiple outputs (e.g., print, ASCII, RTF)
- Graphic support (black-and-white)
- Random questioning output
- Special character support

Web Site

Come visit our Web site at www.Westlegalstudies.com, where you will find valuable information specific to this book and other West Legal Studies texts.

Videos

Free to adopters, the following videos are also available from West Legal Studies.

- *The Drama of the Law II: Paralegal Issues*—Includes a series of five separate dramatizations intended to stimulate classroom discussion about issues and problems faced by paralegals on the job. The dramatizations cover intake interview, client confidentiality, the unauthorized practice of law, and other matters.
- *"I Never Said I Was a Lawyer" Ethics Video*—Non-state specific; can be used in all paralegal programs. It employs hypothetical scenarios to give students experience dealing with ethical dilemmas.
- *The Making of a Case*—Follows a case from the court system to the law library shelf.

ACKNOWLEDGMENTS

I extend special thanks to the many reviewers and editors who helped make this text possible, especially: Janice Hoover, Lynne N. Segal, Joan Gill, Elizabeth Hannon, and Rhonda Dearborn. A special word of thanks also to William Statsky, who allowed me to refer to his legal thesaurus and dictionary throughout this text; and to Debra Orlik, for her encouragement and knowledge of publishing.

Thanks to the following reviewers for their time and helpful suggestions:

Bernadette Agretsi
Gannon University

Joe Atkins
Inver Hills Community College

Teresa Conaway
Pellissippi State Technical
Community College

Leslie McKesson
Western Peidmont Community
College

Constance Ford Mungle
OCU Legal Assistant Program

Kathryn L. Myers
St. Mary of the Woods College

Edward C. O'Boyle
Gwinnett College of Business

Gerald Rogers
Front Range Community College

Sandra Smales
Quincy College

Finally, I must thank my mother for her help; and my husband, John, and sons, Nicholas and Benjamin, for their neverending support and understanding. Thank you.

INTERVIEWING

CHAPTER

1

INTERVIEWING: UNDERSTANDING THE BASICS

OBJECTIVES   After completing this chapter, you will know:

- Interviewing is an interactional communication process.
- The interviewer's role may vary between passive and aggressive.
- Attitude is key to the success of an interview.

- There are many variables in the interviewing process, including two parties, role exchange, perceptions, verbal and nonverbal interactions, listening and feedback, and evaluations.
- Scheduling the interview requires the interviewer to consider date and time, territory, and distractions.

INTRODUCTION

The act of interviewing often causes people as much stress and fear as does public speaking. Because of this fear, some inexperienced interviewers may see their role in conducting an interview as authoritative rather than facilitative. Preconceived ideas about interviewing inhibit the tasks of preparing for, setting up, and conducting an interview, and often create feelings of near-panic. By developing a better understanding of the interviewing process, a person increases his or her chances of conducting a more relaxed and successful interview.

DEFINING INTERVIEW

An **interview** is a communication process between two parties in which at least one of those parties has a predetermined purpose for the communication. An interview is also interactional, meaning that the parties exchange roles, responsibilities, and information during their time together.

A successful interviewer knows the difference between a speech and an interview. When giving a speech, one has an audience; in an interview, speaking time is shared. This does not mean, however, that both parties have equal speaking time. Interviewees do most of the talking. In some interviews this may result in a 70/30 ratio in favor of the interviewee; in other circumstances it may be less.

There are many types of interviews serving many different purposes. Some of them include:

- *Information-giving interviews,* used for:
  - training, coaching, or instruction
  - orientation
  - briefings
- *Information-gathering interviews,* used for:
  - surveys
  - polls
  - research
  - investigations
- *Selection interviews,* used for:
  - screening and placement

- *Problem-solving interviews,* used for:
  - discussing shared problems
  - receiving solutions
- *Persuasion interviews,* used for:
  - selling products and/or services
  - recruiting people

Interviews are dynamic and consist of many ingredients. They include verbal and nonverbal messages, assumptions, feedback, expectations, and evaluations.

Two Parties Create an Interview

Two parties are involved in any interview—but this does not necessarily mean two persons. For instance, an attorney and a paralegal may interview a client. If more than two parties are involved, the encounter ceases to be an interview and becomes a small group meeting.

Each person who takes part in the interview brings his or her own unique background and perspective, influenced by culture, environment, education, and experiences, to the interview. The parties are also motivated by different things and bring with them varying expectations and needs. It is the interviewer's responsibility to understand the differences and similarities between the parties and accentuate them to help facilitate the interview. Inevitably, both parties will share some likenesses, as well as having some differences, and these similarities enhance the quality of the interaction (see Figure 1-1). In contrast, the differences may inhibit the interview. Each interview is unique.

Figure 1-1
Parties to an interview

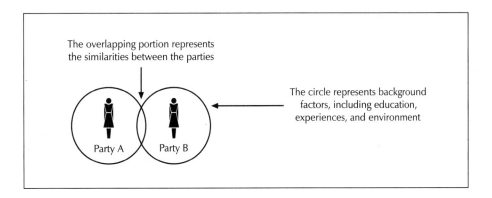

INTERVIEWING ROLES

The roles played by the interviewer and the interviewee often vary during the course of the interview. Both parties will speak and listen, and ask and answer questions. Because the nature of the interview is interactive, neither party should dominate or be able to ignore the process. However, the amount of time a party spends in any one role will depend on the goals the interviewer has pre-determined for the interview and the approach taken to achieve those goals.

There are two fundamental approaches the interviewer may use to manage the interview: the passive approach (nondirective), or the aggressive (directive) approach. A combination is often necessary. Regardless, the interviewer must use these approaches to move the interview forward. Before an interviewer can determine the approach to use, she must evaluate the interviewee, the subject matter of the interview, and her attitude toward the interview.

Attitudes

The interviewer *must* understand that her attitude is one of the most influential components of the interviewing process. She must project a positive image during the interview, always adjusting her demeanor to harmonize with the general mood of the interviewee. An interviewer's image should be one of empathy, impartiality, sincerity, sympathy, objectivity, and firmness. She must be disciplined and observe the following guidelines:

- Subdue personal prejudices
- Keep an open mind; be receptive to all information
- Evaluate each development on its own merit
- Do not try to impress the interviewee
- Be honest
- Do not underestimate the intelligence of the interviewee
- Do not show contempt for the interviewee or her responses
- Do not make promises that you cannot keep
- Be fair
- Avoid body language that expresses personal nervousness
- Possess a pure motivation for truth
- Do not raise your voice
- Do not antagonize the interviewee
- Be a good listener
- Be patient
- Be gentle
- Be persistent
- Be empathetic
- Be professional

Once the interviewer has reviewed these guidelines and adjusted her attitude, she must consider the characteristics of each of the available approaches and determine which best fits the goals of the interview and the temperament of the interviewee.

Passive Role

When employing a passive approach, the interviewer allows the interviewee to control many aspects of the interview, including subject matter, formality, and pace. The passive approach is commonly called a **nondirective interview**. The questions used in the interview are usually open-ended and neutral, permitting the interviewee to respond in almost any way he or she desires. The passive role is frequently used in problem-solving and counseling interviews. The advantages and disadvantages of this approach are outlined in the accompanying table.

Advantages	Disadvantages
Allows interviewer more flexibility	Is time-consuming
Allows interviewer to adapt to each interviewee	May complicate the relationship between the parties
Allows interviewer to probe more deeply into topics	Interviewer may lose control of the interview

The following is a sample dialogue using the passive role:

Interviewer: How did you come to work for ABC Insurance Company?

Answer: I worked at ABC during college and found that I enjoyed writing contracts and researching claims.

Interviewer: Tell me about the contract you wrote for Wilson Crane Company.

Answer: I began drafting portions of the contract in June 1998 and completed it in August 1998. I based my calculations for the premiums on data provided by Mrs. Wilson and checked them against her previous insurance carrier's contracts.

Aggressive Role

The aggressive role requires the interviewer to establish the goals and purpose of the interview at the outset of the interview. She also controls the pace, formality, and subject matter of the interview. An aggressive approach is commonly called a **directive interview**. To employ this approach, the interviewer uses primarily closed or narrow questions, most of which require only short or direct answers. If the interviewee has a strong personality, he or she may attempt to take control of the interview, but the interviewer must work to stay in control. Information-giving and information-gathering interviews, like those used in an investigation, commonly employ the aggressive role. The advantages and disadvantages of this approach are summarized in the accompanying table.

Advantages	Disadvantages
Easy style to learn	Very rigid
Easy to maintain control	Limits interviewer in both variety and depth of subject matter
Takes less time	May hinder interviewee's motivation to participate

The following is a sample dialogue using the aggressive role:

Interviewer: You are currently employed by ABC Insurance Company?

Answer: Yes, I am.

Interviewer: How long have you been with the company?

Answer: Four years, including my time during college.

Interviewer: Did you write the contract for Wilson Construction?

Combining Passive and Aggressive Roles

Realistically, interviewers will usually use a combination of the aggressive and passive approaches during the course of an interview, to minimize the rigidity of the aggressive role and gain some control over the interviewee during passive periods. To facilitate a switch during the interview, the interviewer decides which role best suits a particular topic or subject matter and makes the transition when introducing that topic. For instance, an interviewer may take a passive role when attempting to define an interviewee's general knowledge of data on a topic, then switch to an aggressive role when directing the interviewee into specific details of an event related to the topic.

PERCEPTIONS

Both the interviewer and the interviewee must be aware that they bring perceptions of self, as well as of the other party, into the interview. As the interview progresses, perceptions may change, but they are always present. Understanding the concept of perceptions assists the interviewer in managing both personal perceptions and the perceptions of the interviewee. See Figure 1-2.

The Interviewer

The most basic concept the interviewer must know about her self-perceptions is that they influence the messages she sends and receives. Influences on perceptions include life experiences, beliefs, attitudes, values, and accomplishments. Some of these influences create negative responses and reactions, whereas others are very positive. In the scheme of the interview, the interviewer will find

Figure 1-2
Perceptions and
interactions

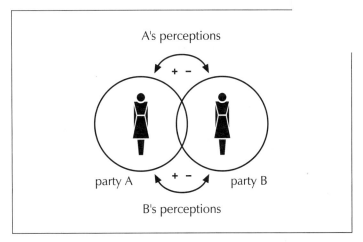

that self-perceptions contribute to both successes and failures. By identifying these perceptions, the interviewer can better understand herself and thus conduct interviews using her best skills and talents.

The Interviewee

The interviewer must recognize that she will also develop perceptions of the interviewee before, during, and after the interview. These perceptions and opinions will be influenced by the interviewee's status, educational background, financial background, manner of dress and speech, and other surface characteristics. They may also be influenced by deeper traits, including age, associations, religious beliefs, and family background. As perceptions change, so may the course of the interview. The interviewer must avoid allowing her perceptions to bias her approach to an interview, because perceptions are not always reliable.

INTERACTIONS

There are three steps or degrees in the interactions between the interviewer and the interviewee, each representing a more sophisticated and personal level of communication. These consist of verbal and nonverbal messages and the expression of emotions (or lack thereof).

Degrees of Interaction

The three steps or degrees of interaction between the interviewer and interviewee represent a variety of commitments and stages of intimacy. See Figure 1-3.

Step 1. The communication that takes place in this step is always found in the opening of the interview, where safe and easy topics are discussed, and is

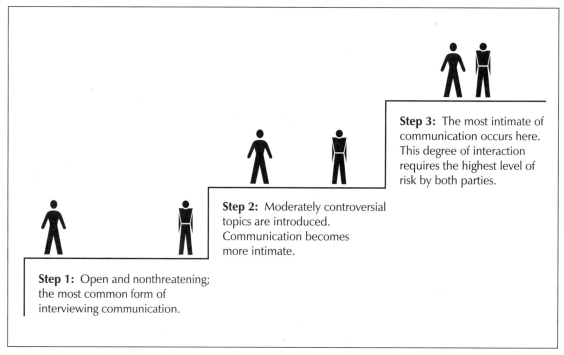

Step 3: The most intimate of communication occurs here. This degree of interaction requires the highest level of risk by both parties.

Step 2: Moderately controversial topics are introduced. Communication becomes more intimate.

Step 1: Open and nonthreatening; the most common form of interviewing communication.

Figure 1-3 Degrees of interaction

used throughout the interview to lighten the interaction when discussing difficult topics. During this step the interviewer and interviewee begin evaluating each other and developing perceptions of each other. Step one may last several minutes or longer, depending on the interviewer and the level of introductory data needed.

Step 2. As the interviewer moves to the next level, she begins probing into attitudes, feelings, and behaviors. The level of risk taken by the interviewee begins to grow at this point in the communication. Interactions during step two are less frequent and require the interviewer to use skillful questioning. The length of interaction at step two also varies and may increase and decrease during the interview. It demonstrates the development of a relationship between the interviewer and interviewee, which is why there is fluctuation. As difficult subjects are discussed, the relationship may weaken, causing the interviewer to need to return to step one briefly. As the relationship builds again, the interviewer may return to step two.

Step 3. The final level of interaction occurs at step three. Only the most difficult, sensitive, and intimate questions and responses happen here. To effectively move to step three, the interviewer must establish a solid relationship with the interviewee based on trust. For the interviewer to be truly successful in any interview, she must motivate the interviewee to move to step three; otherwise, she will never gain access to the interviewee's feelings or insights.

Communication in the interview setting is complicated, dealing as it does with perceptions and feelings. To effectively move an interviewee through the three steps of interaction, the interviewer must:

- Provide clear expectations and avoid tricking or deceiving the interviewee. (Avoid the appearance of deception by clearly stating who your client is and what you need from the interviewee.)
- Demonstrate genuine interest in the interviewee.
- Find a way to spark the interviewee's interest in the topics, the interviewer, and the interview.
- Develop a trust relationship with the interviewee.
- Provide both physical and psychological rewards for the interviewee (compensation for lost wages, recognition, and/or praise).

An interviewer must deal with both verbal and nonverbal messages, and understanding these components enables her to navigate successfully through the steps.

Verbal Communication

The use of spoken language is often the reason many miscommunications occur. Even the simplest words in the English language can mean different things to different people, because there are so many meanings of and connotations for "common" words. Jargon and slang created for specific organizations and professions has only further complicated the process of verbal communication. For example, *AAA* may be taken to mean "American Automobile Association" by many people, but in the medical field it means "abdominal aortic aneurysm." Also, many words in English sound alike yet mean very different things. Consider the examples in the accompanying table.[1]

Word	Meanings
Fair	Good, middle, average, between, indifferent, medium, normal, neutral, moderate, standard, usual
Manipulating	Cunning, deceptive, tricky, handle, use, undermine
Run	Race, lope, speed, leak, creep, trot, smuggle, flow, score, route

These are just a few examples of words that challenge interviewing communication and daily conversation as well. Both use and understanding of words are affected by gender, age, culture, geography, and experiences. An effective interviewer acknowledges these complexities and strives to overcome them with knowledge and strategy. Some strategies to help manage verbal communication problems are:

- Carefully choose the words used to phrase questions, keeping in mind how the interviewee may interpret them.
- Expand your vocabulary to help manage the use of new and often slangy words and meanings.
- Stay aware of changes in words and their uses.
- Use listening techniques to determine the context in which certain words are used.
- Strive to learn the jargon and acronyms of different groups and organizations.
- Rename euphemisms.
- Be sensitive of "labeling" words that antagonize, embarrass, or offend others.
- Be as precise as possible.
- Never assume that another person is using a term in the same way or context as you would without verifying that determination.

Nonverbal Communication

Defining the term *nonverbal communication* is required for the interviewer to understand how it affects interviewing, but doing so is not easy. Randall Harrison provides this explanation:

> The term "nonverbal communication" has been applied to a broad range of phenomena: everything from facial expression and gesture to fashion and status symbol, from dance and drama to music and mime, from the flow of affect to the flow of traffic, from the territoriality of animals to the protocol of diplomats, from extrasensory perception to analog computers, and from the rhetoric of violence to the rhetoric of topless dancers.[2]

For the purpose of this text, *nonverbal communication* means any part of communicative expression outside of the words used to verbalize a response or question—in other words, all physical expression, voice inflections, and other expressive methods of conveying feelings or information.

Some professionals in the field of communication believe that 65 to 95 percent of all communication is conveyed through nonverbal acts, like handshakes, posture, dress, eye contact, and voice inflection.[3] For the interviewer, the messages sent through nonverbal communication are particularly important, because such communication is very intimate and determines the quality or credibility of the interviewee and his or her responses.

There are many common nonverbal cues, and most of these are recognized by professionals in the industry as having a particular meaning. The accompanying table is a list of some of these behaviors and their meanings. However,

be cautious about assuming the applicability of these meanings
situation—no one definition of behavior can always be true.

Action	Meaning
Poor eye contact	Party has something to hide, is a weak interviewee, is insecure.
Limp handshake	Timidity, lack of self-confidence, embarrassment.
Serious facial expression	Sincerity, misunderstanding, agitation, bewilderment, disagreement, confusion.
Touching other party's arm	Understanding, compassion, a sense of relationship, sympathy.
Rate of speaking: Fast Slow Fast and breathless Halting voice	 Urgency, lack of interest. Lack of preparation, gravity of situation. Nervousness. Indecision.
Silence	Encouraging the party to speak, plenty of time for the communication, agreement.
Combination behaviors: Leaning forward, good eye contact, nodding of the head, and serious facial expression	 Interested in the other party and the things he or she is saying.
Fidgeting, crossing and uncrossing the legs, sitting rigidly, looking down, furrowing the brow, using a high pitched voice	Anxiety, fear, and/or agitation.
Drooping body, frowning, speaking slowly	Sadness, resignation, anticipated failure or discipline.
Leaning back, staring, raising eyebrows, shaking head	Disagreement, anger, disgust.
Nodding head yes while answering no	May indicate that respondent is not telling the truth.

Along with these physical aspects, the interviewer must be observant of the dress and appearance of both herself and the interviewee. Appropriate clothing should be worn to the interview. An interviewer must gauge her apparel by the interviewee; she should not wear a suit to interview a farmer in the field nor overalls to meet with an advertising executive in New York City. Clothes should always fit well and be clean and neatly pressed.

Nonverbal communication deals primarily with feelings, whether or not they are intentionally expressed. As the interviewer becomes more attuned to nonverbal communication, she will be better able to identify the feelings behind the behaviors.

Expressed and Unexpressed Emotions

The expression of feelings is a key function in many interviews and a big part of the interaction between the interviewer and interviewee. An interviewee may or may not express the emotions that actually influenced her perception of the events about which she is speaking. When conducting the interview, the interviewer must take adequate time to observe the interviewee's emotional state, to better understand her. The most efficient means of doing this is by offering positive feedback during the interview. For instance, if the interviewee has witnessed a car accident and claims to feel "out of it," the interviewer may offer a response that affirms the statement and clearly defines the feeling. Consider this response to the "out of it" witness:

EXAMPLE

Interviewer: I'm sure it was quite overwhelming to see such an event. Am I understanding you correctly if I say you were confused and temporarily paralyzed after witnessing the event?

Unexpressed Emotions An interviewee's emotions and feelings are not always verbalized during the interview. In some cases, recognizing the interviewee's feelings is very difficult. Occasionally she will give emotionally charged responses with no expression of emotion or feeling at all. When dealing with an interviewee who neglects her feelings during the interview, the interviewer must spend a substantial amount of time building a trust relationship, which enhances the interaction and encourages the interviewee to open up.

It often becomes apparent early in the interview when an interviewee is neglecting or hiding her feelings. Because most people desire to express their feelings when participating in an interview, the interviewer must be leery of the interviewee who does not offer any emotional or subjective information.

Expressing Emotions Active listening enables an interviewer to discover the feelings of a nonemotional interviewee. Develop a common bond with the interviewee by continually affirming his responses; once a relationship has been developed, it is possible to draw on personal data, learned from the interviewee during step one, to regularly reconnect to him. Connecting to the interviewee on a nonthreatening level reassures him that expressing emotion is normal and acceptable, especially when he is discussing sensitive or difficult information.

EXAMPLE ————————————————————

A paralegal is conducting an interview with a witness who has personal knowledge of a white-collar crime. The crime involved a man named Mr. Bill, an employee of a nursery, who stole large sums of money and goods from the nursery's elderly owner. The interviewee, who is a young man, offers details of the theft with no emotional acknowledgment of the acts.

Answer: Mr. Bill took several large maple trees from the nursery and planted them in his mother's yard. He did not pay for the trees. Mr. Bill also paid his sister $35 an hour to water the flowers in the greenhouse. She watered them twice, but was paid for watering fourteen times.

Interviewer: Then what happened?

Answer: Mr. Bill told me that he would continue to take the extra money and goods as long as he could. Mr. Bill worked for the nursery through June 1998, then Mr. Mike, the owner, fired him for stealing.

At this point in the interview, it becomes clear that the interviewee does not intend to express any feelings about the actions of Mr. Bill, Mr. Bill's sister, or Mr. Mike the owner. The paralegal knows that Mr. Bill's actions were so blatant that most people would have some emotional reaction to them; therefore, the paralegal works with the witness to uncover those feelings by using affirmative feedback and active listening. Consider these responses by the paralegal.

EXAMPLE ————————————————————

Interviewer: (1) So Mr. Bill told you he would take what did not belong to him as long as he could?
   (2) Do you think Mr. Bill knew how old Mr. Mike was and that Mr. Mike depended on the proceeds from the nursery to pay his medical bills?
   (3) How much do you believe the maple trees were worth?
   (4) How much do you get paid per hour for your work at the nursery?

All of these questions engage the interviewee's feelings and motivate him to associate the details of his story with his feelings, because the questions associate objective responses, like the cost of maple trees and the interviewee's salary, with subjective responses, such as the injustice of stealing.

Additionally, the interviewer expresses empathy with the interviewee by using voice inflection when asking questions. Imagine the impact of the first question: "So, Mr. Bill *told you* he would take what did not belong to him as long as he could?" By emphasizing "told you," the paralegal expresses both disbelief at Mr. Bill's arrogance and empathy for the witness. Clearly, an interviewee who has valuable yet damaging information will have some feelings about knowing and sharing the information. When this question is asked with an empathetic voice inflection, the interviewee is given permission to express his feelings.

Empathy is also a key component in active listening, and it is important for the interviewer to develop listening skills that encourage the interviewee to share information.

LISTENING SKILLS

Listening during the interview involves both nonverbal and verbal communication. The interviewer must respond verbally and nonverbally while listening to an interviewee, to validate and encourage her to continue speaking. Good listening skills are essential if the interview is to be successful.

Listening strategies are divided into two categories, active and passive listening; both require skill and practice. A description of these techniques suggests how and why an interviewer uses active and passive listening.

Active Listening

Listening, whether active or passive, affirms to the interviewee that he is being heard and that his responses are important. **Active listening** is the process of hearing what is said and repeating that information to the interviewee. During active listening, the interviewer uses **affirmative feedback** to reassure the interviewee that he is being understood. Affirmative feedback is simply a positive response, by the interviewer, acknowledging the specifics of the interviewee's responses. An interviewer must strive to make statements to the interviewee that reflect the content of the information given and the feeling with which the information was given.

Purpose   The purpose of using active listening is to gain information from the interviewee and to help relieve any emotional stress she experiences during the interview. One of the biggest hurdles an interviewer faces is an interviewee's hesitancy to speak because of the emotional stress of the interview. Affirmative feedback and empathy during active listening are critical to obtain the interviewee's full cooperation.

When using active listening, the interviewer creates an open and safe environment for the interviewee to respond in. Here are some guidelines for using affirmative feedback and active listening:

- Listen attentively to each response before asking the next question.
- Be patient, especially when the interviewee is offering boring or unrelated information.
- Clarify what has been said: "That address was 1412 Main Street?"

- Ask for specifics: "What is the company policy regarding worker's compensation claims?"
- Identify feelings: "What is your attitude about age discrimination?"

Empathy   Empathy is one of the most important feelings the interviewer can express during the interview, especially during active listening. When empathy and active listening are combined, the interviewee perceives the interviewer as nonjudgmental. A passive response, in contrast, tends to be interpreted as judgmental, as it does nothing more than acknowledge the receipt of information ("Oh, I see."). Here are some guidelines for using empathy:

- Do not interrupt the interviewee.
- Do not react quickly to topics that create controversy.
- Use candor in all your responses.
- Do not try to comfort the interviewee (for example, by exclaiming, "things will be all right").
- Listen with the intent of providing direction.
- Try to remain nonjudgmental.

Evaluation   While using active listening, the interviewer can evaluate the interviewee's responses for content and emotion. Accumulating data, however, is far easier than identifying and listing an interviewee's feelings. An interviewee's feelings are revealed by the responses she gives to the interviewer's questions.

EXAMPLE

When asked to explain her feelings immediately after witnessing an accident, an interviewee may say, "I was panicked and felt out of it." Such an expression of feeling is vague and poorly articulated, so close attention must be given to better defining these feelings. If an interviewee is "out of it," does that mean she was injured during the accident and lost consciousness? Does it mean she had been drinking before she saw the accident? The interviewer must draw out more definite responses that better describe the interviewee's feelings.

Identifying feelings helps the interviewer identify weaknesses and strengths in the responses. The following are guidelines for evaluation:

- Listen to the *whole* story or response before making a judgment about the data or emotions.
- Closely observe both verbal and nonverbal communication.
- Ask for clarification when necessary.
- Avoid becoming defensive, and do not overreact.
- Refrain from making decisions about the data or emotions until the interview is completed.

Passive Listening

Passive listening, exemplified by silence, is used in all interviews. The word *passive* is defined as being without response to a person or situation that would normally cause expressions of emotion or feeling. An interviewee provides a response with the expectation that the interviewer will provide feedback and show understanding. A passive interviewing style requires self-control and discipline, so that the interviewer avoids speaking but acknowledges the interviewee with eye contact and body language.

Silence   It is common for an interviewee to require quiet to reflect on his thoughts. An interviewer may feel uncomfortable allowing such silence, for fear that the interviewee will lose his train of thought, but this perception is rarely correct. The interviewee uses the silence of a pause to focus on difficult topics or questions.

Interviewers must resist the temptation to interrupt a silence if passive listening is to be successful. Acting precipitously, interrupting an interviewee's silence, and firing off questions rapidly not only destroys the interviewee's concentration, but also damages any trust relationship that has been built between the interviewer and the interviewee. This damage may be difficult to repair.

Passive Questioning   Passive listening uses open-ended questions, with the intent of gathering large amounts of information by encouraging the interviewee to continue thinking and talking without interruption. Often the "thinking" and "talking" portion requires the interviewee to stop frequently and silently review what she has said and what she remembers. During this process, the interviewer may need to acknowledge the interviewee's responses by making a brief, nonintrusive comment such as, "I see." Noncommittal acknowledgments encourage the interviewee by affirming that the interviewer is listening.

Passive listening techniques—silence, open-ended questions, and noncommittal acknowledgments—give the interviewee room to freely express herself but do not offer the same affirming encouragement that active listening does.

EVALUATIONS

Evaluation is used during and after the interview to qualify the credibility of the interviewee and his responses. Developing the skills to evaluate and qualify credibility is one of the most essential tasks of interviewing.

Credibility is influenced by clarity, consistency of responses, personal credibility, competency, knowledge, and status. Virtually every interviewee must be qualified, evaluated, and classified according to: (1) his or her degree of credibility; (2) the amount of support he or she offers the interviewer's goals for the interview; and (3) his or her degree of persuasiveness. Proficiency in identifying these characteristics is not only important but mandatory.

The Interviewee's Credibility

Credible means qualified to be believed or deserving of credit; it applies to both persons and things. Generally, a person who is credible commands belief. Credibility is largely circumstantial, as others must make an inference as to the believability of the responses based on the interviewee's character and demeanor. This is particularly true in journalistic, probing, and persuasive interviews, all of which are commonly used in legal practice.

Influencing Elements Many elements influence the credibility of an interviewee and of her responses. Each piece of the credibility puzzle, which consists of personal characteristics and segments of the story, is interrelated. Therefore, the interviewer must strive to identify the characteristics of the interviewee and her responses and balance them. The following are brief descriptions of the credibility components used to evaluate interviewees and their responses.

Knowledge Level and Status The interviewer will rely on her personal or life experiences to begin evaluating the knowledge level and status of an interviewee. Though not scientific, this method is commonplace, and conclusions can quickly be drawn regarding the interviewee's knowledge of the many subjects to be discussed in the interview.

The interviewer will look for both the interviewee's actual knowledge and his perceived knowledge. Remember, perceptions are not always trustworthy, and unfounded conclusions can be drawn.

Status and knowledge work together to increase credibility, in very similar ways. Society in general fosters the belief that a person is more credible, likable, and worthy of attention when he or she is of high status. Status in turn is often conferred by one's knowledge or perceived knowledge: the college professor enjoys a higher status than the person who cuts the grass on campus; the police detective enjoys a higher status than the officer who writes tickets for parking violations; and so on. Status plagues society and hinders interviews. Yet it is a critical element in establishing an interviewee's credibility.

Motive Motive is an element of personal credibility that greatly affects the value of an interviewee's statements. When evaluating motive, try to understand who the person is, her relationship to the interview, and why she is participating.

Appearance A person's personality is often expressed in his attire and mannerisms. The interviewee's appearance can have a more immediate impact on her audience or interviewer than any other credibility element. Appearance includes clothing, vocabulary, and body language. Generally, a person's appearance affects others' perception of him or her in every setting. In the legal setting, a witness (or client) must strive to make the best possible initial impression on the jury, thereby gaining or enhancing credibility with the jurors.

Mannerisms are deeply intertwined with physical appearance and should also be closely observed. A person is often judged not only by the clothes she wears, but also by how she wears them, when she wears them, and for what reasons she wears them. The same is true with what is said. Demeanor is critical to credibility and can easily be misinterpreted. Immediate decisions on credibility are often based on how quickly the interviewee answers a question, the facial expressions he makes while answering, and on his general body language.

The Credibility of the Interviewee's Responses

Credibility is a primary factor in all aspects of life, from closing a business deal to asking for a date, to telling a story. The interviewer must become proficient at evaluating interviewees and their responses. Specific features by which responses are evaluated include facts, passion, societal issues, clarity, and consistency.

How is the review done? Generally, it begins with the interviewer's inferences regarding the believability of the response, stemming from the evaluation previously made of the interviewee personally. The credibility of a response is circumstantial, so the interviewer must identify the overall purpose of the interviewee's participation in the interview and the data provided. She then starts to probe the facts.

Facts Appraisal of the facts provided in an interview begins when the interviewer creates a mental image of the story told. Separate fact from opinion—there is a danger in allowing vague pictures to be drawn from opinions. Opinions are subjective and vary in meaning, so the interviewer must question the interviewee to uncover facts and clarify the responses.

A fact evaluation can be made when the interviewee provides enough detail, without opinion, to draw a clear picture of an event. In some cases an overeager interviewee may have ulterior motives for participating, and may provide so many details that the responses are not believable. Ideally, the most believable responses have enough detail to define an event.

Passion The passion or emotion with which responses are given greatly affects their believability. A story told with passion, regardless of other credibility problems that may exist, will always be more believable. Passion, however, is not always persuasive in a positive way. For example, the passion of a hostile witness is very powerful—and often damaging precisely because he is so passionate in his opposition. A paralegal should not underestimate the use of hostile data and stories.

Consider the following example of a woman telling a passionate version of her experience at a local hospital:

EXAMPLE ──────────────────────────────────────

During the trial of *Jones v. Memorial Hospital,* which involved an injury Mrs. Jones suffered when she fell from her bed after surgery, Mrs. Jones told the jury the following story:

On January 12, 1998, I underwent surgery for a bleeding ulcer. At my age, 75, the idea of surgery was horrifying. After all, who would take care of my crippled husband if I died? *[Mrs. Jones begins to cry.]*

> The surgery was conducted at 10:30 that morning and by 2:00 that afternoon the nurse told me I could get up and go to the bathroom with her help. I didn't want to go but she insisted that it would be good for me and that she would help me so I wouldn't fall down. *[Regaining her composure, Mrs. Jones continues.]* The nurse took hold of my arm and moved my IV pole so I could walk. I swung my legs around and slid to the edge of the bed. The nurse told me she would count to three and then help me onto my feet. The nurse counted to three and I stood up but she did not have a good hold of me and I fell. *[Mrs. Jones starts crying again.]*
>
> I broke my hip from that fall and wasn't able to walk for three months. My husband had to go to a nursing home until I could walk again. This has been the most horrible ordeal of my life!

Mrs. Jones's story is quite passionate and very affecting. After hearing this, the jury may even forget the nurse's testimony that Mrs. Jones insisted that she did not want help getting out of bed and that she wanted to use a walker to go to the bathroom. There may have been many credibility problems with Mrs. Jones's story, and the defendant's legal team may have pointed out each credibility problem for the jury to evaluate before her testimony. However, the passion with which Mrs. Jones delivered her story may still alter the jury's decision.

Societal Issues   Responses and the credibility of those responses are influenced by many factors, including societal issues and the passions of those who listen to the story. An interviewer must be aware of factors that can influence the projected audience—primarily the presence of cultural and/or political issues within the subjects of the interview.

There are endless categories of cultural and political issues that affect the credibility of an interviewee's responses and overall story. Some societal issues are apparent from the onset of the interview; for example, sexual harassment, job discrimination, and racial violence are all issues that require the interviewer to pay particularly close attention to cultural/political concerns. Other issues, however, are not so obvious. Every story must be examined for overtones of peripheral or underlying subjects. For instance, the example used to describe passion may be burdened by underlying issues such as Medicare injustice, cruelty to the elderly, or insurance fraud.

Those who use data from an interview will bring with them life experiences that they may consciously or subconsciously apply to the facts and stories told. Remember, the credibility of a story is gauged by the perceptions of others, too. Unlike the criteria used to appraise details, evaluation of the effect of these factors may be quite subjective.

Clarity and Consistency   Clarity and consistency focus on the reasons why something happened and why the story should be believed. An interviewee who can provide a story that details what happened and why it happened is a valuable commodity. The "why" details of a story offer an explanation and give the audience the opportunity to make sense out of a series of events.

When evaluating consistency, the interviewer should ask, "Do the pieces of the story fit together?" To determine this, the interviewer will first look at the inner makings of the story. Are the actions and feelings expressed consistent with those of an "average" person? Would the average person experience similar circumstances? Once these inner elements of the story satisfy consistency requirements, the interviewer looks at the outer elements of the story: previous statements and established facts.

Consistency means that the interviewee's story agrees with any informal story he may have offered at a different time. The interviewer must review any statements made by an interviewee prior to a formal interview to accomplish this evaluation.

SCHEDULING THE INTERVIEW

Need is the primary factor in scheduling an interview. The decision to conduct an interview requires the interviewer to decide how soon the interview must take place, under what circumstances it should take place, and what type of environment will best facilitate it. All these factors influence the success of the interview and should be carefully planned.

Date and Time

In selecting the date and time of the interview, use the following guidelines:

- Avoid Monday mornings and Friday afternoons, as people tend to be distracted during these times.
- Avoid scheduling interviews close to or right after a major holiday.
- When contacting the interviewee, ask for or suggest several different dates; this allows a choice and demonstrates respect for the interviewee.
- Avoid scheduling interviews that deal with difficult or complex subjects before lunch, when people are hungry, or late in the afternoon, when people want to go home for the day.
- Attempt to understand the backgrounds of and demands on interviewees, so that you can avoid selecting interviewing times that create a hardship (the student who has finals that week; the professor who is preparing to leave for spring break; the police officer who works third shift).

Territory

When scheduling an interview, the interviewer must recognize that people are territorial by nature, and empathize with the interviewee when arranging the interview. If possible, the interviewer should arrange for the interview to take place in a location that encourages comfort, safety, and motivation to speak.

Territorial concerns also include seating arrangements. If the interviewer needs to take an aggressive role in the interview, she should arrange the seating so that she has an authoritative position. It is not always possible to accommodate the interviewee and meet the goals of the interview. Consider the following seating strategies (see Figure 1-4):

Figure 1-4
Authority and positioning

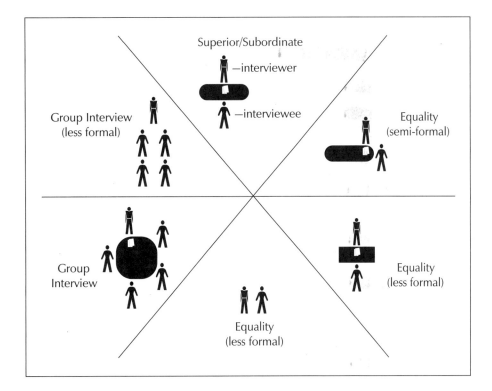

- To take an aggressive role in the interview, the interviewer should sit directly across from the interviewee, with a desk or table between them. This provides adequate distance and communicates the authority of the interviewer.
- To create a less formal situation, the interviewer should set the chairs at a right angle to each other, with a table or desk beside them. This signifies that there is some equality between interviewer and interviewee.
- The interviewer may decide to remove all obstacles from the room, like tables or desks, and bring the chairs into close proximity with each other. This signifies that the authority position of the interviewer has been diminished and that the interview is less formal.

Distractions

Distractions are a very big concern when scheduling an interview. Notify the interviewee that a specific period of uninterrupted time is needed for the interview. This warning is especially important when the interview will be conducted in the interviewee's home or place of business. The interviewer must consider the size of the room to be used, the types of decorations, windows, and possible noise that may distract either party. Minimizing the amount and types of distractions surrounding the interview allows the interview to move smoothly and keeps the participants focused.

SUMMARY

- An interview is an interactional communication process that is initiated by one party who has a predetermined purpose.
- The interview must be scheduled at a time and place that maximize both the interviewer's and interviewee's time.
- The interviewer and interviewee share passive and aggressive roles during the interview in an effort to maximize the effectiveness of the interview.
- Perceptions influence the interaction levels of the interview, as do verbal and nonverbal communication. Emotions, both expressed and unexpressed, also affect this process.
- To fully uncover an interviewee's knowledge and insight into a subject or topic, the interviewer must achieve step three interaction.
- The listening skills of the interviewer are instrumental to her success and are used to support the interviewee. Active listening consists of hearing a message and feeding it back to the interviewee to acknowledge understanding. Passive listening serves the same purpose, but the interviewer uses silence and nonverbal communication to support the interviewee.
- At the conclusion of the interview, the interviewer evaluates the credibility of the interviewee and his or her responses.

ACTIVITIES

1. Think of personal experiences you have had getting and giving affirmative feedback. What actions made the giving or receiving of that feedback positive and successful? What were some of the reasons for giving and getting that feedback? Did anything inhibit the feedback? Develop a list of pros and cons on affirmative feedback and be prepared to discuss your concerns.

2. What should you do if you realize that the interviewee has a different purpose for the interview than you do?

3. Experiment with the concept of perceptions by gathering four different pictures from a variety of sources. For each picture, write down your perceptions of the artist's message in the picture. Then ask two other people to do the same. Log the differences in each person's perception of the picture.

4. Conduct three separate ten-minute interviews with fellow students, all dealing with the same topic. Each interview should be conducted at a different

time of day, in a different type of environment, and in a different type of seating arrangement. Log your impressions of the successes and failures of each interview and what prompted those successes and failures.

CASE STUDY

ABC Subrogation File

This is a new insurance **subrogation** file involving a motor vehicle accident. (*Subrogation* means substituting a third party in place of one who has a claim, demand, or right against another party.) Your firm represents ABC Insurance and its insured, Mr. Michael Dixon (and his wife). The accident occurred on March 1, 1998, on County Road 12. The Dixon vehicle was traveling south on County Road 12 when a car, driven by Jack Peris and owned by Smith's Auto, turned out of the Burger Barn parking lot and headed north on 12. Because of ice and his rapid acceleration, Peris lost control of the vehicle and crossed over the center line, striking the Dixon car head-on. It is not known if either Mr. or Mrs. Dixon suffered any injuries.

Prepare to set up one interview with Mr. Dixon and one with Mr. Peris.

1. Should there be any difference in your attitude toward Mr. Dixon than there is toward Mr. Peris? If so, why? If not, why not?

2. Write down at least ten questions you would ask each of these persons during the interview.

3. What types of listening skills will you use, and why?

4. What type of interview will you arrange with each of these persons? How will you sit, and why? What time of day will you meet, and why?

5. What part of conducting the interview makes you the most nervous? Why?

NOTES

1 This analysis is based on Stanley L. Payne's *The Art of Asking Questions* (Princeton University Press, 1951).

2 Randall Harrison, "Nonverbal Communication," in *Handbook of Communication* (Rand McNally, 1973).

3 Albert Meehrabian, "Communication Without Words," 2 *Psychology Today* 51–52 (1968).

2

THE INTERVIEW STRUCTURE

<u>OBJECTIVES</u>   After completing this chapter, you will know:

- What the three components of the interview are, what purposes they serve, and how to manage them.
- How to identify and use verbal and nonverbal cues and techniques for building rapport with the interviewee.
- How to control the interview.
- How to prepare and use an interview outline.
- How to close an interview successfully.

INTRODUCTION

As discussed in Chapter 1, every interview depends on some level of structure to set it apart from casual conversation. The degree and nature of the interview, which are determined by its type, complexity, length, and purpose, establish its structure. Each interview type, including journalistic, probing, investigative, and those conducted with the client or experts, requires a somewhat different structure, but a number of principles and techniques can be applied to all interview styles. This chapter focuses on these shared principles and techniques, which are divided into the following groups: planning ahead for the interview, opening the interview, the body of the interview, and the closing the interview.

PLANNING AHEAD

Planning ahead is done when the goals of the interview are developed. When planning for an interview, the interviewer focuses on both general and specific data about the interviewee (full name, address, date of birth, etc.), data desired from the interviewee (what was done, heard, seen), and the presumed knowledge of the interviewee (he witnessed the burning of the documents). Before actually conducting the interview, the interviewer must consider these three preparatory components:

- The interviewee's existing knowledge
- The interviewee's perceived knowledge
- The interviewee's background.

Existing Knowledge

Understanding of what existing knowledge an interviewee has is gauged by data received in previous interviews or from outside sources. Commonly, it is not clear what amount of knowledge an interviewee possesses until the end of the first interview.

Perceived Knowledge

The interviewer will also research the interviewee's perceived knowledge. This practical task is accomplished by making inferences and gathering pertinent facts about the subject matter of the interview and the interviewee's background. This material may be used to prompt the interviewee in areas where he is believed to have knowledge.

Determining perceived knowledge sometimes requires a great deal of skill. For instance, a man who lives next door to a house that burns down may know some details about the fire—even if he is not aware that he knows them. These details may include a chronology of events that transpired in the days before the fire and that actually point to the reasons for the fire. His perceived knowledge, because he lives next door, is very important to infer. In many cases the interviewer must make inferences about information an interviewee may have or should possess even when the interviewee does not realize he has such information. Careful attention to detail is essential when evaluating perceived knowledge.

Witness Background

The interviewer should also know as much as possible about the interviewee before conducting the interview. Personal background information is gathered primarily from other interviewees, materials obtained from the client, and subject matter research. Background data helps the interviewer make assumptions about the level of cooperation the interviewee may offer and the barriers that may be encountered during the interview. Life experiences influence the interviewee; for instance, the neighbor in the house fire example may have owned a home that burned in the past or have known someone who experienced difficulty recovering money from an insurance company after a fire. Any personal experiences will inevitably influence the interviewee's responses.

Uncertainty about an interviewee's personal circumstances can lead to disorganized interviews, surprises, and errors. Planning ahead for the interview is done as much for self-preservation as for gaining knowledge of the interviewee. The more understanding the interviewer has of the interviewee, the more likely he is to succeed in obtaining the maximum amount of needed information.

After preparing for the interview, the interviewer must schedule and conduct the interview. The interview structure is common to all interviews: all interviews are made up of an opening, a body, and a closing.

OPENING THE INTERVIEW

The interview is initiated by a greeting. During the rest of the opening, the interviewer establishes a relationship with the interviewee, states the purpose of the interview, and establishes the level of status each party will have during the interaction. He accomplishes these objectives with both verbal and nonverbal communication. The interviewer must keep in mind that his eyes are the primary medium of nonverbal communication during the first four minutes of the meeting.[1] After the first four minutes, the greeting moves into a second phase.[2] During this second phase the interviewer begins using a combination of verbal behavior and physical contact (such as a handshake) to move the interview forward. He also asks his first question(s) during this second phase. This question or series of questions does not necessarily require substantive information, but engages the interviewee in a conversation. A good greeting phase is critical to the success of the rest of the interview.

Once the greeting phase has been completed, the interviewer must again satisfy three objectives: (1) build a rapport with the interviewee and orient her to the specific needs of the interview; (2) break down any barriers that may cause the interviewee to remain silent; and (3) employ nonverbal strategies to move the interview forward. To initiate a rapport with the interviewee, the interviewer can use the common-ground technique, orient the interviewee to the topics or purpose of the interview, and provide her with a clear and concise explanation of what is expected.

Building Rapport and Orienting the Interviewee

The **common-ground technique** is used by the interviewer to bridge any relationship gaps between himself and the interviewee and to begin building a trust relationship. The interviewer selects nonthreatening topics to initiate a conversation (Where did you go to school? Oh, really? So did my brother!). These topics help the interviewer discover personal information about the witness outside of the formality of the interview. Through the common-ground technique, he is able to find similarities between himself and the interviewee. These similarities can be used to make the interviewee feel more comfortable and trust the interviewer. Later, the interviewer can ease into more difficult subject matters by relating back to the trust created between them.

It is essential that the interviewer use easy and simple language to explain the purpose of the interview, and that he not depend on the similarities uncovered by the common-ground technique when explaining the purpose. The interviewer must mix his rapport-building skills with his explanations to create an environment in which the interviewee is well informed. The following is a list of the most effective opening techniques:

- State the purpose

  EXAMPLE —————————————————————————————
  I am investigating the banking dispute between US Savings and Loan and its shareholders.

- Summarize the problem

  EXAMPLE —————————————————————————————
  Because the hospital has lost all of its records regarding Mr. Smith's surgery, I am looking to gain insight into spinal cord operations, the risks that accompany the surgery, and the percentages for full recovery.

- Explain how the problem arose

  EXAMPLE —————————————————————————————
  The stock prospectus arrived three days late and our client was not able to review all the material in a timely fashion. Could you please help answer some of the questions we now have?

- Provide an incentive for participating

  EXAMPLE —————————————————————————————
  I realize that spending time explaining how to roof the apartments takes you away from your job and therefore you do not get a day's salary. I am willing to pay you what your hourly rate is if you will participate in this interview.

- Ask for help

EXAMPLE ——————————————————————————————
Mr. Wexler, I need some help understanding how this land contract for deed will work in relationship to Mr. Sonnet's proposed plan.

- Mention the person who sent you to the interviewee or the organization you represent

EXAMPLE ——————————————————————————————
Jonathan Livingston suggested talking with you. He claims that you are an expert on seagulls.

Mr. Jones, I work with Chrysler Corporation and am interested in learning more about the safety inspections you conducted on mini-vans.

- Mention the position of the interviewee

EXAMPLE ——————————————————————————————
Jim, I understand that you have done a lot of research on amusement park rides and the standards needed to maintain safety. Would you share some of those findings with me?

- Assure the interviewee that only a certain amount of time will be used to conduct the interview

EXAMPLE ——————————————————————————————
Bill, I need just thirty minutes of your time to define the relationship between the stockholders and the union workers.

After a rapport has been established and the purpose of the interview explained, the interviewer must determine if there are any barriers that might inhibit the interviewee from offering all of the information she possesses. To do this, he must identify and break all silence barriers.

Breaking the Silence Barrier

There are endless reasons why interviewees are reluctant to provide complete information, and the most effective method for overcoming silence is to identify the **silence factor**. The silence factor is usually related either to fear of the interview or to fear of certain topics. Each of these can often be identified during the opening of the interview, as they are demonstrated in the interviewee's nonverbal cues.

Nonverbal cues or body language are often indicators of reluctance; for instance, suddenly shifting position during the interview may indicate a feeling of uneasiness. Facial expressions offer insight into the interviewee's concerns or disagreement on a topic or the interpretation of a topic. A change in a person's tone of voice can mean a variety of things, from disgust to uncertainty to vulnerability. Changes in speech patterns also hint at reluctance problems. Most nonverbal indicators can be identified by the interviewer as he explains the purpose of the interview and the topics to be covered. Once the barrier is discovered, it must be dealt with.

Fear of the Interview   During the opening moments of the interview, it may become obvious that the interviewee is uncomfortable; in fact, most people experience some anxiety over being interviewed. To help diminish these feelings, the interviewer should clearly define the purpose of the interview and state what is expected from the interviewee. In most instances, the interviewee will respond to the interviewer's attempts to clarify the situation and begin to relax.

Fear of Certain Topics   After easing the interviewee's fears about the interview process, it may be necessary to address any concerns the interviewee has regarding certain topics. The interviewer should be able to identify obvious problem topics, such as violent crime, education reform, or political issues, immediately and discuss them openly. Many touchy topics, however, are not as easily identified, because they lie under the surface of the interview subject and are very personal. They often involve life experiences that revolve around some part of the subject matter of the interview.

EXAMPLE ───────────────────────────────

A young man is being interviewed about Medicare. Shortly after the greeting phase, the interviewer begins explaining the topics to be covered in the interview and notices that the young man is resisting the topic regarding nursing homes. After a while, the interviewer begins asking about the interviewee's background and finds out that his mother is in a nursing home. The interviewer also discovers that the young man is paying the bills for the nursing home.

Background information on the interviewee will help in identifying these latent fears. The use of empathy by the interviewer will also assist him in handling the interviewee's fears.

Handling the Fear   Dealing with topical fear at the moment it is noticed is the preferred method. Because a rapport between the interviewer and interviewee will already have been initiated, the interviewer can draw on the common-ground technique to "open up" the interviewee and allay her fears. The interviewer may also alter the questioning technique being used. By changing the question style, the interviewer diverts the pressure of upsetting questions and, it is hoped, moves the interview along.

Some interviewees are passive in response to difficult topics. Others talk too much. Overtalking is known as **wandering**, and may or may not be a problem. During some interviewees' wandering, new and unexpected information may be discovered; thus, wandering can actually enhance the interview.

Wandering does not enhance the interview, though, when the i is using it to distract the interviewer's attention from certain details Judging the reason for wandering is the immediate responsibility of th viewer; once he determines that the interviewee is wandering for distracti , ine interviewer must choose a method for handling the wandering. To get the interviewee back on track, the interviewer may have to confront the interviewee by repeating an original question when off-the-subject responses are given. This may require the interviewer to interrupt the interviewee and redirect her attention to the correct topic.

When deciding whether to allow an interviewee to wander, ask these questions:

- Are the extra details being offered in an effort to help?
- Is the interviewee interested in hearing herself talk and nothing else?
- Is the interviewee in need of some education on the purpose or topics of the interview in order to stay focused?

Answering any or all of these questions, as needed, will aid the interviewer in moving the interview forward.

All the techniques discussed here address the verbal communication needs in the opening, but none is effective without the use of nonverbal strategies. It is critical that the interviewer know and use nonverbal strategies.

Nonverbal Strategies

The use of nonverbal communication is critical in the opening, as it creates the first impression. The signals should convey sincerity, respect, interest, empathy, warmth, and seriousness. Nonverbal signals "inform the participants whether or not to move to other forms of interaction."[3] Smiling is believed to be a significant signal among parties who know and trust one another, and therefore it should be used during the interview, especially the opening. See Figure 2-1, which lists the primary forms of verbal and nonverbal communication during the opening of the interview. Each entry in Figure 2-1 is listed in order of importance.

The interviewer's appearance and clothing influence first impressions as well. They should communicate maturity, professionalism, and an understanding of what is appropriate. Voice and facial expressions should adequately reflect the gravity of the situation and topics to be discussed. Be careful of overdoing handshakes, but do not neglect the opportunity to let a firm handshake inform the interviewee of the seriousness of the meeting. Do not touch an interviewee's arm, hand, or shoulder if a relationship has not been built with her. This is reserved for closer relationships.

Finally, do not overestimate the importance of every word and gesture used during the opening. As discussed, all persons involved in the interview bring with them a separate set of perceptions, and projecting those perceptions onto the value or meanings of every message may create problems. Rather, make

Figure 2-1
Primary interactions during the opening. (*See* Krivonos & Knapp, "Initiating Communication" at 122.)

Verbal Variable	Nonverbal Variable
Topic initiation (explanation)	Head gestures
Verbal salute	Mutual glances
Reference to other	Smile
External reference	Grooming
Personal inquiry	Eyebrow flash
Reference to self	Salutes
Witticism	Hand signs
Accentuators	Mutual hand contact
Apologies	Wink
Maintenance	
Compliments	

mental notes of some communications that may be troublesome and watch for them in the body of the interview.

THE BODY OF THE INTERVIEW

Depending on the style of the interview—formal versus informal—the interviewer will design and use an interview outline to conduct the body of the meeting. Informal interviews require little more than a few questions and topics to be outlined. Formal interviews, which typically last longer, require more depth in the outline. Nevertheless, whether the interviewer is spending fifteen minutes or three hours with an interviewee, he must have some type of outline.

The Interview Outline

The **interview outline** functions not only as a guide for the interviewer, but also as a navigational tool, showing the interviewer when to place emphasis on certain topics and questions. The outline is a middle-ground tool. It is not an **interview schedule**, which specifies the questions to be asked, the wording of the questions, the context of the answers to be received, and the degree of the answer. Nor is it an **interview guide**, which is designed to work only in nonscheduled interviews and emphasizes the goals of the interview as well as the relevant and adequate responses to those questions.[4] Instead, the outline is a combination of the interview guide and schedule, applying the best of both to a wider range of uses. The outline is a base for topic development, regardless of the formality of the interview, and is adaptable to any level of interview. This tool is particularly useful in legal interviews, which are generally probing or journalistic in nature, as it allows greater flexibility for the interviewer during the course of the interview.

The paralegal can use the outline to do one or more of the following:

- Build a topical sequence. This strategy allows the paralegal to follow a natural division in issues or topics, which is particularly helpful when breaking down legal issues for evidence research.
- Build a time sequence. This outline strategy helps structure the interview so that it follows a chronological path (see Figure 2-2).
- Build a spatial sequence. This can be done inside the topical or time-sequence outline, to allow the development of details relating to a physical aspect of the interviewee's information. For instance, with a witness to an accident, the interviewer may need a spatial outline that narrows the information on where the witness was at the time of the accident; what time of the day, week, month, year it was; and so on.
- Build a cause-and-effect sequence. An outline using this method may be helpful in interviews dealing with contract disputes, product liability cases, or the like. Each of these depends on a cause and effect, so the paralegal can outline his needs to satisfy the case questions with this strategy.
- Build a problem-solving sequence. This strategy is very useful when dealing with general witnesses and expert witnesses. It allows the paralegal to present a problem and then seek a solution from the interviewee, thereby uncovering needed data.

Figure 2-2

Time sequence interview outline

I. The Day of the Accident

    A. What time did you leave your house?

    B. What were you doing (walking, riding a bike, driving)?

    C. Where were you going?

        1. How long does it normally take to get there?

        2. How often do you go there?

        3. Anything unusual on the day of the accident?

II. The Hour of the Accident

    A. What were you doing between 2 and 3 P.M. on Saturday the 12th of June?

    B. Why were you there?

    C. How do you know what time you were there?

        1. Where are you usually between 2 and 3 on Saturdays?

        2. Why was this Saturday any different or the same?

Note Taking

A paralegal must take some notes during the interview if the witness's testimony is to be preserved. Note taking is a skill as well as a talent and should be practiced as often as possible. To avoid alienating the interviewee, the paralegal must balance note taking with eye contact, and should not begin taking notes until the interviewee has committed to the interview and has begun to open up. If note taking is premature, the interviewee's testimony may be prejudiced.

☑ **PRACTICAL TIP**   A paralegal may create a note-taking tool to expedite this procedure (see Figure 2-3).

Figure 2-3
Note-taking tool

Witness: Mary Jo Smith
Date: April 11, 1997
Location: E&Q Engineering

Dates	Interview Questions	Notes	Conflicts
June 23, 1996, about noon.	Tell me what you heard about Mr. Jones getting fired?	Smith was reluctant, probably scared. Bill Mill, Sue Shoe, Marla Apson, also possible witnesses.	No conflict here, confirm with witnesses she identified.

A blank version of a note-taking tool can be created in pen at the time of the interview, which helps keep the interview comfortable and less rigid.

Formal and Informal Interviews

The interview outline is useful in any type of interview. In an **informal interview**, the conduct of the interview is very relaxed and the interviewer has more time to develop the trust relationship with the interviewee. This type of interview is commonly used in early meetings with the client and with fact witnesses who are providing supportive data to the legal team. This interview style is commonly conducted in an open and nonthreatening environment, such as a conference room in the law office or the interviewee's home, and there usually are no physical barriers between the two parties (e.g., desk or table). There are few time constraints on the informal interview, and the dress and mannerisms of the interviewer are relaxed and welcoming. This style of interview is typical in the early stages of an investigation when large amounts of general data are needed for a possible future lawsuit.

There are also **formal interviews**, in which the environment of the interview is more regulated and the purpose of the interview more structured. These interviews are commonly conducted in the law office and are fairly rigid. The interviewee, whether client, expert witness, or fact witness, is oriented to the purpose of the meeting and then the outline topics are strictly followed. There is less opportunity for the interviewee to wander during the formal interview.

There are advantages and disadvantages to both of these styles and reasons for using each of them (see Figure 2-4). The paralegal/interviewer must choose the interview style that best suits the needs of the investigation. Each requires a different level of skill, so the paralegal should become familiar with his own strengths and weaknesses in interviewing to improve his techniques for both of these styles. It is sometimes necessary to combine aspects of each style in one interview, to meet the unique requirements and time constraints of certain interviewees.

The conclusion of the body of the interview, whether formal or informal, is signaled by completion of the outline. Thereafter the interviewer must move smoothly to the closing. There are specific skills and techniques for handling the closing, all of which the paralegal must know and practice.

Figure 2-4
Formal versus informal interview styles

	Advantages	Disadvantages
Informal	Allows paralegal/interviewer freedom to get to know the interviewee.	Requires paralegal to work harder at establishing his status in the relationship.
	Interview goals are flexible and timeline for communication is open.	Relaxed nature of the environment may distract interviewer and interviewee, thereby wasting time.
	Creates good feeling between interviewer and interviewee.	May not be as productive as formal style.
Formal	Provides structure and ease in establishing status and roles in the interview.	Can create interviewee anxiety due to the formality of the environment.
	More rigid style used makes the expectations of the meeting clear.	Interviewer may encounter more silence barriers than in informal style.
	Often nets large amounts of relevant data.	Does not always foster improved trust relationship between interviewer and interviewee.

CLOSING THE INTERVIEW

There are three primary functions of the closing:[5]

- The closing signals the termination of the interview but not of the relationship between the interviewer and interviewee. This is particularly important to the paralegal when dealing with the client, expert witnesses, and fact witnesses who support the legal team's position.
- The closing supports the relationship and provides a positive ending.
- The closing provides an opportunity for the interviewer to summarize what has transpired between the parties.

Often the success of the interview hinges on its short but professional closing. The paralegal should avoid the temptation to relax at the end of the body of the interview and jeopardize the quality work that has already been done. Abrupt or tactless closings destroy the trust relationship with the interviewee and endanger future interviews with that person. Effective closings enhance relationships and interview results. The interviewer should use the following guidelines for closing the interview:

- Be sincere and honest, especially about future contacts. Witnesses and clients need to know what is expected of them in the future.
- Do not hurry the closing; rather, take time to hear the interviewee's feelings and concerns.
- Avoid introducing any new or unrelated topics at the close of the interview.
- Do not end the interview prematurely. Nonverbal cues can often lead an interviewee to believe that the interviewer is finished when in fact he is not. Pay close attention to the signals being sent as the interview winds down.
- Keep an open-door policy with all interviewees. Avoid making them feel like they have been used and that you no longer have time for them. Offer to meet with them again or be available to speak over the phone if they think of something to add later.

The interviewer should practice or role-play closing the interview. There is no way to describe all the possible situations that can arise when closing an interview; therefore, it is up to the interviewer to anticipate and prepare in advance for a variety of occurrences.

Techniques

When practicing the closing, be creative and imaginative. Consider the following techniques:[6]

- Offer to answer questions.
- Ask a sweeping question, such as: "Can you think of anything we haven't accounted for in this contract?"

- Announce that the goals of the interview have been met: "Well, that's all the questions I have."
- Ask personal questions that move away from the focus of the interview: "Do you leave for the Outer Banks of North Carolina next week?"
- Ask professional questions that move away from the focus of the interview: "When are you giving the seminar on interviewing to the state bar association?"
- Provide a signal indicating that time is up: "Wow, it's 3:30 already and I promised to be finished by then."
- Give a reason for closing: "I'm sorry, I have a class starting very soon and I have to finish now."
- Express gratitude for the interviewee's participation: "Thanks for your feedback; it will help my research."
- Schedule the follow-up interview.
- Summarize the interview: "All right, you have explained that you only saw the accident after it had occurred. Am I forgetting anything?"

Nonverbal Cues

Along with the verbal closing messages, the interviewer must provide nonverbal messages, which are required to bring a psychological closing to the meeting. The following is a list of typical nonverbal closing signals:

- Straightening up in a chair
- Leaning forward
- Standing up
- Moving away from the other party
- Uncrossing legs
- Placing the hands on the knees as if preparing to rise
- Breaking eye contact
- Offering to shake hands
- Making various movements
- Smiling
- Looking at the clock.

The interviewer should not only use these techniques to close the interview, but should also be aware of their use by the interviewee. The interviewer must be keenly conscious of everything he and the interviewee are saying, both physically and vocally. Sending a signal of closure before it is appropriate may inhibit, offend, or anger the interviewee; the interviewer may have the same responses to premature closing signals sent by the interviewee. Staying attuned to nonverbal messages is important if the interviewer intends to control the meeting. Practice using nonverbal closing methods in role-playing situations.

Document the results of any experiments done, for evaluation purposes. The more complete the interviewer's understanding of his nonverbal behavior, the more successful he will be in real interviews.

Signed Statements

Signed statements permanently preserve factual information and memorialize a witness interview. Witnesses benefit from signed statements because they can be used as a memory refresher during the investigation and at the time of trial. Federal Rule of Evidence 612 makes special provision for a witness's use of a signed statement when refreshing her memory (as long as the statement is available to all parties involved in the litigation). The signed statement is also valuable as an impeachment tool, as a substitute for a witness who is unavailable for trial, and as motivation for the witness to tell the same story as originally offered to the legal team.

Experienced paralegals use the interview outline to assist them in creating the signed statement. The outline covers major topics relevant to the legal issue and undisputed facts, and is a convenient method for detailing a witness's testimony both during and after the statement. A copy of the witness's statement is subsequently forwarded to the witness for her approval and signature.

The witness is encouraged to carefully read the statement before signing and to make any necessary corrections to the testimony. Signed statements should be notarized. Care must be given to statements provided by children, illiterate persons, and non-English–speaking persons.

SUMMARY

- The opening of the interview sets the tone for the interview, and is initiated through verbal and nonverbal greetings. Initial impressions occur in the first four minutes. The body of the interview follows the interview outline and satisfies the goals of the meeting. The closing is initiated by verbal and nonverbal messages and sets the stage for a future relationship and interview(s) with the interviewee.

- Rapport is built by using the common-ground technique and orienting the interviewee to the goals of the interview. Trust built during rapport building is used to manage any silence barriers the interviewee may develop regarding the topics of the interview.

- Interview outlines are designed to be adapted to both formal and informal interviews. The outline focuses on topics that are then narrowed to specific questions about the details of an event.

ACTIVITIES

1. Identify the types of nonverbal strategies you personally use regularly in daily conversations. Do you find that you use any of these in formal

interviewing situations? How and when? Do they hinder or help your level of communication? What can you do to improve them?

2. Evaluate your own attempts at planning an interview. After completing the case study assignment in this chapter, reevaluate your ability to plan ahead.

3. Observe several different kinds of interviews on television (for instance, Jay Leno interviewing a guest, Barbara Walters interviewing a guest, and Morley Safer interviewing a guest). Pay particular attention to the opening, body, and closing of the interviews. Log your impressions of the different styles, different results, and responses of the guests to both the verbal and nonverbal techniques used. How could the interviews have been improved? Be specific in your answers and critiques.

CASE STUDY

Murphy v. Schultz Autoplex

Read the following case scenario.[7] When you have finished, prepare to interview any one of the persons involved in this case.

1. Outline the opening you will use, specifically the orienting and nonverbal techniques.

2. Prepare an interview outline identifying the technique you will use and why.

3. Draft your closing.

Murphy v. Schultz Autoplex

David and Leslie Murphy live in a twenty-five-unit apartment building on B Street between Valley View and Castle Drives. David is employed as a teller at Nottingham Bank in Syracuse. He knows a great deal about banking and auto mechanics, but nothing about law or lawyers. He has never been to a lawyer before. Another teller at the bank recommended your supervising attorney to David because the lawyer did a good job in drawing up a will for him.

About four months ago David decided to buy an antique car. What he wanted was a 1930s-vintage Ford or Chrysler. None of the dealers he visited had any such cars available. Finally he went to Schultz Autoplex on Lawton Avenue. Schultz had a 1938 Chrysler, priced at $2,400, that was acceptable to David. In talking with the salesperson, Craig Kingston, David discovered that for an additional $850 Schultz was willing to undertake some substantial reconditioning of the vehicle. After two or three days of negotiation, David

and Kingston came to terms. Under the agreement, for the sum of $3,250 Schultz was to rework the entire upholstery, install a reconditioned clutch, and deliver the car; the work was to be completed within four weeks. The reconditioning was to commence as soon as David made a down payment of $1,000. The balance of the purchase price was to be paid in 12 monthly installments of $206.27 each. These installments included interest at 18 percent per annum. The payments were to begin five weeks from the date the agreement was signed, and the written contract was to be signed when David made the down payment. Schultz said it would hold the car for two weeks to allow David time to get the down payment.

The day after David came to terms with Kingston, he talked with the manager of his bank and arranged to borrow $1,000. About a week later, when he had actually gotten the money, David returned to Schultz to give them the down payment. He noticed immediately that they were already working on the car, and became curious as to why work had begun; under the terms of the agreement, Schultz was not to begin work until David had made his down payment. When David asked Kingston why work had already begun, Kingston stated that they knew he would come up with the money and they had decided to get a head start. David gave Kingston the $1,000, but in the course of all the discussion he forgot to ask for a written agreement. He did, however, get a receipt for the $1,000. He kept the receipt at his home.

A couple of weeks after David made the down payment, he went to Schultz to check the progress on the car. At this time it appeared to him that more work was being done on the car than was called for under his agreement. He could see that the head was off the engine and it seemed to him that some work was being done on the engine itself. Kingston was not present on this occasion, but David spoke with the mechanic who was working on the car. The mechanic, whose name David does not know, said that he had been told grind the valves. David was surprised and indicated to the mechanic that he was the new purchaser of the car and that he did not think any engine work was part of the deal. The mechanic said he did not know anything about any agreement, but he thought the car was being fixed up for Mr. Schultz's daughter. When David heard this, he asked to speak with Schultz himself, but Schultz was not in. Later that day, David reached Kingston and told him of the conversation with the mechanic. Kingston said that there must have been some misunderstanding and that he would call David back. The next day, because he had not heard from Kingston, David called to find out what

was happening. Kingston was not in and David left a message. Kingston never called David.

Three days later, David managed to reach Kingston. Kingston apologized for not getting back to David; he said he had been busy. He indicated that there was some problem because the car had also been sold to Mr. Schultz's former spouse. He said he was trying to work the situation out and would get back to David. After several days of waiting and a series of unreturned phone calls, David went to the dealership and spoke face-to-face with Kingston. Kingston indicated that there was nothing he could do, as the car had already been sold to Schultz's former spouse. He also said that they could no longer sell the car for $3,250, because much more work than agreed on had been put into reconditioning the car. Kingston again apologized and said David's money would be returned in a week. When David asked what extra work had been done and what extra cost was involved, Kingston avoided answering his questions, repeating that the matter was out of his hands.

Finally, David became angry at Kingston and threatened suit. When he did so, Kingston walked into his office and refused to talk with David any more. As David was leaving the lot, he noticed that the Chrysler was not on the lot or in the garage. He therefore decided to ask the mechanic about it. The mechanic told him that as far as he knew the car was being driven by Mr. Schultz's daughter.

David's principal motive is to force Schultz to honor the agreement and sell him the car. He would much rather have the car than have his money back.

NOTES

1 L. Zunin, *Contact: The First Four Minutes* 78 (Nash Publishing, 1972).

2 Paul D. Krivonos & Mark L. Knapp, "Initiating Communication: What Do You Say When You Say Hello?," 26 *Central States Speech J.* 116–17 (1975).

3 *Id.* at 123.

4 Raymond L. Gorden, *Interviewing, Strategy, Techniques, and Tactics* 110 11 (4th ed., Dorsey Press 1987).

5 Mark L. Knapp, Roderick P. Hart, Gustav W. Friedrich, & Gary M. Shulman, "The Rhetoric of Goodbye: Verbal and Nonverbal Correlates of Human Leave Taking," 40 *Speech Monographs* 182–98 (1973).

6 *Id.* at 189.

7 Based on the fact scenario presented by David Binder and Susan Price in the instructor's manual for *Legal Interviewing and Counseling: A Client-Centered Approach* 64–65 (West, 1977).

3

QUESTIONING

OBJECTIVES   After completing this chapter, you will know:

- Why it is important to ask a "good" question.
- What the most general categories of questions are, how questions are used, why they are used, and when they are used.
- How to structure a good question.
- What question types create problems for the interviewer, and why.

INTRODUCTION

The success of any interview is determined in part by the quality of the questions asked. Professional interviewers, also known as "question worders,"[1] understand that the best questions are created by using simple, understandable, bias-free, nonirritating words.[2] They also know that the phrasing of questions is an essential element in research-based interviews, which include most (if not all) legal interviews. However, there are no perfect questions—even if there were, they would not be able to elicit the most complete data from an interviewee. Why? Because questions are only one part of the overall process known as the interview. The other parts of the interview, as discussed in Chapters 1 and 2, include the opening, body, and closing, nonverbal communication, interactions, and perceptions, to name a few.

As an interviewer, it is important to realize that developing "good" questions is first dependent on having an understanding of question types: open/closed, objective/subjective, leading/neutral, and primary/secondary. Second, it is necessary to understand probing techniques: passive, general, and feedback-related. Finally, it is necessary to understand how to structure questions and what types of questions to avoid.

WHY GOOD QUESTIONS ARE REQUIRED

To understand why good questions are required, an interviewer must know what is wrong with so many questions. Quite simply, the most common problem is questions created by an interviewer who assumes that the interviewee knows more than he does. The interviewer takes for granted that the interviewee knows what the subject matter of the interview is and has the ability or basis to provide worthwhile responses—which is often not true. The interviewer trapped in this thought pattern also assumes that the interviewee understands the questions and can therefore respond appropriately.[3]

These assumptions, though not justified, are very natural. To safeguard against them, the paralegal should exercise self-discipline when creating each question. To do so, she need only ask herself one question: "What is being taken for granted in this question?" Answering this question may not be so easy, however. So, the paralegal can then consider these two aspects of the question:

- *The meaningfulness of the question.* Stanley L. Payne, author of *The Art of Asking Questions,* tells us that the more meaningless a question is, the more likely it is to produce inconsistent results. He also claims that interviewers who use words that the interviewee does not understand will only further complicate this problem.

EXAMPLE ————————————————————————

Paralegal: Tell me, Mrs. Barney, regarding the claim of battery, what happened on May 13th between your co-workers?

This question is meaningless because it does not explain what "happened" means, nor does it define *battery*.

- *The assumption, within the question, that widespread knowledge of a certain topic or subject exists.* All persons do not interpret a legislative act, political rhetoric, religious freedom, and many other things in the same way. In general, people will avoid admitting total ignorance on a topic by acknowledging only that they have a limited understanding of the topic. This is particularly true with legal terms and principles.

Remember, it is the interviewer's job to word a question in a manner that is answerable. All of the meanings in the question must be understood by the interviewer and interviewee in the same way. Skillful questioning allows the interviewer to determine an interviewee's knowledge on a topic by first defining the words in the question and then slowly uncovering the interviewee's level of knowledge. These are called **filtering questions**.

EXAMPLE ————————————————————————————————————

Have you ever heard of a summons and complaint?

How would you explain the summons and complaint?

What types of situations would the summons and complaint be used in?

Each level of question is clear and meaningful and is designed to aid the interviewer in discovering the interviewee's base knowledge. None of these questions take anything for granted.

To further her understanding of good questions, the interviewer must know what question types are available and when they are used.

OPEN AND CLOSED QUESTIONS

Closed questions are those that can be answered with a short response. There are three types of closed questions:

- *Selection questions,* which offer the interviewee two or more responses to choose from when responding.

- *Yes/no (bipolar or dichotomous) questions,* which offer the interviewee the chance only to answer yes or no.

- *Identification questions,* which are typically asked in an interrogation style. The interviewee offers a response that answers a who, what, when, where proposition. The answer is usually short.[4]

Open questions are those that do not imply or suggest a specific response, but rather allow the interviewee to offer as much or as little information as she deems appropriate. In theory, all open questions are designed to imply that a longer, more descriptive response is required.

In practice, researchers have used two rules for deciding when to use open questions and when to use closed questions:

- Use a closed question when, to the investigator, it is clear what must be elicited from the interviewee ("Did you see Susan Peltzer shred the corporate records?").
- Use an open question when it is necessary to gain in-depth understanding of the interviewee's motivations and feelings.

For many years, experts in the field of communication and interviewing have debated the effectiveness of open questions over closed questions. Generally, it is believed that open questions provide the interviewee with an opportunity to wander away from the topic of the interview, which is not necessarily good. However, this has not been proven. Open questions are also believed to encourage interviewees to offer more information, because of the nature of the question. Closed questions confine the interviewee's response.

Barbara Snell Dohrenwend, a researcher and professor in the field of social science and communication, has found that the usefulness of one question type over another depends more on the interaction between the interviewer and her use of the question. The interviewer's skill level in questioning is the most influential factor in question type selection. Question type alone plays a secondary role in determining which style is more effective.

Dohrenwend also finds that responses to open questions contain higher amounts of self-revelation than those to closed questions.[5] That is, the interviewee will divulge more information when asked an open/objective question than an open/subjective question, because there is psychological risk in open dialogue on a personal level. However, the nature of the open question, regardless of objectivity or subjectivity, causes the interviewee to reveal more about himself, his thoughts, and his understandings than a closed question does. These findings support the idea that when an investigator needs to know personal information from an interviewee, she is more likely to obtain that information by using open questions (following up, if need be, with closed questions).

Objective versus Subjective Questions

Objective questions and the responses they evoke focus on "observable events, including actions and statements by the respondent and by others, and [on] physical milieu, including objects and their arrangement, as well as the dress and manner of persons."[6] All these elements are necessary to evaluate the credibility of the interviewee and her responses, as discussed in Chapter 1. The use of **subjective questions** allows the interviewer to focus on the interviewee's "thoughts and feelings, and her inferences about others' thoughts and feelings."[7] These also help to determine credibility. To measure the amount of subjective and objective information provided, the interviewer may separate responses into the following descriptive categories.

1. *Objective:* Descriptions of
   - appearance

- behavior
- experience

2. *Subjective:* Descriptions of
  - personal opinions
  - attitudes
  - feelings
  - preferences
  - beliefs
  - value judgments

Dohrenwend and other researchers have found that interviewees tend to resist subjective inquiries. They have also found that skillful interviewers are able to move back and forth between open and closed questions, thereby lowering the interviewee's resistance to subjective topics. Resistance to objective questions, whether open or closed, was not often found. Therefore, to maximize her efforts, the interviewer must balance the use of open and closed questions.

Balancing Open and Closed Questions

To determine when and how often to use open and closed questions, consider this: "There is a significant increase in the length of responses to closed questions when they are in the minority, and a significant decrease in the length of responses to open questions when they are in the minority."[8] The decision on which type of question to use thus depends on the kind and amount of material needed from the interviewee. If closed questions are the most useful when gathering subjective data, the interviewer may want to use more closed questions in the early or opening phase of the interview. A few open questions can be used to offset any discomfort the interviewee may experience while offering subjective data, and at the same time help to limit the amount of time the interviewee takes discussing topics not related to the interview.

During the body of the interview, the interviewer must use more skill in mixing the two styles. She may depend more on objective, open questions to gather larger amounts of information. However, development of good questions will allow her to manage the interviewee and the time he spends responding to these questions.

Subject Matter

The final consideration in choosing between open and closed questions is: "How does the subject matter of the interview affect the question style?" The objectivity or subjectivity of any question, as well as its open or closed nature, influences the responses received. Consider the data Dohrenwend compiled after conducting a research project using a few highly trained interviewers, who conducted four separate fifteen- to twenty-minute interviews balancing the difference between open and closed questions and subjective and objective subject matters (see Figure 3-1). This data reflects the quality of responses based solely on the objectivity or subjectivity of the question.

What this data suggests is that the interviewer must become skillful in adapting open and closed questions to both objective and subjective topics. The subject matter of most investigations and legal cases will be a mixture of both objective and subjective material. Learning to craft skillful questions that accommodate this need is the further objective of this chapter.

Figure 3-1
Balancing of open and closed questions based on the objectivity or subjectivity of the subject matter

Mean Scores for Significant Main Effects of Subject Matter of Questions		
	Subject matter of questions	
Response Property	**Objective %**	**Subjective %**
Specificity of objective reports	85	69
Correctness of objective reports	78	69
Self-revelation	36	85
Inferences concerning others' subjective states	8	57
Specificity of identification of other persons	64	72

Source: Adapted from Barbara Snell Dohrenwend, "Some Effects of Open and Closed Questions on Respondent's Answer," 24 *Field Methods & Techniques, Human Organizations* 175, 182 (1965); courtesy of the Society for Applied Anthropology.

In conclusion, Dohrenwend's experiment showed:

- Subject matter seems to be the most important factor in question style, and questions on objective topics produce more valid responses than those on subjective topics.
- Interviewees with varied educational backgrounds react differently to open and closed questions. The less education the interviewee has, the fewer open questions the interviewer should use, to minimize irrelevant wandering.
- Open questions are less efficient than closed and they do not necessarily provide more depth or validity.
- Open questions used by less experienced interviewers are even more inefficient at preventing interviewees from wandering off the topic.
- In research interviews, closed questions are advantageous.
- When possible, the investigator should use well-tested closed questions in her interviews.

- Investigators who have limited opportunities with an interviewee may be forced to use loosely structured open questions so that the interviewee can establish his own frame of reference for the answers.
- Open questions require more skill in managing the interview.
- Closed questions require more skill in drafting.

LEADING AND NEUTRAL QUESTIONS

Interviewers use **leading questions** to encourage the interviewee to volunteer information that was not specifically asked for. Leading questions may be constructed as either open or closed. A leading question might be phrased something like the following.

EXAMPLE ——
Don't you think taxes should be lower?
You are concerned about environmental regulation, aren't you?
——

Sometimes a nondirective, open question is used to elicit this "volunteered" data.

EXAMPLE ——
Describe your feelings about welfare reform; it is excessive, don't you think?
——

Nondirective questions and interviewing styles let the interviewee take control of the interview and give more than is asked for. The main problem with this type of question is that it allows—and may even encourage—the interviewee to wander off the subject. But there is an alternative: a more direct leading question that is more closed in nature. Stephen A. Richardson, with the Association for the Aid of Crippled Children, conducted a study with twenty student interviewers and found that thirty-one of forty unstructured interviews gathered more volunteered information from interviewees via the leading question than did interviews using the nondirective open approach. He also found that interviewees were less likely to wander off the subject when asked leading questions.[9]

There are varying degrees of leading questions. Consider the following list, which compares leading questions with neutral alternatives:

Neutral	Leading
Do you like to work with people?	I assume you like to work with people?
How do you feel about essay exams?	Do you dislike essay exams as much as I do?
Have you ever cheated on your income taxes?	Have you stopped cheating on your income taxes?[10]

Of these examples, the first two are mild; the last is rather bold and is considered loaded. **Loaded questions** are the most extreme type of leading question. Because leading questions can bias the interviewee, the paralegal should avoid using them without the express approval of the attorney. For example, an introduction like "According to the law,"[11] is very leading, as it encourages the interviewee to respond as he perceives the interviewer wants him to rather than offering his true feelings or knowledge.

There is a strong nonverbal component in leading. If she is not aware of the nonverbal aspect, the interviewer may unconsciously apply a leading push to a neutral question, or she may add emphasis and pressure to a leading question by sending certain nonverbal cues. These cues include hand and body gestures and voice inflection. Guard against this, especially when dealing with a client or hostile witness, as it may damage the trust relationship built with the interviewee during the opening.

PROBING QUESTIONS

Questions come in two general forms, primary and secondary. **Primary questions**[12] introduce a topic or new subject within a topic. They can stand alone when taken out of the interview context.

EXAMPLE ——————————————————————————————

Where were you when the two cars collided?

Tell me about the relationship you had with your ex-husband.

Secondary questions go one step further and probe the interviewee for more detail. These are follow-up questions. Filtering questions are commonly secondary questions. These questions may be open or closed, but are essential when the answers to primary questions lack relevance, are vague, or are incomplete. There are three general types of secondary questions: passive, general, and feedback-related. Each of these is broken down into more specific categories as well.

Passive Probing; Silence and Nudging

The **silent probe** uses nonverbal communication rather than verbal. When an interviewee is giving incomplete responses or is hesitant to respond, as may happen with subjective material, the interviewer can remain silent for a few moments and then probe the interviewee with nonverbal cues. These cues consist of gestures that encourage the person to talk, such as eye contact, head nodding, and hand movements. Silence is a respectful way to probe the interviewee. It demonstrates interest in what the interviewee is saying.

A **nudging probe** is used when a silent probe has failed to stimulate further communication from the interviewee. This is a simple, brief verbal cue used in conjunction with the nonverbal cues given during the silent probe. Nudging uses statements such as:

- Yes?
- What happened then?
- Uh-huh?
- Go on.
- I see.

By employing short, one- or two-word probes, the interviewer avoids mistakenly introducing a new primary question in the effort to move the interviewee along. If a nudging probe is too lengthy, the interviewee may lose his train of thought or neglect to offer information he was trying to figure out how to express.

General Probing; Sweeping and Informational

Sweeping probes are commonly used during the closing of an interview or when the interviewer does not have any more prepared questions to ask. To use a sweeping probe, the interviewer must believe that some information may still be available, even though the interviewee has not been able to express it. Consider the following:

- Have I missed anything that you can think of?
- Is there anything else you would like to add?
- Before we move on, is there anything else you would like to cover on this topic?

The **informational probe** is a tool for gathering explanations, which is particularly important when the interviewee offers superficial information in response to a subjective question. Consider these:

- Tell me more about _____.
- What happened after _____?
- Explain that further for me, please.

Vague or ambiguous answers require something more direct, such as:

- What do you mean by _____?
- I'm not sure I know what you mean by _____?

Finally, use the informational probe when the interviewee offers a subjective response that requires clarification:

- Why do you feel that way?
- What is your attitude about _____?
- How strongly do you feel about _____?

Feedback-Related Probing; Restatement, Reflective, and Mirror

Feedback probes are used by the interviewer when the interviewee offers an irrelevant response to a primary question, refuses to answer the primary question, or answers only part of the primary question. When this happens, the interviewer has three choices: she can restate the original question, reflect the portion of the response that does answer the question, or summarize in a mirror response all that has been said about a particular topic.

Restatement   To use restatement probes properly, the interviewer must be tactful. The **restatement probe** is a method of repeating the original primary question after receiving an incomplete or irrelevant response. If she cannot be tactful, due to the difficulty of the interview, the interviewer may want to try another approach, such as changing the style of the primary question (open to closed; closed to open). Consider this restatement scenario:

Interviewer: How do you feel about joint custody?

Answer: Well, my sister says that joint custody is a joke. She knows a lady who is trying it but hates it.

Interviewer: How do *you* feel about joint custody?

Reflective   Reflective probes are a method of checking accuracy and motivating the interviewee to finish any incomplete answers to primary questions. Again, tact is critical to the success of this technique; reflective probes should be given with nonverbal as well as verbal cues. Consider these examples:

- Was that net or gross income?
- Was that your left or right arm?
- Are you sure there was no clause regarding post-dated checks in the contract?

When unsure about what has been said, try questions that reflect uncertainty:

- Are you defining completion of the contract as the date the carpet was laid in the new house?
- Am I correct when I say that Mary told you she was sexually harassed at least three times during the month of March?

Mirror   The **mirror probe** is used to summarize a series of answers to a series of questions on one topic. Reflective and mirror probes are closely related, but the mirror encompasses a larger scope. It may be most appropriate to use mirror probes when interviewing a client or accepting instructions from an attorney. Consider the following:

> Okay, let me review what you have said about the accident with the ladder. You purchased the ladder on December 12th, used it to fix the lights in the garage, and then stored it until spring. In the spring you used the ladder to clean the gutters on your house and fell because the top rung of the ladder broke when you stood on it. Is that the basics of the accident?

Using Secondary Questions

The use of secondary questions requires skill. A trained, experienced interviewer will not immediately move from one primary question to the next in the interview outline. Instead, she will carefully listen to the response to each question and then determine if the response is adequate. If not, she uses one of the secondary or probing questions to motivate the interviewee to complete the answer. Inexperienced interviewers should practice this skill by slowing down. By slowing the pace of the interview, the interviewer can listen more attentively.

One word of caution when using secondary questions: be patient! An impatient interviewer may ask a secondary question when the interviewee is only carefully thinking through a response to the primary question. The interruption distracts the interviewee, who may completely lose his train of thought and never answer the primary question. Impatience also shows disrespect and inattentiveness.

Voice inflection is also important. Think about how each question is asked, so that undue influence is not placed on the wrong part of the question.

EXAMPLE ────────────────────────────────

<u>Why</u> do you say that?

Why <u>do</u> you say that?

Why do <u>you</u> say that?

Why do you <u>say</u> that?

Why do you say <u>that</u>?[13]

────────────────────────────────

When using the reflective, restatement, or mirror probes, be careful not to **parrot** the interviewee. *Parroting* is the act of restating what has been said in a way that could be perceived as negative or mocking. Guard against this.

⚖ HOW TO STRUCTURE QUESTIONS

As a paralegal begins developing questions for an interview, investigation, or discovery, she will need to consult instructions like these for guidance and direction. As she gains experience, though, these basic rules and ideas will become natural and easy, particularly if she understands the basic types of questions available for use and has a feel for why good questions are required. The following is an overall list of the most basic concepts used to draft good questions.

Subject Matter

- Make the question meaningful by gaining a complete and personal understanding of the subject matter.
- Verify that the subject matter has been defined in the earliest questions in the interview outline.

- State the definition of the subject matter as precisely as possible in the earliest part of the outline.
- Evaluate the subject matter to see if it is meaningful to the interviewee. If not, try to develop a way of presenting the subject in a way that appeals to the interviewee.
- Decide which type or types of questions will net the best responses (e.g., closed questions for subjective material).
- Keep asking yourself, "What am I taking for granted?"

Open Questions

- Attempt to create open questions that are more directive (giving the interviewer control) than nondirective.
- Consider what closed questions or probes can be used to narrow the interviewee's wandering, if necessary.
- Predetermine the amount of response and the specifics within the response that are expected from the question.
- Be prepared to add probes.

Closed Questions

- Practice asking the question so as to avoid emphasizing the wrong word in the question.
- Avoid asking vague or complicated questions that confuse the interviewee.
- Be prepared to alternate closed and open questions by drafting both styles to cover the same subject matter.
- Anticipate the responsiveness of the interviewee by knowing the objective or subjective nature of the question.

Generally

- Phrase questions as concisely, accurately, honestly, and completely as possible.
- Check for relevance in the question. If there is a possibility that the interviewee will not understand the purpose or intent of the question, be prepared to explain or define any language in the question.
- Arrange questions in a logical and flowing sequence. Do not jump from one primary topic to another and back again.
- Understand the knowledge level of the interviewee as completely as possible and write the questions to fit him.
- Draft questions that are as simple as possible, avoiding unnecessary complexities.
- Create questions that the interviewee will find as easy as possible to answer.

- When dealing with sensitive topics (sex, politics, religion, income, etc.) or topics that are very subjective (spousal abuse, criminal behavior, victimization, etc.), strive to understand the relationship with the interviewee. Be keenly aware of all nonverbal messages, from both parties; they will help set the speed and course of the interview regarding these delicate topics.

PROBLEM-PRODUCING QUESTIONS

It is rather easy for the interviewer to avoid creating troublesome questions in advance of the interview, but it is another ball game during the interview. As discussed, probing questions are generally developed on the spot, when an incomplete or irrelevant response is given. To create a good probing question, the interviewer must understand what makes a problem question and know how to avoid them.

The Yes/No (Bipolar) Trap   A yes/no question is bipolar; a **bipolar question** is one that requires an answer from one of two opposites, yes or no. When creating a yes/no trap, the interviewer asks a yes/no-type question when in reality she wants specific information or a long open response.

EXAMPLE

Do you know when he hit his head?

  instead of

When did he hit his head?

Avoid the bipolar trap by using *What, When, Why, How, Explain, Tell me …* to start the sentence.

The Open-and-Closed Exchange   This problem question most commonly arises when the interviewer is attempting to develop primary questions during the actual interview. It happens when she asks an open question but then changes the question before the interviewee responds to the first one. The new question is usually closed or bipolar.

EXAMPLE

Tell me about your property located in the 1800 block of North Main. Have you owned it long?

To avoid creating this problem, the interviewer may do three things: (1) listen to the question as it is being asked; (2) wait silently after asking the question; and (3) give the interviewee ample time to respond to the question.

The Multiple Questions   A multiple question is really several questions combined and asked all at once. This occurs regularly in everyday conversation.

Pay attention to the next casual conversation that occurs with a friend or co-worker and see for yourself.

EXAMPLE

When and how did you obtain the first prospectus?

What type of formal education do you have and where did you get it?

The downside of this kind of question is that the interviewee will most likely be unable to remember all that has been asked, and thus will give an incomplete answer. A hesitant interviewee, especially one dealing with subjective material, will answer only the part of the question that she is comfortable with. Avoid this problem by asking only one question at a time.

The Unintentional Leading Question   Often the interviewer voices a question before realizing that the question is unintentionally leading; that is, it pushes the interviewee to answer in a specific way. This is common with personal injury paralegals, who often conduct spontaneous interviews with persons not known to have information. For instance, a paralegal is conducting her regular investigatory activities when she runs across an unexpected witness, and in the moment of that discovery the paralegal begins a nonscheduled interview with no preplanned questions.

EXAMPLE

From where you were standing, could you see that the blue car was traveling quite a bit faster than the red one?

Don't you think Mrs. Smith was fairly talkative for a woman who had hurt her back so badly?

The interviewer can avoid this by: (1) slowing down during the course of the interview; (2) using short, neutral questions; (3) using a leading question only when the purpose of doing so is clear and she knows what she is doing.

The Inference Game   An inference problem arises when the interviewer has not taken the time to fully understand the subject matter of the interview and is therefore guessing at what the interviewee might know.

EXAMPLE

Could the problem with the contract have been that Mrs. Smith didn't read the last paragraph before she signed it?

In the investigation, the paralegal may need to ask a series of questions that appear to be guessing, but actually are not. She is asking questions to test the interviewee's knowledge of an event that the paralegal already knows about. To avoid inappropriate inference, spend adequate time to understand the subject matter of the interview, prepare an interview outline, and ask questions rather than guessing.

The Yes-Means-No Question   The final problem question appears to be bipolar, but in reality has only one answer. These types of questions have very predictable answers.

EXAMPLE ————————————————————————————————

Do you want to be subpoenaed to the deposition?

Are you telling me that Mrs. Smith never drove her car the day you saw her hit the pole?

To avoid the "yes means no" problem, follow the instructions in the section titled "Why Good Questions Are Required." When creating questions in the midst of the interview, the interviewer can slow down and carefully think through the question before asking it, or she can write it down and read it to herself before asking it.

SUMMARY

- Good questions are required if an interview is to yield its intended results. Good questions are simple, understandable, bias-free, and nonirritating.
- The two general categories of questions are open and closed. Each of these is subcategorized as objective or subjective, leading or neutral, primary or secondary, or probing. Each of these serves specific roles in the interview.
- Structuring a good question is as easy as understanding the subject matter of the interview and the knowledge level of the interviewee. Commonly, an interviewer will take for granted that an interviewee knows more about a topic than he does, or that both interviewer and interviewee share the same understanding of certain terms. When this happens, the interviewer will not prepare good questions.
- The most common problem questions arise when the interviewer does not think carefully about the question before asking it. Avoid yes/no trap questions, inference questions, unintentionally leading questions, yes-means-no questions, and multiple questions by slowing down, pre-reading and mentally testing the question, and allowing the interviewee adequate time to respond.

ACTIVITIES

1. Select a current event or general topic and conduct two ten-minute interviews. In the first interview, use only primary/open questions. In the second interview, use primary/open questions and follow up the responses with secondary questions. Log which questions are objective and which are sub-

jective. Identify the types of secondary questions used to probe the interviewee. In which interview did you have the most success? Why?

2. Select an interview from a leading news magazine or newspaper. Review the article and see if you can identify the question type and a sequence used. Can you decide what determined the question types? If so, explain. Can you decide how the questions influenced the interviewee's responses? If so, explain.

3. Tape-record an interview from the television program *60 Minutes, 20/20,* or *Dateline.* Identify any problem-causing questions. How did the interviewer use them, and why? Did they affect the responses received? Did they affect the climate of the interview?

4. Answer the following questions as an exercise in learning how little can be taken for granted. After you have answered them, ask three other people to do the same. Are the results surprising?

- What color is the complement of blue?
- What is the cube of 2?
- Name the capital of Nebraska.
- Name the five largest cities in the United States.
- Who are the U.S. Senators from this state?
- What date is Arbor Day?
- Without looking, how many keys are on your key ring?
- Without counting, how many teeth do you have?

CASE STUDY

Keller v. Welch

Review the following case details. Assume, for purposes of this assignment, that most of the physical evidence has already been collected. A brief synopsis of each piece of evidence follows the case details.

Your assignment is to evaluate the only eyewitness (as discussed in Chapter 1), Rochelle Tyler, based on the data provided here. Review the witness report attached and also rate the quality of her story. Be specific in your rating. After qualifying her credibility and that of her story, begin preparing to interview her yourself. Determine what the subject matter of the interview will be and then draft a series of questions you will use during the interview, placing them in an interview outline. Identify the questions as either:

- open or closed
- primary or secondary
- objective or subjective
- leading or neutral.

Also outline what type of probing you anticipate needing to use with this witness and why. Once you have finished, be prepared to interview a classmate during role-playing exercises based on this case.

Case Details

On Sunday, March 20, 1994, at 12:40 P.M., Shari Keller was allegedly injured in a car accident. Keller was a passenger in a car driven by her fifteen-year-old son, Calvin. Keller's husband, Bill, was also in the car. At the time of the accident, the Keller vehicle was southbound on Riverside Road and approaching the intersection of Riverside and 4th Avenue. At the same time, Bert Welch was driving his mother's car northbound on Riverside, attempting to make a left-hand turn onto 4th Avenue. The cars collided in the intersection when Welch's front driver's-side bumper hit the Kellers' rear driver's-side door. Shari Keller is complaining of whiplash and pain in the lumbar area of her back. (Review Appendix B for anatomical clarifications.) One eyewitness has been located: Rochelle Tyler. Tyler is an acquaintance of Welch. She is employed at the Salvation Army as the volunteer coordinator.

Physical Evidence

Photographs of the Scene   Photographs show that there are businesses on three corners of the intersection: a Pizza Hut on the southwest corner, an auto body shop on the southeast corner, and a funeral home on the northeast corner. A residential home occupies the northwest corner. The intersection slopes dramatically to the south right at the 4th Avenue crossing. Visibility is somewhat impaired from both angles at 4th Avenue. The view from 4th Avenue onto Riverside is impeded by a two-foot-high retaining wall that lines the sidewalks to the intersection. Neither car was approaching from that angle.

Photographs of the Cars   The Welch car has minimal damage to the front driver's-side bumper. The license plates on this vehicle differ from those listed on the police report; this should be looked into. The Keller car suffered more damage than did the Welch vehicle, but nothing that impairs its use. From the picture it is difficult to visualize how any passenger could have been injured.

Medical Reports   Shari Keller's medical records are extensive and marked by years of back pain and treatment. She is an obese women in her early forties. She works as a receptionist at a local chiropractic office in exchange for free treatment. She claims never to have experienced the kind of back pain she suffers now prior to the accident. There is some question as to the validity of her current claim.

Weather Reports   On March 20th, the roads were clear and the weather was good. It was sunny and 20 degrees Fahrenheit. There had been no snow for more than one week and consequently there were no patches of ice on the road. At 12:40 P.M. the sun was almost directly above the intersection, and thus vision should not have been hindered by the sun's position.

Rochelle Tyler Witness Report

The witness is reluctant to get involved in the case; however, because she is an acquaintance of Welch, she will talk with us. The two know each other through some volunteer work Welch did for the Salvation Army (ringing bells at Christmas).

Tyler was in her car at the southeast corner of the intersection when the accident happened. She was trying to make a southbound turn onto Riverside, and was inching onto Riverside to view oncoming traffic at the time the accident occurred. While attempting to execute her turn, Tyler had moved into the easternmost lane of traffic on Riverside when she noticed Welch making his turn. She waved at him then. It was directly after the wave that Welch and Keller hit.

Tyler completed her turn and pulled into the Pizza Hut parking lot. She completed her turn because she was afraid the Welch and Keller cars might slide into her. She parked parallel to Riverside in the Pizza Hut parking lot. Tyler was at the scene for one hour and during that time spoke with Welch twice. She does not recall speaking with a police officer. (At the completion of the interview, she changed her mind and stated that the police officer may have spoken to her during her hour in the parking lot.)

Tyler has been in two serious car accidents herself, both times suffering back injuries. One of those was a rear-end accident, the other a side-impact collision. Based on those experiences, Tyler was not convinced that Mrs. Keller was injured in the accident, as she appeared alert and mobile. She notes that Keller never complained of back pain directly after the accident.

With regard to the collision, she did not see more than one impact, although she heard Keller

say there were two actual collisions between the cars. Tyler never left her car, however, and cannot verify what the Keller and Welch cars looked like. Tyler did say that the impact was "light" and that there was no broken glass. She did not hear squealing brakes.

Tyler believes both drivers were to blame for the accident. Qualifying that statement, she explains that Keller was driving too fast and that Welch should not have waved to her.

NOTES

1 This term comes from Stanley L. Payne's *The Art of Asking Questions* (Princeton University Press, 1951), and is used throughout his work as a description of persons who use and depend on question style and format in their given professions. These, of course, include attorneys and paralegals.

2 *Id.* at 3.

3 *Id.* at 16–17.

4 Barbara Snell Dohrenwend, "Some Effects of Open and Closed Questions on Respondent's Answer," 24 *Field Methods & Techniques, Human Organizations* 175 (1965).

5 *Id.* at 180.

6 *Id.* at 178.

7 *Id.*

8 Dohrenwend at 182.

9 Barbara Snell Dohrenwend & Stephen A. Richardson, "A Use for Leading Questions in Research Interviewing," 23 *Field Methods & Techniques, Human Organizations* 76 (1964).

10 Charles J. Stewart & William B. Cash, Jr., *Interviewing Principles and Practices* 65 (8th ed., McGraw Hill, 1997).

11 *Id.* at 66.

12 *Id.* at 60.

13 Payne at 204.

4

INTERVIEWING THE CLIENT

OBJECTIVES　After completing this chapter, you will know:

- How the paralegal/client relationship affects the client interview.
- How to initiate the client interview, where to conduct the interview, how to adequately record the interview, and how to prepare a client profile at the conclusion of the interview.
- What types of difficult personalities may be encountered when interviewing clients and how to deal with them.
- What types of questions are used to interview the client.
- What criteria to use when evaluating the client interview.

⚖ INTRODUCTION

Outside of general and expert witness interviews (see Chapters 6 and 5 respectively), the paralegal must be prepared to handle the specific needs of the client. Communication with the client is not limited to one or two interviews—it is continual and progressive. Beginning with the initial client interview, the legal team, and particularly the paralegal, will meet repeatedly with the client over the life of the case. The goal of each meeting is the same: to uncover additional details of the story and continually evaluate the credibility of the client and her claims. Specific strategies unique to the client are used to motivate and deal with her. Before a paralegal can learn client-specific interviewing techniques, though, he must understand his relationship with the client.

The Paralegal/Client Relationship

The paralegal has a unique relationship with the client, partly because the client commonly feels intimidated by the attorney early in the relationship. The client's discomfort is usually based on preconceived ideas regarding the attorney's status and/or demeanor; valid or not, this barrier may interfere with future investigative interviews.

The paralegal is often perceived by the client as less threatening and easier to talk to. This is not a negative reflection on the attorney, but a realistic aspect of the professional relationship. In some instances attorneys do not actively listen to the client during the initial interview, but rather evaluate her and the story being told as to whether they provide the foundation required to support the legal action and theory. This "clinical" type of communication fosters the idea that attorneys are not approachable. This is why paralegals often sit in on initial client interviews (and subsequent interviews) and gather more specific details. Once the attorney has completed the initial probe of the client and her story, the paralegal begins focusing on more specific subjective details.

Experienced paralegals understand the components of the attorney/client and paralegal/client relationships, and work to develop common ground with the client during the early stages of the relationship. During this development phase, the paralegal offers only small talk, avoiding formal or substantive topics of conversation, so as to gain insights into the client and to form a secondary relationship. The secondary relationship, based on trust, develops into a rapport between the paralegal and the client which carries over to the attorney. Psychologically, the client connects the commonality found between herself and the paralegal with the attorney. This same principle can work in reverse: any damage or barriers created with the client during the development of this relationship will work against the attorney.

⚖ THE INITIAL CLIENT INTERVIEW: AN OVERVIEW

The initial client interview is unique, is generally the first meeting with the client, is commonly preceded by a lengthy telephone conversation, and is usually led by the attorney. Often the initial client interview is tense and uncomfortable because trust relationships have not been built between the attorney and the client. In some instances, the attorney obtains the basic facts of the case, discusses the fee, accepts representation, and then leaves the paralegal to collect the full details of the story.

The interview can vary in many aspects. It can be a long, formal interview during which the potential client provides photographs, contracts, and other types of primary evidence; or it can be less formal. It may occur in a hospital room or jail. The client may be willing to talk about the main subject matter, but in some cases is not. Regardless of the circumstances, the primary objective of the initial interview is to gather the facts and obtain the details of the story.

Lawyers approach this interview from a different perspective than does the paralegal. The lawyers want to identify the legal issues and qualify the case from a substantive legal point of view; they commonly look to the paralegal for the layperson's perception of the case, the credibility of the story being told, and the credibility of the potential client.

It is standard practice for the paralegal to bring a phone book to the initial client interview, to help the client identify witnesses, spell the witnesses' names correctly, and specify the witnesses' telephone numbers and addresses. The information obtained in this first meeting is used to begin the investigation.

The purposes of the initial interview are:

- To obtain the client's story in the fullest possible detail
- To evaluate the client's credibility
- To evaluate the credibility of the client's story
- To obtain the names and addresses of potential witnesses and other persons who may have additional information and details
- To develop a timeline or chronology of the events
- To gather evidence already in the possession of the potential client.

The initial interview thus serves a variety of purposes, including allowing the attorney and paralegal to begin deciding what must be done in the investigation. To organize the data gleaned from the interview, the paralegal must create a client information checklist (see Figure 4-1) and complete it during the course of the interview.

CONDUCTING THE INTERVIEW

The client interview, like all interviews, requires the paralegal to be organized, diligent, and patient. Communication with the client is critical to the success of the case. Therefore, when handling a client interview, whether it be the initial interview or a subsequent interview, the paralegal must consider the following basic elements:

- Where to conduct the interview
- The manner in which to conduct the interview

Figure 4-1
Client information
checklist

<u>Initial</u> interview, <u>May 2, 1998</u>, <u>3:30</u> P.M. at <u>Smith Law Offices</u>
<u>Susan Smith</u>, attorney, and <u>Bob Williams</u>, paralegal, in attendance

Plaintiff/Defendant (circle one)
Name of client (full/legal name, including any maiden name):

Date of birth:
Date of accident/occurrence:
Location of accident/occurrence:

Time of day of accident/occurrence:
Spouse's name:
Client's address:

Phone number:
Employer:

    address: phone number:
Supervisor's name:
    phone number:
Dates of employment: (if the employment is less than 1 year, get more
details on past employers)

Spouse's employer:

    address: phone number:

Social Security number:
Driver's license number:
Vehicle registration number: (if accident case)
Name of closest relative:

    address: phone number:

Name of opposing party:

    address: phone number:
Employer:

    address: phone number:

Does the client know this party yes/no
What happened: (in detail)

Any diagram that can be given by the client:

Evidence provided during the interview:
1-
2-
3-

- The paralegal's self-control
- Creation of the client profile.

Where to Conduct the Interview

The paralegal's first concern when interviewing the client is where to hold the interview. Client interviews, initial or otherwise, should always be held in a location and at a time of day that allows a detailed and uninterrupted discussion. Some interviews will be held in the law office, others at the client's home or place of business, and still others in a hospital or other setting. Many factors influence the choice of interview location; for example, a client who was recently injured in an accident may be interviewed in the hospital. In a business case, it may be preferable to hold the meeting at the client's usual place of business or the location where the triggering event occurred. Each scheduled interview should be conducted in a location that maximizes everyone's time and efforts.

Benefits of Certain Locations   The paralegal may find that the less stressful the meeting site, the less stressful the interview. Most people are comfortable in their homes, so meeting at the client's home can be advantageous to the paralegal. Upon arriving at a client's home, the paralegal should begin assessing the client's lifestyle, her credibility status, and how damages suffered from the alleged action are affecting the client.

When interviewing a client in a hospital, the paralegal must be conscious of the hospital staff and treating physician. A casual style and approach in the hospital setting are essential to avoid defensiveness on the part of doctors, nurses, and other hospital staff who may become witnesses.

In a business-related action, it is preferable to conduct an interview as soon as possible at the business office. This allows the paralegal to meet and identify key witnesses (employees) and assess their existing or potential knowledge of the event at the same time. The interviewer also gains a better understanding of the business operation, thus aiding in the development of interviewing questions and topics. Key documents and evidence are also often readily available at the location of the business where a triggering event occurred.

The disadvantage of the business office interview is the possibility of interruption. The client may hold any number of positions inside the company, all of which may require her to answer employee questions, phone calls, or business problems during the interview. It should be made clear to the client that two or more hours of uninterrupted time will be needed for any interview conducted at her office.

Recording the Interview   Regardless of where the client interview is conducted, the attorney must decide if the interview should be recorded, transcribed, or videotaped. Many times the initial client interview is conducted by the attorney, while the paralegal handles the taping or recording. If the interview is to be transcribed, a court reporter will be hired. In subsequent interviews the attorney may determine that note taking is a sufficient means of recording the interview.

The legal team benefits from a permanent record of the interview because law office staff, particularly paralegals and associate attorneys, move in and out of cases (and firms). Recording of client interviews allows legal team members not present at those interviews an opportunity to evaluate the client and her story at a later date.

Note Taking   The paralegal must take some notes if the client's testimony is to be preserved. To avoid alienating the client (or any interviewee), the paralegal must balance note taking with eye contact; therefore, the paralegal may use a practical note-taking tool that will expedite this process. See Figure 4-2.

Figure 4-2

Note-taking tool

Witness: Maxwell Smith
Date: April 11, 1997
Location: E&Q Engineering

Dates	Interview Questions	Notes	Conflicts
June 23, 1996 about noon.	Tell me what you heard about Mr. Jones getting fired?	Smith was reluctant, probably scared. Bill Mill, Sue Shoe, Marla Apson, also possible witnesses.	No conflict here, confirm with witnesses he identified.

A blank version of this note-taking tool can be created at the time of the interview, or it can be prepared before the interview and carried into the interview with a note pad. A preprinted note-taking tool often detracts from the comfortable atmosphere the paralegal tries to create for the client, as it denotes rigidity. If the client is particularly uncomfortable, the paralegal should avoid using a preprinted note-taking outline.

Manner of Conducting the Interview

When conducting a client interview in the law office, the paralegal has more control over the environment and the parties' comfort level. At the onset of the early or first interview, orient the client to the office by taking her around and introducing her to the staff members she will work with. Be friendly and courteous, but maintain professionalism in the relationship. Offer the client coffee, a soft drink, or water. Begin developing a trust relationship with the client by looking for areas of common interest, but not in areas dealing with the specifics of the pending interview or of a stressful nature.

If the attorney has not already done so, the paralegal should explain the duty of confidentiality, to reassure the client about revealing sensitive information. Keep in mind that most jurisdictions permit, or even require, attorneys to disclose certain information.[1] Prior to the client interview, discuss with the attorney whether this ought to be mentioned to the client.

Open the interview by probing the client for details of how she came to your law firm, or what has happened since the last interview. These questions provide background in early interviews and follow-up data in subsequent interviews. Throughout the interview, use the active listening techniques discussed in Chapter 1. Remember, a client carries many burdens when facing litigation and sincerely listening to her story is critical in helping to ease her fears. No matter which interview is occurring (initial, second, or fifteenth), the paralegal should open the meeting by fully listening to the client's whole story. Hear what is and is not being said. The client, like all witnesses, recalls certain parts of a story on some days and other parts on other days; therefore, it is imperative that she tell as much of the story as appropriate each time an interview is conducted. Building a case based on background and historical information requires the client to tell her story a number of times, especially as new information is gathered, interrogatories are answered, and other case-building activities occur.

In the initial interview, the paralegal can open the dialogue by saying, "Tell me what happened and why you are here." In subsequent interviews, the paralegal may ask, "Review for me the confrontation between yourself and Mr. Waxler on June 15th. What has happened since that time?" This type of question allows the client to retell her story and to add new details. Listen intently to the entire story without taking notes, allowing the client to speak uninterrupted. This demonstrates the paralegal's involvement and dedication to the case and respect for the client. When the client believes the paralegal is dedicated to the outcome of the case, the bond or trust relationship grows, and so does the amount of disclosure by the client.

Once the client has stopped talking and has signaled that she is finished, summarize or paraphrase ("rebound") what has been said. A summary of the story gives the client the opportunity to fill in missing or misunderstood information and allows the paralegal to begin taking notes.

After a client has completely given all the facts of the triggering event, she may feel uncomfortable and vulnerable. At this point, the paralegal should explain to the client that what she is saying is protected by the attorney/client privilege unless the client gives written consent for information release. By explaining this protection, the paralegal eases the client's anxiety and again builds the relationship between them.

Self-Control   The client interview is an exercise in self-control. Certain personalities are difficult to handle, and spending extended periods of time with such a client can be a challenge. Some clients are deceptive or hold back information, and the paralegal must be prepared to work with these people. See the more detailed discussion on difficult personalities later in this chapter.

No matter what hurdle the paralegal faces when interviewing the client, he must use professionalism and courtesy. The paralegal's patience will eventually uncover the reason for a difficult client's behavior, at which time the paralegal will be better able to understand the behavior and deal with it.

A client who has suffered a closed-head trauma may struggle with severe personality disorders. The client who has a chemical imbalance, such as insulin-dependent diabetes, may exhibit anxiety, rage, or other extreme behaviors. Clients who have suffered sexual abuse or who are alcohol or drug abusers may also bring personality problems with them, all of which are reflected during the client interview.

To deal with clients who have any of these problems, or a variety of others, the paralegal must adjust his attitude and use self-control.

To manage a difficult client and interview, allow the client to speak freely, investigate the cause of the client's distress, and continue the interview using empathy and compassion. Finding the true reason for difficult behavior in a client may actually change a paralegal's negative feelings about the client to feelings of understanding and motivation to resolve the wrong done to the client.

Creating a Client Profile

At the conclusion of the client interview, a profile must be created. This organizational tool offers a method of quickly referencing the client's biographical information as well as details on the client's character, case problems, case limitations, and the legal issue. Vital statistics and family members are also outlined in this document, which aids the legal team in the search for witnesses.

Attorneys use the client profile when drafting the complaint or answer in the case, when providing background information to expert witnesses, and when drafting opening and closing arguments. A profile will include all of the following information:[2]

- Dates of:
  - marriages
  - divorces
  - deaths
  - births
- Social Security number
- Driver's license number
- Names of fact witnesses
- Names of family members
- Occupations of client, witnesses, family members
- Work experience:
  - names of employers, employers' addresses and telephone numbers
  - names of supervisors
  - dates of employment
  - positions held

- reasons for leaving
    - names of employees who can be used as references
- Special skills
- History of residence
- Educational history:
    - names of schools, dates of attendance, degrees earned
- Armed services history
- Listing of all medical providers (in the case of physical injury):
    - names and addresses of doctors
    - names of clinics or hospitals the doctor is associated with
    - dates of treatment
    - any special facts that may influence the case
    - names of any nurses or medical staff who might serve as witnesses
- Logical sequence diagram
- Any facts that influence the client's credibility:
    - criminal background
    - hobbies
    - talents
    - community service
    - awards
    - favorable qualities
    - negative qualities.

IDENTIFYING DIFFICULT CLIENTS

When interviewing the client, the paralegal must identify personal characteristics of the client that may hinder the interview and the case. These characteristics primarily concern the client's personality and emotional state.

General Evaluation of the Client

Most clients are reliable, cooperative, and dependable. When attempting to identify whether a client has a difficult personality, the paralegal should first identify the client's basic characteristics. As discussed in Chapter 1, this means evaluating credibility, knowledge level and status, motives, and appearance. After completing an initial evaluation of the client based on these criteria, the paralegal begins identifying characteristics that define the client's personality, including passivity, complacency, or dishonesty. An important goal in any interview is to identify personality characteristics of the interviewee that influence his performance; the focus of this section is identifying characteristics that negatively affect the *legal* client.

Naturally, the client's personality will affect a jury's view of the client and his credibility. Ideally, the legal team wants the jurors to see the client as the team presents him to them. This may be hard to do if a difficult client demonstrates personality traits that make it impossible for a jury to believe that he is a victim or a "good guy", therefore, careful evaluation of the client's personality must be done during all interviews and particularly the initial client interview.

In addition to the jury's view of the client, the paralegal must evaluate the client for his own working purposes. Difficult clients are hard to interview!

Difficult Personalities

When a paralegal identifies a client who is difficult to work with, he must do two things:

- Identify the reason why the client is difficult
- Identify the client's personality.

By identifying the reason for a client's misbehavior or resistance in the legal relationship and interview, the paralegal may find out how to create an environment in which the client's tensions are eased. A difficult client is often a fearful client, and the fear is often related to his feelings of being out of control. Remember, the credibility of a client is often greatly diminished if she appears hostile.

To expedite the interview, the paralegal must work to identify any factors in the client's story or experiences that are creating fear or anxiety, to alleviate those feelings, and to move the interview forward. These negative feelings are known as the **fear factor**. Once a "fear" topic is identified, the paralegal (and the legal team) can strive to ease the client's fears and decrease negative behavior and actions by the client.

EXAMPLE

While attending an initial client interview, a paralegal notices that the client is very aggressive toward the attorney. The subject matter of the meeting is sexual discrimination. The client, a man in his thirties, is demanding and overbearing with the attorney and the paralegal. At the conclusion of the meeting, the attorney comments on the potential difficulty she may have in working with this client. The paralegal agrees, but suggests that a second meeting be conducted in an attempt to uncover the root problem.

During the second meeting, the paralegal discovers that the client is a single parent who is afraid of losing custody of his children if he is fired because of the discrimination action. Once the fear factor is identified, the legal team can help ease the client's fear of losing his children. The team can offer to handle any residual legal matter stemming from the discrimination action, offer to contact the ex-spouse's attorney to explain the situation, or offer to find case law to support his retention of the children under such circumstances. By identifying and dealing with the client's fears, the paralegal and the legal team help the client become the kind of witness who helps rather than hinders his case.

To further define a difficult client, it is often necessary to identify a personality trait that best describes the client's behavior. The three most common difficult personalities are:

- The needy client
- The anxious client
- The dishonest client.

Identifying one or more of these traits in a difficult client is critical to the success of all client interviews and possibly the case. Clients who feel out of control tend to scrutinize each interview and be suspicious of the motives behind it. By identifying the difficult client's personality, the paralegal/interviewer is better able to deal with the client's negative actions. Knowing the personality of the client, the paralegal can judge whether to employ active listening, alter questioning styles, change his role from passive to aggressive (or vice versa), or use any other appropriate strategy to conduct a productive interview.

Needy Client The needy client looks at the paralegal/interviewer as a therapist and confidant, especially in family law matters. Empathy is the key to working with the needy client. Because the paralegal spends a large amount of time with the client, both in and out of the interview, he must assist the client in overcoming her neediness. Expressing empathy creates an independence in the relationship between paralegal and client, which is required to accomplish the goals of the interview.

To help relieve the client's neediness, ask her to gather documents, draft a timeline, or compile a witness list to be used during the interview. These tasks place responsibility on the client and create independence. When the client is empowered through strategies such as these, she becomes easier to question and is better able to answer questions.

Anxious Client The anxious client constantly seeks reassurance from the paralegal/interviewer, and demands a great deal of attention both within and outside of the interview. This personality trait may cause the greatest amount of outward conflict between paralegal and client, as it is common for the anxious client to expect all of the interviewer's attention to be devoted to her. Rationally, the client may understand that such a demand is not practical or possible, but emotionally the client expects such treatment. It is critical to the success of this client's case that the paralegal employ empathy and honest communication when dealing with her. Demanding clients respond to logic, especially when logic is explained in an empathetic fashion. To create honest communication with the anxious client, the paralegal must develop a trust relationship with her and depend on it during difficult communication periods.

Anxious clients tend to ask a lot of questions, and in the interview the paralegal may have to struggle to keep the anxious client focused on anything other than these questions. Controlling the interview is key in dealing with the anxious client, and is accomplished by:

- Thoughtfully probing her anxiety
- Listening analytically to the client's questions
- Being respectful of the client's anxiety
- Defining the goals and boundaries of the interview.

Dishonest Client   The last category is the dishonest client. Although the anxious client may be the most conflictual client to deal with, the dishonest client is the most difficult. A dishonest client will say and do whatever it takes to get what she wants. Manipulation is the predominant factor in the interviewer/interviewee relationship, and often the interview is well under way before the paralegal realizes the deception. To deal with the dishonest client, the interviewer must:

- Carefully end the interview when the first dishonesty is discovered
- Arrange for a follow-up interview within a few days
- Carefully plan the topics and subtopics of all subsequent interviews
- Place the topics in chronological order, making it difficult for the client to embellish
- Introduce each topic
- Use **lead-in**[3] questions to direct the client.

A lead-in question is not directly related to the objectives of the interview, but functions as an introduction to the forthcoming relevant question. The purpose of the lead-in is to set the stage for the respondent to provide a more relevant and accurate response.

EXAMPLE

(1) Did you have a chance to draft a timeline of the events?
(2) How far did you get with the timeline?
(3) Did you have any trouble remembering any details?
(4) Can you show me why your timeline of May 18th differs from that on the insurance claim?

In the example, the three lead-in questions allow the client to provide a more truthful response to the objective question regarding the discrepancies on May 18th.

QUESTIONING THE CLIENT

To initiate the discussion on how to question a client, it is appropriate first to remind that clients come in all sizes and shapes and from all different educational and personal backgrounds. Never talk down to or patronize a client—but ensure that he understands the depth and purpose of each question and the words that make up the question. Defining terms, especially legal terms, is necessary during some portions of the client interview, and the paralegal/ interviewer must be careful that he does not damage his relationship with the client in doing so. For instance, in an effort to define the term *income tax,* a paralegal may offer an explanation that helps one client and offends another.

EXAMPLE

How do you feel about your income tax—that is, the amount you have to pay to the government on the money you take in during the year?[4]

By rephrasing such a question and placing the explanation of the term before the term itself, the paralegal will avoid alienating the client, regardless of the client's previous knowledge of the term.

EXAMPLE

How do you feel about the amount you have to pay the government on the money you take in during the year—your income taxes, that is?[5]

By employing a conversational questioning style (like that in the second example), the paralegal will not offend anyone and will still get the job done. A conversational style is usually advantageous throughout the interview.

The Opening

The first few minutes of the client interview set the tone for the remainder of the meeting. Greet the client warmly; reestablish the trust relationship built with the client in previous meetings, telephone conversations, and interviews; state clearly and concisely the goals of the interview and how long the interview will probably last. Setting boundaries lets the client know what to expect and helps her to relax.

Be patient in the early moments of the interview—the client may actually be the party asking the questions. Answer all questions honestly; then, after the client has settled in, ask a very open question like:

- "Do you have any more questions before we begin?"
- "Do you have any new information or evidence to give me since our last meeting?"

Once these niceties have been observed, the paralegal should move on to the body of the interview and begin questioning the client on the substantive topics.

The Body: Questioning Strategies

Questioning requires the paralegal first to develop a trust relationship, which is used to motivate the client and move her to the second stage of the interview interaction. This second level (defined in Chapter 1) deals with intimate and sometimes controversial topics. Eventually, the paralegal must move the client from level two to level three. This last level in the interview deals with highly intimate and controversial topics. To move the client through these phases, the paralegal may need to alternate between a passive and aggressive role in his questioning. (Remember, in the aggressive role the paralegal establishes the purpose for the interview and attempts to control the speed, formality, and flow of the interview. In the passive role, the paralegal allows the client to determine the speed and flow of the interview.)

Use the following guidelines when questioning a client:

- Ask one question at a time.

- Avoid *why* questions whenever possible, as they appear to demand explanations and justifications and may put the client on the defensive.

- Use encouraging probes to move the client forward ("What happened next?", "Go on with your story").

- Avoid embarrassing questions until absolutely necessary (level two or three) and then attempt to ask them in a nonthreatening manner ("I understand you were embarrassed by the failed marriage, but what events kept you from reporting the spousal abuse sooner?").

- Encourage the client to continue answering open questions by using semi-verbal responses. (*Client:* I wanted to tell someone about the abuse but it seemed hopeless. *Paralegal:* Um-hummm. *Client:* What I mean is … .)

- Be aware of all nonverbal behaviors, especially during level two and three questions. Make sure only positive reactions are given to the client.

- When urging a client to elaborate, restate, reflect, or mirror her statements or questions rather than offering ideas or solutions. This will prompt the client to continue answering questions. (*Client:* I didn't know what to do. *Paralegal:* "You didn't know what your options were?")

There are no definitive procedures or plans for conducting or questioning clients. Each situation is dictated by the client, her personality, her needs, and the goals of the interview; the paralegal must choose his questions, style, and behavior based on these variables.

The Closing

Because of the sensitive nature of legal matters and the client's personal investment of time, an interview is closed both consciously and unconsciously. In the opening, the paralegal sets the boundaries for the interview by estimating the approximate length of the interview, which subconsciously prepares the client for a closing to the interview. To close the interview consciously, the paralegal uses a combination of questions and nonverbal actions. Some of the most successful questions for this are:

- "Do you have any more questions for me today?"

- "Are there any concerns you have about the material we covered today?"

- "Would you like to set up another meeting for next week?"
- "Why don't you call me if you think of anything we didn't cover today."

In conjunction with these closing questions, the paralegal may use nonverbal techniques for signaling the end of the meeting, such as:

- preparing to rise
- uncrossing legs
- breaking eye contact
- offering a handshake.

After closing the interview, the paralegal must evaluate the results of the interview.

EVALUATING THE INTERVIEW

Break the evaluation of the interview into six categories.

- Preinterview preparation:
    - How completely was the client background information reviewed prior to the interview?
    - How completely were the questions for the client formulated prior to the meeting, and did they meet the goals of the interview?
    - Were the goals of the interview appropriate?
- Interview structure:
    - How effective was the opening?
    - How effectively were passive and aggressive roles used to motivate the client?
    - How effectively were legal terms and objectives explained?
    - How effective was the closing?
- Was the client profile completed or added to?
- Was a difficult personality identified?
    - If yes, what was the personality type?
    - What methods were used to control the personality?
    - What problems are anticipated in the future based on the personality?
    - What can be done in future interviews to help remove the barriers created by the personality?
- Interview skills:
    - Were the questioning techniques used appropriate and effective?
    - How skillfully were the questioning techniques used?
    - How appropriate were the responses?
    - Was the pace of the interview appropriate? Why or why not?

- Were adequate notes taken or the interview recorded properly?
- Was the client appropriately motivated into level two and three areas? Why or why not?
- How effectively were the paralegal's listening skills used?
- Were the goals of the interview met?

ETHICAL CONSIDERATIONS

The paralegal must demonstrate great respect as he interviews and works with the client. As an agent of the attorney, the paralegal is obligated to function in a manner that parallels the behavior outlined by the American Bar Association in its Model Rules of Professional Conduct (MRPC), as well as those promulgated by the National Association of Legal Assistants and the National Federation of Paralegal Associations. A paralegal's work is a privilege afforded him based on his education, experience, and ethics.

With few exceptions, it is improper for the paralegal or attorney to divulge any secrets and confidences of the client. Model Rule 1.6 of the MRPC defines the duty of confidentiality as two concepts: (1) the client has the right to feel certain that the information she provides to her attorney will remain confidential; (2) the attorney has the right to expect that the client will provide all relevant information. The concepts underlying this rule require express cooperation from the paralegal who works with an attorney. Both attorney and client show the utmost trust when the paralegal is allowed to deal directly with the client, and the privilege of this relationship should never be jeopardized by careless or foolish behavior.

SUMMARY

- The paralegal/client relationship is one that fosters commonality and trust.
- The initial client interview is commonly tense but is soothed by using empathy. It also sets the stage for future interviews.
- The client information checklist and the client profile are valuable tools for managing the data gleaned from each client interview.
- Before arranging for an interview, the paralegal must determine where to conduct the client interview, the manner in which to conduct it, and how to manage his behavior.
- The three most common difficult personalities are the needy client, the anxious client, and the dishonest client. Each of these is dealt with by using various questioning techniques and nonverbal cues.
- To select questions for the client, the paralegal must break the interview into three parts: the opening, the body, and the closing. Each section employs a variety of questions and styles, all of which are chosen based on the client, the goals of the interview, and the pace of the interview.

■■ ACTIVITIES

1. Visit a crisis center in your community or on campus. Observe how volunteer counselors handle telephone counseling. Talk with the counselors about their training techniques and self-evaluations.

2. Contact the local chapter of your state's bar association and ask for the names of pro bono clinics that need volunteers. Volunteer to assist with intake interviews. Spend time with the coordinators of these programs to understand the goals of the interviews and how to conduct them.

3. You have probably been an interviewee in many counseling-type interviews during your lifetime. These may have been between parent and child, employer and employee, or academic counselor and student, to name a few. Pick out two or three of the best and worst counselors you have experienced and list the characteristics of each. Compare these to the principles and techniques described in this chapter.

4. Imagine the first case and investigation you will conduct after you become employed by a law firm. Describe what your strategy will be for interviewing the client.

5. Select a member of your local government or student body government to interview. (Remember to treat this interview as if the interviewee were your client.) Arrange an interview with the person and plan to discuss the death penalty (a highly controversial topic). Map out your strategy for overcoming the fear factor and breaking the silence factor. After conducting the interview, draft a detailed memorandum on the interviewee's feelings and convictions. Also detail in the memo how much motivation the witness needed to continue with the interview and how you handled that need.

6. Describe the ideal mannerisms of a paralegal when interviewing a client.

CASE STUDIES

Henderson v. Eldrich

Review the following case details and prepare to interview the client, Marianne Henderson. Outline the possible difficult personality traits Marianne might exhibit and how they can be handled. List the questions to be used during the opening, body, and closing of the interview to support her parents' claims.

Case Details

This case is brought to the law office by the parents of a sixteen-year-old girl. The parents are seeking action against a school counselor at the girl's high school because they believe the minor child and the counselor have been engaged in a sexual relationship.

Sixteen-year-old Marianne Henderson is believed to be physically and emotionally involved with her school counselor, Jim Eldrich. Henderson has allegedly broken off the relationship with Eldrich and her parents are concerned that he is now harassing her with letters and phone calls. Henderson's parents would like to take civil action against Eldrich, but Marianne will not cooperate by substantiating their suspicion that she and Eldrich had an affair. It is unclear if Marianne is afraid of admitting her sexual activity to her parents (and the rest of the community) by cooperating and bringing charges against Eldrich, or if the parents are incorrect in their assumptions and Marianne and Eldrich have never done anything inappropriate. Eldrich is in his early thirties, is married, and has two small children. He has been with the school district for six years.

Peltz v. Nebraska

Review the case details and then answer the questions following it.

Case Details

In January of 1998, Lennie Peltz and her father, Dave Hill, were driving on a county road in rural Sempter County, Nebraska, when they were struck head-on by a county snowplow. At the time of the accident, visibility was low and both the snowplow and the truck Peltz was driving were traveling at low speeds. As a result of the accident, Peltz suffered a fractured vertebra, a broken arm, and multiple muscle tears along her back and shoulders. She also received many cuts and bruises on her face. She has accumulated many medical expenses since the accident and now Peltz is bringing an action against the county and state for her injuries, lost wages, and loss of consortium.

By the time you enter the case, Peltz has moved to Texas and is again working for the same company she was employed by at the time of the accident. She is continuing to incur medical expenses; however, some of the charges have inadvertently been charged to her HMO plan rather than being held out for payment as related to the litigation. You have been asked to calculate the medical expenses and manage the billing of the services. During the management of the medical expenses, you realize that it is a physician in Texas who is continuing to bill services through the HMO. After contacting the doctor's office, you realize that the dollar amounts being billed are higher than they should be and that many bills may not be covered by the litigation. Some of the services even appear to be unnecessary. After bringing this to the attention of the attorney, you are asked to request new medical records from the doctor to verify what services are being charged. When you do so, the doctor refuses to submit not only the billings but also your client's medical records.

1. Interview the client regarding her medical bills and the questionable actions of her doctor.
2. Outline the questioning sequence you will use and describe why you will use it.
3. Draft a series of questions that will meet your objective and elicit the information needed.
4. How will these same questions motivate the client to level three communication, and why?
5. What difficulties, if any, do you anticipate in the interview, and why?

NOTES

1 *See, e.g.,* Model Rules of Professional Conduct Rule 1.6(b); Arizona State Rules of Professional Conduct ER 1.6(b).

2 Based on a portion of Russ M. Herman, Esq., *Courtroom Persuasion: Winning with Art, Drama, and Science* ch. 1 (Alta Press, 1997). Used by permission.

3 Raymond L. Gordon, *Interviewing Strategies, Techniques, and Tactics* 404 (4th ed., Dorsey Press, 1987).

4 Stanley L. Payne, *The Art of Asking Questions* 116 (2d ed., Princeton University Press, 1951).

5 *Id.*

5

INTERVIEWING THE EXPERT

OBJECTIVES   After completing this chapter, you will know:

- What an expert is and why they figure so prominently in interviewing and investigation.
- How to prepare to interview an expert.
- How to conduct a screening interview while looking for an expert.
- How to conduct the full expert interview.
- What special considerations are involved in working with medical experts.
- What ethical considerations every paralegal must take into account when interviewing an expert.

INTRODUCTION

The increasing complexity of civil litigation has created a great need for expert witnesses, which in turn has created more need for paralegals to interview the experts. The scope of special and technical issues involved in today's lawsuits require jury members to understand a broad range of scientific and technical fields and facts—a requirement that most jurors are incapable of fulfilling without some assistance. Trial lawyers must use every available resource to persuade a jury that the hypothesis offered in a case, regardless of its degree of technical difficulty, is correct. To perform such a task, the legal team turns to the expert witness. An **expert witness** explains and clarifies the facts in the case and offers the jury the benefit of her greater knowledge of the subject at hand. The legal team uses an expert whenever the subject matter is such that an ordinary person serving on the jury would benefit from an "expert" explanation.

Article VII of the Federal Rules of Evidence deals exclusively with expert witnesses and their testimony. Rule 702 states the following:

Rule: Testimony of Experts

If scientific, technical, or other specialized knowledge will assist the trier of fact to understand the evidence or to determine a fact in issue, a witness qualified as an expert by knowledge, skill, experience, training, or education, may testify thereto in the form of an opinion or otherwise.

There is an endless list of technical questions that may require expert testimony in litigation, and an endless list of fields of expertise to be considered. Experts may be needed when a case involves accounting, aeronautics, agriculture, biology, business, chemistry, city planning or zoning, construction, dentistry, dog training, economics, electricity, engineering, finance, foreign law, insurance, investment banking, manufacturing, marketing, mining, motor vehicles, patents, pharmacy, photography, physics, products liability, railways, safety, sociology, statistics, toxicology, and veterinary medicine, to name a few. Experts are not confined to a specific profession; they may include persons possessing special skills or judgment regarding a particular subject. Ordinarily, courts will acknowledge a person as an expert if she can demonstrate considerable experience or reasonable training in the subject matter.

Interviewing an expert is very different from interviewing a fact witness or the client. The interviewer must be cautious of what is said to any expert until she has been qualified as an expert and selected by the legal team for use in the case. To properly and professionally conduct an interview with an expert, the paralegal must understand as much about the subject matter as possible. The paralegal must also conduct thorough screening interviews of all potential expert witnesses, in an effort to evaluate each expert's credibility and ability to communicate with a broad range of listeners (namely, jurors). The paralegal must further determine if the expert has knowledge and opinions that support the legal team's case. All these factors are evaluated by the paralegal during her interviews with the expert.

⚖ PREPARING FOR THE INTERVIEW

As the paralegal begins the search for expert witnesses, she must organize the issues of the case and the investigation and prepare to phone potential experts. This is done to screen the experts and determine who should be selected for use on the case. Because the screening interview occurs over the phone, the paralegal must consider the following guidelines when preparing for the interview.

Before actually phoning a potential expert, the paralegal should prepare a checklist of the data she will need to adequately explain the issues in the lawsuit and, thus, the purpose of the interview. Organization is critical when interviewing an expert witness because both the expert's and the paralegal's time are valuable. The paralegal may also find it intimidating to interview or screen an expert, if the process creates feelings of imbalance or inferiority between the paralegal and expert. Thorough planning will help diminish this feeling.

To get organized and avoid errors, the interviewer should prepare a checklist of the case details, such as that in Figure 5-1. Ready access to these facts

Figure 5-1
Expert checklist:
Case details.
Before beginning a
search for an
expert, list this
information for the
expert. (Give
estimates if exact
data are not
available.)

1. Case name _____
2. Case file # _____
3. Court and case # _____
4. Client's name and position _____
5. Your attorney's name _____
6. Your office # _____
7. Your office address _____
8. Facts of the case: _____
    a) place of incident _____
    b) date of incident _____
    c) time of incident _____
    d) description of incident _____
    e) identification of witnesses _____
    f) statements of witnesses _____
    g) product, if involved _____
          (include model number, year, serial number)
    h) contributing factors _____
          [e.g., no seat belt, alcohol intake, balancing ladder
          on trash can, etc.]
9. Identification of opposing parties _____
10. Last date the expert can decide whether to take the
    assignment _____
11. Anticipated designation date _____
12. Expected deposition date ` _____
13. Scheduled trial date _____
14. Potential length of trial _____

demonstrates the paralegal's knowledge of the case, increases her credibility and professionalism, and saves time. After completing the checklist on case data, she prepares yet another checklist outlining the personal data and background of the potential expert witness (see Figure 5-2). This information is gathered for evaluation purposes and gives the screening interview structure.

While searching for a specific expert, it is critical that the paralegal locate at least three experts in the field to choose from. This is done for three reasons:

- It is easier to evaluate credentials when the paralegal has something to compare them to.

- The paralegal has a back-up source for the case if something happens to the first expert.

Figure 5-2
Expert checklist: Expert personal details. When interviewing a prospective expert, ask for this information

Background
1. Full name and age _____
2. Business address _____
3. Business telephone # _____
4. Home address _____
5. Home telephone # _____
6. Education _____
7. Work history _____
_____
8. Specific area of expertise _____
9. Published articles and books _____
10. Professional affiliations _____
11. Professional magazines subscribed to _____

Prior Legal Experience
12. Prior clients (dates, defendant or plaintiff) _____
13. Types of investigations (with dates) _____
14. Reports (oral and written and dates) _____
15. Deposition testimony _____
16. Court testimony _____
17. References _____

Availability
18. Vacation plans and dates _____
19. Seminar plans and dates _____
20. Potential meeting dates with your attorney _____

Miscellaneous
21. Referrals to other potential experts _____
22. Personal feelings about potential expert _____
_____

- The paralegal gets more than one view of the issues by conducting the initial interviews with the experts.

A separate checklist (see Figure 5-2) should be created for each expert. Save copies of the completed checklists in a three-ring binder for future use; keep the originals in the file and clearly mark them "expert witness."

The paralegal plays a key role in the selection of expert witnesses. She is able to offer the legal team some insight into the expert's ability to communicate, as a result of her preparation and the screening interview. As a general rule, if the expert cannot get along with or communicate with the paralegal, that expert will not be a credible or useable witness before a jury.

THE SCREENING INTERVIEW

State, at the onset of the phone conversation with the expert, that the legal team is looking for someone to testify in whatever capacity has been determined. If the potential expert is not interested, the phone call goes no further; however, before hanging up the paralegal should ask the expert for names of other experts in the field who may be willing to testify. If the expert shows an interest in testifying or offering an opinion in the case, the paralegal should explain that she has approximately ten to fifteen minutes' worth of questions to ask as part of her initial research on the subject matter. During this phone conversation, she should be gathering the details outlined in the personal data checklist (Figure 5-2) and requesting the expert's **curriculum vita**. A curriculum vita is a written description of a person's qualifications as an expert, including educational background, work experience, publications, memberships in professional associations, and professional awards or recognitions. The curriculum vita is similar to a résumé. The paralegal will also begin to assess the expert's credibility, flexibility, and communication abilities.

The information offered to the potential expert during a screening interview should be limited. The only case details shared with the expert should be undisputed facts and items found on the checklist previously created in preparation for the interview (Figure 5-1). The express purposes of the first phone conversation are to:

- Find out if the witness is interested in testifying or consulting
- Determine the general strengths and weakness of the witness in relation to the needs of the case
- Qualify the witness's credentials.

After conducting the screening interview and gathering the curriculum vita, the paralegal should begin verifying the credentials the expert has cited. It is essential that all of an expert's qualifications be verified before she is hired.

The following guidelines will help in handling the screening interview:

- Prepare the checklists described, using clear and simple language.

- Prepare an interview outline, using any of the previously described options (see Chapter 2). Be certain that the questions drafted for the outline are simple, nonbiased, and relevant, and that they do not take anything for granted.
- Restrict questions to essential information only.
- Ask short questions that minimize the time the expert must spend on them; this avoids offending or angering the expert.
- Have a positive attitude when the call is placed and during the interview. Review Chapter 1 for guidelines on perceptions, interactions, and verbal and nonverbal communication.
- Ask questions in the exact order and style as prepared on the outline. Remember, the expert is very familiar with the subject matter of the interview; if the interviewer misuses any terminology or speaks out of context, she may diminish her credibility.
- Do not express surprise at or disapproval of the expert's responses.
- Carefully guard against negative voice inflection.
- Be prepared to probe when necessary.

CONDUCTING THE FULL EXPERT INTERVIEW

Once the paralegal has provided a list of three experts for each legal area deemed necessary, the team will select one or more of the experts for further interviews. Then the paralegal prepares to interview the chosen expert(s). The second, or "full," interview will be more formal and takes the form of a regularly structured interview as described in Chapter 2. This includes preparing an opening, body, and closing for the interview. A new and more fully developed interview outline is created, adding more primary questions about the specifics of the case.

The expert interview itself is similar to what professionals in interviewing call the **survey interview**. During a survey interview, "[i]nterviewers do nothing but ask people all kinds of questions about their attitudes, behaviours, knowledge, and personal characteristics."[1] The difference between the survey interview and an expert interview is that during the expert interview the interviewer focuses on only one (or a few) expert in a particular field of study, rather than a wide variety of respondents. Remember, both parties in a lawsuit will present one or more experts with differing opinions on the same topic. The survey form of interviewing gathers each expert's attitudes and knowledge and compares them. For instance, after preparing the interview outline for the expert's interview, the paralegal may offer the same questions to the attorney for use in deposing the opposing party's expert. In so doing, the legal team compares both experts' responses to the same set of questions. This comparison helps the legal team determine which expert holds a more respected and believable opinion and why.

Because of the impact of the expert interview and the aptitude of the interviewee, the interviewer takes unusually extreme precautions to formulate good questions. By definition, the survey or expert interview "is a task-oriented question-answer exchange between an interviewer and respondent who are strangers."[2] The "stranger" will probably know more about the subject matter of the interview than the interviewer, and because of this the interviewer must take the appropriate steps to develop quality questions for the interview.

Planning Ahead

The first step in planning for the full interview is not to write questions, but to define the purpose of asking the questions. The paralegal asks herself the following questions:

- What is the legal issue?
- What are the damages?
- What does the jury need to know to find in favor of the client?
- What does the legal team need from the expert?

If the interviewer does not ask and answer these questions before preparing questions for the interview, she will endanger the results of the interview. Expert testimony and participation are expensive, so the interviewer costs the client money if she conducts an interview without following these simple steps. Responses to haphazardly or illogically drafted questions are a waste of time.

After defining the purpose of the interview, the interviewer will begin formulating questions via the interview outline. This is done by asking two questions:

- Why is the question being asked?
  For each question drafted, the interviewer must be able to explain how or why the question relates to the purpose of the interview—that is, the legal issue, the damages, the needs of the jury, and/or the needs of the legal team. If it is not clear what purpose a question serves, it will be impossible to gain a useable response from the expert.
- Is anything being taken for granted in the question?
  Asking this during development of the interview outline and the questions that make up the outline helps the interviewer to create good questions that expedite the interview.

Once the interview outline is developed and the questioning strategy is in place, the interviewer is ready to conduct the interview.

Opening

The opening of the expert interview is very structured. In the first minutes of the interview, the interviewer must establish the status of each of the parties and set the tone for the meeting. The opening consists of a greeting, a statement of purpose, a simple request, and qualifier questions.[3]

EXAMPLE ————————————————————————————————————

Hello. I am Joan VanHorn, Ms. Wilson's paralegal. Ms. Wilson represents Julie Jackson in an action against Material World, and I have asked you to meet with me today to discuss your opinion of the evidence in the lawsuit. Have you had time to review the material I sent you? Good. I will begin by asking you some general questions about yourself and your background.

(1) Have you ever testified regarding structural engineering issues before?
(2) Tell me what types of cases you have testified in.
(3) Were you paid for your participation in those cases?

————————————————————————————————————

This opening identifies the interviewer, her affiliation with the lawyer and the law firm, and states the purpose of the interview. The first three questions immediately begin defining the expert's background and competency to testify.

What happens next is dictated by the participation of the interviewee and by the interview outline. In some cases, the interviewer will need to ask many qualifying questions to determine the expert's educational background, experiences, and attitudes. If the screening interview was conducted properly, most of these qualifying questions will already have been answered. If not, the interviewer will need to gather the data during the opening. The interviewer will probably use a combination of open and closed questions during this phase and will stay away from leading questions. Once finished, the interviewer may move to the body of the interview.

Body

As discussed in Chapter 3, all questions are either open or closed, and are either primary or secondary, objective or subjective, leading or neutral. When and how to use each of these question types depends on the interviewer's purpose for the interview and her skills.

Determining how to question an expert is a very important decision. While questioning the expert during the opening, the interviewer is merely qualifying the interviewee and little probing is required; this is not so during the body of the interview. The interviewer must evaluate her skill in keeping the expert from wandering during open questions and her ability to extract information with closed questions. This helps the interviewer decide what questioning strategy to employ.

Both open and closed questions are useful in the body of the expert interview:

- Open questions are used to discover and develop categories of information that are then narrowed by closed questions. It is advisable to ask open questions when introducing new topics (primary questions).

EXAMPLE ————————————————————————————————————

(1) How would you explain the density of a plate glass window?
(2) Are plate glass windows commonly used in high-rise buildings?

(3) Was the use of a plate glass window in Ms. Jackson's 14th-floor apartment appropriate, in your opinion?

- Closed question are used to quickly move through areas where the expert is not able to offer helpful data. This is particularly necessary when more than one expert is used in the case. For example, in a case involving the construction of an office building, the paralegal may need experts in the fields of structural engineering, building codes and practices, and physics. Closed questions may be used during portions of the interview that involve a specialty area of one expert but not necessarily that of another. This enables the interviewer to quickly evaluate each expert's specific and general knowledge. She can then pursue her questioning on the subjects on which the expert is able to provide valid data.

- Open questions are good for gathering data on objective subjects.

- Closed questions are good for gathering data on subjective matters. Remember, attitudes are important, as jurors use them to help determine the expert's credibility.

- Beware of questions that are perceived as being right or wrong. Even experts want to respond in a way that gains approval. The interviewer must keep this in mind when structuring questions, because the expert is very aware of the responses the legal team wants. Intentionally or not, the expert may provide answers that are in line with the legal team's position but are not accurate or supportable. This does not happen often, but should always be guarded against.

- Use caution when employing bipolar questions. A simple "yes" answer will often be taken as sufficient; "no" answers are commonly expected to have a follow-up explanation attached. Providing a "yes" answer may allow the expert to avoid a long or complex explanation. Unfortunately, some experts are not eager to participate in long interviews, and may use the "yes" answer as a way of shortening the interview.

- When asking primary questions, the interviewer should watch for responses that make professional assumptions. As discussed in Chapter 1, assumptions or perceptions are not always reliable and are seldom shared by large numbers of people. If the expert is not careful, she may assume that her audience—the interviewer and ultimately the jury—shares her understandings and beliefs on the subject. This probably is not so. The expert is hired not to offer assumptions but rather to give an educated opinion or thought based on supportable data and interpretation. The danger in allowing such assumptions to go unqualified and unexplored is that the opposing expert may challenge them; also, the jury may be offended or confused. Check all data provided by the expert.

After satisfying all the items on the interview outline, the paralegal makes the transition to the closing of the interview.

Closing

The closing should be brief and express professional gratitude for the expert's willingness to participate. Use sweeping questions to assess the expert's feelings on the topics covered, and make sure the expert does not have any unanswered questions. Using nonverbal cues to signal the end of the interview is necessary, as it brings a psychological ending to the meeting. A friendly, positive closing ensures that the next interaction with the expert will be cooperative and productive.

MEDICAL EXPERTS

As the need for medical experts in litigation grows, the paralegal must be particularly aware of the special needs and requirements for handling these witnesses. The medical experts encountered in civil litigation are as varied as the general categories of all experts, ranging from neurologists to urologists, doctors to nurses, psychologists to dentists, and endocrinologists to pharmacists.

The interviewer must be aware of the unique relationship between the medical expert and her audience: the medical expert will testify at trial before a jury of people who have undoubtedly had some interaction with medical personnel. The interviewer must conduct pretrial interviews that help pinpoint problematic areas of the expert's testimony or personality.

Additionally, the paralegal needs to find ways to translate complex and difficult medical terminology and practices into lay terms. Follow these general guidelines when interviewing the medical expert:

- Understand as completely as possible the medical subject matter of the interview.
- Ask questions that enhance the medical expert's relationship with the interviewer and ultimately the expert's audience. Use subjective questions to uncover the expert's feelings and attitudes about certain aspects of medical treatment and diagnosis. This is particularly helpful when controversial treatments or techniques are at issue in the case.
- Ask questions that define the expert's ability to communicate in interpersonal environments. Many jurors have had negative experiences with medical professionals who lacked interpersonal communication skills. Open questions regarding the expert's background with patients can be used to determine if the legal team needs to work with the expert to improve her ability to relate to the jury or if another expert is needed.
- Use a formal interview style with medical experts—and all experts—to maintain control over the interview and to introduce the expert to the authority structure found in trials. If the expert is not willing to accept the appearance of the interviewer's authority, the paralegal should inform the attorney that a potential problem in deposition or trial may exist.

- Spend adequate time during the opening of the interview to identify and label the perceptions, values, beliefs, and attitudes of the expert. This evaluation includes the expert's feelings about the subject matter, the interviewer, the client, the opposing party, and nonmedical persons in general.

The paralegal will be responsible for providing very confidential and personal data to the medical expert, so respect and integrity must be used. Medical records are confidential and the patient must give express permission for their use.

The medical expert may have very specific requirements about material to be reviewed before the interview. This may mean that the legal team has to produce volumes of medical records, a variety of tests and test results, x-rays, CT scans, and laboratory work. During the screening interview it is imperative that the paralegal verify what the expert needs for medical review in order to participate in the full interview. Any material requested must be forwarded immediately to the expert. Because of the sensitive nature of such material, the paralegal must make some record of what has been sent to the expert, where it originated from, when it was sent, and when it is expected to be returned. Medical records summaries, created by paralegals when reviewing medical records, should not be sent to medical experts without the express instruction of the attorney. Material forwarded to the expert may be discoverable, so do not send anything that jeopardizes work product material, such as working indexes or summaries of medical records.

Finally, with the increased demand for medical experts in litigation (due in part to the increasing number of medically related suits), the paralegal must acquire a good understanding of basic anatomy, medical tests and procedures, and medical terminology. Appendix B of this text offers a desk reference section on anatomy, complete with illustrations, basic terminology, and general medical principles. The paralegal should use the self-testing material in the appendix to further comprehend the medical expert and the wide variety of medical issues in civil litigation.

DISCLOSURE OF INFORMATION

There are three main considerations when viewing the expert interview in terms of the work product doctrine, confidentiality, and the attorney/client privilege. The work product doctrine protects from discovery documents and items prepared in anticipation of litigation.[4] The duty of confidentiality is an ethical obligation imposed by bar regulators to prevent attorneys from divulging client confidences.[5] The attorney/client privilege is an evidentiary rule providing that neither an attorney nor a client can be forced to disclose the contents of confidential communications in a judicial proceeding.[6] Each of these separate but interrelated issues requires the paralegal to use due diligence and reasonable care to avoid violating these privileges and duties.

Work Product Doctrine

The work product doctrine is designed to protect all documents, notes, indexes, memoranda, and papers created by attorneys or members of their staff in preparation for litigation.

Rule: Federal Rule of Civil Procedure 26(b)(3)

Subject to [certain exceptions], a party may obtain discovery of documents and tangible things otherwise discoverable ... and prepared in anticipation of litigation or for trial by or for another party or by or for that other party's representative ... only upon a showing that the party seeking discovery has substantial need of the materials in the preparation of the party's case and that the party is unable without undue hardship to obtain the substantial equivalent of the materials by other means.

Thus, the work product doctrine protects from disclosure material prepared in anticipation of litigation by or for a party or by or for that party's attorney acting for the client.

With few exceptions, the paralegal does not remove or forward from the law office any documents protected by the work product doctrine. However, when interviewing an expert witness for a case, the paralegal is often forced to provide the expert with material containing many details of the investigation and case, which often includes some privileged information. For instance, in a medical case, the expert needs to have copies of all medical records, x-rays, test results, and so forth. Because these materials are often voluminous and the expert charges high fees for reviewing the data, the attorney may ask that a copy of an index created for the records and a summary of what is in the records accompany the material. When this happens, the privilege protecting the index and summary may be threatened. A paralegal should never provide this type of privileged documentation to any third party, even an expert, without the express instruction of the attorney.

Confidentiality and the Attorney/Client Privilege

The duty of confidentiality incorporates two different but related ideas: (1) The client must feel that the information she provides to the attorney will remain confidential. (2) To function at the highest level, the attorney must obtain all relevant information from the client. If a paralegal jeopardizes the client's confidentiality when dealing with third parties, such as experts, he also jeopardizes the attorney's ability to function well. Confidentiality and the attorney/client privilege are closely related, and the paralegal must understand that the codes, canons, and rules promulgated by the American Bar Association and state and federal law apply to him with regard to these issues.

To fulfill the duty of confidentiality, the paralegal must fully understand what confidentiality is and how it applies to the attorney/client privilege:

- An attorney's duty of confidentiality protects "information relating to the representation of a client. [7]

- Confidential information is not limited to "personal secrets." A *confidence* has been defined as "information protected by the attorney-client privilege under applicable law"; *secret* refers to "other information gained in the professional relationship that the client has requested be held inviolate or the disclosure of which would be embarrassing or would be likely to be detrimental to the client."[8]
- There are differences between the attorney/client privilege and confidentiality.
- The attorney/client privilege cannot protect information that is otherwise available to the public, but it does encompass information that the attorney obtains from the client.
- Confidentiality is an obligation to keep information, even public information, confidential when it comes directly from the client. This includes all "information relating to representation of a client."

SUMMARY

- Expert witnesses are persons who, by training, experience, education, or skill in a subject matter, are deemed qualified to offer opinion testimony. A steady increase in complex civil litigation has forced lawyers to use more and more expert witnesses to explain the cases to juries.
- The paralegal prepares for the expert interview by creating a case-specific checklist and a background checklist for the expert. She also depends on a well-developed interview outline.
- Screening interviews are conducted over the phone, are short, and seek qualifying data about the expert.
- Using a mix of open and closed questions, the paralegal meets the needs of the opening, body, and closing portions of the interview with questions that expand the primary issues of the case and narrowly define the details.
- Unlike with other experts, the paralegal must closely evaluate the medical expert's interpersonal communication skills, biases, perceptions, values, and attitudes. Sensitive material regarding the plaintiff and sometimes the defendant is exchanged with the medical expert, and great care must be taken to protect all parties' rights to privacy.
- The work product doctrine, confidentiality, and the attorney/client privilege must all be taken into account when conducting an expert interview.

ACTIVITIES

1. Interview some professional interviewers and find out what phone techniques they use.

2. Discuss your own experiences with telephone surveys. What kinds of things did the interviewer do that (a) made you want to participate; (b) caused you to refuse to participate?

3. If you were a senior paralegal training new paralegals, what procedures would you set up to ensure that only the best screening interviews and full expert interviews occurred?

4. What do you perceive to be the most difficult barrier when interviewing medical experts? How is this different from any other expert? Why?

5. Return to the case study, *Peltz v. Nebraska,* in Chapter 4 and answer the following questions. Consider the interviews with the doctor and nurse to be those of experts.

   ▪ Plan an interview with the doctor and his nurse. Map out your strategy and the questions you will ask.

   ▪ Describe in detail how you will conduct the interview.

   ▪ Write out the questions you will ask.

   ▪ Explain how you will deal with any silence problems from the doctor, as opposed to those from the nurse.

   ▪ What types of questions or strategies will you use to motivate both of these witnesses to participate?

CASE STUDY

Huggem v. Tuttle Railroad

Review the following case details and then complete these assignments:

1. Prepare an outline for an interview with an expert in this case. You select the type of expert to be interviewed based on the fact scenario—be creative!

2. What information do you hope to get from the witness, and why?

3. What types of questions will you use to meet your goals in the interview?

4. Do you foresee any problems? If so, what problems and why?

Case Details

In July of 1998, Ms. Joyce Huggem died at a railroad crossing in rural Milton County. The train crossing is surrounded by cornfields and a few farmsteads. The crossing is also approximately 10 miles north of Wickster, a town of approximately 4,000 people. It is reported that over the last ten years, four people have died at this crossing. Five years ago, Tuttle Railroad installed new signals, which feature lights and bells, at this and several other crossings. In addition, the railroad strictly enforces a rule requiring all engineers to blow the train whistle beginning two miles prior to entering any crossing.

To date, your legal team has been retained by the railroad to defend against a wrongful death case brought by the heirs of Huggem. It has been discovered that:

1. Huggem was hit at 3:10 P.M., Thursday, July 9th.

2. Huggem was depressed and was taking Prozac at the time of the accident.

3. Several witnesses were standing at a road-side fruit stand at the time of the accident.

4. Some of the witnesses claim that Huggem was parked on the track when the train hit her.

5. In interviews of persons who regularly travel the crossing, it is discovered that underbrush was often overgrown at the crossing. This foliage commonly blocked the view of drivers trying to cross the tracks.

6. Within four months of the accident, the railroad burned down the foliage.

7. The railroad has pictures of the foliage just prior to the burning of the brush.

8. Huggem's life insurance carriers have not paid on her policy because they suspect that Huggem committed suicide.

9. Tuttle Railroad denies responsibility for the death, saying that the signals were working that day, that the engineer blew his whistle as required, and that Huggem's vision was not blocked.

NOTES

1 J.T. Dillon, *The Practice of Questioning* 109 (Routledge, 1990).

2 *Id.* at 110.

3 Charles J. Stewart & William B. Cash, Jr., *Interviewing Principles and Practices* 120 (8th ed., McGraw Hill, 1997).

4 *See* Fed. R. Civ. P. 26(b)(3).

5 *See* Model Rule of Professional Conduct 1.6.

6 *See* Fed. R. Evid. 501 and applicable principles of common law.

7 Model Rule of Professional Conduct 1.6.

8 Model Code DR 4-101(A).

6

THE INVESTIGATIVE INTERVIEW

<u>OBJECTIVES</u> After completing this chapter, you will know:

- What the purpose of the investigative interview is.
- How to conduct an investigative interview.

- How to employ investigative questioning techniques during witness interviews.
- What types of body language are important during the interview.
- How to analyze an investigative interview.

INTRODUCTION

An **investigative interview** seeks details and information from a witness during the course of an investigation. The main goals of the investigative interview are to focus exclusively on witnesses and preserve the witnesses' testimony. Civil litigation often extends for long periods of time before a trial takes place, and there is a risk that witnesses will forget certain details, move away, die, or even change their stories. By conducting and memorializing an investigative interview, the paralegal provides the legal team with an opportunity to forecast a witness's testimony. In addition, the investigative interview provides the first opportunity for the paralegal and legal team to analyze the witness and his story.

One must recognize and understand the different parts of the investigative interview before one can begin conducting such interviews. These components include understanding the body language of both interviewer and interviewee, what the objectives of the interview are, how to question an interviewee, how to conduct the interview, and how to analyze the interview.

Body Language

Author and professor Raymond L. Gorden claims that "nonverbal cues are essential ingredients in both interviewer-to-respondent and respondent-to-interviewer communication."[1] He also believes that the verbal expression of the question is the most primary function of the interview. Nevertheless, a great deal of experimentation in nonverbal language has proven that the interviewer must not concentrate all his efforts in the area of verbal communication. If an interviewer neglects the signals and meanings of nonverbal communication, he closes himself off to greater insight into himself and the interviewee, which means that learning to understand and use nonverbal cues or body language is yet another tool for executing a good interview.

Interviewer   The body language of the interviewer reveals many things, including his attitudes, that can greatly influence the interviewee, regardless of the type of interview conducted or the style of questions used. For instance, the interviewer who approaches an interviewee with his hands jammed into his pockets projects an image that says, "Don't bother me." Artificial smiles can be interpreted to mean anything from insincerity to anger. When conducting an interview, even over the phone, body language influences the way a witness feels about talking.

EXAMPLE ———————————————————————————————

Consider a telephone interview with a witness who is believed t(
paralegal may express an attitude of dislike and distrust toward
by his tone of voice. A person really can determine, over the ph(
person is smiling and positive.

What the interviewer says is just as important as what he does. Experts in the field of body language and facial expression claim that nonverbal communication is more effective in business relationships than most people think—this is particularly true in legal interviews. The paralegal who regularly deals with witnesses and clients must be keenly aware of the messages he is sending if he is to achieve the greatest level of investigative success. He must be equally alert to the signals others, particularly witnesses, are sending about his body language. If a witness shrinks back, the paralegal may have invaded the interviewee's personal space or created a defensive attitude in her by appearing defensive himself. If the interviewee steps back, takes a deep breath, or stands taller, it is possible that she is wary of the interviewer. When the interviewer notices these actions during the interview, he should use a friendly expression and eye contact to win back the trust of the witness.

If a paralegal wants an interviewee to like him, he should be open and friendly, smile frequently, sit or stand facing the other person, and keep hands and arms relaxed. He should also look directly into the interviewee's eyes, reflecting a genuine liking for her.

Interviewee   Analyzing the interviewee's body language is as important to the interviewer as monitoring his own body language. The balance between the interviewee and the interviewer is often established through body language and is the interviewer's responsibility. In the analysis phase of the investigative interview, the paralegal should note body language clues bearing on the witness's credibility, strength, or effectiveness. During the opening of the interview, the interviewer will gauge his questioning techniques, pace, and flow based on the nonverbal cues the interviewee provides.

When evaluating an interviewee, the interviewer should note if the interviewee has a weak demeanor or strong personality; both are influential in the subsequent use of the witness at trial or deposition. This determination can be made by observing the interviewee's behavior, including eye contact or lack thereof, slumping shoulders, and a soft or hesitant voice. Make special note of strong witnesses, such as those who repeatedly look at the interviewer when disagreeing with statements or questions. An interviewee willing to use direct eye contact while disagreeing has a strong position and intensity. Good eye contact during the discussion of difficult topics suggests that the interviewee is strong and assured in her story.

Defining an interviewee's characteristics through body language helps the paralegal to determine how much damage or assistance the witness will be to the case. A weak witness with a strong opinion against (or for) the case is not nearly as damaging (or helpful) as the strong witness with a mild opinion against (or for) the case. Experience demonstrates that juries are more responsive to strong witnesses, regardless of the strength of the witness's beliefs. Weak witnesses are not often respected or believed, because a weak witness lacks power and sincerity.

Characteristics   A person's credibility is based on her tone of voice, vocabulary, and body posture, all of which denote status and knowledge. Another characteristic often overlooked is facial expression. "More than any other part of the human body, the face is the primary physical key to understanding people's emotional expression," says Paul Ekman, Ph.D., professor of psychology and director of the Human Interaction Laboratory of the University of California Medical School in San Francisco.[2] During the investigative interview, the interviewer must watch the interviewee's facial expressions closely. Interpretation of facial expressions may be difficult, though most people are able to understand basic expressions of displeasure, discomfort, intensity, and passivity. Dr. Ekman suggests the following tips for interpreting facial expression:

- Do not take a smile at face value. A smile may represent anything from contempt to joy to misery to fear.
- Watch for masking. A person may cover or hide a true emotion with another, artificial emotion. For instance, a witness may mask guilt with anger.
- Watch for **micro-expressions**, facial postures that appear for only a moment and then are quickly removed. These usually occur without the conscious decision of the interviewee. Typically, a smile occurs almost instantly after a micro-expression, which is a hint for the interviewer. A micro-expression is a signal that the interviewee may be concealing a feeling.
- Learn to "read lips" for emotional cues. In other words watch for twitching or pursed lips. These are a sign that the interviewee is attempting to control her emotions.

Ekman suggests practicing face reading by watching television with the sound turned off. Attempt to determine what is happening based solely on the actors' facial expressions.

Other body language clues include:

- folded arms
- fidgeting
- the amount of personal space the witness requires.

THE FIVE WS OF THE INVESTIGATIVE INTERVIEW

Before beginning investigative interviews, the legal team jointly selects the witnesses to be interviewed and decides when to interview them. The paralegal provides background information for those decisions based on his current knowledge of the case and any informal investigation done after the initial client interview. The process used to select a witness for interview, along with the information needed from the witness, is to ask the *Five Ws:* who, what, when, where, and why.

Who

The *who* segment of the Five Ws focuses on who should be interviewed and who the witnesses are.

General Witnesses   Early in the investigation, the legal team must decide which witnesses to interview. The task of determining witnesses can be laborious, but it is doable when the paralegal is organized. Originally, the client provides a base list of witnesses (during the initial client interview) from which the team works. A timeline of the client's story, also known as a *logical sequence diagram,* is then used to map out the sequence of events in the case and locate witnesses and physical evidence. The team also uses a deductive reasoning process called the *proximate probability theory* during this process. The proximate probability theory identifies specific types of witnesses, such as character witnesses and collateral witnesses. The theory requires the paralegal to ask two questions: (1) "Who could be a witness?" and (2) "Who should be a witness?" These questions are answered by reviewing the logical sequence diagram.

Next, the paralegal lists every possible witness or hypothetical witness he can think of. After the initial witness list is compiled, including hypothetical witnesses identified through proximate probability analysis, the legal team begins arranging the witnesses in an interview order, to maximize interviewing efforts and avoid subsequent interviews with witnesses who are not cooperative (i.e., hostile witnesses last, friendly witnesses first). The paralegal also lists all known background on each witness, completing any missing details during the interview.

The Client   The *who* portion of the investigation also deals with the client. It is important that the legal team evaluate the client early in the investigation—certainly before any witness interviews are conducted. To execute a thorough and productive investigation, the paralegal must first know who the client is within the general confines of the case, as a subject of the case, and outside of the case. These factors, together and individually, influence the manner in which other witnesses and the opposing party are handled by the legal team.

EXAMPLE ───

If the legal team determines that the client has a difficult personality, they can prepare for possible negative reactions from witnesses regarding the client. To better understand this concept, consider this fact scenario.

Details   A paralegal attends the initial client interview in an assault case involving an elderly man and his neighbor. The client, Mr. Smith, claims that his neighbor, Mr. Jones, regularly assaults him. Smith claims that Jones uses filthy language and often threatens him. Smith owns a dog that is kept outside and often barks, and Jones's primary problem with Smith is the dog's barking. When asked specifically if other neighbors have complained about the dog, Smith says, "Well, everybody complains about something, either the dog's barking, or where my dog goes to the bathroom on his walks, or the music I play in my garage at night." Smith adds, "Everyone in my neighborhood has a problem."

After the initial client interview, the legal team evaluates Smith according to "who" he is both inside and outside of the case. From the initial impression Smith gave the legal team, they determine that Smith may have difficulties with most people, including the witnesses in this case.

It is valuable for the paralegal to determine "who" the client is, because the paralegal has to deal with the client and because witnesses will be biased regarding the client due to past experiences with him. In the preceding example, the legal team may have difficulty interviewing the witnesses in the case, most of whom will be neighbors, because of the problems the client has had with many of them. Even neighbors who have not personally had problems with the client will probably have heard of him, and this reputation may bias them.

Who determinations should be done for all persons involved in an investigation, including persons not actually interviewed as witnesses. For example, neighbors who have no knowledge of the facts of the case, but who know one or both parties, may offer valuable insights into the behaviors and motivations of the parties. These same persons may influence (albeit indirectly) the problematic relationship between Smith and Jones. It is critical that the paralegal know and understand all of the players in the drama, whether they are easily identifiable or not.

What

The *what* segment of an investigative interview can mean a variety of things:

- What does the witness know in general about the case?
- What does the witness know specifically about the legal issue and its elements?
- What does the witness know in general about the client and the other party?
- What does the witness know specifically about the client and the other party?
- What barriers does the witness bring to the interview and future trial testimony?

All of the *what* factors aid the legal team in qualifying the witness, while allowing them to test their hypothesis and legal theory at the same time. Answering each of these questions also helps the paralegal to rank the witness, according to her value to the investigation (and case), and to draft a complete chronology. A *chronology* is a detailed timeline of the case that includes the client's version of the events and all of the witnesses' versions.

When

Evaluating *when* during an investigative interview depends on the strategy of the legal team. *When* focuses on many things, including:

- When the witness saw or heard something relating to the triggering event
- When the witness first came to know the client or other party
- When the witness became aware of the pending legal action
- When the witness believes the triggering event happened.

Each of these *when* questions is answered by the witness and serves either as the basis for furthering the legal team's objectives, or as a means of building rebuttal evidence. Rebuttal evidence is often accentuated during the *when* portion of the interview, because the paralegal asks narrow and specific questions, focusing on the information the witness may possess, to prove one or more legal elements.

Never be critical of the witness during this segment of the investigative interview. Rather, strive to identify weaknesses and strengths in the story by asking questions that pin down time and specific pieces of the triggering event. These define when something did or did not happen.

EXAMPLE

When interviewing Mr. Smith about the alleged assault, the interviewer structures his questions in a way that moves Smith away from his personal problems with the neighbors and on to the specific triggering event. This is done by using a combination of passive and aggressive roles.

Paralegal: Mr. Smith, you said Mr. Jones assaulted you on Friday, May 11th?

Do you remember what time of day that was?

What are your normal activities on Friday mornings?

Do you normally see Mr. Jones on Friday mornings?

Tell me why you believe he was home that morning and why he felt inclined to assault you.

By using narrow questions that pin down an approximate time frame and then asking an open-ended question, the paralegal has guided the witness (in this case the client) in a direction focusing on a specific time while allowing him to freely explain himself. By using the combination approach, the paralegal also helps eliminate any stress the more difficult questions may have created.

Where

The focus of the *where* segment of the investigative interview emphasizes specific pieces of the story being told. The goal during this portion of the questioning is to give the witness flexibility in answering questions while guiding her toward specific details of the story. For instance, an eyewitness to a car accident is able to provide a great deal of *where* detail in her story. Unfortunately, many eyewitnesses do not realize the amount of detail they possess. The paralegal has to structure the investigative interview in a way that allows the witness to freely discuss the events creating the story, while drawing the witness's attention to pieces of the story that demand clarification. Such an examination consists of open-ended questions followed by narrow questions.

EXAMPLE ————————————————————————————————

When interviewing an eyewitness to a car accident, the paralegal may ask, "Where were you the morning of the accident?" or "Where were you at the time of the accident?" This open-ended question allows the witness to narrate a list of information that can then be used to narrow the scope of the witness's recollections. The details gleaned from the answer can be discussed at the conclusion of the narrative interview, as the witness and the paralegal complete a timeline of the triggering event. This type of questioning helps fill in the gaps of timelines provided by other witnesses and initiates development of the interviewee's own timeline. Once the witness has completed her story of the events, the paralegal can ferret out specific details, such as "Where were you standing at the time of the collision?"

When the paralegal asks an initial open-ended question followed by several moderately narrow questions, he sets the stage for the witness to recall specific details.

EXAMPLE ————————————————————————————————

The paralegal may now ask the eyewitness, "At what place on the curb were you standing at the time of the collision?" or "Were you five feet from the cars or closer?"

The purpose of *where* is to gradually narrow the scope of the questions and develop a very specific picture of the event. In cases in which the witness has been traumatized by the events, it is helpful to ask her to draw pictures or diagrams of the locations of people or objects. This strategy not only relaxes the mood of the interview, but also offers the witness an opportunity to take a break and think.

Why

The final section of the investigative interview, which deals with *why,* may be the most difficult. *Why* requires the witness to share her personal views of the story and the triggering event. The civil investigation is built on inferences and circumstantial evidence and the legal team's ability to support such inferences and evidence with witness testimony and "real" evidence; therefore, *why* is critical. Also remember that juries tend to respond more positively when they are told why something happened. The object of the *why* section of the interview is to identify the witness's inferences in the story and test them against the legal theory. Also, during the *why* segment, alliances with the witness must be made, regardless of the inferences she draws, by offering nonjudgmental feedback on the story she is telling.

When asking for a witness's opinion on why certain events occurred, the interviewer must show empathy for the witness. It is a stressful situation for a witness when she is asked to voice an opinion about a fact scenario. In some cases, the witness may first need reassurance as to her anonymity and safety; in other circumstances, the witness will require other motivations before she will explain why she believes something happened. Interviewers must be patient with the witness during this type of questioning, and appeal to the witness's ego by stressing her intelligence and insight into the subject matter. The witness's value to the case may hinge on her ability to explain why something she saw or heard happened.

QUINTAMENSIONAL QUESTIONING TECHNIQUE

Once the interviewer/paralegal understands what the goals of the investigative interview are, he can begin preparing questions and objectives for each interview. Learning how to question an interviewee, however, is sometimes difficult, and interviewers are encouraged to use the *quintamensional questioning technique*[3] to guide their interviews. This five-question strategy was designed to help the interviewer identify interviewees who are not properly informed on the topics being covered. It is particularly helpful during witness interviews.

The five categories of questions that make up the quintamensional questioning technique are designed to complement each other and offer the interviewer a variety of question choices in order to accomplish his goals. This questioning strategy is flexible and can be expanded or contracted to meet the needs of each individual interview. The creator of this plan, George Gallup, originally designed the strategy to be used in public opinion interviews, but it has become a valued tool in probing and investigative interviews as well. He suggests using the following five question types, in the order presented here, to achieve maximum results:

- Filter or information questions
- Open or free-answer questions
- Dichotomous or specific-issue questions
- Reason-why questions
- Intensity questions.

Although Gallup suggested that there is room for some variation in this structure, he recommended designing probing interviews, like the investigative interview, in this fashion to maximize the interviewer's chances of reaching an interviewee's true knowledge of a subject.

Filter Questions

Opening questions for the investigative interview are used to identify who the witness is and, generally, what she knows. The filter question asks for a general opinion.

EXAMPLE

Have you heard about the lawsuit between Mr. White and Mr. Black?

Depending on the subject matter of the interview and the interviewer's goals, the filter questions may focus on specific events or general topic areas. These early questions allow the interviewer to quickly identify and discard interviewees who lack sufficient knowledge to further the investigation. When the interviewee is being used as a support witness (such as a character witness), the interviewer may need to use the filter questions to identify the extent of the person's knowledge on a subject and educate her enough to continue the interview. The goal is to move the interviewee far enough along that the true purpose of the interview can be met.

After opening with a broad filter question, the interviewer must probe the level of the interviewee's knowledge on a subject.

EXAMPLE

What do you know about the allegations Mr. White is making in this case?

The interviewer can ask any number of narrowing questions to further develop an understanding of the interviewee's knowledge. To achieve this goal, the interviewer asks a number of two-part questions requiring the interviewee to demonstrate her understanding of the events or subjects.

EXAMPLE

Please explain to me what you understand to be Mr. White's complaints about Mr. Black and Mr. Black's complaints about Mr. White.

Filter questions that continue to narrow, like the examples given here, give the interviewer a sense of the interviewee's depth of thought on an issue. To continue in the quintamensional strategy, the interviewer uses open questions on the same subjects, which allows the interviewer to balance the amount and nature of the interviewee's information with her opinions.

Open Questions

Open questions help bring to light the interviewee's general attitudes and motivate her to share ideas and thoughts that might otherwise go unsaid. The interviewer moves to this level of questioning, with little interruption in the flow, by asking questions that no longer qualify the interviewee personally but qualify the amount of data the interviewee knows.

EXAMPLE

Tell me what you know about the events of June 12, 1998, involving Mr. White and Mr. Black.

In the investigative interview, a large number of open questions are used to begin forming a timeline of the interviewee's knowledge. In some cases only one or two open questions will be needed, but when the interviewee knows a great deal about the facts surrounding an event, the bulk of the interview may consist of open questions.

Yes/No (Dichotomous) Questions

The third step in the quintamensional process narrows the questioning technique. This strategy is used to gauge the interviewee's ability to be used in a trial or deposition setting. Can the interviewee be believed? Does her behavior support the statements she has already made in the interview? Will she be credible and believable to a jury? Complex issues in the investigative interview should be broken down into categorical questions.

EXAMPLE ──

Did you hear Mr. White ask Mr. Black to leave his business?

Did you see Mr. Black push Mr. White?

From what you saw, was Mr. White injured when Mr. Black pushed him?

When complicated legal issues are involved, it may be necessary for the interviewer to ask questions in simple language, helping to break down any educational barriers between the subject and the interviewee. This also helps the interviewer gauge the status and general knowledge of the interviewee for future uses.

It is useful for the interviewer to judge the quality of yes/no questions by comparing them to the broad answers provided in response to the open questions. Without using the filter and open questions first, the interviewer cannot determine the true quality of the interviewee's information or formulate follow-up questions.

Why Questions

As previously discussed (see Chapter 1), the interviewer must determine the interviewee's motives during the course of the interview. This is done for many reasons, but in the case of the investigative interview the interviewer must be sure that the data gathered from the interviewee is as unbiased as possible. Without unbiased data, the investigation may be jeopardized and valuable time wasted. Therefore, the fourth category of questions is the *why* questions, which aid in describing the opinions voiced during the interview and qualifying those opinions.

The quintamensional technique allows some variance, especially with *why* questions. A combination of open and closed questions can be used to gather a large number of opinion responses from an interviewee and then narrow the opinion into topic-specific responses. Using closed questions (specifically dichotomous questions) helps the interviewer focus the respondent's attention on key details. This is necessary because the interviewer must determine if the interviewee has any hidden or biased motives for providing certain details or versions of the story. Without a varied approach to the *why* question, the interviewer may inadvertently allow the interviewee with hidden motives to mislead or bias the investigation.

Use open *why* questions to gain a deeper understanding of the interviewee and her response; this is also useful after narrow yes/no questions. Determination of when and where to use *why* questions is up to the interviewer and depends on his overall needs during the interview.

Intensity Questions

As the interview winds down, the interviewer determines the *intensity* of the interviewee. Information gathered from an interviewee who is perceived to be weak is often less valuable, because such an interviewee's credibility is shaky, and the interviewer will need to ask only a few intensity questions to determine the interviewee's feelings. The majority of the interview provides the interviewer with opportunities to evaluate the quality of the witness, and intensity questions simply support the interviewer's conclusions.

Applications of the Technique

The quintamensional technique can be applied to most investigations. Drafting questions to fit into each of these categories requires time and patience on the part of the interviewer, but with few exceptions, use of the technique should produce a quality interview. The accompanying table is an example of how this technique was used for the interview of an employee of a large corporation. The interview was scheduled after a co-worker of the employee filed a complaint with the Equal Employment Opportunity Commission.

Issue: Wrongful Discharge	
Question Style	**Question**
Filter	Have you heard or read about Jim Green's claims against the company? What do you think his chief complaints are? What do you think the company's attitudes are?
Open	What are your feelings about Green's position and what he should do?
Yes/No (Dichotomous)	Would you like to see Green resolve this matter within the EEOC? Would you like to see Green take this problem to court?
Why	Why do you feel this way?
Intensity	How strongly do you feel about this problem Green is having?

Filter questions are used to determine which interviewees are worth spending time with. With such questions the interviewer can quickly and easily determine who will be useful in an investigation, and this knowledge facilitates the task of conducting the interview. The technique provides a practical and useable overall approach to the investigative interview.

CONDUCTING THE INTERVIEW

Conducting the interview requires the interviewer to be flexible enough to adapt to any situation. This requires analytical ability—specifically, "[t]he ability to analyze what is happening while you are participating in the interaction itself."[4] It is not easy for the paralegal to be both observer and participant. Therefore, he must gain a complete understanding of the three components of the interview (opening, body, and closing). The following descriptions provide a basic strategy for using these three elements in the investigative (witness) interview.

Opening

All witnesses, even the client, need some time early in the interview to become familiar with the paralegal and his questioning style. Thus, a generous amount of time should be allocated to the opening of the interview. During this level-one phase, the goal of the interviewer is to build trust with the interviewee and amass general details about her. Introductory questions, which are nonthreatening and open, are used for this purpose. The purpose of these general questions is twofold. First, there are no right or wrong answers, so the interviewee can gain confidence in the interviewer and the questions he will ask. Also, introductory questions garner the interviewee's statistical information (name, birth date, address, telephone number, Social Security number, etc.). Second, introductory questions are used to give the interviewer a general feeling for the openness and cooperativeness of the interviewee. Use of common-ground topics during the opening allows a connection to develop between the witness and the interviewer.

When forming open questions for this phase of the interview, the paralegal should remember to gather the following details:

- Full name
- Address
- Telephone number for both daytime and evening
- Place of employment, including telephone number, address, supervisor's name, and other data regarding if and when the interviewee may be contacted while at work
- Name of spouse, spouse's employer, address, and so on
- Driver's license number
- Social Security number

- Age and date of birth
- Any other information relevant to the pending investigation.

Remember, open questions allow the witness freedom to speak and a feeling of power over the conversation. They also provide large amounts of information as personally narrated by the witness. During these nonthreatening questions, the interviewer begins evaluating any credibility issues he perceives with the interviewee and her information. Generally, interviewees respond well to open questions. Using introductory questions, some of which are filtering questions, during the opening of the interview builds a foundation for the interview and allows a transition to the more difficult topics in levels two and three.

Body

During the middle portion or *body* of the interview, the interviewer attempts to accomplish two things: (1) focus on overall topics central to the investigation; and (2) develop a timeline of the events the interviewee is recounting. Recall the Five Ws of the investigative interview when preparing for the body of the interview. During the opening phase, the interviewee answers questions about herself, helping to further define the *who* portion of the Five Ws. During the body of the interview, the interviewee will be answering the other Ws: *what, when, where,* and *why.* Use the following descriptions to help form questions central to the legal investigation topics.

Focusing on the Central Topics   Continue using open questions during this stage to encourage the interviewee to talk. It may also be necessary to alter questioning techniques to accommodate the goals of the interview. Often, during the body of the investigative interview, a wise interviewer will ask questions that do not sound like questions.[5]

EXAMPLE ───────────────────────────────────

Describe your position in the company.
Tell me about your relationship with the shareholders.

Try to make the interviewee the star of the interview.

Investigative interviews are flexible by nature and require the interviewer to use both primary questions, for stand-alone topics, and secondary questions, for follow-up information. A variety of probing techniques should be used to motivate the interviewee beyond her initial reactions to questions.

EXAMPLE ───────────────────────────────────

Go on ... (nudging probe)
And then what happened? (nudging probe)
Who is William Randolph? (informational probe)
How do you know about that? (informational probe)

Limit closed questions to the timeline development activity, to avoid dominating the time allotted for answers. At this stage, it is too soon to close the interviewee down with such narrow responses, because primary topics are the focus. Primary questions require the interviewee to provide large amounts of more general information, which the paralegal will evaluate at the conclusion of the interview.

Timeline Development   When developing the timeline, large amounts of data are needed to gauge the witness's emotions and general knowledge of the event. After gathering the story through open questions, the interviewer uses closed or narrow questions to focus on parts of the story that are confusing or contradictory. The gradual narrowing of questions takes control of the interview away from the interviewee and returns it to the interviewer. In some cases the questions are so narrow that they require nothing more than a yes or no response. The quintamensional questioning technique is very helpful here. During this continued shift in questioning, the interviewer begins asking questions he prepared prior to the interview dealing with specific topics central to the investigation.

When developing and asking questions about the timeline the paralegal should be tactful, nonargumentative, and courteous. Do not get into a debate over details that are not consistent with other information. Instead, use sweeping and reflective probes to verify the interviewee's responses.

EXAMPLE ─────────────────────────────

Is there anything else you can recall about this incident? (sweeping probe)
You think, then, the fire started near the sofa in the family room? (reflective probe)

─────────────────────────────

Be prepared to back off if the interviewee becomes emotional or angry. Overuse of probing techniques at this point may damage the trust relationship built with the interviewee and destroy any future relationship with her.

During the development of the timeline, the paralegal needs to create questions on the spot. As discussed in Chapter 3, some questions almost always create problems. The paralegal must be careful to avoid using them during the building of the timeline, because such questions may tempt the interviewee to guess or force her to answer in a way she might not have otherwise.

EXAMPLE ─────────────────────────────

Guessing:

Bad: Did you decide to withhold information about the accident because you were afraid or because you didn't see anything?

Good: Why did you decide to withhold information on the accident?

Pushy-leading:

Bad: Shouldn't the plaintiff in this case win because the defendant is a bad guy?

Good: What is your opinion of the plaintiff's claims in this case?

─────────────────────────────

It may also be necessary to ask obvious questions. This must be done, however, in a way that does not appear condescending to the interviewee.

Why is your company considering breaking the contract with the plaintiff?
I understand you saw the accident at the corner of Third and Maple on Friday night.

Closing

The closing portion of the interview is used to reestablish the trust relationship built with the interviewee during the opening. Return to nonthreatening topics of conversation to "cool down" the interview and gradually close it.

In preparing for the closing, the interviewer must pay careful attention to the time parameters set for the investigative interview and close it when promised. To elicit the most cooperation from an interviewee, the interviewer must respect the boundaries set. Nevertheless, it is not always possible to finish in the prearranged time frame. If, at the end of the scheduled meeting, more questions remain to be asked, ask the interviewee for a specific amount of additional time, or schedule a second or follow-up meeting.

SPECIAL CONSIDERATIONS

During a legal investigation, many types of witnesses are encountered, many of whom are lay witnesses. The term **lay witness** is used during the investigation to describe any person who will testify in the case and who is not an expert. These persons may include the client (discussed in Chapter 4), children, illiterate witnesses, and non-English–speaking witnesses. Aside from these general witness categories, the paralegal must remember that some witnesses will be friendly and easy to interview and others will be hostile. The following special considerations are a guide to effective interviews of each of these unique categories of witnesses.

Children

When dealing with child witnesses, the legal team must address their special needs and prove that they are competent to testify (review Federal Rule of Evidence 601 for issues concerning competency). Children are placed in a category of their own because they think and act very differently than adults, and therefore present very different challenges for the interviewer. Some social scientists believe that children have better memories than adults, and that their memories are often in the form of picture images. The images children retain can provide a great deal of important detail to an investigation; however, these vivid images may be laced with imagination. Commonly, when children are asked to recount an event, particularly a emotionally difficult event, they will make up details if they do not remember clearly what happened. The problem with this—besides the obvious—is that children often are wholly convinced that what they "remember" is the truth.

When interviewing children, speak with them in the presence of an adult whom they trust, and who is not directly involved in the investigation. Any statement a paralegal takes from a child witness should be documented in a signed statement, to increase the value of the testimony for impeachment or memory stimulation purposes later. If possible, it should be drafted by the child. If the child is not capable of drafting such a document, the paralegal must create the statement for the child, using the child's vocabulary.

Illiterate Witnesses

Illiterate witnesses are yet another unique category. A surprising number of persons fall into this classification. The paralegal must carefully aid the illiterate witness in the telling of her story and in documenting it. The use of an illiterate witness may be further complicated by her embarrassment or shame at her handicap. The paralegal may find working with these witnesses difficult, but he can overcome their self-protective reactions by using empathetic and tactful questioning. While preparing such a witness for trial testimony, the paralegal must help the witness feel comfortable with her ability to tell the story as she knows it and not to be ashamed or self-conscious about her illiteracy.

Non-English–Speaking Witnesses

Non-English–speaking witnesses again challenge the capabilities of the interviewer, but are nonetheless important to the outcome of some investigations. When confronted with a non-English–speaking witness, the paralegal should first locate a translator and then create a **translator's affidavit**. The affidavit should:

1. Indicate that the translator has read the statement made in the affidavit to the witness, in the witness's own language
2. Indicate that the witness understood the statement as it was read to her
3. Indicate that the witness affirms that the statement is true and correct.

The affidavit is attached to the end of the signed statement and is considered to be part of the statement. The translator will sign the affidavit and the witness will sign the statement. If the translator is not a notary public, the affidavit should be sworn to before a notary. If the witness does not speak any English, the statement must be taken in the native language of the witness and then translated into English. The translator is then required to attest to the quality and accuracy of the translation.

Hostile Witnesses

A **hostile witness** is also known as an *adverse witness*. By definition, this category of witness has a prejudiced relationship to the opposing party, so her testimony is always suspect for bias. A witness declared to be hostile may be asked leading questions and is subject to cross-examination by the party that called her. Although the hostile witness is treated as a separate and distinct category of witness here, in actuality the hostile witness may be a lay witness or an expert witness. The qualities that make a witness hostile can range from a mild difference of opinion between the witness and one or both legal teams, to aggressive emotional tension between the witness and one or both legal teams. A hostile witness may originate from either party's witness pool. The level of hostility between a party and a witness is usually heightened by certain interactions (namely interviews) between the two during the investigation.

When dealing with the hostile witness, the paralegal must employ empathy and active listening. He must also carefully prepare for any interviews with that witness by creating questions that challenge but respect the witness, to minimize any tension during the interview. Additionally, the paralegal should be patient, act professionally, and use common sense. The following lists techniques for handling the hostile witness:

- Prepare ahead.
- Use the common-ground technique to build rapport.
- Use open-ended questions.
- Try to identify the "hostility factor" in the witness; that is, find out why the witness is hostile.
- Be honest and do not threaten the witness.
- Terminate the interview if the hostility increases during the interaction, thereby avoiding further damage to the relationship.

ANALYZING THE INVESTIGATIVE INTERVIEW

The final step after the investigative interview is to analyze the quality of the interview. To perform the evaluation, compare the questions and answers. The interviewer can do this by asking himself four questions and comparing his thoughts to the information gleaned from the interviewee:

- Was the purpose of the interview made clear?
- Were questions relevant to the stated purpose?
- Was the interviewer a good listener?
- Did the interviewee feel free to be honest and candid?[6]

After answering these questions, the interviewer may document any other thoughts or feelings about the interview he deems important. This may include credibility issues, conflicts in responses, or the like.

ETHICAL CONSIDERATIONS

While conducting the investigative interview, the paralegal must stay keenly aware of his ethical responsibilities. Never suggest, encourage, or persuade a witness to testify to things that are not true or that the witness does not have personal knowledge of. The paralegal's conduct should be modeled after the many codes, canons, and guidelines adopted by the American Bar Association, the National Association of Legal Assistants, and the National Federation of Paralegal Associations. Numerous sources outline ethical conduct and discuss the great variety of circumstances that can present themselves during investigative interviews, so it is suggested that the paralegal review these and local, state, and national guidelines for ethical considerations regarding:

- confidentiality
- attorney/client privilege
- work product doctrine
- other forms of privileged communication.

SUMMARY

- The body language of the interviewer and the interviewee sets the tone for the interview and acts as an evaluation tool for the interviewer.
- The *who, what, when, where,* and *why* of the investigative interview set the goals of the interview and help create an outline for the interviewer to use in preparing questions.
- The quintamensional questioning technique allows the interviewer to evaluate the worth and knowledge of the interviewee within minutes of beginning the interview, and provides a structure for moving smoothly through the interview.
- When conducting the interview, the paralegal will:
  - Open with filter and introductory questions
  - Use a variety of questioning techniques during the body of the interview to focus on the central topics of the investigation and to develop a timeline
  - Provide a closing that allows both interviewer and interviewee an opportunity to reestablish or strengthen the trust relationship they have built.
- To analyze the interview, the interviewer need only ask himself four evaluative questions and compare his thoughts to the responses received during the interview.

ACTIVITIES

Explain the following concepts:
1. The body language of the interviewee.
2. The *when* segment of the investigative interview.

Perform the following tasks:

3. Make several phone calls to three different department stores and ask for help locating a particular clothing item. Note the feelings you have about each clerk at the conclusion of the phone call, and review your findings. Record your impression and identify questioning techniques that might have influenced the conversation.

4. Select one of the following topics and prepare a list of questions regarding the topic. Define the goals of your interview by determining what you would like to discover about the interviewee's knowledge and attitudes on the subject. Use the quintamensional structure and interview a classmate.

   - Campus politics
   - Legal drinking ages
   - The marketing of cigarettes to minors

   At the conclusion of the first interview, have the classmate interview you. When you both have finished, critique each other based on the question structure and answerability of the questions.

5. Select a classmate to interview. Determine if the interviewee has ever had a difficult experience with a professor in another subject area. Once you have targeted a particular event to investigate, employ the techniques described in this chapter to uncover all of the details of the story. At the completion of the interview, prepare to share with the class the difficulties you experienced uncovering hidden information.

6. Review the following deposition transcript and document the purpose of each question. At the conclusion of your review, rewrite the questions for yourself to use with this witness during an investigative interview. What are the differences between your needs in the interview and those of the attorney performing the deposition? Is it necessary for there to be a difference between the two styles and approaches? Why or why not?

Line	Dialogue
1	THE WITNESS: I guess I expected, driving at a reasonable rate
2	of speed, which I was doing, that a car ahead of me was
3	traveling at a rate of speed that would have been similar
4	to the speed of my car. There were no lights of any kind
5	that would indicate she was going to turn or was going
6	to stop and I expected she was going to continue on as I
7	was doing.
8	
9	(BY MR. ALPHA, CONTINUING)
10	
11	Q: That's what we are going to get to right now. In reference
12	to that vehicle that you saw in front of you, the taillights
13	on, did you ever see any signal lights?
14	A. There were no signal lights to see

Line	Dialogue
15	Q: Did you ever have a conversation with her mother in
16	which you stated that the right signal light was on?
17	A: I did not. I had a conversation with her mother. I called to
18	find out the names and ages of the children as occupants
19	of the car and to get the proper spelling of her name and
20	her driver's license number for my accident report to the
21	state. I did not discuss the accident with her in any way.
22	Q: All right. Now, let's get back to the next question then.
23	Did you see any signal lights on?
24	A: There were no signal lights to be seen.
25	Q: Did you see any brake lights?
26	A: There were no brake lights on either to warn me that
27	there was something ahead to caution us of.
page 2	
1	Q: All right. What happened then, Mrs. Beta?
2	A: As I came traveling closer to her car, I was looking closely
3	to try and figure out what she was doing and all of a
4	sudden, I realized, "My God, that girl is stopped in the
5	middle of the road," and I grabbed my wheel and in one
6	flash, I hit my brakes hard and I turned to go off into the
7	right ditch.
8	Q: Did you make it?
9	A: No, I didn't quite make it.
10	Q: What happened?
11	A: My left front end of my car, the left fender and the left
12	part of my car hit the right rear panel of her car. I tensed
13	myself, I grabbed for the wheel tightly, which I probably
14	shouldn't have done, but when you see an impending
15	accident, I grabbed the wheel hard and went forward and
16	hit my head on the windshield.
17	Q: Did you try to avoid the accident?
18	A: I did everything humanly possible to try to avoid that
19	accident.
20	Q: As you were approaching this vehicle ahead of you, Mrs.
21	Beta, which you later found out to be driven by Jane
22	Delta, were there vehicles coming in the opposite
23	direction?
24	A: Yes, there were. There were two cars, possibly three.
25	Q: After your vehicle collided with the vehicle driven by Ms.
26	Delta, what happened after that?
27	A: I tried to reach for my C.B. radio to see if I could reach
28	someone to call for help and I could not pick myself up
29	off the back of the seat.

Line	Dialogue
30 31 32 33	Q: Let's wait a minute. Let's be more specific about this. What I am asking you is, right after the collision, then what happened? Your vehicle came to a stop after that or shortly after that?
page 3	
1	A: A split second. My vehicle was completely stopped.
2	Q: Where did your vehicle stop, or did you see that?
3 4 5 6	A: I did not say that I saw it because I was taken—the men took me from my car and put me right directly on the backboard or stretcher to go to the ambulance to the hospital.
7	Q: Now at the time of the collision, what happened to you?
8 9 10	A: I flew up over the steering wheel and I hit my head sharply against the windshield and broke the windshield with my head.
11	Q: Did you receive a bump as a result of that?
12 13	A: I had a big goose egg on the top of my head right in this area here
14	*[indicating]*.
15 16 17	Q: When your car came to a stop then, Mrs. Beta, where did you end up in the vehicle, to the best of your recollection?
18 19 20	A: I was sitting behind the steering wheel with my head laying sideways on the back of the seat. I could not pick up my neck off of the car seat. I could not lift my head.
21	Q: What's the next thing you remember after that?
22 23 24 25 26 27	A: The next thing I remember was this man came to the car door and opened the door and said he was a doctor and asked if he could give me first aid and check me to see how serious I was injured, if I would object, and I said, "NO," that I would not object and it would be all right, he could check me.
28	Q: Did he do that then?
29	A: Yes, he did.

--- **CASE STUDY** ---

Keller v. Welch

Return to the case study in Chapter 3 entitled *Keller v. Welch.*

1. Describe in detail the interviewing approach you would have used for the first interview with Rochelle Tyler.

2. How or why would you use this approach?

3. What question types do you believe would have motivated this witness, and why?

4. What interviewing problems do you perceive, and why?

5. How would your approach be different if Rochelle were the client? Why?

--- **NOTES** ---

1 Raymond L. Gorden, *Interviewing, Strategy, Techniques, and Tactics* 347 (4th ed., Dorsey Press, 1987).

2 Quoted in Myrna Lewis, "Body Language: How to Tell What Others Are Really Thinking," *New Choices* ____ (1996).

3 George Gallup, "The Quintamensional Plan of Question Design," *Public Opinion Q.* 385 (Fall 1947).

4 Cal W. Downs, G. Paul Smeyak & Ernest Martin, *Professional Interviewing* 73 (Harper & Row, 1980).

5 Charles J. Stewart & William B. Cash, Jr., *Interviewing Principles and Practices* 91 (8th ed., McGraw Hill, 1997).

6 J.T. Dillon, *The Practice of Questioning* 107 (Routledge, 1990).

INVESTIGATION

INVESTIGATION: UNDERSTANDING THE BASICS

<u>OBJECTIVES</u>   After completing this chapter, you will know:

- What a civil investigation is and who uses it.
- The roles paralegals play in civil investigation.
- The eight objectives of the investigation.
- Techniques for thinking like an investigator.
- The role of the skiptracer in the investigation and how to accomplish some of those activities.

⚖ INTRODUCTION

What Is a Civil Investigation?

The civil investigation is the backbone of today's civil litigation. Cases presented to a judge and/or jury are only as good as the information and evidence gathered during the investigation. To better understand the investigation, realize first that it is an ongoing process, beginning with the initial client interview and continuing throughout the life of the case. At the conclusion of the trial and/or postjudgment activities, the investigation is finished. Paralegal functions during the investigation include identifying and locating witnesses, identifying and preserving evidence, and creating a hypothesis for the investigation. Proficiency in investigation is achieved when critical thinking skills are developed.

Who Uses Civil Investigation?

All paralegals will investigate something during their careers, whether it be a witness's credibility, a missing piece of evidence, or the value of a claim. Investigation is such an integral part of the paralegal's work that it is virtually impossible to name or describe all the possible activities one could be assigned. Many investigative functions overlap into legal specialty areas, as discussed later in this chapter. Here are five common areas of paralegal employment and the investigative functions performed therein.

Family Law   Family law represents a unique challenge for the paralegal. This area deals with highly emotional issues and clients, and investigations is sometimes directed at sensitive issues requiring the utmost confidentiality. It is not uncommon for the family law paralegal to search for property titles, assets a spouse may have hidden, children who have been illegally taken, or private records dealing with a party's past.

These investigations require a higher level of detective skills than those used to resolve a contract dispute. A person may not disclose all the information he has, even when he is the client, for a myriad of reasons that include subject matter, ignorance, and embarrassment—all of which make the paralegal's job very difficult.

The paralegal investigating family law matters needs a good working knowledge of the court system, public records, personal and real property matters, and the police system. Personal relationships with courthouse staff and police agencies enhance the paralegal's ability to collect material and uncover evidence. This task requires the investigator to be able to detach from the client and be objective.

Real Estate   Real estate law requires specialty skills. The real estate paralegal's investigations are often complex and lengthy. They require patience; diligence; and specific knowledge of deeds, mortgages, and contracts. These skills must be used regularly to be maintained. Following a chain of title, for instance, requires intense concentration and a willingness to review volumes of material many times. Much research is done in the courthouse or in the Deed of Records office, but many searches can now be handled on the computer in the paralegal's office. Plat maps and titles are complicated and take practice and experience to adequately evaluate and investigate. This area of law requires a paralegal who likes paper-intensive work and deals well with it.

Probate   Probate law requires a skill level similar to that needed for real estate positions; however, the paralegal must also be proficient at locating hidden assets. Wills can be contested and people may hide financial items during a dispute; therefore, the probate paralegal needs skills in finding and locating moneys and goods, including tracking bank records, investments, and other such assets. The probate paralegal must also possess excellent mathematical and organizational skills.

Personal Injury   Personal injury (PI) law is one of the highest-demand specialty areas of law for paralegals, and the caseload is large. The investigation portion of the personal injury case is continuous and often multilayered, with more than one investigation being done on the same case at the same time.

   The PI paralegal may need to investigate the client as well as the substantive aspects of his case. Specialty knowledge of anatomy, chiropractic care, mechanics, engineering, product types, and other subjects may be needed for a complicated investigation, and cases may also include subrogation claims, collection investigations, underinsured motorist claims, and/or uninsured motorist claims.

Business/Corporate   The law relating to corporations and other business organizations has a unique set of investigative requirements regarding the issuance of stock, prospectuses, intellectual property, and other special subjects. The corporate paralegal needs a working knowledge of the federal systems and how to research and investigate federal filings. The Freedom of Information Act and other such statutes are often used to obtain information to provide a solid base for investigation. The corporate/business paralegal must be flexible and willing to constantly learn new and often difficult subject matters and laws; for instance, she may need to know how to adequately research patents, trademarks, and copyrights. This field is expanding, as many corporations now handle their own litigation matters in-house.

Generally   Many specialty areas not mentioned here also use investigation regularly, including environmental law and intellectual property law. The amount of investigation required in any paralegal position depends on the specialty area of practice and the paralegal's relationship with the supervising attorney.

UNDERSTANDING THE INVESTIGATION

Understanding the goals and rules of the investigation and how to achieve them is critical to success. The goals of the investigation are to:

1. Identify and obtain the facts
2. Identify and find evidence to prove the facts.

Included in the goals are three general rules: (1) The case is only as good as the evidence produced in the investigation. (2) The first side to find the best evidence usually has the advantage. (3) Empathy motivates the investigation.

Attorneys want to win their cases, as do paralegals. To accomplish the investigative goals and follow the rules, attorneys and paralegals must work together. To initiate a quality investigation, the paralegal must understand the attorney's position on the case, what is needed to prove the legal theory, and how much time is to be spent on the investigation. The attorney must know the status of the paralegal's investigation and provide guidance and supervision. Quality communication is critical.

The final rule of investigation concerns empathy. Every paralegal must understand the importance of using empathy during an investigation; it makes the investigation personal and adds the drive needed to ensure that all facts and details are thoroughly reviewed and new leads considered. Empathetic insight promotes better use of evidence gathered from the client and perspicacity as to missing and unknown evidence. Empathy is an important tool in the investigation and should never be forgotten or neglected.

The Paralegal's Role

The paralegal's role in the investigation is diverse. She is responsible for managing, collecting, and preserving evidence; identifying, locating, and interviewing witnesses; and dealing with formal discovery. In fact, the paralegal's role as investigator and litigation assistant overlap, making it difficult to distinguish which tasks are investigatory and which are litigation functions. The most comprehensive definition of the paralegal's role in investigation may include all of the following:

- Interview the client and manage all evidence provided by the client.
- Develop a hypothesis to support the cause of action and drive the investigation.
- Prepare formal discovery to be served on the opposing party.
- Answer formal discovery served by the opposing party.
- Identify, locate, and interview witnesses.
- Identify, locate, and preserve evidence.
- Analyze evidence for use in the investigation and at trial.
- Review documents and summarize them for application in the investigation.
- Take photographs, locate maps, and collect other demonstrative evidence as applicable.
- In general, perform any and all tasks required to support the attorney and the cause of action.

THE OBJECTIVE OF THE CIVIL INVESTIGATION

The overall objectives the paralegal must accomplish when conducting an investigation are listed based on the priorities of the civil lawsuit:

- Understand the goals of the investigation.
- Identify the legal theories and what is required to prove them.
- Prepare a client profile.
- Research and understand the subject matter of the case.
- Use fact analysis to determine the components of the client's claim.
- Prepare organizational tools for the investigation (e.g., witness lists, tickler systems, and case management charts).
- Obtain all evidence already in the client's possession and outline where additional evidence may be found.
- Note any credibility issues involving the client and her story.

Understand the Goals of the Investigation

The paralegal must understand the parameters of the investigation and the supervising attorney's goals at the onset of the investigation. She must know what points of law the attorney will be dealing with and what type of investigation and evidence are required. The attorney provides additional detail on subject matter issues. The paralegal should never guess what is needed for the case and spend valuable time going in the wrong direction. A good rule of thumb is: "The first side to find the best evidence (usually) wins the case."

Every paralegal should strive for a better understanding of how to prove or defend against such actions as negligence, wage loss, fraud, and other torts. Ask questions when necessary. If the paralegal does not understand the **cause of action**, she should not continue with the investigation. A *cause of action* is "[t]he fact or facts that give a person a right to judicial redress or relief against another; a legally acceptable reason for suing."[1] Paralegals must be proficient in procedural law and the laws of evidence. Without a good understanding and strict observance of these rules, the pieces of evidence may be of no use to the attorney, or evidence may be overlooked. Lack of information on substantive matters causes errors.

Identify the Legal Theory and Facts Necessary for Its Support

The main goal of an investigation is to provide the attorney with the evidence needed to support the cause of action or defenses. To identify one or both of these items, the paralegal reviews the standards for the legal issues claimed in the action and researches data dealing with the subject matter of the lawsuit, such as stock purchases or engineering statistics. Competent paralegals must increase their knowledge in areas not taught as part of their formal paralegal education.

EXAMPLE ———————————————————————

An investigation has been started involving a client (contractor) and a window company that sold and installed windows for a large building. It is alleged that the windows were inadequate and consequently caused damage to the property.

The paralegal needs to understand the legal elements of each cause of action, such as breach of contract, contemplated by the attorney. The paralegal also needs a working understanding of windows and structural engineering.

The overall knowledge required in this example is quite extensive and complex, including knowledge of windows, their installation, types of glass, building codes, costs of repair, ordering systems and timelines, and structural safety requirements. To obtain this data, the paralegal contacts building inspectors and manufacturers, collects engineering materials dealing with window construction, and taps other sources as needed. Pre-investigation can be slow, but there is no way to avoid the need for such information. Good communication between the attorney and the paralegal helps. The paralegal must fully understand the goals of the investigation, as set by the supervising attorney, and adhere to them. This eliminates searches for unneeded material and details. Understanding the substantive law being applied to a case, and its requirements, greatly aids an efficient, timely investigation.

Prepare a Client Profile

The client profile is based on data gathered during the initial interview. As discussed in Chapter 4, the information gleaned from that interview provides a base outline about the client, the opposing party, the action or event itself, and the evidence available to date.

Participating in the initial client interview is the most effective means of uncovering this material. While gaining experience in collecting this data and interviewing clients, the paralegal depends on common sense and the attorney's help in determining the strengths and weaknesses of a client, her story, and the evidence required in a case. Think logically about the story being told and use personal life experiences to aid in identifying evidence.

Understand the Subject Matter

After putting together the client profile, begin gathering research materials on the subject matter of the case. These materials should both support the case and offer education on the subject. Attorneys and/or law offices often have books and resources for this purpose, but be creative when searching for materials. Use sources such as the Internet, the public library, and others. It is not uncommon for paralegals to contact others knowledgeable in a field to discover where information may be located and how to get it; sometimes information can be gathered from that person himself. However, the paralegal should be cautious about obtaining information from a source who may be adverse or who may later be used as an expert witness by the opposing party. Once resource material has been gathered, keep it in a file marked "save."

After obtaining the material, review and apply it to the case details, being as objective as possible so that holes in the client's story and missing evidence become obvious. With thorough research, it is possible for the paralegal to know more about the client's story than he does. When an investigative paralegal understands the subject matter of a case, she can ask questions that jog or enhance the memories of the client and witnesses. Detailed knowledge of any subject matter should always be outlined in a memo for the attorney so that she can use the research as well.

Do Fact Analysis

With an understanding of the legal theories and subject matter, the paralegal begins to do a fact analysis of the existing details of the case story, to determine what is needed to support the legal issues. The analysis is begun by first identifying the fundamental characteristics of the facts in a case:

- The triggering event
- The client's version of the story
- Witness stories, each of which supplies different pieces of the whole story
- Existing documentary evidence.

The second step in fact analysis is to chart the different witness stories and the witnesses' potential motivation for involvement. At the same time, note any credibility issues regarding a witness's testimony; these notes can be used to qualify each witness and aid in identifying, overlapping and contradicting details in the witnesses' testimony.

Prepare Organizational Tools for the Investigation

During the early stages of an investigation, various checklists, charts, and graphs are developed to help manage the investigation. Chapter 8 explains these many tools and how to use them. The paralegal simply recognizes the need for organization during an active investigation, and begins the management process early in the case to avoid evidence and witness problems and to adequately handle time deadlines.

A variety of organizational tools are used in investigation, each tailored to a specific topic or issue. As evidence is gathered, it is logged on checklists; the same is true for witnesses. The paralegal is entrusted with all of the evidence in a case and must use the utmost care and integrity in managing it.

Gather Evidence and Outline Sources of Additional Evidence

The first evidence is collected from the client at the initial interview. Each item collected must be logged on an appropriate chart or list and its value and use described. The items must then be preserved. For instance, photographs must be placed in a climate-controlled environment and original documents kept in the firm's safe. The location of preserved evidence must also appear on the evidence log.

After dealing with the existing evidence, the paralegal creates a second evidence list for items suggested by the client as potential evidence. These items have yet to be gathered, so an organizational list is created to monitor the paralegal's progress in finding and securing them. On this list the paralegal identifies such things as photographs to be taken at the location of the triggering event, documents to be produced by the opposing party, and witness interviews to be conducted. How and where to gather these evidentiary items are also logged on this list or chart.

The purpose of logging such information is twofold. First, the log manages the search and keeps the paralegal moving at a timely speed. Second, if the lead paralegal becomes unable to handle all the investigative duties herself, another member of the legal team or another paralegal may use this document as a guide in gathering the evidence.

Note Credibility Issues

As part of the investigation, and as discussed in Chapters 1 and 4, the credibility of every interviewee (witness) must be evaluated, especially the client. The legal team has agreed to represent the client, so the paralegal needs to critically review the client and his story for any areas the opposing party may use as rebuttal evidence.

EXAMPLE ————————————————————————————

In a case involving securities fraud, the legal team representing the plaintiff claims that the defendant issued a deceptive prospectus that induced the plaintiff to invest in a bogus venture. After researching the subject matter of the case (stock investments), the paralegal finds that, by law, the client is considered a "sophisticated" investor who should have been able to identify the problems with the allegedly defective prospectus.

In this scenario, the paralegal has noted a potential credibility issue with the client and his story, which she believes the opposing party will use. The legal team expects the paralegal to make this type of critical review throughout the investigation.

THINKING LIKE AN INVESTIGATOR

Learning to think like an investigator can be difficult. It requires the paralegal to use her creative mind in conjunction with her legal knowledge. She must permit herself some freedom in the investigation to expand and explore evidence, story details, and subject matter details. To think like an investigator, the paralegal must:

- Have a sense of humor
- Learn to make assumptions about case details and evidence
- Learn to evaluate the case.

Adopt a Sense of Humor

Like most of the tasks paralegals are asked to perform, investigations may become stressful, cumbersome, and even tedious. A sense of humor is almost mandatory if the paralegal is to eliminate these barriers and remain productive. Within the confines of the investigation, humor is particularly valuable: it can help identify the finest pieces of the client's or opposing party's story for further investigation.

EXAMPLE

While reviewing several boxes of documents during an investigation, the paralegal finds repeated phone messages from the plaintiff to the defendant (client). The paralegal also notices that the secretary taking the messages for the client made marginal comments to her boss regarding the plaintiff's phone calls. Some of these comments are quite funny, like, "She wants to know if you are ever here except to sell insurance contracts." Although these messages are initially humorous and lighten the paralegal's task, the fact is that the paralegal has stumbled onto potential evidence. By using her sense of humor during the document review, the paralegal begins to integrate the secretary's notes into potential evidence. How? She begins to develop theories about the plaintiff: if the plaintiff was making many calls after the triggering event, perhaps she also made several phone calls before the triggering event. In addition, the paralegal may assume that the plaintiff made other such comments to the secretary early in the plaintiff/defendant relationship, many of which may be of value to the investigation.

The paralegal should focus on the finer points of the investigation, often those that amuse her, which can lighten the stress of the assignment and allow her to begin developing theories about the case and its evidence.

Learn to Make Assumptions About Case Details and Evidence

The paralegal must be able to critically review evidence and story details and make assumptions about them. Use brainstorming to spark new ideas about the evidence and the investigation. The paralegal begins by recording all of her impressions about the client, the client's story, the witnesses and their stories, existing evidence, and documents produced by or to the client—and develops the habit of listening to her intuition. This procedure will help her uncover missing or deleted details of the triggering event.

Learn to Evaluate the Case

Evaluate the case and its evidence throughout the life of the case by reading the file as a "normal," uninvolved person would. To do this evaluation, detach from the case and lay out all the information, including the client's story, the opposing party's story, all evidence (existing and potential), and all witness stories; review them as if you were a jury member hearing them for the first time. Impressions of the strengths and weaknesses of the case must be recorded for later analysis. The paralegal should practice this detachment so that judgments are not biased. A nonbiased opinion is critical when researching the investigation, because it allows the legal team to weigh both positive and negative information and use it accordingly.

SKIPTRACING

The duties of the skiptracer are time-consuming and cumbersome. The skiptracer finds missing witnesses, parties, and pieces of evidence an attorney and/or paralegal need for a case but are unable to locate. Skiptracers have found a place in the law office because of their specialized abilities to investigate and to use technology unique to finding missing persons and assets. In the last decade, the skiptracer has offered services traditional paralegals were unable or too inexperienced to handle.

The technology the skiptracer commonly uses includes computerized databases and specialty software. (See Chapter 9 for more details on using databases and the Internet as investigative tools.) Because technologically advanced equipment is expensive, the cost of using skiptracers has become prohibitive to many law firms and clients. Therefore, paralegals are learning to function as in-house skiptracers for many firms. The majority of the tasks skiptracers perform can be done within the law office; however, memberships and subscriptions to specialized computer companies dealing in marginally private information, and specialty software, are required.

The skiptracer does primarily electronic or computer-type research; thus, a paralegal performing skiptracing tasks needs these specific skills. The skiptracer follows asset trails through computerized banking data; traces ownership of motor vehicles and other items by means of state and federal registration agencies; and locates and copies driving records, among other things. These are but a few of the many data banks available for investigators. See Appendix A for a list of the many state and federal agencies that aid in public information searches.

As paralegals take on the responsibility of in-house skiptracing, the relationship between the paralegal and attorney changes. New timelines for skiptracing reduce the amount of time available for traditional paralegal duties. This can create a conflict, so it is not uncommon for one or more paralegals to handle all skiptracing duties for the firm. This practice promotes higher quality results from the in-house paralegal/skiptracer, because she is handling only those duties and staying current with techniques, which constantly evolve in this specialty area.

Skiptracing Activities

What does the paralegal do as a skiptracer? The most efficient way to look at skiptracing is through an example.

EXAMPLE

Take the case of a missing witness, who is key to the law firm's case. A skiptracer could be hired to evaluate the witness's personal traits and find her. The paralegal/skiptracer does the same thing. The obvious difference is that the paralegal is already familiar with the case, its facts, and some details about the witness. In this situation, the paralegal saves the client and the firm money and time by logically reviewing previously gathered data for information that might lead to the witness. This same review would be done by an outside skiptracer, but would take longer and probably cost more. Fact analysis of the material requires some natural sense and "street smarts," if the witness is to be found.

The missing witness is a well-known trainer of field retrievers. No one in the law firm has talked to her, but she would be very valuable to the investigation because of her personal knowledge and expertise in training dogs. The witness has many ties to the original venue of the case, which is within the same county as the law office (this also makes travel practical and affordable for the paralegal). The paralegal has interviewed several persons who have worked with this trainer and understands that the trainer does not want to be involved in the case because of the volatile nature of the opposing party.

The information from the interviews helps the paralegal understand the missing dog trainer and her motivations. In the interviews the paralegal has begun developing trust relationships with the interviewees. The paralegal can use these relationships to open doors to the missing trainer.

During repeated conversations with other witnesses, it is clear that the trainer has recently married and moved out of state. Although the witnesses have not given the paralegal any direct information regarding the missing trainer/witness, they have told the paralegal when the trainer was married and when she moved. The paralegal can then use this information to search public records (e.g., marriage licenses) via the Internet and possibly find the trainer's new name.

Assume that the trainer specializes in Labrador retrievers and has been in the business for fifteen years. In addition, she has written several articles about training these dogs. A computer search of periodicals on dog training reveals that there are three nationally known magazines relating to dog training and Labrador retrievers. The computer search also provides the phone numbers of each of the magazines' editors. A call to each of the editors provides information on the articles the trainer has written—they may even know her current residence.

Thus, the paralegal provided skiptracing services in less time and at less expense by using existing investigation data, her relationships with other witnesses (already developed in the case), and various computerized services.

The specialty skills acquired by the paralegal skiptracer are applicable in many civil law fields. Paralegals are using these skills in areas like bankruptcy law, family law, and personal injury practices.

SUMMARY

- The civil investigation is the very backbone of the civil lawsuit. It is an ongoing process of critical thinking and evaluation that involves various investigative duties and functions and may be needed in all specialty areas.

- The civil investigation is based on two goals and three general rules. The goals are: (1) identify and obtain the facts; and (2) identify and find evidence to prove the facts. The rules are: (1) the case is only as good as the investigation; (2) the first side to find the best evidence usually has the advantage; and (3) empathy motivates the investigation.

- The eight objectives of the investigation define a step-by-step procedure for the paralegal to follow in doing a quality investigation. They include understanding the goals of the investigation, identifying the legal theories, preparing the client profile, understanding the subject matter of the case, using fact analysis, preparing organizational tools, gathering the client's evidence, and identifying the client's credibility issues.

- The paralegal must strive to develop the skills to think like an investigator. These skills include having a sense of humor, learning to make assumptions about the case and evidence, and learning to evaluate the case.

- Skiptracing has become a major investigative function for many paralegals and private companies. The in-house paralegal adds her specialty skills in technology, including use of specialty software and databases, to her existing skills in litigating a case to enhance the civil investigation.

ACTIVITIES

1. Choose one specialty area in which you are considering seeking employment when you finish school. Research law firms in your area that handle this type of law. Contact a senior paralegal within that firm and schedule an interview with him or her. Ask specific questions about the types of daily investigation he or she does and what types he or she rarely has the opportunity to do. Ask him or her what continuing legal education to seek out regarding investigation in this particular type of law. Find out what types of technology she or he regularly uses to further the work in this field.

2. Prepare a five- to ten-minute presentation on the findings from your interview. Present them to the class and support your data with real-life case examples provided by the interviewee. Also, research at least one of the technological tools the interviewee suggested to you; explain its uses, strengths and weaknesses, and how much it costs to use.

3. Refer to the first example in this chapter, which deals with the client contractor and the window problem. Satisfy each of the eight objectives required for the investigation; be specific. Discuss where you might research the subject matter. Also use investigative thinking strategies to move this investigation into action.

CASE STUDY

Jim and Joan Klosty

After reading the details of this case, complete the following assignments.

1. Find your state's laws regarding real estate transactions and disclosure statements. Research what laws may apply to the Klostys' case.
2. Using the laws you have found, list the evidence you will need to gather to support the Klostys' case. Note which of those items you will get from the Klostys.
3. Research the topics of the case (siding for the house, rotted window frames, and so on). Gather enough detail on the cost of replacement for those items so that you can educate the class on the specifics of the subject matter.

Case Details

Jim and Joan Klosty bought a home in March of 1998. The previous owners claimed that there was no current damage and no problems with the home at the time of the sale. The real estate agent, Joyce Allswell, supported the previous owners, stating that she knew a lot about houses and that this one was fine. Joyce also told the Klostys that they did not need to have the house inspected and that it was not standard practice to do so in this state. The Klostys, who were new to the state, believed the real estate agent and went ahead with the home purchase. After moving in, the Klostys found several problems, including rotted siding on the outside, rotted window frames, broken pipes that had been taped together, and holes in the walls that were covered with wallpaper. The Klostys are now asking for legal representation and wish to sue the previous owners for $20,000, which is the approximate cost of repairing the damage.

NOTES

[1] William Statsky, *Legal Thesaurus/Dictionary* (West, 1985).

8 ORGANIZATION AND THE SUCCESSFUL INVESTIGATION

OBJECTIVES   After completing this chapter, you will know:

- Why organizational tools are critical to the success of the investigation.
- How to create and use tickler systems, calendars, and dockets.
- What types of charts, lists, and tables to use for specific investigative and case functions, such as evidence and witness management.
- How to use computerization in case management and case investigation.

INTRODUCTION

One of the most important investigative jobs the paralegal has is that of information manager. While conducting an investigation, and generally when handling any case, the paralegal is responsible for the management and control of documents, evidence, and witness data. This responsibility reaches beyond the investigation to encompass all formal discovery and general pleadings work.

It is an unwritten law that when a paralegal is managing the information on a case, that information should be quickly accessible. For this to be accomplished, the paralegal creates an organizational framework within which he places all of a case's documents, data, and materials. In addition to these functions, the paralegal takes responsibility (under the attorney's supervision) for managing the case calendar and ensuring that discovery deadlines and other such court-ordered timelines are never missed or neglected. These tasks are handled through methodical planning and the use of tickler systems, charts and graphs, witness and exhibit lists, discovery plans, databases, and case reference manuals. Each of these sources is used in a variety of different case and investigation situations.

TICKLER SYSTEMS

General Office Systems

Every law office has a method of keeping and maintaining a general calendar. A **tickler system**, by definition, is a memorandum, reference work, or the like maintained to "tickle" or jog memories about happenings and activities. In some law offices, the tickler system is known as a *diary system.*

In addition to the tickler systems, the paralegal also uses a docketing system. Items found on a legal calendar, commonly referred to as a **docket**, include meetings, depositions, court dates, and due dates for pleadings. All these systems are used to manage the attorney's responsibilities to the client and the court. Although the attorney is ultimately responsible for case management, these responsibilities are often delegated to the paralegal, so a general calendar is needed to provide a quick and broad overview of a day, week, or month as deadlines are met and new appointments scheduled.

In many law offices it is standard procedure for a physically maintained, annual calendar to be kept with the office manager (the hub of the office). However, technological advances have now prompted most firms to move their docket and tickler systems onto computers. The computer systems offer automatic alarm notices on individual computers, which allows the person directly related to a deadline to be notified automatically when that deadline draws near. Such systems provide a daily, weekly, or monthly printout of the entire office schedule, so everyone in the office is made aware of all upcoming events and schedule requirements. Docket and tickler systems afford attorneys, paralegals, legal secretaries, and other office personnel an understanding of each office member's commitments and workload.

Individual Systems

Individual tickler systems provide many services to paralegals, especially those handling the cases of many attorneys at one time. By using a **manual tickler system**, in addition to the computerized or general office system, the paralegal can track the attorney's deadlines and his own as well. The most common manual tickler system works off a desk calendar or note cards.

Manual Systems   It is most efficient for the paralegal to break the manual system into two or more separate systems. Generally, the daily needs of the attorney are placed on a desk calendar, particularly daily case deadlines. Entries on the calendar range from depositions to trial dates, and include all the many smaller tasks that fall in between (such as the issuance and service of subpoenas). If these needs and events are noted on the desktop calendar, any member of the legal team can have ready access to the paralegal's deadlines, even in his absence.

After covering very general commitments on the desk calendar, the paralegal creates a more specific system for individual cases. One way to do this is with 3 × 5 index cards and a box to hold them. Divide the cards by case, client name, subject, or urgency, depending on your personal management preference, or use a combination of these categories. Also create a dated index system that will work like a perpetual calendar—thirty-one days' worth of cards or slots that do not refer to a specific month. Behind each date, place a card with detailed information on what has to be done on a particular case. Several cards can be placed behind each date. That way the paralegal can check each day for projects to be completed on that day. This system offers an opportunity to calendar such small tasks as returning phone calls, as well as larger duties such as completing a draft of a pleading.

For example, using an index file created and managed under case name, the paralegal places a general calendar in the front of the file and subcategorizes subsequent cards dealing with specific topics or needs, like the last date for filing a witness list before trial. A general calendar card may include the name of the case, the case number, the court where the case is located, critical dates in the case, and the attorneys involved. See Figure 8-1.

Figure 8-1
Sample index card from a case-based tickler system

Williamson v. Merrick, Case No. 98-4567-CV

5th District, Big Blue County

Discovery Deadline: May 15, 1998
IME Deadline: June 20, 1998
Trial Date: Sept. 23, 1998

Attorney: Mary Stockton and Tony Jones
Opposing: Arter & Haden, Doug Robinson

This type of indexing is very effective and almost always ensures that material is quickly available when needed. The card system also ensures that the specifics of any case are available to other legal team members who need them.

The utility of a card system can be enhanced by color-coding cards to signify specific tasks. For instance, all witness cards can be color-coded blue, general case schedules color-coded yellow, and problem areas color-coded green. Color coding is easily done by using colored cards or simply making a colored line across the top of a white card.

Computerizing Many firms are computerizing all data; however, there is some uncertainty about the safety and security of data-based files. If all critical date materials (and maybe even some of the less critical dates) have been placed on the computerized firm calendar, what happens if the computer crashes? There may be no way to access the material. Of course, this risk is minimal if the system is backed up each day, but it is still useful to have manual files that can be substituted for computerized data when needed. Each paralegal should develop his own system to handle these situations; most will end up with a combination of both computerized and manual systems.

Creating a System When creating a tickler system, the paralegal must also invent a simple coding or abbreviation system. Coding helps shorten entries and keep them specific. For instance, Figure 8-2 shows an entry on the personal calendar noting that the *Williamson v. Merrick* case has a deadline for all discovery one week from the third of the month.

The desk calendar in Figure 8-2 shows many different entries and abbreviations. The paralegal has any number of choices when creating the system, but a key should be easily available for those who do not know the system or understand the coding. The accompanying table lists some sample abbreviations.

MON	TUE	WED	THUR	FRI	SAT	SUN
1	2	3 ck/w atty. Re: disc. D/1W; Williamson	4 meeting for alt. Service due; Jones case	5	6	7
8	9	10 disc. Due Williamson case	11	12 serve S&C in Henry case	13	14
15 Contact CT. For new trial DT.; Jones case	16	17	18	19	20	21

Figure 8-2 Desk calendar system with standard abbreviations

Abbreviations	*Explanation*
CK/W	check with
D/1D	due in one day
D/1W	due in one week
F	file
RMND	remind
RVS	revise
S	serve
S/B	should be
W/O	without
S&C	summons and complaint

Many of these abbreviations are common shorthand for everyday legal terminology. Each paralegal will develop his own abbreviations to add to this list. The benefit of such a system is that it shortens the amount of time spent entering items in the tickler system and reduces the time needed to interpret the notations.

CHARTS AND GRAPHS

Effective management of a case is reflected in the quality of the work and billable hours the paralegal produces. By using effective, efficient management tools, the paralegal is assured that he is doing all he can to complete a thorough investigation. Cases move along more efficiently and deadlines are less likely to be overlooked or forgotten when charts and graphs map the way.

When preparing charts and graphs for a case, first break out specific categories of items for which individual charts will be needed. For instance, a general pleadings log is required for every case, but may have to be individualized for certain complex cases. A general index and a specific discovery index (and other individualized indexes) may or may not be required. Charts dealing with evidence, general documents, depositions, and formal discovery items will also be required; in some cases, even time sheets for billable hours are included (this is particularly important for the in-house paralegal/skiptracer).

Many different phases of litigation should be managed via chart, graph, or log: depositions, interrogatories, requests for admissions, requests for production, and the individual investigation. These areas are closely interconnected, and their purpose and management require individual treatment so as to minimize time and effort. For example, questions asked in the deposition are often prompted (and even necessitated) by information found in the formal and informal investigations; therefore, good management of the investigation material is critical. Keep these interconnections in mind during the following brief overview of specific uses for charts, graphs, and logs in four formal investigation (discovery) categories.

Pleadings

When logging or charting pleadings, first determine the complexity of the case. Sometimes it is necessary to bring additional paralegals into a case for the investigation or trial preparation; the more carefully the charting system has been implemented, the easier it will be to add support personnel to the case. When working on a simple case file (i.e., one plaintiff and one defendant), it will usually be sufficient to use the indices produced by the legal secretary for the pleadings and kept in the litigation file itself. Most indices merely list the names of the pleadings, the date they were filed, and corresponding tab numbers. When starting the investigation, use this pleadings index to create a pleadings log similar to the one shown in Figure 8-3.

Figure 8-3
Pleadings log, simple form

PLEADINGS LOG

Tab number	Description (propounding party names)	Date	Corresponding tab number
2	Defendant's Original Answer	11/5/95	1—Plaintiff's S&C

Case Name: Williamson v. Merrick
Case Number: 95-4567-CV

The first two columns are virtually the same as those in the pleadings index from the case file. The description lists the originating party's name and the title of the pleading (for example, "Defendant's Original Answer"). Due dates are noted for all documents except the summons and complaint. Extensions are common in the litigation system, so use pencil when filling in due dates. Corresponding pleadings are listed in the last column, and direct interested persons to pleadings that are responsive to documents already entered. For example, the corresponding pleading for Defendant's Original Answer is Plaintiff's Complaint. More complex litigation may require immediate preparation of a pleadings log for quick desk reference—particularly true for cases involving ten or more parties and consolidated cases. The more complicated the case, the simpler the logging system must be. These logs and charts help avoid confusion during the investigation and during witness and trial preparation. Complex cases are best served by a separate log for each type of pleading, with the type clearly marked at the top of the log. See Figure 8-4.

These tools are adaptable to any situation. The key to using these tools is to acknowledge the due dates as listed, use the data to help overlap the formal and informal investigations, and maintain a functional calendar.

PLEADINGS LOG

Type of pleading:

Originating party and date	Responding party/due date	Date received	Inspected by and date	Actions taken and by whom	Comments

Case Name: _____
Case Number: _____

Figure 8-4   Pleadings log, complex form

Depositions

Expenses for the court reporter, the attorney's time, subpoena for the witness, and other items all contribute to the high cost of a deposition. To avoid additional costs, while achieving the purpose of the deposition, preparation is required. Checklists serve as a quick reference tool for timetables within the court, availability of the witness and counsel, and information or exhibits needed at the deposition.

Two general deposition charts should be used. The first is usable in all depositions, regardless of the case. This chart, known as a **jurisdictional timetable**, affords the paralegal and the legal team quick reference to the state, local, or federal authority having jurisdictional control over the case, the deposition, and applicable rules. For instance, Federal Rules of Civil Procedure 27–32 apply to depositions taken in federal court cases, but the legal practitioner must follow state procedural rules in state courts. Rules may vary from one state to the next, and may cover everything from the deposition of the party, to the deposition of a witness, to the deposition of persons located in other states. Rather than constantly consulting the library or rule book, prepare a chart outlining the basics of these rules and citing sources of extra material on the issue. At a glance, this chart allows the paralegal to verify how many days he has to serve a subpoena prior to the event, and how many days are needed to notice a deposition.

In addition to these uses, a timetable can be adapted to individual cases as a means of tracking the paralegal's completion of tasks. Figure 8-5 is a sample **deposition timetable**. Like all charts, this one may be altered to fit specific legal work and the applicable procedural rules. This same outline format can be used to manage many rule/guideline requirements within the civil lawsuit, such as interrogatories, requests for admissions, and requests for production of documents.

Deposition Log   The second most productive tool for depositions will be the **deposition log**. If a case has five or more total parties and/or potential witnesses, a deposition log is needed (this includes most cases). The principal function of the log is to provide the paralegal and legal team with a tool for

DEPOSITION TIMETABLE

Discovery	Days	Court/Calendar	Authority
Notice of deposition			
Extra time given if mailed			
Extra time given if mailed out of state			
Subpoena in state			
Subpoena out of state			
Letters rogatory			
Notice			
Commission			
Notice of deposition before trial			
Motion to compel			
Motion for protective orders			
Notice of motion			
Extra if mailed			
Extra if mailed out of state			
Extra if mailed out of country			
Opposition to motion			
Reply to opposition			
Proof of service			
Motions deadline before trial			

Figure 8-5   Deposition timetable (adapted for long-term usability)

recording deposition status and information as it is happening, so that they need not constantly review the physical file. It takes less time to deal with new data immediately than to repeatedly dig for details buried in a file. Once the deposition log has been created, the paralegal can update information with little effort or expenditure of billable time. The deposition log contains approximately eight categories of information (see Figure 8-6). Additional abbreviations can be created to minimize the space used on the log.

Once deposition scheduling begins, use this log to note the name of the deponent, date of the deposition, need for a subpoena or notice, and other critical information. Also note the name of the court reporter, in case the deposition is canceled or rescheduled. Once the transcript is back, update the log to include

DEPOSITION LOG

Deponent	Deposition date	Noticed by	Document prepared	Volume/ Pages	Exhibit numbers	Attorney Paralegal	Notes/ Comment

Case Name: _____   Legend: "N/A" = not attached
Case Number: _____   "N/N" = not necessary
                                                 "S/B" = separate binder

Figure 8-6   Deposition log, used for ready reference in cases with at least five parties or witnesses

when it was received, if it must be summarized, who will summarize it, and what the deadline for the summary is. Include in the log a note as to whether the deposition transcript is on disk and when the deponent is required to have read and corrected the transcript. As a standard practice, always fill out organizational tools in pencil. By initialing and dating information when it is entered in the log, the paralegal provides a quick reference as to who was working with the materials at a particular time and what materials were used.

Requests for Production of Documents

As for depositions, some type of timetable is required for a request for production of documents. The paralegal chooses whether to include a place for individual case status in that table; there are benefits to handling a case either way. An alternative is to complete a master timetable for every formal discovery function and make copies to be used for status in individual cases. A master list of timetables can be kept in a personal data notebook, discussed later in this chapter. An adapted version of the timetable appears in Appendix B.

Document Log   The need for a document log varies from case to case, though one is usually used in any case for which the legal team expects to receive a large number of documents. If needed, prepare a log of the critical documents and how they pertain to the legal issues.

EXAMPLE ————————————————————————————————————

While managing a case that involves an unsuccessful international adoption, the paralegal is told that a large batch of documents is coming from the plaintiffs. The documents eventually arrive in five **bankers boxes**. (A *bankers box* is a large cardboard box commonly used in legal matters to hold several hundred pages at a time; it is very similar to a single large filing drawer.)

Several years have passed since the adoption fell through and the documents being produced span a long time period. The case originally involved several different parties, some of whom have documents from seven or more judicial districts—all of which the plaintiffs have now produced. The complexity of the documents is quite apparent. Although these documents will have to be managed by Bates stamping and indexing, they will also have to be logged somehow. (A **Bates stamp** is a six (or more) digit number placed in the bottom corner of the document, using a numbering machine of the type first made by the Bates company. Note: There are now many products, software packages, and vendors for this process.) The numbers can include an alpha series to identify the producing party, if there are multiple parties. A larger series of numbers can be used when there are more than 1 million documents.

A document log may look like the sample in Figure 8-7. However, it is an adaptable tool and should be adjusted to fit the needs of each individual case. Documents are material evidence, and material evidence is vital to any case. Every effort must be made to manage the documents so that they can be used to their fullest potential and so that they are protected.

DOCUMENT LOG

Requested by and date	Produced by and date	Received, inspected/date	Document numbers, if stamped	Summarized/ computerized/ indexed	Subject matter/ comments

Case Name: _____

Case Number: _____

Figure 8-7   Detailed document log

Master Document Index   In cases like the adoption example, a master index is required, because of the sheer volume of the documents and the complexity of the issues. A **master document index** records the general number groupings used as they relate to the documents produced and received. A numbering system will show who produced what documents, especially if some documents are duplicated.

EXAMPLE ——————————————————————————————————

Assume in the adoption example that your firm represents the adoption agency, one of five original defendants. All other parties have settled with the plaintiffs, but the agency wants to litigate the matter. Documents from all the other defendants will likely be produced by the plaintiffs during formal discovery, as the plaintiffs are probably depending on some of those documents to prove their claim. In a case like this, where a large portion of the investigation takes place "inside the documents," the documents must be logged by file, location, and other pertinent information.

Figure 8-8 shows how a master index may be put together.

MASTER DOCUMENT INDEX

File title and inclusive document numbers list	Reviewed/ summarized/ computerized	Requesting party and producing party (dates of both)	Location of documents
Adoption plaintiff (000000-012345)	Reviewed and computerized	R = defendant "A" P = plaintiff	Database disk in central safe, physical file in war room 2.

Case Name: _____
Case Number: _____

Figure 8-8 Master document index

The master index is a convenient management tool that minimizes the time and effort needed to initiate and maintain document productions and investigations. Update this index in pencil when new documents arrive or when the status of a document changes.

Computerization The computerization of documents is usually done after many of the basic organizational tools have been prepared. However, preparation work is needed for the computerizing of documents, too. This includes identifying the cast of characters (persons and entities involved), identifying the types of documents being handled, and preparing a list of the issues. The attorney decides the issues to be listed and what document types will be investigated to support those issues. (A more detailed discussion of document databases appears later in this chapter.)

Interrogatories

In general, interrogatories are one of the most effective and least expensive discovery tools available. The use of paralegals to develop and answer interrogatories is common because it is a cost-effective use of the client's money and the firm's time. Once again, checklists provide an easy and efficient method of accessing information. A basic timetable should be drafted for the interrogatory phase of discovery, as for the deposition and request-for-production phases. A sample specific interrogatory timetable appears in Appendix B.

Interrogatory Log   The interrogatory log is used to maintain a schedule and record of when certain parties exchanged interrogatories. When interrogatory answers are computerized, a log to identify document numbers is used. The log will have categories such as:

- Propounding party/Pleading tab number
- Date
- Responding party/Pleading tab number
- Date
- Set number and interrogatory numbers
- Summarized/Computerized
- Subject matter and comments.

Federal Rules and Computerization   The Federal Rules of Civil Procedure allow (under Rule 33) up to twenty-five interrogatories to be issued at any one time, and several sets of interrogatories may be exchanged between parties, if permitted by the court. If there are several parties in a case, there can be vast numbers of answers and questions to be managed, and computerization of this material is expensive. If it is not possible to computerize interrogatory answers, due to financial restraints or other reasons, they can easily be maintained through a standard summary procedure.

To computerize responses, a numbering system (*identifier*) is needed to expedite retrieval. This system depends solely on the case and the object of the case. A basic identifier format is a seven- or eight-digit number. Figure 8-9 shows a sample identifier, A0101001, broken down into its meaningful components.

Requests for Admissions

Like every other discovery tool, a timetable for requests for admission must be drafted so that critical dates can be tracked and met, and so that the amount of time spent managing organizational tools for requests is minimized. Appendix B shows a generalized request for admissions timetable and log. The log tracks material to be included in the request and when other parties served requests for admissions. If requests for admissions are computerized, include the numbering system in the log.

Figure 8-9
Components of
eight-digit
alphanumeric
coding system

A =	The letter that clearly identifies that the information is coming from an interrogatory answer.
01 =	Number representing the propounding party. *[This is optional if you are identifying the propounding party in the interrogatory log. The shorter the identifier, the better.]*
01 =	Number given to the responding party from the master list of characters (the master list was originally drafted when the case/file was put on a computer database). *[This number indicates who has said something happened, without the paralegal's having to specifically write the person's name each time. Remember that the identifier can have only two characters when there are more than nine parties on the master index.]*
001 or **01** =	The last two to three numbers are arbitrarily used to identify specific responses. When interrogatories are numbered consecutively, save three spaces to correlate these last numbers with the interrogatory number. This creates the simplest referral method. If more than one set of interrogatories is issued to a party, use the first space to identify the "set" of interrogatories and the next two to identify the specific question number (e.g., set 1, question 12 = 112).

Federal Rule of Civil Procedure 33 clearly states that there should not be more than twenty-five interrogatories per set. If this rule is observed, this numbering system will never be insufficient.[1]

[1] Dianne Dupre Zalewski, *Paralegal Discovery* (Cross Publishing, 1987).

Computerization   Computerized management of requests for admissions requires use of the same "cast of characters" keys and indices as for the databased discovery tools discussed earlier. The numbering system created should be as simple as possible, to avoid confusion. One good system uses an alpha index to start the numbering: R-01-3-015. The "R" signifies requests for admissions, "01" the propounding party, "3" the third set of requests, and "015" the fifteenth request. If there are only a few parties, or the parties are using relatively few requests for admissions, a simpler numbering system can be used. In many instances, requests for admissions are tracked manually, though this system may still require some form of identifying number.

Miscellaneous Charts and Graphs

Regardless of the type of litigation a paralegal works on, he needs a variety of methods for charting a great number of different data sources and data types. In the area of intellectual property law, for example, a paralegal uses timetables, logs, and charts to manage patent laws and schedules rather than state rules for litigation. In personal injury litigation, a paralegal needs all the charts and graphs mentioned thus far, and also needs case-specific logs, such as for employment and medical records. These fit into a master index and need special attention. Specific subject-matter logs (like those used for medicine or engineering) require a legend so that any legal team member can easily interpret the log. All these logs are kept with the documents, and a copy of each is maintained in a case file holding all indexes, summaries, and organizational data.

General Case Management

Charts and graphs can also greatly aid in the management of general case responsibilities. In addition to the specific pleadings log(s) discussed so far, a **case checklist** offers a visual summary of the whole case, featuring standard pleadings and trial preparation materials. At one glance, the case checklist or status sheet gives the status of discovery, eliminating the need to read the pleadings every time there is a question. During an investigation, the paralegal may have to search out pleading dates several times to coordinate new information with existing information. A good checklist saves hours of time that would otherwise be spent thumbing through the physical file. See Figure 8-10.

Case status sheets can be fairly elaborate and contain several pieces of information, such as the legal elements and issues, the date of accident or injury, damage assessments, witness lists, and dates for depositions in the case. A detailed status sheet is shown in Appendix B. The degree of detail in the case status or checklist sheet depends on many variables, as no two cases have the same needs. Smaller cases usually take less intricate status sheets and a shortened version of the checklist (shown in Figure 8-10).

Case Reference Manuals   Case reference manuals may be used to provide a ready reference for all critical information. Every case reference manual is developed based on the complexity of the case, but all manuals should have sections for parties, court, and pleadings. For a complex case, add sections for witnesses, timelines, deposition tables, document logs, and the like. In cases where witnesses may be difficult to work with, keep copies of the witnesses' signatures along with any documents or testimony being preserved. After a case has been completed, store the reference manual for history purposes. When a new case deals with similar issues or has similar complexities, the old manuals serve as easy, quick reference guides. The manual also helps in appeal and other postjudgment work. Finally, with permission and appropriate attention to confidentiality, such management materials and tools can be used at seminars or other education opportunities.

Personal Data Notebook   The paralegal is responsible for knowing and understanding a wide variety of information sources during the investigation. All this information must be managed and should be carefully maintained in a **personal data notebook**. The personal data notebook is something the paralegal begins creating while still in school. The notebook is most efficiently housed in a three-ring binder, so materials can easily be added.

CASE CHECKLIST

Date	Pleading	Responsible Person	Done
_____	Complaint: _____ v. _____	_____	_____
_____	Answer	_____	_____
_____	Cross-claim: _____ v. _____	_____	_____
_____	Answer to cross-claim	_____	_____
_____	Interrogatories to: _____	_____	_____
_____	Interrogatories to: _____	_____	_____
_____	Interrogatories to: _____	_____	_____
_____	Response to Inter. from: _____	_____	_____
_____	Response to Inter. from: _____	_____	_____
_____	Response to Inter. from: _____	_____	_____
_____	Request to produce to: _____	_____	_____
_____	Request to produce to: _____	_____	_____
_____	Response to RTP from: _____	_____	_____
_____	Response to RTP from: _____	_____	_____
_____	Request for admissions to: _____	_____	_____
_____	Response to admissions from: _____	_____	_____
_____	Miscellaneous:_____	_____	_____

Figure 8-10   Simple case status checklist

Information source lists (Figure 8-11) are created and added as new information is gathered, and must be updated periodically for easier use. It can take
years to compile a thorough listing of information sources, but drafting blank
charts is a good way to begin such a list.

In addition to information sources, the paralegal needs sample pleadings, organized in a binder and indexed. Standard versions of complaints and answers,
interrogatory definitions and questions, and the like all typically use **boilerplate
language**. *Boilerplate* is standard (and sometimes mandatory) verbiage used in
almost all documents of a kind (all pleadings or all contracts, for example); it is
often drawn directly from statutory language and time-tested, well-known legal
phraseology.

Among the general charts created for a personal data notebook, it is useful
for the paralegal to create a statute of limitations chart, which provides an overview of the state laws affecting many different actions and serves as a quick

Figure 8-11
Personal data
notebook
worksheet

INFORMATION SOURCE LIST

Source	Address/ Phone	Contact Name	Comments
CITY:			
Mayor's Office			
Assessor's Office			
Tax Office			
COUNTY:			
Courthouse			
Board of Health			
Registrar of Voters			
Sheriff's Office			
STATE:			
Governor			
Dept. Motor Vehicles			
Sec'y of State			
Senator			
FEDERAL:			
Bankruptcy Court			

guide for assessing data early in a case. The timelines established for civil matters are set by the court or the Federal Rules of Civil Procedure; depending on who set the rules, the timelines may be altered.

WITNESS AND EVIDENCE LISTS

Although the idea of creating a large number of charting systems may seem overwhelming, they are necessary to handle the daily demands of the paralegal's job. Many indexes, charts, and logs are used universally, yet this is not the case with witness and evidence lists. The general format for these lists is often drafted ahead of time, but the details are left open and adjusted to fit each unique case. These subjects and categories require a unique management system to manage constantly changing subject matter. Each list helps the paralegal and legal team prepare for depositions, pretrial conferences, and the trial.

Preliminary Lists

The initial assignment of a new case requires the paralegal to review all data from the client and begin collecting evidence and names of potential witnesses; it is immediately obvious that this information needs management. In the initial client interview the paralegal uses a ready-made witness and exhibit list to document what the client identifies. Thereafter this list is used to begin the informal investigation. All cases have some type of preliminary list for witnesses and evidence. See Figure 8-12.

WITNESS LIST		
Name	**Address/Phone Number**	**Purpose**
1. Alexander Wilkes	1312 W. Pine 555-8989	Agrees that plaintiff hit defendant first.
2.		
3.		
4.		

Figure 8-12   Preliminary witness list

Evidence lists look very much the same, except that they provide information on the location or perceived location of the evidence (exhibit). Figure 8-13 shows a sample preliminary evidence list. These preliminary lists are used as a base when the attorney reviews the facts and supporting evidence to date and makes decisions on the case. This same data provides the paralegal with a starting place in the informal investigation.

Specific Lists

As witnesses are located, a more specific witness list must be created. This list allows the paralegal a systematic means of managing the location of the witnesses and the legal team's use of those witnesses (e.g., deposition, trial, or investigative interview). Figure 8-14 is an example of this second type of list.

The same idea is used with the evidence lists. Once the investigation has begun to take shape, it will be necessary to adjust the witness and evidence lists. Both the witness and evidence lists will be placed in a trial notebook (created well before the actual trial).

EVIDENCE LIST

Document	Location	Use(s)
1. Contract	Original in client's vault, copies in the office and with defendant	Contains provisions that support breach of contract issue.
2.		
3.		
4.		

Figure 8-13   Preliminary evidence list

WITNESS LIST #2

Name	Address/Phone	Date talked to	Results
1. Alex Wilkes	1312 Pine 555-8989	10/11/98	Friendly but nervous, may be helpful, can call at work, 565-0900 after 2.
2.			
3.			

Figure 8-14   Second-level witness list, detailing individual witness needs and uses

☑ **PRACTICAL TIP**   Evidence lists will be titled *exhibit lists* at the trial.

The witness list provides the names of the witnesses intended to be called; their addresses and telephone numbers; if they gave a deposition and when; what evidence they will help to introduce; and when they were served with a subpoena to appear. In addition to these details, the witnesses are placed on the list in the order the attorney intends to call them at the trial. In some cases, it is even necessary to estimate the date and time the witnesses will be called. All of this is helpful not only to the legal team, but to the witnesses as well. A more detailed witness list, as described here, appears in Appendix B. Other varieties of witness lists may be used for experts and when attempting to locate witnesses.

Evidence   Evidence and witness lists are both molded to the needs of the case. However, evidence lists have different variables and rarely evolve at the same pace as the witness list. Once the general evidence list has been compiled, the attorney asks that specific evidence, selected for use at the depositions and trial, be gathered together in a safe location (provided all of the evidence can be accommodated in the same location). Once this has been done, the evidence list is re-created to reflect:

- When the evidence was collected
- From whom it was collected
- If it is in its original form
- What use will be made of it
- Any other specific comments regarding the individual object.

Evidence lists may require diversity, and paralegals may need a more personal evidence list while conducting the investigation. This personal list may include such things as the size and specifics of a blow-up diagram or chronology for trial, or it may include a description of what service will prepare evidence for trial, and any costs associated with the evidence.

CREATIVITY AND ORGANIZATION

Creativity in the investigation has taken on a new meaning over the last ten years. With the introduction of a wide variety of software packages for the law office, particularly in litigation, the paralegal and attorney have gained a number of resources that greatly enhance creative management of legal files.

Computerization

The primary factor for evaluating whether to computerize a file is not the cost of software, but the cost of its application and the additional costs of computerizing. There are several other functional costs to be considered, including the initial review of the file, the coding and summarizing of documents, and data input. All these can be very costly (and time-consuming) procedures and each raises the cost of a case. Law firms that regularly handle large cases with thousands of documents can use the same basic software over and over, but the firm that rarely has a case large enough to warrant purchasing litigation-specific software may find the cost prohibitive. When a firm already owns the software, the billable time used to manage the case on computer may not be any greater than if management were done manually. Nevertheless, all the previously mentioned expenses must be reviewed before a decision is made to place a document- and witness-intensive case on computer, regardless of the size of the firm.

Often immensely complex cases are better served by computerization. Still, when a firm is faced with purchasing software and additional staff to input documents and other data, it may be more cost-effective to use a very detailed manual system or to hire a private litigation management team to work with the paralegal on the case. Regardless of the manner in which a firm decides to handle a case, the paralegal must be prepared to deal with complex coding, summarizing, and indexing systems.

The computerization of a file directly influences all aspects of the case, including the investigation. With the huge increase in complex, paper-intensive cases, legal teams and especially paralegals have found that litigation support databases allow them to locate vital information about the facts, sort factual information into categories that fit the issues, and print out that data in useful formats. It is common for the litigation team to analyze critical documents early in a case to guide them in the litigation process and at the same time to select the material to be placed in a database. At this same time, the paralegal begins identifying key words, names, and document types to be used for coding. Once this has been done, and the material placed on the system, the paralegal reviews and sorts reports focusing on investigative needs, discovery requests, or database expansion. When the documents deal with discrete matters and sensitive documents are the core group of documents to be coded, the paralegal focuses on subjective analysis and abstract summaries rather than the individual documents.

Databases

There are two types of databases: **full-text** and **abstract**. The full-text system allows full inputting of all documents; that is, every word of every document is input into a system (commonly with the use of a scanner). The abstract system requires that all documents be reviewed, broken into categories or fields, and the information abstracted. This is commonly done when select topics, dates, names, and types of documents are identified by the legal team as important. Then, all documents are reviewed and numbered, and the information correlating to the document is entered into the system.

These two systems can be combined. Some materials may have to be fully input because of the complexity of their nature; for example, expert testimony on the function of a nuclear reactor. Other material can be abstracted into the system; for instance, portions of medical records. Several areas of litigation are best served by the full-text system:

1. testimony management
2. witness impeachment
3. discovery responses.

All three areas depend on the ability to locate exact language within the many documents involved in the litigation. The credibility of a witness is of paramount importance, and when his testimony is inconsistent, the most efficient way to find the conflicts is on a database. After doing word searches on all materials from a witness, it is possible to print a report showing all inconsistencies. This data makes good impeachment material and great trial exhibits. Many court reporters now offer depositions on diskette, greatly enhancing the usefulness of this system.

Abstract System   The abstract system, which is the most widely used, focuses on subject matter when searches are performed by subject title. When searching under this system, the paralegal requests all documents identified during input that deal with a specific subject matter. A listing of all the documents in this category can be searched and retrieved for a specific detail (like a date or specific person). This is especially helpful when (1) controlling evidentiary material, (2) documenting production history, or (3) tracking discovery responses. This system is particularly advantageous for heavy-document cases in which voluminous boxes of documents are produced. With the abstract system, all documents are computerized, thus eliminating the need for cross-indexing. A well-designed system allows access to documents from several entry points, and with the swiftness of the computer and a solid numbering system, retrieval of documents from a hard-copy repository is expeditious. When preparing for trial or deposition, it is often necessary to locate and review all documents on a particular subject or with regard to a certain person; the abstract system can print a variety of different reports on one subject, linking together people, testimony, subject, and timelines.

Coding

The biggest job the paralegal faces is creating the numbering and coding systems. A coding system handles the documents, regardless of the method (manual, full-text, or abstract). The simpler the system is, the better, regardless of the management tool used. As a standard rule, all documents are Bates stamped. Once the documents are numbered, the legal team needs to decide what characters, issues, dates, and other fields will be used to break down the documents for review after input. In the abstract system, the identifier titles or subjects chosen become even more critical, because outside data entry personnel will be used to review documents for coded material and input them into the system. If there is any question on the part of an unknowing coder, critical data could be overlooked. To avoid this problem, a list is made of the types of documents found in the production during the initial review of the documents. This list is the second coding system created after numbering. Consider the following examples of document codes for a medical case.

Medical Case	*Document Codes*
ACRT	accident report
ADMR	admission records
AMBR	ambulance report
AMBI	ambulance invoice
AUTR	autopsy report
CONR	consultation report
DS	discharge summary
EKG	electrocardiogram report
H&P	history and physical

Medical Case	*Document Codes*
PATH	pathology report
UST	ultrasound treatment records
XRAY	x-ray report

Characters   The cast of characters is the next field created. A complete list of all of the parties or witnesses, regardless of their status, is required so that the legal team can search for specific impeachment and supportive evidence once the material has been entered into the system. This list can be added to as the need arises. Consider the following example of name coding.

Character Coding	
ABC	ABC Company
BAE	Barry Allan Elson
CJSR	Christian James, Sr.
GG	Gary Gretsner
GEO	Gary's Garage
MP	Mary Pahlen
MPD	Muncie Police Department
NES	Nests Exterminating Services

Fields   Fields are predetermined areas of a computer record into which portions of documents are entered. For example, if a securities fraud occurred on November 10, 1989, then 11/10/89 would be one field (a date field) used in the design of the database. Each time a document is scanned, regardless of the means used for managing documents, the date 11/10/89 is watched for, coded, and input. Fields should be carefully selected. If too many fields are created, the system slows down and searches may net more information than is usable. The following is a list of possible fields, with their descriptions.

Fields	
Document date	Use the date the document is signed or sent.
Document type	Select the one word that best describes the document.
Author	Identify the person who signed or authorized the document.
Addressee	Identify the person(s) receiving the document.
Mentioned names	List the names of persons receiving a copy of the document.
Issues	Assign predetermined numbers for each issue to indicate which issue(s) applies to the document.

Smoking gun   Select a symbol for a particularly critical document.
                     If your system allows the use of additional alpha
                     prefixes with a symbol, code the document to show
                     if it is advantageous to your client or not.

Issues Issue lists follow the same principle as field lists; however, a numbering system may be needed. Ideally, what is wanted is to assign each issue a
heading number, like 100, and to designate specific happenings or events
(within that heading number) with a more specific but related number.

EXAMPLE ──

The paralegal is working on a structural engineering case involving large windows installed in a city building. The windows were allegedly installed incorrectly, causing them to fall from the building. This resulted in injured bystanders
and damage to the building. The issue coding might look something like this:

ISSUES

100	**Negligence**
101	*Contracts:* outlining the contractor's responsibility.
102	*Correspondence:* anything showing that the contractor was told the windows were right.
103	*Correspondence:* anything showing that the contractor was told the windows were wrong.
104	Reserved for future use.
200	**Windows**
201	*Caulking:* include information regarding condition, presence, or absence of caulking.
202	*Inferior Materials:* include information on cost, type, and materials used.
203	Reserved for future use.

The issue list is particularly useful in the abstract system. Each time a document is reviewed, it is coded with the applicable numbers; once all the codes
and fields have been determined, indexed, and logged, inputting may begin. A
document input log is needed, along with a master index, to ensure that input
documents are replaced in the proper physical location and that originals are
protected. See Figure 8-15.

Conclusion

There are pros and cons to both of the database types available, as well as
to the manual system outlined here. Regardless of the method implemented, organization is the key to success. Take into consideration all variables in a case

Figure 8-15
Input log for use
after coding
documents

INPUT LOG				
Associated files	**Copied**	**Numbers**	**Computerized**	**Entered**
Incident rpts.	Some	1001–1094	same	
Condo. Handbook	all	1101–1133		
Ass'n rules	None	1204–1308	N/A	N/A
Brochures	half	2234–3000	same	same

before suggesting that a case file be computerized; make sure the case qualifies
for a database. If unable to use a database, implement these same ideas into a
manual system and create indexes and charts to maintain the system.

SUMMARY

- Tickler systems offer a variety of calendar strategies that afford the legal
  team, law office, and individual paralegal control over daily, weekly, and
  monthly workloads.
- The paralegal should make a series of standardized charts and logs, to be
  used with any file and completed as a case progresses. Many time sheets, judicial timetables, and other such tools fit into this category.
- A vast supply of litigation software allows for the paralegal to use creativity
  in daily tasks to eliminate problems in caring for critical case evidence, witnesses, and investigative functions.
- All of the charts, logs, and other resource tools discussed in this chapter are
  adaptable to any size caseload and type of practice. These tools are valuable
  assets the paralegal will use throughout her career.

ACTIVITIES

1. Research both local and national software companies for products dealing
   with organizational tools for litigation.
2. Narrow your research to one specific category of material requiring organization (e.g., witness lists, any variety of resources, or some form of formal
   discovery). Once you have selected your specialty area, apply the data you
   have found to the adoption case study presented in this chapter.
3. Prepare a list of questions or concerns you have about organization and the
   investigation and management of the adoption case. Be prepared to present
   these to the class for discussion.

4. Explain why a paralegal would consider using a manual tickler system rather than a computerized tickler system. Should all paralegals use a manual system? Why or why not?

5. Case reference manuals serve a vital purpose in the life of a litigation paralegal. Explain what makes up a case reference manual and how paralegals working in areas other than litigation may benefit from such a tool.

6. Identify the area of legal practice you anticipate specializing in. Name the four organizational tools that you think will be the most important for that specialty field and explain how you will use those tools after accepting your first job.

7. Explain what the following number sequence stands for and how you would apply it A0101001.

8. Describe the difference between a computerized full-text system and an abstract system. When and why would you use each of these?

CASE STUDIES

Adoption Case

Refer to the adoption case study discussed in this chapter. In this case, volumes of documents have been produced by the plaintiff in response to a request for production. Assume you are the paralegal handling this case. You have been asked to code and index the documents. As it stands, 10,000 individual pieces of paper have been produced by the plaintiff, covering a variety of topics and concerning different people involved in the failed adoption. As far as you know, the documents deal with:

- preadoption matters
- postadoption matters
- the adoption agency
- state courts in New Jersey, California, Montana, Nebraska, and Texas
- the plaintiff
- the defendant
- a third-party defendant
- a bank that loaned the plaintiff money for the adoption.

Given this list of characters and possible subjects, what is the best method of indexing and coding this case? Be specific.

Murphy v. Schultz Autoplex

Return to the case study introduced in Chapter 2, entitled *Murphy v. Schultz Autoplex*. Create a preliminary witness and exhibit list. Also draft a simple case checklist, using your knowledge of litigation to anticipate the timelines needed to complete such a checklist. Will you need a document log? If so, draft one, making it as complete as possible based on the story facts and investigation you have done to date. If not, explain why you feel that such a tool is not needed.

9

SOURCES FOR THE INVESTIGATION

OUTLINE

Introduction

Public Records

Specific Records

Freedom of Information Act
Confidential and Privileged Records
Personnel and Medical Records
Personnel Files
Medical Records

Public Agencies
Federal Register

The Internet and Databases
The Internet
Search Engines
Public Records
Companies

Printed Material
Telephone Directory
City Directories
American Medical Association Directory
American Dental Association
Directory of Newspapers and Periodicals
Handbook of Scientific and Technological Societies
Biographical Resources
Mailing Lists
Advertising and Instructional Material
Miscellaneous Sources

Related and Nonrelated People

<u>**OBJECTIVES**</u>   After completing this chapter, you will know:

- The difference between a public record and a private record.

- How to deal with records custodians.

- How to handle public records and what the rights of the public are for copying those records.

- Which city, county, and state records are available for use and what is contained in those records.

- The difference between confidential and privileged private records.

- What the Freedom of Information Act is and why it is needed.

- How many varieties of printed material are available to the paralegal.

- How to use the Internet and various databases to research information vital to the investigation.

INTRODUCTION

The civil investigation focuses on identifying facts and finding and gathering evidence to support facts. This chapter explains the many sources available to the investigator, how they are used, and where they are located; it includes public and private records, printed materials, public agencies and their records, the Internet and databases, and people not related to the case.

All information collected for an investigation is categorized as either public or private. The data can range from medical records to motor vehicle records to birth records to weather reports. Some information sources have rules for release of data, which are based on law and agency regulations. For instance, federal agencies are required, under the Administrative Procedure Act, to provide adequate notice of any meeting to be held, so that the public may attend.[1] This same statute requires the agency to make available to the public any minutes of most meetings.[2] State agencies are bound by similar state statutes. Understanding the rules that govern public agencies and knowing how to obtain records helps the paralegal conduct a thorough investigation.

PUBLIC RECORDS

Formal Definition of Public Records

A **public record** is a record that a government unit is required by law to keep or that it finds necessary to keep to discharge its duties imposed by law. A **record** is a note, chart, or some written document used for the purpose of memorializing evidence of an event. The event can be something written, like a contract; or said, like a board meeting; or done, like the approval of a new zoning commission or a court proceeding. In some circumstances, a public record is required by law, which means that minutes of a public agency's meetings are public records. This also means that the pleadings in civil suits and court rulings are public record. However, the law provides some shields when material within a public record is known to be damaging or requires protection, so not all public records are available upon request. An example of this is the records of juvenile court systems, which protect from disclosure otherwise public records of minor children, thus shielding the minors from undue harm. Paralegals should monitor public records laws, as well as case law affecting access to records and their availability for an investigation.

Public records include legislative, judicial, and executive records, and further include, under the category of executive and legislative records, books of records for transactions of towns, city councils, and other municipal bodies. Additionally, some public officials may be required to maintain a memorial of certain transactions involving the office; these too are public records. Other public records or documents include census reports; recommendations for liquor licenses; pollbooks of special elections; state papers published under the authority of Congress or state legislatures; communications to a public officer relative to a public business, when such communications are within the terms of a law making them public; statistical information that public officers are required to gather as part of their duties; records of official park boards or authorized employees; records of marriage licenses; licenses of motor vehicles issued by the motor vehicle registrar's office; and documents dealing with title to property. Each state's secretary of state maintains the articles of incorporation (and amendments thereto) for corporations, as well as records of fictitious and trade names of businesses.

When looking for a public record, the paralegal should remember that the nature and purpose of a document determine its status as a public record, not where it is kept.[3]

Practical Definition of Public Records

The definition of *public record* given earlier does not provide much practical assistance to the paralegal, because records may be publicly available under some circumstances but not under others.

EXAMPLE ————————————————————————————————

The County Health Department is holding its annual board meeting and you are attending the meeting to gather information on a particular issue that will affect a client at the law firm. When you arrive at the meeting, you take a seat and listen to the many topics on the agenda that come before the one in which you are interested. Once the topic you have come to hear about is introduced, the board requests that all nonboard-member attendees leave for the discussion on your topic. In other words, the board closes its meeting to the public for this one topic. It is safe to say that the minutes of the otherwise open meeting, which are also supposed to be public records, will not provide details on the closed part of the session. Once the board's reasoning for closing the meeting is determined, the attorney will decide if the board's ruling should be challenged in court so that the records (i.e., the minutes of the closed portion of the meeting) will be made public.

This example demonstrates that the public-record status of a document will depend on the purposes and interpretations of the law in each individual situation. All states have legislation outlining what is public, and the paralegal must follow these guidelines for determining a document's status.

Records Custodians

Public records come primarily from agencies or governing bodies (legislative, judicial, or executive), which appoint a custodian of records to handle all records requests. The physical records must be maintained for the protection of the documents and to ensure public access. The officer appointed with responsibility over such records is merely a custodian and is at all times subject to the will of the state governing the records; he or she must allow any person access per the instruction of state or federal law. Records are never private property. Once a public document (e.g., an agency file) has reached its intended destination, it may not be removed, destroyed, altered, or falsified by the custodian or anyone else unless permitted by law.

In theory, the information found in a public document is true and correct, but it is common to find records, as originally filed, with incorrect information. To safeguard against such false information, the paralegal should always verify the data in the record.

EXAMPLE ———————————————————————

A paralegal is researching marriage licenses in an attempt to find a missing witness in a case. He believes the witness was married shortly before he began looking for her. He searches by maiden name and a general date of marriage in the county believed to be the witness's residence prior to the marriage. He finds a marriage certificate that matches the witness by name, but the date is dramatically different from what was expected. Because this data is critical, he needs to find another source to verify that the right person is located. There are many options in public records to accomplish this task, including the local newspaper, where marriages (and dates of marriage) are regularly printed. These can be accessed through the newspapers' offices or at the public library. If this does not yield an answer, a search of the department of motor vehicles may give a new name for the witness and an issuance date for a new license, narrowing when the marriage occurred. Unfortunately, it is also quite possible that the paralegal does not have correct information, and that he will have to use other sources to locate the witness.

Obtaining Records from the Custodian   The records custodian may not provide data to a requesting party without first following "proper" procedures. For example, when seeking a judicial record on a juvenile offender (assuming the information is applicable), the attorney must first petition the court to open the records and release the data.

☑ **PRACTICAL TIP**   In many jurisdictions, juvenile records are rarely opened. The petitioning party must show good cause, and may need authorization from the defendant, before the material will be released.

An attorney or paralegal cannot just go to the clerk of the court's desk and request a protected file (like a juvenile record) for review, as in a regular civil suit; instead, the clerk (custodian) must follow protocol and protect the "special" material. Without an order by the court granting the opening of these records, a custodian will not honor a standard request for the material.

Status by Location   Records are not deemed public merely by location; records attain "public" status based primarily on their nature and purpose as well. For example, delinquent property tax records show when the taxes on a piece of property became delinquent and when the property was sold by the city/county. These records are public not because they are kept at the city/county treasurer's office, but because they contain public information. Many documents and reports compiled by public officers are public only because of the data they contain, not because of where the records are stored.

Court Records

Records of the court, in some states, are considered notice to the public, and it is assumed that all persons are able to know the facts these records disclose.[4] There is an exception to this rule, though: a public record is deemed effective notice when and only when the record contains properly placed information. Any information illegally placed within the document, making it false or incompetent, negates the notice it might otherwise have created.[5] Additionally, outside of instruments affecting title to land, simply filing a record in a public office does not constitute notice to the public.[6]

Ownership of Public Records

Public records and the documents constituting them belong to the particular government entity that holds them, and include those held by the record's keeper for a long period of time.[7] Documents are deposited in a designated location, and remain there until an act of the legislature provides the authority for them to be removed, which also determines how they will be removed.[8] An example is a criminal indictment: once this document has been duly filed, it cannot legitimately be removed by anyone except a judge. When a judge is authorized to remove the record, and does so, he has **expunged** it. To *expunge* is to erase, delete, or strike. Another illustration of this involves prison records.

EXAMPLE

By law, the photograph and description of a person convicted of a crime and imprisoned, along with the measurement of her sentence, are required to be held by the superintendent of prisons during and after the prisoner's stay. It is part of the public record and the superintendent does not have the power or authority to remove or destroy it even when the prisoner's sentence is reversed or she is acquitted. However, the governor or judge may, under certain circumstances, expunge this record.[9]

In some states persons are allowed to seal some records, such as adoption papers. An attorney must seek permission from the court to open such records.

Handling of Public Records

It is a criminal act to willfully and unlawfully remove, mutilate, destroy, conceal, alter, or obliterate a record, paper, document, or other thing filed or deposited in a public office or with any public officer, by authority of law.[10] In some instances, the crime is grand larceny (for unlawfully removing and confiscating a court record), and a person charged with this offense may not claim that a court officer granted her permission to do so.

The falsification of public records is also a crime. This applies to writings that serve as evidence of a completed act of a public servant (e.g., minutes of court proceedings or public boards) and to legal documents that must be recorded by a public officer (e.g., a will). Under federal statutes, the concealment, removal, mutilation, or falsification of a record deposited with a United States office or officer is prosecutable under federal statutes.

Ethical Considerations

Ethics are of paramount importance to the legal professional. When responsible for any original public or private record, the paralegal must demonstrate professional respect for the record and its contents.

Inspection of Records

Rules and laws regarding the inspection of public records call for the majority of records to be open for public inspection, but not all records, documents, and writings possessed by the government are available. In some jurisdictions a person requesting to inspect records must show that she has a special interest in the document(s).[11] Other jurisdictions hold that there is an absolute right to inspect public documents when there is no specific reason why inspection should be denied.[12] Yet another approach to document inspection provides that the right to inspection is dictated by benefit versus harm: if release will cause a harm to the public interest, and that harm outweighs the benefits of releasing the documents, access will be denied. Nevertheless, the common law favors the right to inspection, and only in exceptional cases is access denied.[13] When the legislature manifests an intention that documents be available for inspection, it is an absolute right, and the custodian has no authority to deny inspection.[14]

The right to inspect does not extend to all public records. Public policy has determined that some records, though public, must be kept secret and free from inspection. These include records dealing with diplomatic correspondence, letters or dispatches in police services, and anything relating to the seizure, prosecution, and arrest of criminals.[15] Police records are confidential, except when there are statutory requirements to the contrary; motor vehicle departments may allow only limited access, to protect information that, if revealed, might hamper effective law enforcement or bias the efforts of a public body to protect itself in a court action.[16] Some states have now discontinued access to birth and death records, in an effort to minimize the creation of false identification. Adoption and juvenile records often come under the protection of a "privacy" umbrella. Grand jury proceedings are considered secret. Some states statutes allow an indicted person to obtain a stenographic transcript of the testimony heard before the grand jury, but it is understood that the grand jury may remove the transcript, which is a public record, to ensure protection from prejudicial publicity.

The public has a right to inspect the records of criminal court proceedings when they have been completed and entered in the docket. This right may be limited, by the court, when the judge feels that justice requires it.[17] Similarly, government reports on statutes and regulations are often declared confidential, and access to them is regularly denied.

Copying Public Records   The right to copy public records is also implied by the records and recording laws and is considered a basic privilege—otherwise, access is useless.[18] When a statute grants public access to records, during regular business hours, it also permits them to be copied. The right to inspect carries with it the following privileges:

- The right to photograph the records as a modern method of copying them accurately, harmlessly, noiselessly, and rapidly.
- The right to hand-copy documents.
- The statutory right of access *usually* includes a reasonable opportunity for the assistance of experts and other persons (copy services).[19]

Rules and Regulations   In most jurisdictions, there are reasonable rules and regulations for copying records, including when, where, and how to inspect and copy them. The purposes are to guard against loss or destruction of the records and to avoid unreasonable disruption of the office in which the records are maintained. When no specific rules for inspection and copying exist, the right of inspection implies that document users may not take possession of nor monopolize the records or record books.[20]

When a records custodian is required to make the copies, particularly inside her own offices, she is not under any mandate to provide them without a proper demand or request, which usually means a formal written request. When making this type of request, the paralegal should state the timeline she is working under and by what date she needs the records to be copied and provided. These time parameters do not necessarily have to be followed by the custodian, but a response should be received in a reasonably timely manner. Any fee for the copies must be paid promptly when the records are delivered, and sometimes prepayment is required. Statutory provisions outline standard costs for retrieval, copying, and certifying, and are systematically set by state statutes. The following is the Minnesota statute regarding copying fees.

Rule: Minn. Stat. Ann. § 144.335(5) (West 1998)

When a patient requests a copy of the patient's record for purposes of reviewing current medical care, the provider must not charge a fee. When a provider or its representative makes copies of patient records upon a patient's request under this section, the provider or its representative may charge the patient or the patient's representative no more than 75 cents per page, plus $10 for time spent retrieving and copying the records, unless other law or a rule or contract provide for a lower maximum charge.

The statutory fee schedule is adjusted each year, if necessary, to stay consistent with increases in copying expenses and inflation. It is not uncommon for the IRS and Social Security Administration to personally copy their records.

Ethical Consideration   Anything researched or desired for an investigation must be gathered with the utmost respect for the agency or judicial body from which it comes. This attitude creates a better working relationship between the paralegal and the record holder(s).

Inspection by Special Interest Groups Some questions have been raised about specialized groups that regularly search and copy public records. This does not relate to paralegals and attorneys, but rather refers to newspapers (reporters) and businesses engaged in record searching. A newspaper has no right to inspect records that are not open to the public; however, when records are public and citizens have a right to inspect them, any refusal of access to a newspaper (particularly if the privilege is accorded to a competitor) is a denial of equal protection of the law.[21] When records deal with how the government is operated, and there is a legitimate desire to inform the public of the operation, inspection is granted.[22] As a matter of statute or judicial construction, the right to inspect and copy public records is generally extended to any businesses (and their representatives) engaged in searching public records and copying them for profit.[23] These businesses operate primarily in the field of abstracting and title insurance, but over the past ten years, new sources have developed, focusing on a broader scope of research and retrieval of documents. The Internet is a perfect example: it now includes court documents, marriage licenses, motor vehicle documents, and other public records.

SPECIFIC RECORDS

To apply the statutory rules about records and their availability, it is necessary to identify what records are public, what office houses the records, and exactly what these records mean to an investigation. Each individual state has rules regarding the location and release of public records, so the information in this section is necessarily a broad overview; it is the responsibility of each paralegal to research the specific state rules regarding location and release of any public record. This section identifies as many offices and holders of general categories of documents as possible.

Public records are virtually limitless, as will be demonstrated in this section. They include weather and accident reports; birth and death records; Social Security, municipal, and health records; and patents, among many others. The following sections describe a variety of commonly sought public records, along with where to find them, how to go about accessing them, and what can be found inside them.

Municipal and County Records

Unless specifically legislated, all municipal and county records are available to the public for review. These include books and records of the municipality, accounts, the "doings" of the officers and the office, and files.[24] Freedom of access is, of course, regulated when reasonable doubt regarding the safety of the records or the purpose for gathering the records is in question. A municipal corporation can have no private books, and in some jurisdictions access to municipal records is regulated by statute.

☑ **PRACTICAL TIP** The retrieval of these records will require the paralegal to make a personal appearance at the municipal or county office where the records are located, so that she may review the specific file and copy the records herself at a copy machine in that office. If the paralegal knows precisely which records are needed, a courier or document delivery service may be dispatched instead, or the office may be willing to mail the copies. By handling files this way, the municipal or county office maintains control over who has the records, where they review the records, and where the copies are made. These measures help to ensure that the records will not be removed or destroyed by the person seeking the information.

County Recorder

(Search the Internet by "county recorder," looking for individual state listing, or go to http://www.cdb.com)

The county recorder offers the following types of materials and sources for the investigation:

- Books of record
- Maps
- Charts
- Surveys
- Other papers that may be on file (general).

These records help to identify ownership of properties, property divisions, municipality boundaries, and other such data needed for many types of litigation. For example, when the paralegal needs to identify a property line relating to an easement dispute, these records provide information and proof. When dealing with the collection of a civil judgment, these records can be used to identify property or ownership rights held by the judgment debtor.

A further breakdown of documents that may be found with the county recorder is as follows:

- Deeds, grants, transfers, and mortgages of real estate; releases of mortgages; powers of attorney to convey real estate
- Mortgages of personal property
- Marriage contracts
- Wills admitted to probate
- Official bonds
- Notices of mechanics' liens
- Transcripts or abstracts of judgments creating liens on real estate
- Notices of the pendency of actions affecting real estate
- Instruments describing or relating to the separate property of married women
- Births and deaths (not available in all states)

- Certified copies of petitions, orders, or decrees relating to proceedings under the Bankruptcy Act
- Certified copies of decrees and judgments of courts of record.

Many other records may also be located here, and rules regarding the use and life of some of the documents can be learned through the county recorder.

EXAMPLE

If a paralegal is attempting to sell an automobile that has been totaled in an accident, she may need to clear the title to sell the car to a salvage yard. To do this, she needs to check for mechanics' and other liens. She calls the county recorder and asks if a mechanic's lien has been filed, when it was filed, the amount of the lien, and when the lien will expire. Some mechanics' liens have a short life—less than five years—and must be reinstituted if the initial time lapses. The county recorder's office can help with many of these details when investigating property.

County Clerk

(Search the Internet by specific state or county, or at
http://www.nasire.org/ss/)

Documents in the possession or control of the county clerk can include any number of court-related documents, *including criminal files and adoption files, both of which are available only to a select group of people.* The clerk's office prepares certified copies of original documents, or can certify copies already in the possession of the paralegal once they are compared to the original in the file. The clerk answers telephone inquiries in many jurisdictions, but the phone query should deal with general data, such as the existence of a particular file or proceeding or dates and times of a litigation proceeding. Confidential information will not be released over the phone, and the clerk must limit her time on the phone to providing short, easy-to-retrieve answers and information. The paralegal should expect to pay a fee for the copies. Payment in full is due upon receipt of the copies. In some instances the paralegal must pay for the copies in advance. If the paralegal is involved in an in-depth investigation of a prospective client, defendant, or witness, it may be the best use of her time to personally visit the clerk's office and review all of the material available.

Register of Actions

(Search the Internet by specific state or county, or at
http://www.nasire.org/ss/)

In many states, a register of actions is used to index court proceedings. The register includes "plaintiff and defendant" indices, which are valuable to the investigator because they provide a guide to all actions within a jurisdiction, listing them by case number, date of commencement, and names of the parties. These are often cross-referenced by plaintiff and defendant, so the person searching is not forced to labor for hours when she has the name of only one party. The register of actions contains a description of each document filed relating to the specific case, as well as a summary of the case up to the time of the examination. The register is in chronological order, separated by division, for every matter before the court and entered under date or order of commencement. A chronological listing of each proceeding in the action is also available. The actions are individually bound and broken into groups (most commonly civil, probate, and criminal).

It is common to find plaintiff and defendant indices on computer databases in the general civil clerk's office. If they are not on computer, each index is bound and kept in the appropriate clerk's office. Some court indices and dockets are computerized, going back five or so years, and some are now available on the Internet or through commercial online services.

☑ **PRACTICAL TIP**   Each volume commonly represents at least one year. To use these registries, the paralegal needs to know the case or file number of the action or the date of its commencement. The alphabetical plaintiff and defendant indices provide the action number or commencement date and thus can be used to preface a search at the register's office. When searching computerized databases, the paralegal may be able to locate dockets by party name.

Clerks are generally helpful in answering questions regarding policy and fee schedules for filing a variety of documents.

Abstracts of Judgment

The *abstract of judgment* is an original document prepared by the clerk or judge who issued the judgment. It is used to execute on a judgment or to transfer a judgment to another jurisdiction. The following information is found within the judgment:

- Case number (number of action)
- Date of entry of the judgment
- Names of the judgment debtor and creditor
- Amount of judgment
- Location of the judgment in the judgment book, minutes, or docket (whichever the particular court uses).

If a certified copy is required, request it from the clerk.

Records of the Assessor

(Search the Internet by specific state or county or at
http://www.nasire.org/ss/)

In many states there are three levels of assessors—state, county, and city—with each being responsible for maintaining records showing the ownership of all taxable property within their particular governmental segment. At the state assessor's office, the paralegal will find records reflecting the following:

- Public utility property
- Pipelines
- Canals
- Other types of properties.

The county assessor is responsible for the taxable property within the county, except for property located inside the city limits, which defaults to the city assessor. The county assessor may assess inside the city, however, when a transfer of that function is deemed necessary by the city assessor.

Assessment rolls are open to the general public and are available in the appropriate assessor's office upon request. Some confidential records are also held inside the assessor's office, including annual property statements; the only access to these records is given to the assessee or her attorney. The assessment roll is divided into **secured** and **unsecured rolls**. The secured roll catalogues property on which the assessed taxes constitute a lien. All of the rest is considered unsecured, consisting of personal property.

The following is a listing of the data commonly found on the assessment roll:

- Name and address of the owner of a particular parcel of property
- The property and interest in property owned by a person within a county.

The interests mentioned in this second category of data include:

- Improvements to the property
- Mineral rights
- Leaseholds.

These records show legal ownership, not equitable ownership.[25]

The county assessor normally has possession of a detailed map of the county, which shows specifics of the area (including blocks, tracts, and rural areas). The assessor keeps appropriate indices, which provide a means of ascertaining the exact location of land.[26] This is valuable to real estate, probate, and bankruptcy paralegals, who regularly handle real property, and to the litigation paralegal who may be looking for a witness or party who is hiding. These tools also help answer venue questions, because venue is sometimes complicated; knowing where current and historical city, county, and state maps are located is an asset.

In urban areas, the paralegal may find **block books** or *plats,* which contain maps of every block, the size of the numbered or lettered parcels or lots, and the name of the person to whom taxes are assessed. She can even find the names of the adjacent streets. When researching the sale of property, **sale books** are used to find the name of the purchaser, a particular sale, and the date of recordation of the instrument of conveyance. These books are maintained by location of the lot, not by purchaser's name.[27]

In some jurisdictions, the assessor also holds boat ownership information.[28] When a paralegal is working in an area where many boats are used by the public, this is a valuable source. This information will be located in the sale book.

The name and street indices also help in researching and locating property. These list property by owner's name (**name index**) or by street (**street index**). Name indices are usually revised annually and provide access to information in the assessment roll, block book, sale books, and county maps, and each type of record serves as a cross-reference to the others. Telephone and written requests for information within this office will be honored, and generally there is no fee for a simple search, but complicated searches require advance warning and prepayment.[29]

Motor Vehicle Records

(Search the Internet by specific state or county, or at http://www.cdb.com, or at http://www.investigations.net/page16.htm)

The right to inspect motor vehicle records is governed by state statutes, and is commonly extended only to those records that are public or official.[30] In many jurisdictions, the requesting party is required to show special interest in the information; in other jurisdictions, the right of inspection is unlimited, making a record available to anyone who seeks it, even for curiosity's sake.[31] A person can request title and registration information over the phone, go to the office in person, make a request for copies of the information in writing, or use the Internet (in many states).

☑ **PRACTICAL TIP**   Only written requests are accepted in some states, and it can take a long time to receive copies. It is advisable to make a call to the local or state office and verify the specific requirements and timelines before ordering data.

Within the motor vehicle records one can find registration and regulati[on of] the motor vehicles, licensing of drivers, and related subjects prescribed [by] state vehicle code or statutes. The records provide an alphabetical index [of] license applications and their status (granted, denied, etc.); the indices are [man-] aged by vehicle registration number or by alphabetical listing of the own[er's] name. An index of motor numbers, serial numbers, or other permanent identi[fy-] ing numbers of the vehicles may also be found, and are valuable sources for certain investigations.

Not all states give their motor vehicle departments the same name. Here is a list of common names of departments responsible for motor vehicles:

- Motor Vehicle Division
- Motor Vehicle Commission
- Motor Vehicle Registry
- Bureau of Motor Vehicles
- Department of Public Safety

- Bureau/Department of Revenue
- Department/Secretary of State
- Department of Law Enforcement.

License and Registration Applications Motor Vehicle Records

(Search the Internet by specific state or county, or at http://www.cdb.com, or at http://www.investigations.net/page16.htm)

Where available for public inspection, driver's license applications may provide the following details about the person applying:

- Full name
- Date of birth
- Mailing address
- Marital status
- Residence address
- Height
- Age
- Weight
- Color of eyes and hair
- Military status.

If the driver is also licensed to drive in another state, it is possible to find out:

- Length of time he or she has had a license
- Prior state licenses
- Applications for licenses under another name
- Failure to pass a driver's test
- Refusal of a license and cancellation, suspension, or revocation of a prior license.

Generally, the license and the application will be signed by the applicant. This may be useful for comparison purposes.

For vehicle registration, an application includes the name and address of the owner and a description of the vehicle. When the legal owner is different from the actual owner, that person's or entity's name and address will also appear. The loan holder (i.e., bank or mortgagor) is required by statute (in most jurisdictions) to file a properly endorsed certificate of title and application for registration, and as a general rule the only lien or encumbrance on the registration will come from such a secured transaction. A variety of forms found in registration files may be used to determine how the vehicle was purchased or where it was purchased. For instance, if a car was formerly registered in another state, or if it was purchased at a sheriff's sale, the appropriate paper trail will accompany the registration.

Individual Income Tax Returns

(Search the Internet at http://www.investigations.net/page16.htm
or at http://www.cdb.com)

The manner in which federal and state income tax returns are inspected, and who may have access to them, are determined by federal Treasury regulations. Federal income tax returns require an applicant to apply, in writing, to the Internal Revenue officer with whom the return was filed, and set forth the following information:

- Name and address of person for whom the return was made
- Kind of tax reported on the return
- Taxable period covered by the return
- Reason why inspection is desired
- Statements showing that the applicant is entitled to inspection under Treasury regulations.

The court having authority over a pending civil action may require one party to produce a copy of federal or state income tax returns for inspection by the adverse party. Federal and state statutes generally provide that no government officer or employee shall disclose any information revealed by the return except to the taxpayer or her representative, but this does not mean that the taxpayer has an absolute privilege. Therefore, the court can order the taxpayer to provide copies of the returns, eliminating the need to go through public officers and employees. When the taxpayer has not retained copies of the returns, she provides an authorization to the adverse party permitting the government office to release the information.

Birth Records

(Search the Internet at http://www.vitalcheck.com
or at http://www.cdb.com)

The bureau of vital statistics in many states, counties, and cities houses birth records for persons born in that state, county, or city.

☑ **PRACTICAL TIP**   Some states limit access to birth records, so check with each individual state office for verification.

Physicians, hospital authorities, or other birth attendants prepare birth certificates and file them. Information contained in the certificate can be obtained by writing to the vital statistics office in the county where the person was born, and pre-paying for the cost of copying and certifying the document. The fee for additional certified copies is minimal if the copies are ordered at the same time as the original request, so check the number of copies needed before ordering, to avoid unnecessary expense. The paralegal may also need to outline in her letter why she is seeking the record.

Three types of certified copies of birth certificates are available; depending on why the document is needed, the requesting party must choose the appropriate type. Typically the categories of certification are:

- A certified copy that contains all items reported on the official certificate
- Birth card that is certified as to the name, sex, date, and place of birth, and date of original filings
- Short-form certificate that varies in content but usually contains the items included on the birth card, in addition to parentage.

Each of these certifications varies in degree of information and how the information is delivered. When planning to file anything with the court, the paralegal should always request a document in its full and complete form.

The letter requesting birth records should contain these facts:

- Full name of the person as given on the birth record
- Sex
- Parents' names, including maiden name of mother
- Month, day, and year of the birth
- Place of birth (city or town, county, state, and name of hospital, if any).

When a birth is not recorded, the following records, though not necessarily public, may be researched to verify the date of birth, place of birth, and parentage:

- Hospital records of the birth. Request a certified statement from the person who has charge of the official hospital records. (This may be the medical records supervisor.)
- Physician's record of the birth. If the doctor who delivered the baby has a record, procure a certified statement from her or him.
- Baptismal or other church records. If the baby was baptized, or underwent some other church rite, request an official statement from the custodian of the church records.
- School records. It is possible to procure an official statement from the person in charge of the school records, especially early school records, giving age (birth date) and parent's name. (Private school records are more complicated to obtain without express permission. In many states, school records are now closed to the public without express permission of the student or parent or guardian.)
- Insurance records. When applicable, seek out insurance applications showing the birth information data on a person. You can ask for an official statement from the insurance company for the birth facts as given on the insurance records. (Check your state private records act for availability of these records.)
- Selective Service records. For persons registered during World War I, write to the Federal Records Center, 1557 St. Joseph Avenue, East Point, GA

30344; for those registered during and since World War II, write to the Selective Service Board of the state in which the persons are registered. In either case, the following information should be provided: name of the person, date of registration, place of registration, and date of birth as given on the registration.

- Census records. Request Form 10-611, "Application for Search of Census Records," at your regional Census Bureau (United States Bureau of Census). The regional office will search decennial population census records for age and place-of-birth information.

- Other federal records. The National Archives and Records Service, 7th & Pennsylvania Avenue NW, Washington, DC, 20408 (201-501-5400 or 202-501-5500) maintains records that may prove a person's age or citizenship (for example, homestead application, ship passenger lists, seamen's protection-certificate application, pension application, and personnel records). At the suggestion of the National Archives, consider contacting a regional office for quicker service; they are located in California, Georgia, Illinois, Michigan, Missouri, and Washington.

- Other personal records. Driver's licenses, marriage records, employment records, and records of fraternal organizations usually contain birth information.

Death Records

(Search the Internet at http://www.vitalcheck.com
or at http://www.cdb.com)

Death certificates are an official certificate recorded in the place where the death occurred. These, like birth certificates, are prepared by physicians, funeral directors, coroners, medical examiners, hospital authorities, or other professional attendants, and are filed in the central office of the bureau of vital statistics (registrar or division). This office may be at the state, county, or city level, depending on the jurisdiction.

A request is needed to receive a certified copy of a death certificate, and some states have privacy laws prohibiting the release of these documents. If the records are accessible, the paralegal will send, to the bureau of vital statistics in the place where the death occurred, prepaid fees for the certification and copies and a brief letter stating why a copy of the document is needed. The type of copy issued will vary depending on the purpose for the document, so the letter should provide the following information:

- Full name of the person as given on the death record
- Sex
- Parents' names, including maiden name of mother
- Month, day, and year of death
- Place of death (city or town, county, state, and name of hospital, if any).

Autopsy Reports

The need for autopsy reports in litigation is usually self-evident, as questions about the death of a person can be critical. A medical examiner or a coroner has the legal authority to perform autopsies when the cause of death is in question. To request autopsy reports, consult your local (state) medical examiner for instruction, as state guidelines vary greatly.

Marriage Records

(Search the Internet at http://www.vitalcheck.com
or at http://cdb.com)

The location of marriage license filing varies from state to state. Licenses may be kept in the county clerk's office or the marriage license division of the county where the marriage took place; filed with the bureau of vital statistics (registrar or division) at the state level; or filed in city or other local offices. When the records are located in the county system but the paralegal does not know which county to search, she must write to each individual county requesting a search and copy of any document found. Many states have now recognized the onerous time and personnel requirements for such searches and have centralized marriage records.

When writing for a certified copy of a marriage license, enclose prepayment for the cost of copying and certifying the record (the amount can be determined by first calling the clerk), and provide the necessary information to identify the correct marriage record, including:

- Full names of both bride and groom (including nicknames)
- Residence addresses at the time of marriage
- Ages at the time of marriage (or dates of birth)
- Places of birth (state or foreign country)
- Date and place of marriage.

Divorce and Annulment Records

(Search the Internet at http://www.investigations.net/page16.htm,
or at http://www.vitalcheck.com, or at http://www.cdb.com)

Divorce and annulment records for a state are usually kept by the bureau of vital statistics and in the court system where the decree was granted. If it is not possible to locate the decree in the plaintiff and defendant indices at the courthouse, or it is not known what county court granted the decree, the paralegal may search the bureau of vital statistics. Some states file these reports in any number of different county court offices (county clerk, recorder, etc.), so it may require several phone calls to locate the records. Because of this problem, centralization of these records has been undertaken in most states.

When writing for a certified copy, it is a good idea to include prepayment for the copy and the following information:

- Full names of husband and wife (including nicknames)
- Present residence addresses
- Former addresses (as in court records)
- Ages at the time of divorce or annulment (or dates of birth)
- Places of birth (state or foreign country)
- Date and place of divorce or annulment
- Type of final decree.

Voter Registration

When locating a witness—especially the elusive witness—voter registration[32] documents can provide valuable data. These records are kept by the registrar of voters, and limited information may be available to the public within the discretion of the registrar or clerk.

☑ **PRACTICAL TIP** Developing good relationships with the clerks in this department (and all agencies) allows the paralegal to access a tremendous amount of information and to receive help and guidance from these contacts.

In some states voters are automatically registered to vote when they apply for and receive a driver's license. This further expands the available records.

The primary source of information from the voter's registration office is the **affidavit of registration** (this title may vary in different states), which may include:

- Name of registrant
  - When a change of name, other than by marriage, has been made within one year before registration, this fact and the former name and date of change may appear in the affidavit.
- Current address
- Last prior address (in some cases)
  - In some areas, the registrar of the county from which the registrant moved will receive an affidavit of cancellation from the registrar of the county to which the registrant has moved; this is ordinarily attached to the canceled affidavit of registration. In many instances, the county from which a registrant comes will be noted, with varying degrees of completeness of address, on the current affidavit of registration.
- Occupation of registrant
- State or county of birth

- If the registrant is foreign-born, the affidavit may show the manner of acquisition of citizenship. Also shown may be the place and date of acquisition of citizenship.
- Name of spouse and date and place of marriage (in some cases)
- Names of registrant's parents
- Height of registrant
- Physical disability that might prevent marking of ballot
- Signature of registrant.

Canceled affidavits of registration may also be retained, which may contain information on a criminal conviction (which bars voting privileges), voter's death, or a judicial determination of insanity or incompetence. Canceled copies of affidavits of registration are filed alphabetically by name, whereas current (original) affidavits are normally kept by precinct address in a bound precinct book. Cross-referencing allows the paralegal to search for an individual when she only has details of the person's past history. Searches dealing with older records require at least the person's name and a possible address.

Voter registration records can be personally viewed, but the clerk can and should help in the search. Certified copies of the affidavits and other records are available. If the paralegal has an extensive search to do, it is a good idea to call ahead and check on search fees before going to the office. In most counties there is a charge for certified copies and a charge for uncertified photocopies.

Social Security Records

(Search the Internet at http://www.ssa.gov
or at http://www.cdb.com)

Access to Social Security records is very limited and the majority are considered private by nature.[33] 20 C.F.R. §§ 401.3–401.190 (1988) sets forth guidelines specifying to whom access is granted and under what conditions. For the general acquisition of these records, the paralegal needs authorization from the party to whom the records apply.[34] Disclosure may be made to a claimant, prospective claimant, or the claimant's authorized representative, in matters directly concerning the prospective claimant (other than medical information), when consistent with the proper and efficient administration of the law. Social Security regulations allow access to anyone to whom the person the records concern grants permission; access is given via a specific authorization.[35] See Chapter 10 for a detailed discussion on authorizations.

Veterans Administration Records

Within the Veterans Administration,[36] a file exists for every veteran who has filed a claim for compensation, pension, or hospitalization. These files contain a variety of information, including medical data (both background and current), Social Security status and payment received, and the nature of the treatment the veteran is receiving. Through the data in these files, many types of cases, like worker's compensation, personal injury, and wrongful death, have been investigated. The United States Code provides levels of guidance regarding veterans' records and copying of these records.[37]

Rule: 38 U.S.C. § 5701 (1994)

(a) All files, records, reports, and other papers and documents pertaining to any claim under any of the laws administered by the Secretary ... shall be confidential and privileged, and no disclosure thereof shall be made except as provided in this section.

(b) The secretary shall make disclosure [of information] as follows:

    (1) To a claimant or duly authorized agent or representative of a claimant matters concerning the claimant alone when, in the judgment of the Secretary, such disclosure would not be injurious to the physical or mental health of the claimant.

    (2) When required by process of a United States court to be produced in any suit or proceeding therein pending.

    (3) When required by any department or other agency of the United States Government.

    (4) In all proceedings in the nature of an inquest into the mental competency of a claimant.

    (5) In any suit or other judicial proceeding when in the judgment of the Secretary such disclosure is deemed necessary and proper.

With regard to the "furnishing of records," 38 U.S.C. § 5702 (1994) says in part:

Any person desiring a copy of any record, paper, and so forth, in the custody of the Secretary, which may be disclosed under section 5701 of this title, must make written application therefore to the Secretary, stating specifically—

    (1) the particular record, paper, and so forth, a copy of which is desired and whether certified or uncertified; and

    (2) the purpose for which such copy is desired to be used. ...

(b) The Secretary is authorized to fix a schedule of fees for copies and certification of such records.

When the request for information comes from the veteran or her authorized representative, 38 C.F.R. § 1.503 implements the statute:

Rule: 38 C.F.R. § 1.503 (1998)

Information may be disclosed to a veteran or his or her duly authorized representative as to matters concerning himself or herself alone when such disclosure would not be injurious to the physical health or mental health of the veteran. If the veteran be deceased, matters concerning him or her may be disclosed to his [or her] widow[(er)], children, or next of kin if such disclosure will not be injurious to the physical or mental health of the person in whose behalf information is sought or cause repugnance or resentment toward the decedent.

The Veterans Administration will determine whether requested information will be released based on the intended use of the information, and if it will adversely affect the veteran.

Business Organization Documents

(Search the Internet for the specific secretary of state's office at http://www.nasire.org/ss/)

Corporate documents can be located in county offices (county clerk's office), or in the secretary of State's office, usually under the title "Corporate Division." With technological advances, many secretary of state offices have now created Web pages to help meet the public's need for information, and include corporate filings, fictitious/trade names, and partnerships in their Internet-accessible materials. Certified copies of corporate documents are filed with the secretary of state or other appropriate office, and may be required to be filed with the county clerk's office in the county where the corporation has its principal place of business. It is not uncommon to find these papers also filed in the county where a business owns property.

The following is a list of noncorporate entities' filings that may be found in the county clerk's office:

- Certificates of doing business under a fictitious name
- Certificates of abandonment of fictitious name
- Affidavits of publication
- Certificates of limited partnership and amendments of such certificates
- Affidavits of publication of notices of dissolution of partnership.

If the paralegal is investigating a business name, the research is not complete until she has examined the files for corporate and fictitious names, assumed names, and corporations that are not in good standing. When searching county records rather than a statewide registry at the secretary of state's office, she may need to examine many county files to determine if the name being researched has been the subject of a fictitious name filing or partnership filing.

The most common resource on the state level is the secretary of state, but in some jurisdictions this office goes by the name commissioner of corporations, department of commerce or investments, or something similar relating to corporations. The office serves as a custodian of all basic corporate documents that are required to be filed. Depending on the jurisdiction, the paralegal can receive updated telephone information on the status of a corporation, including:

- Names and addresses of the first directors
- Names of predecessor or merged corporations
- Location of the principal office as specified in the articles of incorporation (also known as the principal place of business)
- Name and address of the corporate agent for service of process (if any)

- Names and addresses of the corporation's principal officers, and the location and address of its principal office, if a statement has been filed under the statute
- The law under which the corporation was organized (General Corporate Law, General Nonprofit Corporation Law, or any other special law or act)
- The term of corporate existence, if a fixed term is stated in the articles
- The nature of any defects in incorporation.

In the majority of secretary of state offices, the clerk will inform the requester of the current standing of the corporation (good standing or not). If the company is not in good standing, it is because they have not met one of the provisions of incorporation or have not filed required reports. If the paralegal needs evidence regarding a corporation's good standing, she can request a **certificate of good standing** or a **certificate of existence**. These prove that a corporation has not been dissolved or suspended and that its existence is not impaired.

Paralegals may also obtain a certificate listing all corporate documents on file with the secretary's office; this can be used for any number of purposes, ranging from verifying the agent for service, to piercing the corporate veil, to setting up public financing for a corporation. The fees charged by the secretary of state are often set by statute, and in some states are printed in a pamphlet that can be procured directly from the secretary's office. When an attorney needs documents promptly and the paralegal is not close enough to go to the secretary's office, a clerk there will often certify and copy records, send them directly to the attorney, and bill the attorney. However, in some jurisdictions, requests must be made in writing and paid for in advance. In such cases it is faster (although more expensive) to obtain the information through a commercial online service such as WESTLAW.

Commission on Corporations/Corporate Taxing Authority

The state commission on corporations and the corporate taxing authority hold information on corporations, including data found on the corporation's application, its ability to sell shares, or whether or not it has paid state income taxes.

☑ **PRACTICAL TIP**   This data may be available via phone request.

At the appropriate commission on corporations, the paralegal can personally inspect a file or request specific data if she knows what is in the file. Such data may include:

- The names and addresses of the corporation's officers at the time of filing of the application
- The provisions of the corporation's bylaws, as well as its articles of incorporation (check for individual state variations)
- The provisions of any trust indenture or other document identifying or limiting the rights of the corporation's security holders (check for individual state variations)

- The nature and amount of consideration for which the corporation was authorized to issue its securities

- Any conditions imposed by the commissioner on the corporation in connection with the issuance of securities; if the corporation's securities are being held in escrow, the name of the escrow holder (check for individual state variations)

- The business address and the nature of the business of the corporation at the time it applied for a permit (check for individual state variations).

A wide variety of other information can be found in both of these offices. By contacting the individual office with a specific request, the paralegal can further her understanding of the many sources available from these two agencies.

Automobile Accident Records

Automobile accident reports[38] are filed when an injury or death occurs or when property damage occurs in excess of a statutory amount. The report is filed with the motor vehicle department. Some information may be available to the public, for example:

- Names and addresses of persons involved in the accident, the registration numbers, and description of vehicles involved

- Date and time of the accident

- Basis for exemption from security requirements

- Names and addresses of insurance carriers

- Names and addresses of witnesses to the accident.

Similar reports can also be obtained from the police department or other investigative agencies who were at the scene of an accident or handled the accident. These reports are public records.

Weather Reports

Meteorologists are regarded as the most accurate and reliable sources of evidence when weather is an issue. The United States Weather Bureau (National Weather Service and National Oceanic and Aviation Association), which falls under the auspices of the Department of Commerce, employs meteorologists in its weather stations, located in major cities and arctic regions. Hourly observations are recorded at these stations and significant changes in weather conditions are noted at the time of their occurrence. It is not uncommon for forest rangers or fire lookout observers to make periodic reports of their observations, too. Persons making these observations may be paid by the Weather Bureau, so their observations fall within the scope of official records and are presumed to be accurate. The paralegal may obtain weather information for a particular day and locality from the nearest weather bureau office. Hourly precipitation and climatological data can also be procured from the Superintendent of Documents, Government Printing Office, Washington, DC 20408. Payment is required but is usually minimal. The National Weather Service also offers climate data over the phone or by written request. This data is valuable in defending against or initiating a civil suit in which weather-related circumstance may mitigate damages or further prove a cause of action.

FREEDOM OF INFORMATION ACT

State statutes, the federal **Freedom of Information Act (FOIA)**,[39] and the Privacy Act of 1974[40] carefully classify and regulate what government documents can be released to the public. The FOIA is a legislative act dealing specifically with how and when such records will be released.

The FOIA is not a substitute for or supplement to the formal civil discovery process. In the same vein, the private litigant cannot be denied materials under the FOIA when access would normally be granted to a public agency or other governmental body.[41] Discovery rights in civil suits are governed by the applicable rules of civil procedure rather than the FOIA[42] and state law is considered authority. There are nine exemptions found in the FOIA, all offering protection to certain records:

1. Classified documents

2. Internal personnel rules and practices

3. Information exempt under other statutes

4. Trade secrets and confidential business information

5. Internal government documents regarding the policy-making process

6. Personal privacy (such as personnel, medical, and similar files, disclosure of which would constitute an invasion of privacy)

7. Law enforcement records that would interfere with the law enforcement process, would deprive a person of fair adjudication, would invade privacy, or would disclose a confidential source, or the like

8. Banking or financial institution information

9. Geographical and geophysical information, data, and maps about wells.[43]

As a general rule, the FOIA cannot be used as a formal discovery tool. However, it is a valuable source of evidence.

Confidential and Privileged Records

Confidential and **privileged** documents are two categories in the FOIA, which are also broken down into specific types of records deemed private, such as trade secrets and medical records. Both of these immunities are based on FOIA exemption 4.

Confidential Records   Commercial and financial records are defined as confidential when, if disclosed, they would:

1. "impair the government's ability to obtain necessary information in the future"

   2. "cause substantial harm to the competitive position of the parties supplying the information"

Some courts have "recognized a third prong protecting other governmental interests, such as compliance and program effectiveness."[44]

Denial of confidential information of this nature requires any party opposing disclosure to "demonstrate that disclosure will harm a specific interest that Congress sought to protect by enacting the exemption."[45] Therefore, information or records may be withheld only "when the affirmative interests in disclosure are outweighed by factors mitigating against disclosure."[46] A reviewing court may consider the perspective of the person who first provided the information and, for example, may ask:

- Is the information of a type that would not customarily be released to the public by the person from whom it was obtained?

- Was the information specifically procured by the agency in confidence?[47]

If the information sought is considered confidential but the material or data has previously become available to the public, it is no longer confidential.[48] Usually, the burden of proving that a document or record is confidential rests with the party opposing disclosure.[49] In the case of confidential commercial information, FOIA exemption 5 can also be invoked. This exemption deals specifically with qualified privileges like the attorney/client privilege. The FOIA has many general and specific provisions and applications with regard to confidentiality; if there is any question, the FOIA and state freedom of information laws should be consulted, along with the attorney.

Privileged Records   Privileged records may also be protected under any one of the FOIA exemptions. Specifically, exemption 4 defines the term "privileged document." *Confidential* and *privileged* are not synonymous, and data found to be free of confidentiality barriers may still be privileged and not producible. *Privileged* refers to information that cannot be disclosed in a legal proceeding based on provisions of the Constitution or a statute, or by common law. For example, the attorney/client privilege protects much material from disclosure. In some instances the court may review documents, whether confidential or privileged, **in camera** to determine their status. *In camera* is a Latin term meaning "in chambers." The court may use this method to determine whether a document or record should be protected by the freedom of information regulations or during the course of regular formal discovery procedures.

State statutes and the federal Freedom of Information Act are looked to for guidance when dealing with a wide variety of records that are either wholly or partially private. Some of those records include:

- Criminal and juvenile offense files

- Health and examiner reports

- Sensitive judicial proceedings

- Personnel records, including disciplinary proceedings

- Prison, probation, and parole records
- Tax records or investigation reports
- Unemployment insurance records
- Welfare records.

For specific details on any one of these record types, consult state freedom of information laws or the regulations of the appropriate federal or state agencies.

Personnel and Medical Records

Within the federal FOIA, there are many exemptions for the private records found in federal agencies, some of which have been discussed. Though this act was not written with the private business community in mind, it will not allow persons to invade the privacy of business records held by federal agencies, either. As for personnel, medical, and other related records, relief for private records is found under FOIA exemption 6. Congress drafted this protection for the purpose of preserving the *individual* privacy of persons from disclosure of the "great quantities of files" held by administrative agencies.[50] These files may contain "intimate details" of individuals' lives, which in the past had been protected by agency rules. Some individual states have sought legislation that mimics exemption 6 of the FOIA, except that the state exclusion covers the personal privacy of specific individuals. Under exemption 6, individuals are shielded from a wide range of embarrassing disclosures, including derogatory information and highly personal information; under the state laws, the exemption goes one step further to protect private information in public records that is not embarrassing or intimate, but simply private.

For the second prong of the exemption to apply, the request for information must clearly threaten the privacy interest of the information holder. An unintentional encroachment is not considered a "clearly unwarranted" invasion of privacy.[51] Information found inside a discloseable record will not be protected under exemption 6 when the person's name cannot be determined by examining the record. This often affects the production of sensitive documents that have first been reviewed in camera. Once a court has made a determination that particular records can and should be produced, but that the names of certain persons within those records should not be produced, the party producing the records will commonly "black" those names out, copy the related documents, and produce the copies. The individual is thus protected, yet the bulk of the producible documents are in fact produced. The FOIA, with related regulations and case law, carefully outlines a multitude of possible distinctions. All of these can be researched and exercised, if applicable, in any investigation.

Personnel Files

The term *personnel files* has not been specifically defined by the FOIA. However, the Supreme Court has narrowed the scope of such records to include those that contain "vast amounts" of personal data on an individual which creates a profile of the person.[52] In reviewing all of the information that can be located in these types of files, a researcher will see why this is so. For instance, many personnel files include a person's school records, work evaluations, and a history of where he or she has lived. Federal law differs from state law and recognizes that the following information qualifies as "intimate" or private under exemption 6 and therefore is not to be disclosed:

- Marital status
- Medical conditions
- Welfare payments
- Alcohol consumption
- Family fights
- Reputations
- Legitimacy of children.[53]

If this type of information can be deleted from files that are requested for production, the files may be allowed to be produced.

State laws vary regarding whether disclosure of personal matters, job applications, and other job-related information is considered an "invasion of personal privacy" and therefore exempt. As has been the rule with other exemptions, the courts have found it necessary to make many determinations on file availability based on the balance between the privacy interest and the public interest. Some courts apply the **reasonable person standard** when using the **balancing method** to make a decision. The reasonable person standard is based on a hypothetical person who demonstrates the characteristics of attention, scholarship, aptitude, and discernment that society requires of its members. These same characteristics protect both society and the interests of the individual.

Agencies in particular may "sanitize" (black out or redact) information from files that are not truly relevant to the request. Exemption 6 can, of course, be waived by the party whom the request involves, if that person signs an authorization for the release of such files. This does not mean that confidential information relating specifically to the agency or employer will not still be removed from the file before production. Information is not usually blacked out on job applications, but may be from performance reviews or other detailed data.

Medical Records

Exemption 6 and state laws on information production also apply to medical records. There is no solid definition of *medical records,* and the use of exemption 6 in regard to this category of records is quite varied. For instance, the National Institute for Occupational Safety and Health believes that its possession of medical information about cancer risks in the workplace is immune under exemption 6. Individual state laws may exempt autopsy reports, worker's compensation data, and questionnaire facts gathered from a person. In a few instances, the court has ordered such records to be released to a district attorney who was carrying out official duties, or in cases of compelling public interest. In general, the best method for obtaining such records is by authorization of the person to whom the records relate.

PUBLIC AGENCIES

Federal Register

(Search the Internet at http://www.nara.gov/fedreg, or at http://www.citation.com, or at http://www/access.gpo.gov)

The federal Freedom of Information Act requires all agencies to publish in the *Federal Register* the following information, which will serve as a guide to the public:

- Descriptions of the agency's central and field organizations. This must tell the public whom to contact and at what locations. It should also describe the methods to be followed to obtain information, to make submittals or requests, or to obtain decisions.

- Statements of the general course and methods by which an agency's functions are channeled and determined, including the nature and requirements of all formal and informal procedures available.

- Rules of procedure, descriptions of forms available (or the places where the forms may be obtained), and instructions as to the scope and contents of all papers, reports, or examinations.

- Substantive rules of general applicability adopted as authorized by law, and statements of general policy or interpretations of general applicability formulated and adopted by the agency.

- Each amendment, revision, or repeal of the foregoing.[54]

Purpose   The purpose of disclosing descriptions of the agency organization is to provide the public with a means of knowing the nature and requirements for all formal and informal procedures and how they may obtain information thereon. The method by which the agency makes decisions regarding data requests is set out in the agency's entry in the *Federal Register.* An agency may find some relief, granted under exemption 2, for data relating to internal personnel rules and practices. The publishing of the agency's procedural rules gives notice to the public of how and under what circumstances an agency may take action against a party. The agency is required to use only those procedures listed in the *Federal Register* when it seeks to act against any person.[55] This shields the public and provides evidentiary material for civil litigation in the event of wrongful discharge or other such action allegedly done by the agency.

Rules   Substantive rules must be published in the *Federal Register.* This provides the public with access to the contents of such rules at a definite location and avoids agency delay in providing such material. This is particularly helpful in the civil investigation and lawsuit. When there is a question as to the writing, use, or misuse of a particular agency rule, the agency cannot delay production of such material—it is already public and available. This also provides a solid groundwork for determining the validity of any procedures questioned in a civil lawsuit. This same general principle applies to the publishing of statements of general policy and their application. These rules can and do affect the substantive rights of individuals. All the agency requirements that are published in the *Federal Register* can also be located in the Code of Federal Regulations.

Additional Public Material   Aside from the material required to be published in the *Federal Register,* agencies must make public all indices to any material that is available for inspection and copying, and must promptly identify and make available any other record properly requested.[56] This, of course, means that the requested item must first be identified as a public record (the definition of which was outlined earlier in this chapter). Examples of agency records include the following:

- Reports prepared by an agency
- Investigative and consultant's reports, assuming the record is considered an agency record and is not exempt
- Accident reports
- Autopsy reports
- Inventory of evidence used against a criminal defendant
- Telephone directory at a defense plant operated by a defense contractor
- Copies of a motion-picture film depicting an experiment conducted on behalf of the government
- Photographs, at least insofar as they are used in the operations or decision-making functions of an agency
- Actuarial tables used by a state retirement system to calculate pension benefits
- Medical and hospital records
- Records regarding the use of public funds, and budget information
- Public contracts
- Settlement agreements
- Grant or loan applications
- License and permit applications
- Lists of registered or licensed individuals
- Minutes of meetings of public bodies
- Records of the schedule of a Cabinet Secretary prepared by agency staff
- Personnel records
- IRS letter rulings
- Lists of tax delinquents
- Real estate inspection reports, assessments, and appraisals.[57]

Agency Records Only "agency records" need be produced or disclosed under the FOIA. The term **agency records** includes only those created or compiled by an agency in the course of its work. If the agency seeks to deny access to any record requested, the agency and not the requester must prove why the material sought is not an "agency record."[58] The following is a short list of some records not considered to be agency records:

- A city assessor's field books
- Appointment calendars, phone logs, and daily agendas of government officials
- Physical objects or evidence
- Library reference material, such as a computerized bibliography and index.[59]

Agencies Involved A variety of agencies fall under the rules set forth by the FOIA. For a better understanding of the rules as they apply to each of these individual agencies, look to the federal Freedom of Information Act and to each agency's FOIA regulations. Here is a listing of some federal agencies included in this legislation:

- Central Intelligence Agency
- Commerce Department (including the Bureau of Census)
- Commodity Futures Trading Commission
- Consumer Product Safety Commission
- Defense Department
- Equal Employment Opportunity Commission
- Federal Aviation Administration
- Health and Human Services Department
- Internal Revenue Service.

THE INTERNET AND DATABASES

Electronic technology advances have now made it possible for all persons, and especially paralegals, to use computers for searching out material on witnesses and evidence. Global searches on any number of Internet servers open doors to chat rooms, investigative services, document retrieval services, databases, and others. These opportunities allow the paralegal to search local, state, and federal records, as well as other resource materials, from her desk; the time needed to research, order, and receive material and documents through the Internet is usually short and cost-effective. To adequately utilize this resource, the paralegal must become familiar with the Internet, search engines, databases, and software products. All Web site and database information herein was current as of the printing of this text, but constant change on the Internet prohibits any guarantee that these cites and references will remain valid.

The Internet

Using the Internet and a variety of databases, the paralegal is able to search for information in three main categories: persons, companies, and public records. (A discussion on people searches appears in Chapter 14, on locating witnesses.) The accompanying figure compares the advantages and disadvantages of these systems.

Advantages	Disadvantages
Saves time.	Can waste time if irrelevant information distracts or interferes with the paralegal's search.
Provides a lot of information from a vast number of sources.	So much information is available, from such a wide variety of sources, that the paralegal may be overwhelmed and actually miss good material.
Most information is available at no cost.	Some searches lead to document and information retrieval companies that charge large sums of money for the data requested; discretion must be used.

☑ **PRACTICAL TIP**   The Internet is both a great time-saver and a terrible time-waster. A paralegal may spend hours searching for information and not find what she is looking for, so she should plan her search carefully.

It is possible to find one piece of the information immediately and then waste hours looking at other sites in an effort to ensure that no additional information has been missed. To avoid this, the paralegal should:

- Know what is wanted and how much is wanted.
- Stay focused on the type of information needed and avoid being distracted by the advertising found on search pages.
- Make a plan for the search and specifically allot a certain amount of time for the search. This helps to limit the time wasted in looking at irrelevant information.
- Decide if and how much money is available for the search.
- Keep track of where the search has been and what sites provided the best information. It is often possible to search only sites similar to the ones found to be the most useful.

Search Engines

To date, there are more than 1,800 search engines on the Web. Some of the most used engines are:

- Yahoo: http://www.yahoo.com
- Infoseek: http://www.infoseek.com
- Excite: http://www.excite.com
- AltaVista: http://www.altavista.com
- HotBot: http://www.hotbot.com
- Lycos: http://www.lycos.com
- Netscape (see Figure 9-1).

Search engines are designed to make a statistical analysis of the data requested and apply it to a general audience. The amount and degree of analysis vary greatly from engine to engine.

- The engines rank the data they find based on a relevancy rating by topic.
- The data received from the engines is a conglomerate of everything on the Internet, from very scientific data from prestigious institutions to the very worst information from the most unreliable sources.

Figure 9-1
Netscape search screen, showing many search engines

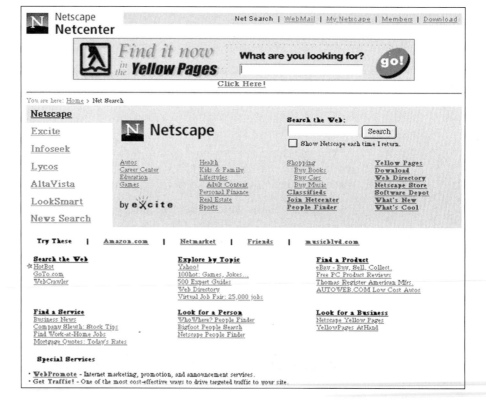

- The researcher can easily get much more than she asked for.

- No one engine can do a full search of all the data on a specific subject. To best accommodate any search, the paralegal should use more than one search engine.

- Netscape Navigator lists many search engines and allows the researcher to select which one(s) to use. It also allows the researcher to choose more than one.

- Metasearch is a relatively new engine that allows the researcher to enter the key word or search items once and then have that entry applied or submitted to all available engines. However, this can provide too much information, and the researcher may become overwhelmed.

- Dogpile is another application, like Metasearch, that allows the researcher to input the key words for the search once and then move through all of the engines. The difference between Dogpile and Metasearch is that Dogpile has a timer, which allows the researcher to limit the time and amount of the search. Dogpile searches for the data in all of the engines simultaneously; it then provides a list of the hits and engines that hold the hits, all within the time frame specified.

- Yahoo is really more a directory than a search engine.

- Excite is very easy to use and provides channels of information to ease the search.

- AltaVista offers a big screen for the search and can take extra commands to narrow the search at the beginning of the process. It is also possible to do a people search from here.

- The Internet and the search engines change daily. It behooves the paralegal to stay informed on those changes as they apply to public records, company, and people searches.

- The paralegal is responsible for learning which sites can be trusted. Build a "library" by getting referrals from other paralegals, attorneys, the ABA, NALA, NFPA, and other professional legal organizations.

Once the paralegal has an understanding of what the search engines are, who runs them, and what they provide, she must be able to conduct the search. Searching is done by entering the name of the person, company, subject, or topic.

- Be as specific as possible, using first and last names, full company names and acronyms, or other applicable titles.

- Use the directories provided by the search engine to narrow the search. For instance, when searching *umbilical cord blood,* the paralegal may add to her search *blood research, national organ donation, medical research,* or the names of any researchers, clinics, or hospitals known to specialize in this area.

- Use the directories to "drill down" (and narrow) the search by interchanging subjects and topics with the names of people.

- Keep track of the sites that have been of interest and provided good and useable information. Many engines will ask the researcher if she would like to see more sites like the ones she has picked. By selecting yes, the paralegal can weed out wasteful sites.

When the paralegal does not need a person or general information, but instead needs a public record or company data, she can do many things, the most common of which are explained here.

Public Records

Due to the heavy—and ever-increasing—demand for public records, many agencies and offices are using the Internet to provide public access to data. Although this is good news for the paralegal and the public, it has sometimes been detrimental to the privacy of some individuals. Because of the sensitivity of some records, like those found at the Social Security office, some agencies (including the Social Security Administration) are now leaving the Internet and returning to more traditional methods of providing public access to their records. As public offices leave the Web, it is critical that the paralegal remember that Web sites can be put together by anyone; before paying for anything, determine the value of the material to be delivered, and use caution with regard to the expense of a service. The paralegal is responsible for determining fees and obtaining permission to spend money before continuing on the Web. When searching for public records, the paralegal should become familiar with the following Web sites and services:

- **Knowx: http://www.knowx.com:** This is perhaps the best public-records search company. It offers reliable records at a low price, and it has comprehensive coverage, including the ability to use multiple databases to search for licenses, assets, people, and businesses all at the same time. If a large search is not required, the paralegal can use a single database. Knowx is easy to use and provides detailed pricing information. Some of the categories found there include:
  - Aircraft
  - Bankruptcy
  - Corporate
  - Lawsuits
  - Professional licenses
  - Real property
  - UCC filings.
- **Edgar Online (SEC): http://www.edgar-online.com/:** Edgar provides data on patents and trademarks. There is a fee for Edgar services. The paralegal can search by company name or ticker symbol; choose all filings or specify the type; or choose a time period (Edgar automatically defaults to one month). See Figure 9-2.

Figure 9-2
EDGAR™ Online:
The Source for
Today's SEC
Information.
(Courtesy of
Cybernet Data
Systems)

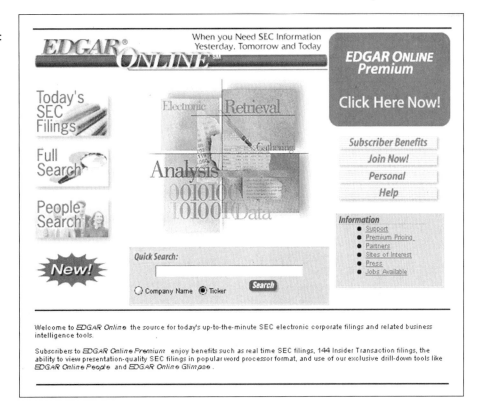

- The *Federal Register:* http://law.house.gov/7.htm
- **Internal Revenue Service:** http://www.irs.ustreas.gov
- **National Association of State Resource Executives:**
  http://www.nasire.org
- State and national court sites:
  - Federal Judicial Center: http://www.fjc.gov
  - US Federal Courts: http://www.uscourts.gov
  - National Center for State Courts: http://www.ncsc.dni.us
    (see Figure 9-3)
  - Federal Court Link: http://www.txlegal.com/Fedlnk.htm
  - BK Court Link: http://www.bkauthority.com/courts.htm
  - USSC+: US Supreme Court Decisions; Infosynthesis, Inc.:
    http://www.usscplus.com
- **Court Link: http://www.focuscorp.com/courts.htm:** In this site
  (see Figure 9-4) the paralegal will find:
  - Dates for court motions
  - Past and pending litigation

Figure 9-3
National Center for
State Courts Web
site

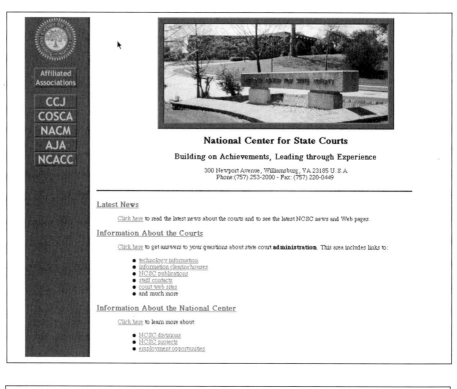

Figure 9-4
Focus Systems'
Court Link Web
site. (Courtesy of
Focus Systems)

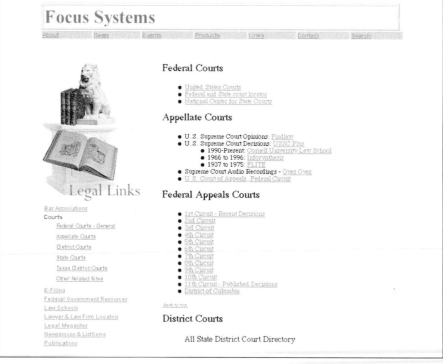

- Court dockets
  - United States District Court
  - United States Bankruptcy Court
  - United States Circuit Court of Appeals
- **LEXIS/NEXIS: http://www.lexis-nexis.com**.

Companies

When searching for data on companies, the paralegal should know that search engines list the data by industry. Once the industry directory has been browsed and the company identified, she can find the following information:

- Stock quotes, price changes, and dates
  - Silicon Investor: http://www.techstocks.com/
  - Investor Guide Research: http://www.investorguide.com/Research.html
- Company news and press releases
  - CompanyLink: http://www.companylink.com/ (industry news and research company information)
  - WSRN.com: http://www.wsrn.com/home/companyResearch.html (research a United States or Canadian company)
  - CorpTech: http://www.corptech.com/ (search 45,000 technology manufacturers and developers of high-tech products)
- Market snapshots
- Listings of officers
- Price histories
- Accounting statistics
- Portfolio information
  - Infoseek Portfolio tracker: http://infoseek.moneynet.com/content/infoseek/Signup/PTSignup.asp (this free service will track up to ten personalized portfolios with up to thirty securities in each; sign up and enter the symbols of the stocks, mutual funds, and options desired)
  - Hoover's Online: http://www.hoovers.com/
  - ComFind: http://comfind.com/
  - Companies Online: http://www.companiesonline.com (see Figure 9-5).

Paralegals may also find the names and titles of a company's executives, which may be available from press releases furnished by the company online. The paralegal may also be able to track executive careers within the company via these press releases.

When conducting a company search, use the following steps:

- First try to locate the company's Web site, if it has one (or more). This is often done by using the company's name followed by ".com".

Figure 9-5
Dun & Bradstreet's Companies Online Web site. (Courtesy of Dun & Bradstreet, a company of The Dun & Bradstreet Corporation, 1998)

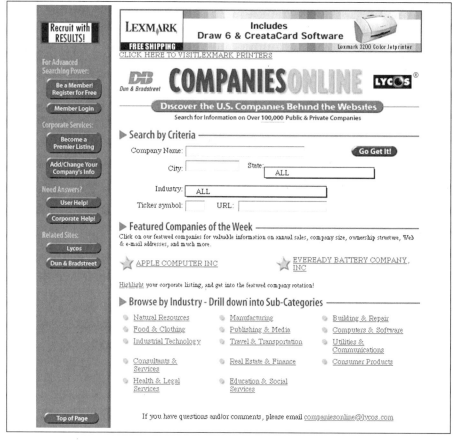

- Browse the search engine listings organized by industry if the first search does not work.
- Search for the company name using a favorite engine.
- Use a combination of search engines and browsing. This is the most helpful and expedient process. It is also possible to search organizations for data on companies, by using the organization's name followed by ".org".

The paralegal must use her best judgment when gathering and using material from the Internet. Sources have to be verified and data checked for accuracy. Verification can be done through traditional sources, like those discussed in the public records section of this chapter, and/or through the many printed materials available to the public.

PRINTED MATERIAL

With little effort, the paralegal can amass a wide variety of printed materials that serve as a tremendous investigative resource. Some of the materials that she may want to include in her personal library will include various different directories, which are so common and attainable that they are often overlooked. Do not be fooled into thinking that the more obvious a resource tool is, the less effective it will be—that type of thinking will often make finding a witness or particular piece of evidence difficult. In other areas, if something appears "too good to be true, it probably is," but this is not always the case with investigative resources. The paralegal must take time to find and understand the many types of directories available to the public and how to use them.

Telephone Directory

(Search the Internet at http://www.abii.com,
or at http://www.angelfire.com/pages0/ultimates,
or at http://www.worldpages.com)

Certainly, telephone books fall into the category of very obvious information. Many law firms maintain a collection of phone books for the surrounding areas and may even keep old books for reference. What the paralegal may not know is that local libraries also have copies of phone books; their selection is usually quite large and in some libraries includes most major United States cities. The library may keep older copies of phone books, as will local chambers of commerce. If not at the local chamber, check the chamber within the city where the search is being conducted. The telephone company itself usually stocks old issues of phone books.

It is reasonable to assume that a paralegal can contact directory assistance for telephone numbers and addresses; however, this service is often time-consuming and expensive. It is often more helpful—and sometimes necessary—to physically look at a phone book for cross-references and other data. When information is unlisted, the paralegal must find another method of uncovering the data, as unlisted phone numbers are private and require a court order for release.

City Directories

(Search the Internet at http://www.virtualvoyages.com/usa/us_city.sht
or at http://www.citypubco.com)

At least two private companies compile and sell city directories, for almost every metropolitan area and many smaller cities and towns. These are commonly referred to by the publishers' names (i.e., the Polk Directory and the Coles Directory). The many uses for these directories make them an invaluable resource tool, but the directories are costly, especially if one or more is regularly used, as is true in many large metropolitan law firms where clients are scattered all over the country. Therefore, this is one resource the average paralegal will not have in her personal library, though they are available at some libraries and law firms.

A city directory lists phone numbers for a particular city in three ways:

- In numerical order, starting with the first prefix applicable to the phoning area of that urban region

- By street address for the city (a city map is usually found in the front of the book)
- Alphabetically by household or business name.

All of these listings allow cross-referencing if the paralegal has only one particular piece of the information with which to begin the search.

EXAMPLE ————————————————————————————————

A paralegal is looking for a witness to an accident. She knows, from the client, that the witness recently moved into the neighborhood where the accident occurred. She also knows that his name is Bob and that he works at an engineering firm in town. At first the paralegal may think it will be difficult to locate this person: after all, she does not have his name, phone number, or address. However, if she uses the city directory, she can determine the names of the streets close to the accident scene, look up those streets, and search for all the "Roberts" or "Bobs" who live there. What she may not know is that the city directories also provide information on the persons who live at each address, including where they work, how many people are in the home, and how long they have lived in the home. She can narrow her search to all of the "Bobs" who have lived in their homes less than a year and work for an engineering firm in town. If more than one Bob fitting those requirements is found, she can begin calling them until she locates the right one.

American Medical Association Directory

(Search the Internet at http://www.ama-assn.org)

Within the AMA directory, statistical information on doctors is found, including:

- Name
- Home and office addresses
- Medical organization memberships
- Licensing data
- Birth date
- Dates of school graduations.

Each city and county has a listing of member doctors in the local association, but local listings may not satisfy all of the needs for locating doctors in a litigation investigation. State medical associations also have the names of many doctors, but the paralegal may not be able to obtain the data over the phone; the associations may require a written request. In addition, deceased doctors are dropped from the listings within about five years from the date of death. Collecting this directory and updating it periodically provides the paralegal with access to doctors currently practicing, barred from practicing, or deceased for a period of time longer than current records cover.

American Dental Association

(Search the Internet at http://www.ada.org)

The American Dental Association (ADA) is a national organization that strives to maintain listings for the many licensed dentists across the United States. The ADA can be contacted at: 211 East Chicago Avenue, Chicago, IL 60611. In addition to the listings available from the ADA, listings may be found through local dental societies and the licensing board in each state.

Directory of Newspapers and Periodicals

(Search the Internet at http://www.rollins.edu/olin/olinref.htm)

The Directory of Newspapers and Periodicals offers an in-depth guide to periodicals and newspapers nationwide. It provides a description of the periodical or paper; where it is published, including the city name and population; and a summary of the publication statistics, such as name of the issue, the dates of issue, the column information, price, and circulation. This directory also provides access to authors, reports, photographs, and other valuable evidence and sources of evidence.

Handbook of Scientific and Technological Societies

This directory is published by the National Research Council at the National Academy of Sciences in Washington, DC. The Handbook of Scientific and Technical Societies, which covers all of the United States and Canada, publishes the names of organizations involved in the natural sciences. The directory lists information on the organizations, their structure, their officers, and their publications.

Biographical Resources

A variety of publications are available that provide autobiographies of individuals in different classifications. An example is the "Who's Who" series. At the request of the publishers who create these resources, the individuals listed write their own personal data entries. Specifics on these people should therefore be accurate, but in some cases the entries are not verified by the publisher, so use caution before believing all that is printed. This material may be published in a variety of ways, including national editions; state, county, and local versions; and student versions (high-school or college-level participants).

Mailing Lists

Although this source is not technically a directory, the paralegal can compile a great number of mailing lists and create her own directory from them. Many companies sell mailing lists for nominal fees, and one can request lists with specific requirements. For instance, request recent subscribers to a magazine, or the names of the fifty most recent catalog purchasers' names; or narrow the search to a small alphabetical, geographical, or age grouping. Once a paralegal has begun procuring these types of sources, she can place them in a binder or on a computer and create her own directory.

Advertising and Instructional Material

Much like mailing lists, advertising and instructional materials are not found in directory form, but can be collected over the course of years of work, or may be provided to novice paralegals by a senior paralegal. In this category, the paralegal may find a manufacturer's advertising or instructional manuals that accompany mechanical or chemical products at purchase. She may also obtain this type of material for other specific litigation matters (such as engineering maintenance for amusement park rides), all of which will be included in a directory created for management of this material. The purpose of creating a directory for these sources is, fairly obviously, to identify product information and experts in special fields.

Miscellaneous Sources

The types of sources that could be detailed in this category are endless and in no way does this list represent a complete outline. What this list does outline is the many possibilities of sources, how to identify them, and what to do with them when found. The paralegal should make it a practice to log the names and descriptions of any data collected in an investigation that she did not already have access to; three-ring binders provide excellent storage for this material. Sources the paralegal may regularly contact and find useful include:

- City library names, telephone numbers, and librarian names. (Search the Internet at http://ipl.sils.umich.ed, or the Library of Congress at http://lcweb.loc.gov/homepage/lchp.html, or Libraries Unlimited at lueditorial@lu.com)
- Law libraries, by name, location, telephone number, and specifics on what is available. (Search the Internet at http://www.washlaw.edu)
- Better Business Bureaus across the country.
- Local news reporters and weather announcers.
- Court districts and the names of staff members whom you deal with regularly.
- Court reporters.
- Skiptracers.
- Secretary of state offices.
- Expert witness directories, files, and referrals.
- Fellow paralegals who specialize in a unique legal field.
- Seminar material.

A paralegal should never have to repeat a search for material if she maintains a system to manage her valuable data, except to keep the data current.

RELATED AND NONRELATED PEOPLE

An enormous supply of information, available to any investigation, is often overlooked or tremendously downplayed: that source is people. People can be directly related to a case or piece of evidence, but generally, *any* person may help an investigation, including witnesses, records keepers, treating physicians, neighbors, friends, relatives, and even people who are totally uninvolved.

EXAMPLE

A paralegal who is researching the property assets of a judgment debtor has spent the day in the county assessor's office, poring over data, with little luck. While she is looking through the block book, she starts a conversation with the clerk, who is filing some new maps, and during the conversation she describes what she is looking for. The clerk tells the paralegal that there was some construction work three years earlier on the parcel of property she is researching, and that the property changed ownership during that time. This is information the paralegal could have gotten from the clerk at any time, but the clerk goes further and tells her about the company that bought the property from the original owner (the judgment debtor). She even discloses details about the sale that are not recorded in the county's documents, including trouble clearing the title, the judgment debtor's difficult personality, and the name of the contact person at the company.

This example shows that the paralegal could have conducted her search for the property without ever talking to the clerk—but she would have missed the opportunity to find out a wealth of details. This is but one of many examples of the kinds of serendipitous sources that a paralegal may tap, with luck and a little effort.

Many people in the courthouse may be available to provide information, including clerks who handle the everyday work on civil files and members of the sheriff's office who serve process. The communication skills discussed in the first section of this text make it possible for the paralegal to uncover information by openly probing people she comes into contact with during the investigation. Never assume that any person within the immediate proximity of the investigation (clerks, sheriff's staff, and others) does not have helpful information.

EXAMPLE

A paralegal is reviewing medical records in a wrongful death case concerning a woman who was hit and killed by a train. As she reviews the records, she finds an entry made by a doctor concerning what appears to be an unrelated medical condition, but the entry is illegible. She contacts the doctor's office and speaks with the nurse, asking for clarification of the physician's notes. After the nurse explains what the record says, the paralegal asks for a definition of the condition described. The nurse explains that it is a mental condition connected to depression and is often seen in suicidal patients. The paralegal has now gathered, from this unrelated person, enough data to begin an investigation into the possibility that the "wrongful death" was actually a suicide.

This is a perfect example of why potential sources of information should never be left unused. It is quite possible that the paralegal could have taken the information from the nurse and never asked for more detail; in the hypothetical, of course, this would have been an error in judgment. It is not possible for the paralegal to interview every person she comes into contact with, but she can develop communication skills that help her quickly assess a person's knowledge on a subject and, when necessary, spend more time speaking with that person. Consider every person encountered during an investigation a potential source of information. The amount of data that can be discovered is amazing!

SUMMARY

- Public records are found in many places within city, county, state, and federal venues. They are not identified as such merely by where they are located, but rather by what they contain.
- The right to copy records is associated with the right to inspect records. Copying of public records can be done by the requesting party or, in some instances, by the records custodian. Each agency and public office has a policy on how copying will be handled.
- Records held by government agencies may be confidential or privileged. The FOIA and state laws determine which records will be released. The goal is to allow as many records as possible to be released to the public.
- Printed material is easily obtained and valuable to the investigation.
- People are an excellent but often overlooked source of information.

ACTIVITIES

Answer the following questions pertaining to public records:

1. Who are the primary holders of public records?
2. After identifying certain public records as useful to the investigation, the paralegal must gather and review those records. How would she go about that, and who would she talk to? (Select any two types of public records to answer this question.)
3. What ethical considerations must the paralegal remember when handling public records, and why?
4. As you know, there are state rules regulating the copying of records. Research your state laws regarding such copying and list the current fees for copying.

Contact the local offices listed here and identify some of the primary information each has available:

5. County recorder
6. Records of the assessor

7. Voter registration

8. Business organization documents

9. Weather reports

Answer the following questions regarding private records:

10. List the nine exemptions found in the FOIA.

11. Select a section of the Freedom of Information Act that you find particularly interesting and research your state laws regarding the same general topic. Outline the differences you found between the state regulations and the federal rulings dealing with that topic. (Consider looking for such subjects as public meetings, personnel records, executive privilege, or telephone records and confidentiality issues.)

Use your local library to answer the following questions:

12. How many state telephone directories are found in your local library?

13. How many city telephone directories are found in your local library?

14. List three other directories found at your library and what they are used for.

CASE STUDIES

Christian Lowd, Minor

Read the following case scenario details, and then answer the questions using information learned from this chapter.

Case Details

A notice is received from the court regarding the docketing of a judgment against a defendant, Christian Lowd. The law firm represented an insurance company in a subrogation case against Lowd several years earlier, when Lowd, with another person, stole a car belonging to the insurance company's client. The car was totaled in a collision while Lowd was driving; Lowd and the other person were both minors at the time of the original judgment. The court has now issued judgment in the civil case, ordering full restitution for the car to be paid by Lowd to the plaintiff. When the judgment is received, the named plaintiff in the judgment is the owner of the vehicle rather than the insurance company; however, the owner was paid in full by the insurance company at the time of the claim. The paralegal is asked to do the following:

- Have the judgment amended so that it reflects the name of the insurance company and not the owner of the vehicle.
- Collect financial data on Lowd so that restitution can be collected.

1. Do you foresee any problem obtaining the juvenile court records in order to change the judgment?

2. What records will be needed to begin locating financial records on Mr. Lowd?

3. What resources are available to the paralegal (both public and private) to search for financial data on Mr. Lowd?

4. Are any other resources available to the paralegal when looking for Mr. Lowd and his money?

Hart v. Spoker

Review the following case study. After your review, identify the public and/or private records you would need to review to answer these questions (include in your answer the method you would use to obtain the records, and identify any problems you anticipate in gathering the information).

Hart v. Spoker

This case comes to the litigation department via the probate section, and deals with a very complicated dram shop lawsuit in which a Mr. Lester Hart—or rather his estate and heirs—is the plaintiff. Jason Spoker is the owner of the Zoo Bar, who is being sued by Hart's heirs.

Lester Hart was married for some time to Jenny Jenkins. He and Jenkins have three children, but are now divorced, and Jenkins allegedly never received any child support payments after the divorce. Sometime later, Hart met another woman, Sally Felder, and either married her or planned to marry her in February of 1998. She was expecting his child. During the time of the new marriage, Jenkins filed a suit against Hart for back child support and asked the court to garnish his wages. During the period of this court activity, Hart went to the Zoo Bar for a few drinks. After consuming several drinks on the night of March 1, 1998, Hart was killed in a car accident on his way home. Now both the ex-wife and the alleged new wife are fighting over his estate and the damages that may be awarded to the estate in the case against the bar.

1. What are the dates of the deceased's marriages? What are the dates of his divorces?

2. What are his children's birth dates and what hospitals were they born in?

3. What counties have jurisdiction over his marriages and divorces?

4. Obtain copies or records of all child support payments he made.

5. Research the deceased's criminal and/or civil litigation history.

NOTES

1 5 U.S.C. § 552b(e) (1994, as amended).

2 5 U.S.C. § 552b(f)(2).

3 5 U.S.C. § 552b(f)(3).

4 66 Am. Jur. 2d *Records and Recording Laws* § 6.

5 *Id.*

6 *Id.*

7 66 Am. Jur. 2d *Records and Recording Laws* § 10.

8 *Id.*

9 *Id.*

10 *Id.*

11 66 Am. Jur. 2d *Records and Recording Laws* § 12.

12 *Id.*

13 *Id.*

14 *Id.*

15 66 Am. Jur. 2d *Records and Recording Laws* § 27.

16 *Id.*

17 *Id.*

18 66 Am. Jur. 2d *Records and Recording Laws* § 13.

19 66 Am. Jur. 2d *Records and Recording Laws* at 349–50.

20 66 Am. Jur. 2d *Records and Recording Laws* § 14.

21 66 Am. Jur. 2d *Records and Recording Laws* § 16.

22 *Id.*

23 66 Am. Jur. 2d *Records and Recording Laws* § 17.

24 66 Am. Jur. 2d *Records and Recording Laws* at 356.

25 2 Am. Jur. Trials, *Locating Public Records* § 16 (1964).

26 *Id.*

27 *Id.*

28 *Id.*

29 *Id.*

30 2 Am. Jur. Trials, *Locating Public Records* § 23 (1964).

31 *Id.*

32 2 Am. Jur. Trials, *Locating Public Records* § 17 (1964).

33 *See, e.g.,* 42 U.S.C. § 1306(a) (1994).

34 20 C.F.R. § 401.100(a) (1988).

35 *Id.*

36 2 Am. Jur. Trials, *Locating Public Records* § 29 (1964).

37 38 U.S.C. § 5701 (1994); *see also* 2 Am. Jur. Trials, *Locating Public Records* at 28–29.

38 2 Am. Jur. Trials, *Locating Public Records* § 25 (1964).

39 5 U.S.C. § 552 (1994, as amended).

40 5 U.S.C. § 552a (1994, as amended).

41 37A Am. Jur. 2d *Freedom of Information Acts* § 27.

42 *Id.*

43 5 U.S.C. § 552(b).

44 37A Am. Jur. 2d *Freedom of Information Acts* § 158.

45 *Id.* § 152.

46 *Id.* § 152.

47 *Id.* § 153.

48 *Id.* § 156.

49 *Id.*

50 37A Am. Jur. 2d *Freedom of Information Acts* at 238–39.

51 *Id.* at 251.

52 *Department of Air Force v. Rose,* 425 U.S. 352, 48 L. Ed 2d 11, 96 S. Ct. 1592, 1 Media L. Rep. 2509 (1976).

53 37A Am. Jur. 2d *Freedom of Information Acts* § 259 (1994).

54 37A Am. Jur. 2d *Freedom of Information Acts* §§ 42–46 (1994).

55 37A Am. Jur. 2d *Freedom of Information Acts* § 43 (1994).

56 37A Am. Jur. 2d *Freedom of Information Acts* § 57 (1994).

57 37A Am. Jur. 2d *Freedom of Information Acts* § 66 (1994).

58 *Id.*

59 37A Am. Jur. 2d *Freedom of Information Acts* at 102–04.

10 CONDUCTING THE INVESTIGATION

OBJECTIVES After completing this chapter, you will know:

- An investigation is initiated when the paralegal makes a plan based on an investigative outline.

- The objectives of the investigative outline are to identify the facts to be obtained and to identify all the required evidence and witnesses.

- There are six basic investigative strategies that ensure organization and competence in the investigation.

- Chronologies and timelines are used to manage witness information and all the case details and facts.

- Authorizations are used to obtain a party's private data from a third party.
- The paralegal is ethically responsible for conducting his investigation and personally behaving in a manner that meets the standards set out by the American Bar Association and the two national paralegal associations.

MAKING A PLAN

An organizational plan is the first tool needed to begin an investigation. The plan focuses on the two main objectives for the investigation:

- Identifying and obtaining the facts
- Identifying and finding all of the required evidence and witnesses.

To complete these two primary objectives, an **investigative outline** must be created.

Investigative Outline

The investigative outline provides a visual method for planning the investigation strategy, prioritizing tasks, and ranking witnesses and evidence. Figure 10-1 is a model of an investigative outline in an employment dispute dealing with wrongful discharge.

Developing the investigative outline requires creativity and individualization, as every investigation and case are different. The sample outline shown in Figure 10-1 is very preliminary and will be revised several times as the investigation progresses. This is necessary because no solid details are available for the initial outline. Specific and unknown witnesses, and evidence uncovered through timeline interviews, are listed and ranked when determined, as are a variety of administrative tasks. The paralegal looks to the attorney for all requirements needed to prove the legal theory, ranking them as instructed. Substantive legal work is handled by the attorney. The paralegal's main objective is to explore evidence.

Exploring Evidence   Conducting an investigation means, primarily, probing and exploring the stories gathered from witness interviews and from the client. By creating a general plan for the investigation, the paralegal can plan where and how to expand the investigation. The paralegal determines what questions to ask and what evidence to seek by following the investigative outline.

An investigative outline aims to generate topics for specific inquiries, rather than focusing on recording information. By means of the outline, the paralegal surveys gaps in the information and decides which evidence or witnesses may help provide the answers needed to prove certain legal theories. By classifying evidence and witnesses as affirmative (supportive) or rebuttal, it is possible to keep the objectives of the investigation clear and fresh. Outlining an investigation as completely as possible helps the legal team uncover the evidence and

Figure 10-1
Investigative
outline

Smith v. Williams Construction
Investigative Outline

1. **Legal Issue:** Breach of contract by wrongful discharge from employment (plaintiff's case). Requirements to be proved (elements):
   a. Evidence that Smith had an employment contract with Williams that required good cause for termination
   b. Evidence that the employee performed his duties adequately and otherwise fulfilled his contract
   c. Evidence that Williams terminated Smith without good cause, in violation of the contract
   d. Evidence showing the degree to which the client, Mr. Smith, was damaged.

2. Evaluate witnesses and rank them by credibility.
   a.
   b.
   c.
   d.

3. Evaluate existing evidence and rank it by relevance as to legal issues.
   a.
   b.
   c.
   d.

4. Summarize the story (chronology) and identify which evidence or witness supports each fact.

5. What information must be explored further?
   a.
   b.
   c.
   d.

6. What administrative tasks must be completed? Rank them in terms of importance and length of time needed to complete them.
   a.
   b.
   c.
   d.

testimony needed to produce the desired results. Look at the specific features of the *Smith v. Williams Construction* outline (Figure 10-1) to better understand the components of the outline—but first review the case study.

CASE STUDY

Smith v. Williams Construction

Smith worked at Williams Construction for ten years as a structural engineer. He was very close to his first supervisor, who is no longer at the company, but has never gotten along with Mr. Williams, the owner. He also does not get along with his new supervisor. Smith believes that the animosity between the supervisor, Williams, and himself is caused by disagreement on work ethics and standards. On several occasions Smith and Williams have disagreed about cost issues on projects and possible sacrifice of building standards.

Ultimately, Williams terminated Smith's employment. Smith claims that Williams had told the supervisor he wanted Smith fired in violation of Smith's employment contract. Smith also claims that he always performed his work responsibilities fully.

Smith does not know the current whereabouts of his original supervisor, who could verify his claims against Williams. What he does know is the name of the personnel manager who worked at Williams Construction at the same time as Smith and the original supervisor.

Legal Issue   Each investigative outline begins by defining the legal issue of the case. In the *Smith v. Williams Construction* outline, the cause of action is breach of contract. As mentioned earlier, the paralegal gathers all substantive details of the legal theory from the attorney. For the Smith outline, those are:

- Evidence that Smith had an employment contract with Williams that required good cause for termination
- Evidence that the employee performed his duties adequately and otherwise fulfilled his contract
- Evidence that Williams terminated Smith without good cause, in violation of the contract
- Evidence showing the degree to which the client, Mr. Smith, was damaged.

The paralegal needs evidence of Williams intent to wrongfully discharge Smith, as well as evidence to support the claim that Smith was a good employee during his time at Williams Construction and performed his job adequately. In addition, Smith must prove the amount of damages he suffered due to the unjust firing. To more specifically reveal what supporting evidence is required for the plaintiff, the paralegal may wish to further break down the subcategories of the outline, as shown in the accompanying outline.

1. **Legal Issue:**
   c. Evidence that Williams intended to violate the employment
      contract:
      i. Any correspondence in which Williams claims to want
         Smith fired
      ii. Any personnel records showing tampering by Mr. Williams
      iii. Any witnesses who will testify that Williams wanted Smith
         fired

The more defined the outline, the easier it will be to look for specific information—but be careful not to depend solely on the items listed in the outline early in the investigation. By limiting the investigation to these items alone, the paralegal is assuming that no other evidence categories are available. In reality, new evidence may just be waiting to be discovered. Overconfidence in one's logic plagues any investigation and may cause the paralegal to overlook valuable evidence.

Sources of Evidence   The paralegal breaks down the legal issue to include possible sources of proof for the evidence sought, thus expanding the outline. By doing so, the paralegal stays on track and eliminates the possibility of missing an information source. The expanded outline might look like the accompanying outline.

1. **Legal Issue:**
   c. Evidence that Williams intended to violate the employment
      contract:
      i. Any correspondence in which Williams claims to want
         Smith fired
         a. personnel files or memos
         b. phone messages between Williams and any other party
            whom Smith tells the law firm wanted him fired too
         c. personnel evaluations or notes taken by Smith
         d. taped conversations between Smith and Williams in
            which Williams acknowledges he wants Smith fired
         e. other witnesses who may have been told or overheard
            Williams say he wanted Smith fired
         f. e-mail messages containing any information regarding
            Smith or Williams

As the paralegal gains experience in investigating, he will find that many preliminary steps in creating the investigative outline become second nature and require less forethought. He also will almost automatically know what sources of information are available early and routinely in most investigations, such as informal witness interviews, police reports, or employment records; all these will be identified in the investigative outline.

Ranking Witnesses and Evidence   In the next two sections of the outline, the paralegal develops a ranking of witnesses and evidence. This process is like brainstorming and can be done with or without the attorney. Experienced paralegals create the value ranking of witnesses and evidence before meeting with the attorney for a strategy session, thus saving valuable billing and investigation time. Nonetheless, the attorney does the final ranking of all evidence and witnesses, as this is a substantive task.

As events and information unfold in the investigation, all are susceptible to changes in value and ranking.

CASE STUDY

Details

In *Smith v. Williams Construction,* the personnel manager is a key witness, or is assumed to be a key witness, and so is placed at the top of the witness list. The personnel manager is critical because she has information pivotal to proving the legal issue and winning the case. She says Williams told her on several occasions that he wanted anything he could find on Smith so he could fire Smith. This witness provides evidence that Williams planned to fire Smith and was going to do so with or without adequate reason. During the discovery phase of litigation, the paralegal finds out from yet another witness that Williams and the personnel manager were having an affair at the time he told her he wanted Smith fired; but Williams broke it off just days before the paralegal approached the personnel manager seeking information on Williams's desire to fire Smith. If that second witness proves credible, the information seriously damages the personnel manager's credibility and casts doubt on her motives for testifying against Williams. The personnel manager may no longer be a prime witness, because of her damaged credibility.

When such a problem occurs, the outline for the investigation must be readjusted and a new element added to counter the negative information found.

Summarizing the Story and Determining What Information to Explore   The next sections of the outline deal with the story itself, including where the details of the story come from and what information must to be explored further. When itemizing the story in outline form, the paralegal includes the details gathered during witness and client interviews to build a timeline of the story and note where the facts were obtained. By doing this, the paralegal identifies topics worth probing and notes topics that are key to the investigation and the case. He also gathers documents that may help witnesses (especially hostile witnesses) focus on particular parts of the story.

The story outline serves a dual purpose: it provides an organized topic reference for interviews and document searches, and it defines the story in a way that helps the legal team develop demonstrative evidence for trial or depositions. For example, a similar outline may be created as a trial exhibit, to be verified by testimony, when the subject matter is complicated and the jury will benefit from an easy-to-read chart on the issue(s).

Expanding the Story   The story outline and details originated thereby are critical when expanding the story. A paralegal *must* expand the story (and the investigation) to find additional facts to support or undermine the legal theory and case. These additional facts may help or harm the credibility and utility of the client, witness, or physical evidence. It is important to know where information comes from so that additional witnesses can be located and the story can be clarified. When using an outline, the legal team identifies topics of concern and areas of strength, and assists witnesses in expanding their stories and the depth of the case.

Details are needed to support a legal hypothesis of the story and/or test the strength of the adversary's theory. The paralegal uses the investigative outline to select topics and events for further discussion; he stimulates the witness's memory by asking open-ended questions dealing with a specific topic. When interviewing an unemployment office clerk, for example, he might say, "Tell me how the procedure for filing unemployment claims works."

Events and Topics   Events establish context, which provides an opportunity for witnesses to recall details of a story. Distinguish the difference between a topic and event:

- An **event** deals with an occurrence at a specific moment in time, like Smith's being fired or his filing an unemployment claim.
- A **topic** is the whole of a certain subject matter, like unemployment records.

Questions concerning topics may seek information to pinpoint when an event occurred. For instance, the clerk may say the plaintiff filed unemployment claims on three different occasions; with that knowledge, the paralegal can investigate three different events (the unemployment filings). Use separate questions for topics and events, steering topical probes away from specific events. For instance, the paralegal asks the clerk for details on how to file an unemployment claim, and what criteria are used to approve or deny a claim. By using this topical probe early in the interview, he lays the groundwork for specific questions on the plaintiff's unemployment claim(s).

The main purpose of topic- and event-oriented questioning is to stimulate the witness's recall. The paralegal should not spend a lot of time defining a question based on its category (i.e., topic or event); instead, he should concentrate on the goal, which is to expand the story via the witness.

Administrative Tasks   Finally, the outline takes a very practical approach to the paralegal's job duties. Although last in line, ranking the tasks necessary to gather, preserve, and care for evidence and witnesses is critical. Discovery and other deadlines are imposed by the court to ensure a speedy judicial process,[1] and the paralegal may be responsible for developing these deadlines. These deadlines often limit the time a paralegal has to conduct a thorough investigation, but do not reduce the need for a complete investigation.

When the paralegal creates this portion of the outline, he provides the attorney with a realistic look at the time required to perform the most basic litigation functions. To prioritize a paralegal's duties in the investigation, the attorney must have a timetable of the tasks required, which aids both attorney and paralegal in delegating parts of the investigation to others in the law office and ensures that all litigation functions are handled in a timely manner. Look at a sample outline of the tasks a paralegal may do:

6. Tasks for discovery:

   a. Obtain all necessary authorizations from the client and/or other party (2 weeks, approx.)

   b. Request all the medical, employment, Social Security, and other specific records needed for the investigation and discovery phase of litigation (up to 6 weeks)

   c. Request all other documents available, such as ambulance reports, police reports, weather reports, newspaper and other news media stories dealing with the event or occurrence (2–3 days and up to 2 weeks)

   d. Draft any discovery documents needed or other general pleadings required (varies)

   e. Serve all documents as required (varies)

   f. File all documents with the court according to the applicable court rules (varies)

   g. Prepare all records received for potential deposition and/or trial (e.g., summarize medical reports, etc.) (up to 2 weeks from receipt)

   h. Schedule all depositions and serve subpoenas on the appropriate parties (varies)

   i. Begin informal interviews with potential witnesses (varies).

The list of possible investigative tasks is extensive; in no way is this particular list all-inclusive.

In addition to the many basic tasks a paralegal handles, he must also develop and become familiar with the timeline for accomplishing these tasks. For instance, scheduling depositions can take days, as participating attorneys, the court reporter, and the witness attempt to reach each other and agree on dates, times, and terms. Serving a subpoena on the deponent (witness) can likewise be a frustrating and time-consuming process. A witness who does not wish to be part of a lawsuit and does not intend to be served with a subpoena can cost the paralegal weeks, just in getting this one task accomplished. Depositions must be conducted regardless of the deponent's desire—or lack of desire—to be deposed. It is common to hire a private detective to serve elusive witnesses in difficult cases. The coordination of this one task drains a great deal of time from the investigation; however, a paralegal does more than one task at a time. If the paralegal does not have a working understanding of the many functional timelines for these and other litigation tasks, he should seek the advice of a more experienced paralegal or the attorney when drafting this portion of the investigative outline.

STRATEGIES FOR CONDUCTING THE INVESTIGATION

To conduct a successful investigation, a paralegal must be competent and organized. The basic strategies listed in Figure 10-2 are helpful, time-tested means for efficient and effective organization.

Organization guides the search for information. Each strategy is a way to sort through materials and information and manage the investigation. All six of the tasks named in Figure 10-2 are intertwined with one another and sometimes they are difficult to recognize separately. For example, while identifying physical evidence, the paralegal also stores and preserves the evidence. The same can be true for creating timelines and chronologies; during the creation of these organizational tools, the paralegal also develops leads and identifies witnesses. In any investigation, many of these activities happen simultaneously. We will examine each of these strategies more closely, for a more detailed explanation of how each strategy works, why it is important, and why they all work together to produce a competent investigation.

Figure 10-2
Six strategies for conducting a competent, organized investigation

1. Diagram a logical sequence of events that defines the client's version of the event or occurrence, which is the subject of the investigation.

2. Early in the investigation, identify physical evidence and create an evidence log to manage it.

3. Properly store and preserve all physical evidence as it is gathered.

4. Identify witnesses, interview them, and prepare detailed reports on the witnesses.

5. Develop leads.

6. Begin creating a chronology of the whole (overall) event or occurrence.

The Logical Sequence Procedure

The purpose of the **logical sequence procedure** is to help the paralegal think through the story provided by the client and draw a picture of the event. The logical sequence procedure is drawn up in diagram format after the initial client interview has been conducted. The **logical sequence diagram (LSD)** is a visual, written organization of the client's story and is used to review the story for any problems and to identify missing evidence and information.

CASE STUDY

Slip and Fall

A client who owns an apartment building comes to the law firm seeking help to defend against a "slip and fall" claim. During the winter a renter slipped on the building's outside steps leading down to the parking lot and injured herself. During the initial client interview, details of the fall and injury are sketched out, along with the renter's history at the apartment complex, the owner/client's history of owning and operating the apartment complex, and the physical layout of the steps and sidewalk where the fall occurred. After this first meeting, all information gained from the client is charted in an initial timeline of the story, and a logical sequence diagram is created.

The client says the renter is always complaining about the apartment and has wanted to break her lease for several months. The client also says the renter is clumsy and fell because she was not paying attention to where she was going, not because the steps were slippery.

For the purpose of the LSD, the paralegal should note the time of day the fall occurred, the day of the week on which it occurred, and what the client claims the weather conditions were when it occurred. See Figure 10-3.

Logical Sequence Diagram   The logical sequence diagram allows the legal team to review the client's story and pinpoint what is missing or problematic. The paralegal creates this diagram while the attorney develops the cause of action or defense best fitting the fact scenario presented by the client. When the paralegal and attorney meet later with their separate data (i.e., LSD and legal theory), the attorney decides whether to take the case and what investigation should be started. For the hypothetical slip-and-fall case, the diagram details the client's definitive statements about the fall and the renter, all of which must be supported by evidence. For example, the condition of the steps and sidewalk on the morning of the fall will be an issue; evidence is required to prove that there was no ice on the steps and therefore no neglect or negligence on the part of the owner/client. The following information also requires investigation:

- Look at the data on Dec. 17th at 7:57: the client says the renter walked away from the fall when the client arrived, saying she was fine.
- Now look at the data on Dec. 21st at 10:30: the renter claims that she broke her ankle and missed several days of work due to the accident.

It is obvious that the extent of the renter's injury must be investigated.

Figure 10-3
Logical sequence
diagram

Day of the Week	Date	Time of Day	Description of Event
Tuesday	Dec. 17, 1997	7:45 A.M.	Renter leaves the building; it is clear and cold outside.
		7:48 A.M.	Renter steps off the second of four steps and slips and falls. Renter injures left ankle and wrist.
		7:50 A.M.	A second tenant finds the first renter lying on the ground, in pain. The injured renter cannot get up. The uninjured tenant calls the owner/client.
		7:57 A.M.	The owner/client arrives at the scene. The injured renter is up and moving around. The sidewalk is clear and salted, no ice is present. The second tenant (uninjured) leaves for work. The injured renter says she is fine and goes to the parking lot to leave for work. The client re-salts the steps.
Saturday	Dec. 21, 1997	10:30 A.M.	The injured renter calls the client and says she has missed work since she fell, because of a fractured ankle and sprained wrist. She wants the client to pay the medical bills.
		12:00 P.M.	The client contacts his insurance agent about his liability coverage and the injured renter.
		2:45 P.M.	The insurance agent calls back and tells the client he is covered for the injuries the renter sustained, but he does not have coverage against any negligence claims the renter may file for the allegedly unmaintained steps and sidewalk.

Figure 10-3
(*continued*)

Day of the Week	Date	Time of Day	Description of Event
Monday	Dec. 23, 1997	8:00 A.M.	The renter informs the client that she is breaking her lease because of the poorly maintained steps/sidewalk and their dangers. The client tells the renter he will keep the security deposit and pursue full payment of the remainder of the lease if she breaks the lease.
		1:00 P.M.	The client contacts the law firm and schedules an appointment for possible representation.
Friday	Jan. 23, 1998	9:30 A.M.	The initial client interview is conducted.

Proximate Probability The LSD also helps the paralegal identify witnesses and evidence by a means known, for purposes of this text, as **proximate probability**. This theory is applied to case scenarios to locate people and/or evidence logically involved in a specific event. Proximate probability points to people and evidence that would, could, or should be able to provide details or otherwise figure in the investigation. Thus, it encourages expansion of the investigation.

In the slip-and-fall case, one such witness is the second tenant who showed up immediately after the fall. Other witnesses could include other tenants in the building who used the same doorway and stairs where the fall happened, specifically on the morning of December 17th. The LSD may also suggest to the paralegal that the injured renter's co-workers are potential witnesses, because they could or should have seen the injured renter after the accident. Additionally, guests of tenants at the apartment complex, mail carriers, delivery persons, utility employees servicing the building, and others using the building regularly will be important potential witnesses, as they can testify to any ongoing safety precautions on the steps. Any potential witness may provide support for the client's claim that the steps in question were safe on December 17, 1997, and the day just prior to the accident.

Other witnesses located by means of the proximate probability process include persons having information about weather conditions, building codes, and/or previous lawsuits at the complex. There will probably be credibility or character witnesses for both the client and the renter. Each potential witness may provide base information for the case and, possibly, mitigating circumstances in favor of the client. **Mitigating circumstances** are those "surrounding the commission of an act, which in fairness can be considered as extenuating or reducing the severity or degree of moral culpability of the act, but do not serve to excuse or justify it." The information provided by these witnesses is referred to in this text as **collateral evidence**.

Collateral Evidence Of the types of evidence identified by proximate probability, most is collateral evidence, providing secondary proof of a primary principle. Any type of evidence that supports or improves a client's position or claims can be considered collateral evidence. For example, the lease contract is collateral evidence in the slip-and-fall case because it relates to three separate points of dispute:

- It contains provisions regarding the renter's ability to break her lease.
- It provides guidelines for negligence claims against the owner/client.
- It defines the owner/client's position if the renter terminates the lease and the client decides to **counterclaim** for breach of contract.

A *counterclaim* is a counteraction by the defendant against the plaintiff once the plaintiff has initiated a civil suit. It is not an answer to the original complaint, but a new and independent cause of action.

Primary Evidence Primary, or material evidence directly supports the legal issues of a case. For example:

- Weather reports for the morning of the accident (or even the days prior to the accident) may help prove the condition of the steps on the morning of the fall.
- Photographs taken at the time of the accident or in the general time frame of the accident may provide visual proof of the condition of the steps.
- Police reports may provide details of the accident, if the injured party contacted them.
- Medical reports may provide specific data on the severity of the renter's injury and future injury-related problems.

Creativity is needed to find proximate probability sources of primary evidence. For the slip-and-fall case, primary evidence includes weather reports showing there was no snow and consequently no failure to remove snow, and building codes showing that the steps were safe by city standards.

A tremendous amount of information and investigative work is generated from the LSD, which is developed from the client's original story. New details are uncovered as the LSD is applied to other portions of the client's story (such as the renter's history at the apartment complex and previous apartment complexes). Ultimately, the client's story is expanded by the details uncovered, which concentrate on smaller parts of the overall story and are used to create alternative diagrams.

Alternative Diagrams Diagrams similar to the LSD can be created for information on the peripheral parts of the event being investigated. In the slip-and-fall case, this might include the renter's history at the apartment complex and other complexes. An LSD can be used to diagram the client's history of owning, renting, and managing apartments, or for help in forming a picture of the steps, sidewalk, parking lot, and surrounding areas where the fall occurred. Separate diagrams can eventually be brought together to provide a complete picture of the accident. The paralegal should remember that the purpose of these diagrams is to "see" the details of the event and the persons making up the event. See Figures 10-4, 10-5, and 10-6 for examples of alternative diagrams.

Once data like that described in Figures 10-4, 10-5, and 10-6 has been gathered, a more complete sequence of events is developed, and problems in the client's and adversary's stories appear. Additionally, the paralegal may use this very detailed description to prepare interview outlines and questions for witnesses, and to create drawings of the event to be used as exhibits at trial.

RENTER'S HISTORY

Place of Abode	Time at Location	Details
Garden Apartments 1234 Main St. Gardenville, MN Owner: our client (basement apartment, #5; south side of building)	May 1994 to present	Injured renter leases apartment alone. She has no record of late rent payments and is thought of as quiet. She has made some complaints about the other tenants. She would have preferred an apartment on the other side of the complex. She regularly calls for maintenance work on the apartment and is picky about the quality of services offered at the complex (e.g., quiet and clean laundry facilities, swimming pool area, security system).
Hilltop Condominiums 1589 Sierra View Gardenville, MN Owner: Jim Nesbitt	October 1991– May 1994	Renter shared unit with one other person (Sharon Murphy) for first two years in condo. The co-renter moved after a disagreement with the renter in May 1993. When this happened the renter tried to break her lease and leave. After being threatened with a breach-of-contract suit by the owner, the renter decided to stay. The remaining lease term of one year ended in May 1994, when she moved to Garden Apartments. The owner, Nesbitt, said the renter was difficult.

Figure 10-4 This alternative diagram deals with the renter's leasing history.

OWNER'S HISTORY

Date	Description of History
July 1989 to present	Client has owned and managed the Garden Apartments for over six years. During that time he has owned two other properties in Gardenville, but does not manage them on site. He makes all final decisions at the three properties. The client has had many dealings with the renter regarding maintenance problems, the location of her apartment, and noise problems. The client is firm in his dealings with this renter and all other tenants. He responds promptly to all requests or complaints by tenants. He lives on the property and does most of the snow removal himself. He says it is standard procedure to salt all the steps and sidewalks and claims that he keeps the parking lots clear of snow. As a standard procedure, he salts all the stairs and sidewalks around midnight, to ensure safety early in the morning. The client admits to having exchanged words with the renter on other occasions when he felt the renter was being unrealistic and demanding. The client has also had problems with other tenants, but claims that these problems involve noise and disturbance issues.

Figure 10-5   This alternative diagram focuses on the client's previous history.

PHYSICAL DESCRIPTIONS

Area	Description
Sidewalk	There are four sidewalks leading out of the building at the Garden Apartments where the injured renter lives. The sidewalks are 3 feet wide and approximately 20 feet long, leading to the curb and parking lot areas or a sidewalk that circles the perimeter of the building. There are four steps leading down from the building to the sidewalk. These steps have wrought-iron hand railings, which are firmly attached to the steps. The steps are 36 inches wide and 8 high. These are all standard according to the city code.
Parking Lot	The parking lots are located on three sides of the building: east, west, and south. Garages line the outside perimeter of the parking lot. Parking spaces for guests and tenants who do not rent garages are located directly across the parking lot from the garages and line the curb, which is parallel to the sidewalk. According to at least six tenants, the parking spaces are regularly filled, making it difficult to cross the parking lot from the curb in slippery conditions.
Surrounding Areas	There is a grassy area next to each sidewalk leading from the building to the parking lot, which is sometimes used for walking when the sidewalks are slick. There are no hand rails along any of the sidewalks.

Figure 10-6   This alternative diagram focuses on the physical property at the apartment complex where the renter fell.

A visual display of the events is almost always useful. Information detailed in the LSD and alternative diagrams commonly sparks investigative ideas as well. A concluding diagram can also be created, putting together all of the old and new data (see Figure 10-7).

Thus, a story is built with the logical sequence procedure, always encouraging greater detail and generating more information for the attorney to use. Case strengths and weaknesses can also be identified thereby.

CONCLUDING DIAGRAM

Day of the Week	Date	Time of the Day	Description of What Happened
	June 1997		Renter (who is later injured) wants to move from currently rented apartment in Garden Apts. because she does not like living on the south side of the building. There are no empty units now and the client/owner says she will have to wait. The renter and owner exchange words. Renter makes several phone calls thereafter for various maintenance problems with her apt. The renter wants to break her lease. Owner says no.
Tuesday	Dec. 17, 1997	7:45 A.M.	Renter leaves her building from the north entrance. It is cold. She goes down the first 2 of 4 steps and then falls. She is not holding onto the hand rail. The client salted the stairs at midnight, almost 8 hours earlier.
	Dec. 17, 1997	7:50 A.M.	Second tenant finds the injured renter on the north steps, sitting next to the hand railing.
	Dec. 17, 1997	7:57 A.M.	Client/owner arrives. The injured renter is up and holding onto the hand rail. There are salt stains on the injured renter's pants and salt is still on the steps from midnight. The second tenant leaves, going down the sidewalk to his car parked in one of the garages on the south side of the parking lot. The injured renter goes to her car in the south parking lot, via the sidewalk. She does not having a garage. Client and renter are not friendly and do not communicate well during this meeting.

Figure 10-7   A concluding diagram ties together all the information displayed in the previous subdiagrams.

Physical Evidence

When the LSD is completed, the paralegal begins identifying the physical evidence needed and deciding how to gather it. In civil and criminal law, **real and physical** are used synonymously to describe a type of evidence. Physical evidence is evidence that is demonstrative in nature and not witness testimony; physical evidence can be touched, inspected, and handled. The bumper of a smashed car and a lease agreement are physical evidence. When the paralegal reviews information in a case, he is looking for physical or other evidence required to prove and support a cause of action or defense.

Gathering Evidence   One of the most important purposes of the investigation is to decide what physical evidence is available, where it might be, and what must be done to obtain it. Physical evidence is critical to the success of the investigation, which is why it ranks so high on the six basic strategies list. Understanding the client's problem is the paralegal's primary goal early in the investigation; then he begins finding and obtaining evidence to support the case. In the initial client interview, or when talking with a witness, the paralegal asks for any documents, pictures, or other physical evidence concerning the events being described. In the slip-and-fall example, the paralegal investigating the case asks the client to provide a copy of the renter's lease at the initial interview, along with any repair records for the property.

Once he has identified physical evidence, the paralegal decides how to obtain it. The avenues available for gathering physical evidence fall into four broad categories:

1. Public records—usually obtained by written request, but sometimes by personally going to the agency in possession of the records and asking for a copy. Some records can even be requested by telephone.

2. Private records—authorization from the client or opposing party is needed to receive copies of these documents. Examples of private records are medical records, employment records, and Social Security records.

3. Formal discovery—interrogatories, requests for production of documents, depositions with a subpoena duces tecum, etc.

4. Traditional "private detective" methods of gathering evidence—visiting the scene of the accident or event and taking pictures, talking with potential witnesses, and so on.

All these methods of identifying and obtaining physical evidence should be used throughout the investigation.

Organizing Evidence   Charting or diagramming is necessary during the collection of evidence, to ensure competency and completeness. An evidence chart is easy to make and provides the paralegal and attorney with ready reference to the evidence and its status, uses, and location. After evidence is identified, the paralegal prepares to receive the evidence, at which time he drafts an evidence chart like that shown in Figure 10-8.

Figure 10-8
Evidence chart

EVIDENCE CHART
Owner v. Injured Renter

Evidence	Purpose (Location)	Received From
Lease contract	Use: breach-of-contract case (in office vault)	Provided by client on 1/23/98
Photographs of steps and sidewalk	Shows scene and condition of steps, show lack of negligence on client's part (in office vault)	Taken 3/98 at 4:30 P.M. By Nick George, paralegal
Building code	Verifies status of steps at time of accident (in office vault)	Copied from city clerk's office 2-15-98
Medical records on plaintiff	Shows preexisting ankle condition and lack of injury from fall (kept in file)	Received from Mercy Hospital, Gardenville Clinic, and Jerry Walker Family Clinic (dates vary)

Storing and Preserving Physical Evidence

When a paralegal is dealing with physical evidence, he uses the utmost care to protect it. Once an original piece of evidence is obtained, there is no other. For example, an original stock certificate or prospectus in a security fraud case is a one-of-a-kind document; losing it could mean losing the case. *Original evidence* includes more than an "original" contract or stock certificate. It can mean a one-of-a-kind photograph of a totaled vehicle before a salvage company destroyed it, or a photograph of a bush blocking the view of a railroad crossing before it was cut down. The Federal Rules of Evidence require that parties produce original documentation if the authenticity of a duplicate is in question, or if it would be unfair to admit a duplicate into evidence.

Guard photographs and other physical evidence to ensure their integrity and value. The level of responsibility placed on the paralegal for the collection and preservation of all evidence is tremendous.

Methods of Preservation   What methods of preservation are available for physical evidence? The answer is as open-ended as the types and varieties of possible physical evidence. There are many ways to store and preserve evidence, but a few methods are fairly standard. It is quite common in big-document cases—cases that focus on great volumes of documents as evidence—for the paralegal to Bates stamp all documents received and produced (that is, to stamp each page of evidence with a unique, consecutive number). Once the documents have been numbered, they are reviewed and summarized. The summaries provide the legal team with a synopsis of the individual documents, where the documents came from, and their value to the case. Particular documents that will be used as evidence, or that will greatly influence the case, are pulled from the general body of documents. They are then copied for work use, returned to the group of original documents, logged on an evidence sheet, and placed in a safe environment. A safe environment does not necessarily mean the paralegal's or attorney's office; it might be a vault, safe, or other designated location. Refer to Chapter 8 for examples of organizational tools appropriate to evidence management.

Coverings and Copying   Some documents require protective coverings, like plastic, to keep them from being stained, faded, or damaged. Paralegals should educate themselves on the types of plastics used for document protection, to avoid using a covering that may damage or destroy a document. Acid-free paper and coatings should be used when storing photographs, to prevent the photos from sticking to anything, fading, or otherwise deteriorating. In many metropolitan areas, there are private businesses that specialize in the care and preservation of litigation documents; it is useful to know where these companies are located, what they will do, and how they charge. In reality, the paralegal will not only hire this vendor, but will also supervise the copying of documents, along with a paralegal working for the producing party, to ensure the safety and confidentiality of the documents. This is commonly done when neither party wants full responsibility for the copying of sensitive material.

Document Integrity   Another category of protection applies to paper documents, dealing with the integrity of the paper itself. In some jurisdictions, for example, a document will not be admitted into evidence if it has been drawn on, colored or highlighted, or punched with holes. These are but a few examples of the many rules governing the handling of evidence.

As a standard rule, never disturb the original condition of a document without specific instruction from an attorney. It is also a good practice, when instructed to violate an original document's integrity, to check with a court administrator or law clerk to identify the judge handling the case and verify what rules or standards that judge uses to govern paper evidence. If the judge has specific conditions for documents to be submitted to the court as evidence, notify the attorney before continuing with the task.

A primary function of the paralegal is to continually research the particular standards of individual judges, courts, and jurisdictions for this specific data. This knowledge helps the attorney and paralegal avoid critical errors.

Nonpaper Evidence   When dealing with physical evidence other than documents (such as a ladder, artificial limb, or car bumper), different types of organization and protection are required. In these instances, the paralegal may need to make special arrangements with a storage company to seal evidence and protect it from theft or fire damage. Any number of things can happen to evidence once it is beyond the control of the paralegal or attorney, so diligent effort must be made to protect all evidence.

Evidence Management   To handle special evidence properly, the legal team must develop a document log. If something accidentally destroys or damages original evidence, the document log offers support for the admission of replacement evidence. It may also help establish a chain of custody. Paralegals may be directly responsible for handling physical evidence, and are accountable to the attorney for lost or damaged evidence.

EXAMPLE

A paralegal is assigned to a case involving a stepladder. The client fell off the ladder while using it. The client claims that the ladder company did not give proper instructions and precautions for using the ladder, and that is why he fell and injured himself. Clearly, the portion of the ladder that contains usage instructions and precautions must be carefully maintained, along with the rest of the ladder, even if the ladder was damaged at the time of the client's fall.

The client was using the ladder to reach the gutters on his home. He stood the ladder on four cement blocks, one under each foot of the ladder. The cement blocks will also be needed as physical evidence. The assessment of the physical evidence is relatively easy, but collecting and storing the evidence may not be so simple. The first problem is the ladder: the client did not bring the case to the law office until six months after the accident, and he used the ladder several times during that period. The original integrity of the ladder is in question, because the ladder is not exactly as it was on the day of the accident and the instructions on the side of the ladder have been worn down with use.

The body of the ladder appears to have been weakened by inappropriate use. The paralegal must store the ladder so that its condition (its integrity) is maintained. He will also need to locate an identical new ladder, to replicate the client's use of the original ladder at the time of the accident.

The cement blocks present yet another problem. They have remained in the ground since the time of the accident. The paralegal is faced with several questions about the blocks: Should the blocks be left in the ground where they were at the time of the accident, and pictures or videotape be taken of them? Should the blocks be removed and used in a simulation of the ground on the day of the accident, so that the jury can estimate their stability at the time of the accident?

These questions will be answered by the attorney, but the paralegal must execute the attorney's instructions. Thus, the paralegal will need to be adequately prepared to gather and preserve the evidence. The blocks, ladder, and instructions all have to be evaluated by the attorney once they have been gathered, so the items must be handled gently.

Both the original and replica ladders must be stored somewhere, in the law office or another appropriate location, where they will not be used. Both ladders will have to be flagged as evidence, especially if they are kept in the office, to avoid accidental use. Photographs of the original ladder should be taken as supporting evidence, showing that the ladder was not tampered with during storage. Evidence photographs should always be taken with a camera that prints the date and time of day on the photograph.

Standard Procedures   Standard methods for handling evidence, though useful, should be individualized for each case; the paralegal should first think about the evidence and potential problems. By routinely using standard handling procedures for all evidence, the paralegal may jeopardize a unique piece of evidence.

EXAMPLE ───────────────────────────────────────

Some types of artwork and photographs should only be stored in temperature-controlled environments. The law office vault, which is the standard holding location for evidence, may destroy the evidence rather than preserve it; too much humidity or heat in the vault can damage delicate or unusual evidence. By evaluating each piece of physical evidence for vulnerability, the paralegal ensures its safety during storage.

There are many opportunities, whether through professional seminars or literature, for paralegals and attorneys to increase their knowledge of evidence storage and preservation methods. The paralegal should seek any available chance to learn more about specialized procedures for storing and preserving evidence.

Identifying Witnesses

Witness identification is an important part of the investigation that helps to expand the client's story with extra details. To begin this task, the paralegal does two things:

- Asks the client for a list of witnesses.
- Uses the LSD to identify unknown witnesses.

All witnesses, especially those identified by the client early in the case, are used as a source for identifying other witnesses, via the investigative interview. The idea behind the LSD is to create a timeline, based on the client's details of the event, that helps to display the strengths and weaknesses of the story being told. This helps to identify **credibility witnesses** and **evidence witnesses**. For purposes of this text, a *credibility witness* is a person who testifies regarding the good or bad characteristics of another person; such a witness is used to lay a foundation either for or against a party in the lawsuit or another witness in the case. An *evidence witness* testifies about details of the case or about physical evidence. For example, an evidence witness may testify to the time he saw a defendant enter or leave a building.

By reviewing the LSD, the paralegal drafts a list of witnesses who fall into one of these two broad categories. The parties, people known to have been at the scene of an accident or triggering event, police and other emergency personnel, spouses, children, employees of a business, and other persons can all be identified via the LSD and the client's supporting evidence (contract, photographs, insurance proposals, fire report, etc.). Additional documents not provided by the client (police report, ambulance report, etc.) also provide witness information.

Credibility Witnesses   Locating credibility witnesses involves reviewing the story diagram and developing a mental picture of the parties involved and the triggering event. Once the paralegal has a picture of the event in his mind, he asks himself, "Who could, should, or would be able to offer character testimony?" In the slip-and-fall case, the injured renter's previous landlord and other tenants would be the first such witnesses to consider.

EXAMPLE

While interviewing the person who lives in the apartment above the injured renter's, the paralegal discovers that the injured renter was unhappy with the landlord because he refused to give her a new apartment. The interviewee says the injured renter wanted an apartment on the second floor facing the north, the opposite of the direction she currently faces. At a recent party in the apartment complex lounge, the injured renter told this interviewee that she would do anything to get back at the landlord and get the apartment she wanted, including breaking her lease. This information can be used to develop testimony in support of the theory that the injured renter is fabricating her claim in an effort to break her lease.

The paralegal should always remember, when identifying witnesses, that each witness has the potential to lead him to yet another witness. He should always ask each witness for the names, addresses, and telephone numbers of anyone else who may have information.

Once the witnesses have been identified, the paralegal prepares a witness table to manage the information. See Figure 10-9.

Figure 10-9
Witness data
table

WITNESS TABLE

Name of Witness	Phone Number	Address	Connection
Mary Richards	555-8907	1234 Main St., Apt. 1B	Friend of renter; may support our idea that renter wanted to break the lease and was not really hurt.
Sheila Friske	555-0032	567 Walnut	UPS delivery worker; regularly delivers to the complex using the south entrance; was there the morning of the fall.
Tony Ginger	555-9898	1234 Main St., Apt. 2B	He found the renter the morning of the fall.
Jim Nesbitt	567-3412	1589 Sierra View	Previous landlord of injured renter; she may have been a problem renter for him.

Interviewing Witnesses   After reviewing the data in the witness data table with the attorney and client, a strategy is developed and a priority list created regarding which witnesses will be contacted first, and why. The paralegal closely follows the priority list, because story details accumulate as each interview is conducted. The order in which information is gathered can be critical. A primary goal of this strategy is to avoid re-interviewing a witness who does not wish to be involved in the case. Preparation and forethought are the keys to success. If there is any indication that a witness does not want to talk, the paralegal should interview that witness last. By doing so, the paralegal will already have collected a reasonably complete set of details, which can be used to draft an interview outline and thereby avoid the need for a second interview in light of any newly discovered information. Some witnesses must be interviewed first; their identities will normally be quite obvious. Once these special, primary witnesses have been located and interviewed, the interview strategy just described should be employed.

The paralegal should not be surprised, after starting the interviews, if questions regarding the existing LSD develop. When this happens (and it should happen frequently), the paralegal knows he is gaining valuable data and expanding the investigation, and should verify the expanded details by contacting previously interviewed witnesses and probing their knowledge of the new details. This should be done whenever two or more witnesses disagree on details. After reviewing any new data with the client, the paralegal may have to draft a new LSD that allows better management of the expanded story.

The process of contacting and interviewing witnesses can be long and difficult. Witnesses work and have other commitments that can make them hard to reach. It is not uncommon for the paralegal to work during evening hours or weekends when interviewing witnesses, and he should prepare ahead for such demands. The paralegal must accommodate the witnesses as much as possible to keep them cooperative—unhappy witnesses are not helpful!

Witness Reports   After each witness is interviewed, the paralegal drafts a **witness report**. Witness reports detail the information provided by each witness, strengths and weaknesses of the story and the witness, and any other attributes deemed appropriate. The paralegal should include personal feelings on the witness's overall credibility, the witness's motivation for being involved in the case, and any problems perceived with the witness. He must also include where the witness can be reached (at any time). The location of the witness, whether it be home, work, or somewhere else, is important for the service of subpoenas or other court papers as the litigation progresses. The attorney receives a witness report after each interview and gets the information again in a combined form when all witnesses have been interviewed. The paralegal uses the reports as a medium to share with the attorney any thoughts he has on which witnesses best support (or damage) the client and why. Witness reports are used as preparation material for trial and deposition; they can help the paralegal refresh the witness's memory or be used to challenge her honesty. By far, the witness reports are one of the most valuable investigation tools for the legal team.

Developing Leads

The development of leads is an ongoing process in the investigation, for both attorney and paralegal. The paralegal's role in lead development is different from the attorney's. The job of the paralegal is to uncover the details of the case story and find information relating to the attorney's legal theory, which helps (or hinders) the attorney in proving the client's story. The paralegal is sometimes asked to look at the client's story from a number of different angles, as a jury might. The attorney will be doing this too, but the paralegal often tests these other viewpoints in hopes of finding and using evidence supporting the attorney's theory. The attorney reviews the different points of view developed by the paralegal and decides which is the strongest and best supports the objectives.

The development of leads depends on each of the steps used in the investigation strategy, just as the investigation depends on the development of leads. The development of leads is directly related to witness interviews, but it is equally related to the collection of relevant evidence.

Collecting Documents   When any investigation begins, the primary goal is to find out what happened and why. Once the story has been told, it must be supported by evidence. In the majority of cases, some types of paper documents will be used as evidence, whether a lease, an accident report, a stock certificate, or other document. There is a virtually endless list of documents that may be used in litigation, and a wide variety of documents and reports are available to legal teams.

Some reports and documents are private and must be obtained through discovery, following the Federal Rules of Civil Procedure. Generally, the parties must meet and plan for required disclosures and discovery, before formal discovery can actually commence.[2] For private records, the paralegal must obtain authorizations from the party (whichever that may be) before documents can be collected. Because a superior investigation is demonstrated by attention to detail, and physical evidence can disappear very quickly, the collection of reports and documents must be expedient.

When reports and documents are public rather than private, no authorization is needed, and the paralegal can obtain the material without the express knowledge or consent of the opposing party. Some public records custodians do require written requests, so the timeline for receiving these documents can be long. For example, when a paralegal is looking for licensing information on a vehicle, he makes a written request to the motor vehicle department in the appropriate state to receive a listing of title and licensing information; he may even access some of this data via the Internet. The only problem is that government agencies are often slow to respond to written requests. This is why the paralegal must act quickly, in the early stages of the investigation, to begin gathering reports and documents. A more detailed discussion on records requests and authorizations appears later in this chapter.

Creating the Chronology and Timeline

The *chronology* is a timeline encompassing all of the client's and witnesses' information and all data gathered from evidence. Begin developing this as soon as information is available, but keep it separate from the client-specific LSD.

⚖ TIMELINES AND CHRONOLOGIES

The chronology and timeline are essentially the same thing as the LSD discussed earlier in this chapter. The chronology is the most comprehensive tool of the three, because it is a detailed listing of all facts and information gathered from all sources. The timeline is a listing of a single witness's description of the story events or details. Like the LSD, the chronology and timeline are used to set the details of a story out on paper for review and investigation. The critical differences among the chronology, timeline, and LSD is that the chronology is developed over time and encompasses the entire fact scenario; the timeline focuses on one specific witness; and the LSD focuses on the client's story. All three tools include supporting and damaging evidence, testimony, and facts.

Timelines

The paralegal uses the timeline to place a witness's narrative story in a logical, sequential order. This is necessary because a witness or client may not tell a story in the exact order it happened, without a little help. A witness may refrain from telling everything that happened because, in the heat of the interview, he forgot it; or he may simply not realize that the information he was withholding is important. A timeline also gives a visual reminder of the events for both the witness and the paralegal. The paralegal drafts a timeline by writing down the details the witness gives, in the order they are given, and comparing them to the client's details recorded in the LSD. He is thus able to see what makes sense and what information needs more clarification during the interview. See Figure 10-10.

When drafting a timeline, the paralegal heads the document with the name of the witness, the case, and the date. When applicable, he identifies the sources of any evidence uncovered during the interview.

Using the data from Figure 10-10, the paralegal develops a time sequence of the events described, to create a precise timeline. He needs to know:

Figure 10-10
A chart-style timeline

Green v. Brown **Juanita Hidalgo** **11/17/98**	
Detail 1	**Detail 2**
Red car is headed toward the light really fast; light turns yellow. The driver taps the breaks.	White car goes to the corner to turn right, stops for a second, and turns on the red light.

- Where the red car was in relationship to the white car when the white car got to the intersection.
- Does the witness know how long the "second" really was that the white car stopped before entering the intersection?
- Does the witness know how long the light for the red car had been yellow?
- Does the witness know if the light turned from yellow to red before the red car came into the intersection?
- Was the witness watching the white car or the red car at the time of the accident?
- How long had the witness been at the corner before the accident?
- Where did the witness come from?
- How long does it take to get to the corner from where the witness was coming from?
- Does the witness use this crosswalk often? If so, how often?
- If the witness uses the crosswalk often, were the street lights working properly that day?
- If not, what was different?
- At any time prior to, during, or shortly after these events, did the witness look at her watch for a time reference?

Witnesses usually attempt to give as much detail as possible during interviews; however, witnesses may not always think in a logical time pattern. In the rush to tell all he knows during the interview, a witness may inadvertently leave out some important details. All questions developed for the example, in response to the data in Figure 10-10, must be answered; but when and how they are answered must be carefully planned by the paralegal, to obtain the most complete timeline possible. Creating and following the interview outline aids the paralegal in making those decisions.

Timelines promote the organization of a witness's data. Without a timeline, the paralegal wastes a lot of time wading through interview notes in an effort to draft the witness report. The timeline also helps stimulate the witness's memory. When the paralegal designs a timeline and asks questions relating to it, the witness is forced to focus on specific events, which helps her remember details that might otherwise be neglected. The expansion of details through memory stimulation also produces more details. A method called **backtracking** is used during timeline development to trace the witness's memory and activities when recalling an event. For example, when someone loses his car keys, he retraces his activities and whereabouts (either physically or mentally) for a specific amount of time to locate the last moment he had the keys.[3] This same method works with the witness and the story she tells. While backtracking the event in memory, the witness may "find" other items she lost (pieces of the story), even if she did not realize they were missing. By guiding a witness with backtracking questions, it is possible to uncover details that neither the paralegal nor the witness realized could influence the event. It is also quite possible that backtracking will help the paralegal identify additional witnesses. Once the paralegal has accumulated a list of events in the timeline, he can thoroughly explore the witness's story and develop a plan for further investigation.

Timeline as a Tool The timeline is a powerful tool in the investigation, allowing the investigator to draw inferences about an event, witness, or party in the case. As important as the timeline is for evaluation, it is even more important at trial. Logically speaking, people tend to think in sequence; for instance, when asked how his day was, a person usually begins thinking from morning till evening. It simply makes sense to think in this manner and to dictate the story a witness tells in the same manner. When a witness is asked to recall a series of events in sequential order, she is being asked to perform or behave in a natural and nonthreatening way. It is comfortable to think in sequence, so the witness usually responds to requests for such information with greater cooperation. It is this same sensibility that makes the timeline valuable to a jury: juries are much more receptive to a clear picture of an event.

Conducting the Timeline Interview Questioning during the timeline interview is the skill most critical to the success of the interview. Once the LSD is created, the paralegal may approach witness interviews too zealously, focusing too closely on specifics. This is a natural tendency—after all, the paralegal is an advocate for the client and has a good idea of the information that will help the client's position. However, the paralegal must refrain from asking pointed, narrow questions early in the investigation. It is not until the creation of the chronology that specifics are requested. General narratives and open responses offer many avenues for finding specifics that would never be uncovered by closed questions. There is no way to develop a complete story and a chronology or timeline without allowing the witness to freely narrate his experiences surrounding a particular event.

After the interview, the story has to be evaluated. The paralegal can, if necessary, conduct a second interview to clear up any problems or gaps discovered in the course of the evaluation. When the gaps are very small, the paralegal may contact the witness by phone and ask about the missing details. The rapport developed with the witness during the first interview increases the likelihood that the witness will disclose previously withheld information during the second inquiry. Interviewers seek to maintain quality in all conversations with witnesses. A witness may conceal information if overly specific questions are asked before a relationship or rapport has been developed between the interviewer and interviewee. The best strategy in the timeline interview is: Stop, Look, and Listen to the witness.

Chronologies

When developing the chronology, the paralegal merges all of the data from the witness timelines and the LSD to create a full, complete story.

AUTHORIZATIONS AND RECORDS REQUESTS

Many types of **authorizations** are used in litigation, including the medical authorization, Social Security authorization, and employment records authorization. The purpose of the authorization is to allow each party access to the personal and private records of the plaintiff in a lawsuit. Often the defendant may have records that the plaintiff needs to establish a legal cause of action or rebuttal theory. Whatever the reason, the receiving party is seeking to obtain records dealing with the opposing party, either directly related to the cause of action in a civil suit or that may lead to collateral evidence. Authorizations are generally sought during the early stages of the litigation process.

It is a cumbersome and time-consuming process to gather authorizations, forward them to records custodians, and manage the records. See Figure 10-11 for a standard authorization.

As mentioned earlier, many different types of records can be obtained only by means of an authorization. The specific authorization shown in Figure 10-11 is used for medical records, but can be adapted to apply to personnel records, Social Security records, or unemployment records.

Certification

As a standard rule, the paralegal sends to the document provider (1) the authorization signed by the party releasing the information, (2) the request for the records, and (3) a **certification**. The certification is a formally signed, notarized document stating that the record holder has provided a complete and accurate copy of the entire file requested. In some states the requirements for certification are less stringent than in others; additionally, certain states use a "business records" affidavit to certify business records. In many jurisdictions the legal team will not be able to use records as evidence if the records have not been certified. Neglecting to get a certification is an error the paralegal cannot afford to make. Verify the need for certified records with the attorney before requesting any records.

The cost of certification varies from facility to facility and state to state. Some states have legislation that sets costs for retrieving, copying, and certifying records. These prices are periodically increased to track inflation, so stay updated on the costs of retrieving and copying records. Attorneys should be informed if problems arise in collecting information or if billings from records keepers are higher than expected. Figure 10-12 is a standard records request letter. Notice the last paragraph, which attempts to limit the cost of collecting records.

The second paragraph of the sample letter states that the records custodian should not provide records not generated by his or her own facility. This is necessary because the custodian has no authorization to release records from any other facility. For example, a hospital may (with proper authorization) release its own records; it may *not* release records belonging to its staff physicians, even if it has physical custody of those files. By demonstrating good faith in the

Figure 10-11

Patient authorization for release of private information

PATIENT AUTHORIZATION FOR RELEASE OF INFORMATION

Metro Clinic _____   Re: Mary Wilkins _____

1234 Main Street _____   Date of Birth: 8-27-31 _____

West Village, TX 75123 _____   Social Sec. #: XXX-XX-XXXX _____

This is your full and sufficient authorization, pursuant to (whatever state law applies), to release to (whatever law firm or agency is seeking the information), their representatives or employees, all medical information (including but not limited to that which involves treatment for alcohol or drug abuse, sickle cell anemia, or mental problems) maintained while I was a patient at your facility on any date, with the following exceptions: _____ (this can be used to place restrictions on the release of records, if any apply).

This information is needed for the purpose of pending litigation.

This authorization specifically includes records prepared prior to the authorization during the pendency of this proceeding (including claims and potential claims). I do not authorize re-release of this information by the third party.

I understand that I may revoke this consent in writing at any time, but that such revocation may adversely affect the course of the proceeding requiring these records. Upon the fulfillment of the above stated purpose, a photocopy of this authorization will be treated in the same manner as an original. Conversations by the bearer of this authorization with physicians are not authorized by this release form.

Dated: _____   _____
                                          Signature of Patient/Guardian

                                          _____
                                          Relationship to Patient

                                          _____
                                          Reason Patient Unable to Sign

ATTENTION PUBLIC FACILITIES: _____ state statute requires automatic expiration of this authorization one (1) year from date of authorization.

Figure 10-12
Standard records
request letter

Name of Provider _____

Address of Provider_____

Re: Patient Name: _____

      Date of Birth: _____

      Our File: _____

Dear Medical Records Custodian:

　　Enclosed is a medical authorization signed by __(name of the
patient)__. Please provide certified copies of all medical records and
narrative reports, including all correspondence, in your possession
relative to your care and treatment of __(name of patient)__. [Specify
particular dates if necessary, e.g., from 9-1-61 through 9-1-87.]

　　Please do not copy records from other facilities. However, on the
enclosed certification form, please list the names of the medical
facilities whose records are also in this patient's file. If for some
reason you do not send a complete copy of your facility's entire chart,
I would appreciate knowing your reason for doing so.

　　Please return these to our office within ten (10) working days.
Should this be a problem, please contact me. If the copying charges
for these records will exceed $50.00, please call me for prior approval.
Thank you for your prompt attention and cooperation in providing
these records.

Sincerely,

__[Paralegal's name]__
Paralegal

request and asking only for preapproved records, the paralegal maintains his integrity and ethics.

Notice that paragraph two requests the names of any other facilities for which the queried custodian holds records. If he receives the names of other providers, the paralegal can discover additional records, getting the appropriate authorizations and subsequent records through legitimate means.

Figure 10-13 is a standard certification that can be adapted to any type of records requested. Many government agencies prefer to use their own certification forms and thus will not use the one provided; it is irrelevant who provides the certification form, as long as one is properly completed.

Managing Requests

Once the process of gathering authorizations, records, and certifications has begun, the paralegal manages the records received. On occasion a provider may

Figure 10-13
Standard records
certification form
(accompanies all
records requests)

CERTIFICATION OF MEDICAL RECORDS

Date:_____

Re: _____
              Patient Name

_____
Date of Birth / Social Security Number

     I, _____, Custodian of Medical Records, do hereby
certify that the attached photographic copy of the medical records
covering the period from _____ has been compared
with the original on file and that the attached photographic copy is a
legible, true, and complete duplicate of said medical records.

     Further, I certify these are:

          _____   Complete copies of the patient's medical record.

          _____   Complete copies of specific parts of the patient's
                    medical record as requested. Specific parts are
                    listed below.

                    _____

                    _____

Further, I understand that this certification is made pursuant to <u>(give
name of appropriate state)</u> statute <u>(give appropriate state statute
number)</u> and I understand that these records will or may be used as
evidence in a court of law.

Records from other facilities in our possession but not sent:

_____   _____

_____   _____

                                     _____
                                     Record Custodian

                                     _____
                                     Medical Provider

                                     _____
                                     Address/Telephone Number

_____ x-rays included

lose a request, respond slowly, or decide not to respond at all; additional litigation procedures may be needed to obtain records that are being withheld. One method for handling this cumbersome task is to create a request management chart or tickler system. Figure 10-14 is an example of a medical records request tickler.

Use of authorizations and certifications is important to any investigation. Organizing and managing these requests and records is paramount to the success of the case. The success of any civil suit depends on evidence used to support each party's position, so the paralegal must develop tools to adequately manage that evidence. Becoming proficient in the use and management of records authorizations is a simple and practical method for initiating a thorough investigation.

Figure 10-14

Medical records tickler system, an organizational tool adaptable to any type of evidence management

Name of Patient: _____   Case no.:_____

Name of Case: _____

Date of Birth: _____

Name of Provider	Date of Request	Status	Date Records Received	Updated	Update
1.					
2.					

⚖ ETHICAL CONSIDERATIONS

When the paralegal undertakes the responsibilities of an investigation, he also agrees to conduct himself in a manner that reflects the attorney's ethical obligations. In every aspect of the paralegal's career, he will be faced with ethical dilemmas; during the course of an investigation, the paralegal may be confronted with situations that challenge his honesty, integrity, and professionalism. When dealing with the client, witnesses, records keepers, opposing counsel, and court personnel, the paralegal must constantly choose between honest and dishonest methods of obtaining data and evidence. In every situation the paralegal should remember these basic standard rules:

- Do not participate in the unauthorized practice of law.
- Do not threaten, lie to, or coerce a witness, records keeper, or the client.
- Do not suppress evidence or information.
- Keep all client confidences and secrets.

SUMMARY

- A plan for the investigation is created through an investigative outline.

- Conducting an investigation takes competence and organization, which are achieved by following the six basic investigative strategies: (1) diagram a logical sequence of events based on the client's story; (2) identify physical evidence; (3) store and preserve evidence; (4) identify witnesses, interview them, and prepare witness reports; (5) develop leads; (6) begin creating a chronology.

- The chronology is created over time and encompasses the entire fact scenario of the case. The chronology is more thorough than the witness timeline or LSD; it includes details and evidence from all parties and witnesses.

- The timeline is made up of all relevant details known by a single witness, placed in sequential order. It also helps a witness overcome memory problems.

ACTIVITIES

1. Clip an article from a local newspaper regarding a recent civil matter. After reading the article, create a logical sequence diagram of the details of the event as you imagine the client might have presented them. Be as specific as you would hope the client would be in real life. Develop an investigative outline. After you have developed the outline, practice questioning techniques and methods for developing questions for use with witnesses in the case.

2. Using the same article from exercise 1, chart the witnesses you would expect to locate using proximate probability. Specifically name what sources would lead you to the witnesses, and why.

3. Identify the evidence the LSD points to.

4. Create a chronology based on hypothetical information gathered from the witnesses, client, and any evidence gathered.

CASE STUDY

Smith v. Williams Construction

Consider the sample case, *Smith v. Williams Construction,* presented in this chapter. What information would you look for using the proximate probability process? How might this information influence your investigative outline? What details would you put in your logical sequence diagram based on what you were told? What inferences might you draw from this diagram?

NOTES

1 *See* Fed. R. Civ. P. 16(b); *see also* Fed. R. Civ. P. 26(f) (planning for discovery).

2 Fed. R. Civ. P. 26(d), (f).

3 David A. Binder & Paul Bergman, *Fact Investigation from Hypothesis to Proof* 265 (West, 1984). Used with permission of the West Publishing Corporation.

IDENTIFYING EVIDENCE

OBJECTIVES   After completing this chapter, you will know:

- A cause of action and its elements are the backbone of evidence identification. After developing an understanding of the many causes of action and their elements, the paralegal can drive the search for evidence by matching legal elements to facts.

- The damages in a civil case are used as a method of compensating a wrong done to another party. In relation to the search for evidence, the paralegal must assess the type of damages incurred and evaluate them, in order to find evidence to support or mitigate those damages.

- All evidence will fall into one of two broad categories, affirmative or rebuttal. Once classified as affirmative or rebuttal, the evidence is placed in one of four subcategories and then identified under a specific evidence category (such as circumstantial or direct).

- The term *fact* is the most widely used expression in investigation. Facts influence the usability of evidence and testimony, and they must be distinguished from opinion.

- The primary use of evidence is to prove facts. The paralegal needs to understand the many types and categories of evidence so she can apply evidence to the facts and support the causes of action and elements.

INTRODUCTION

Learning to identify evidence can be challenging, because it requires the paralegal to understand the case's cause(s) of action and its elements. In addition, the paralegal needs to understand the damages in the case. All three of these components point the paralegal in the direction of evidence, but are substantive in nature and depend on rules and laws for definition. Different types of evidence, used to support different types of damages and causes of action, require special consideration and understanding to be used properly.

After identifying the issues and assessing the damages, the paralegal separates the evidence into broad and specific categories. **Evidence** is commonly defined as "[a]ny kind of proof offered to establish the existence or nonexistence of a fact in dispute, e.g., testimony, writings, other material objects, demonstrations." Because the general definition of evidence is broad, evidence must be classified in descriptive categories, such as relevant and irrelevant, circumstantial and direct. In gaining an understanding of these descriptive categories of evidence, the paralegal equips herself with the knowledge needed to identify evidence.

CAUSES OF ACTION AND ELEMENTS

Before a case is accepted by a legal team, the attorney reviews the information on the triggering event and determines what causes of action are involved, in preparation for the investigation. Pleadings filed with the court must be based on a cause of action and supported by evidence proving the elements of the action. A **cause of action** is defined as "[t]he facts that give a person a right to judicial relief[; a] legally acceptable reason for suing." Therefore, a lawsuit is commonly called an *action*.

There are many types of civil actions, and each is based on some measure of duty or contractual obligation owed to the plaintiff (injured party) by the defendant. For every cause of action, there is a remedy—but to receive the right to use the remedy, the legal team must prove the action by satisfying the elements defining it.

The constituent parts of a cause of action that must be proved, if the plaintiff is to prevail, are called **elements**. Federal Rule of Civil Procedure 12(b) requires an action to be dismissed if the legal team fails to file a complaint that properly alleges all the elements of the relevant cause of action. The cause of action or defense provides the parameters for the investigation; the evidence supporting (or undermining) each element provides the proof.

What often complicates the breakdown of the elements in an action is the need to identify them. The paralegal is not responsible for defining the cause of action or elements in the case, but should be able to diagram or chart them in a way that will enhance the investigation and guarantee that all of the elements have evidentiary support. Consider the action of negligence and its elements and subelements (see Figure 11-1).

Negligence breaks down into four primary elements and then into subelements. In the diagram, "duty to use reasonable care" has been selected as the primary element for further review. As shown in Figure 11-1, to prove the

Figure 11-1
Visual breakdown of negligence cause of action and its elements

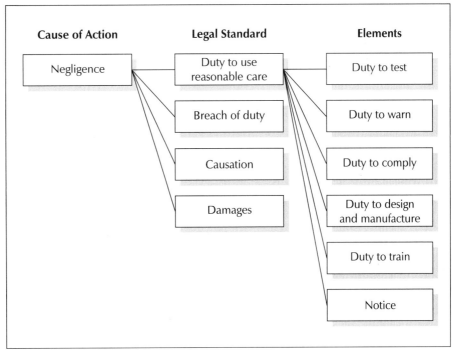

primary element of duty to use reasonable care, the legal team must find evidence demonstrating that the defendant either performed all of the subelements or did not (depending on the team's position). Evidence is sought to show that the required elements have or have not been met; this is done for each primary element and its subelements.

Primary Elements

The primary elements in Figure 11-1 are duty to use reasonable care, breach of duty, causation, and damages. Each element is investigated individually to prove the overall action of negligence. In some cases, elements such as causation and damages require nothing more than the presentation of undisputed facts (e.g., a car accident and subsequent injuries to the plaintiff). Other standards, such as reasonable care and breach of duty, require more investigation. In still other cases, all primary elements require in-depth investigation. Whatever the circumstances of the case, a diagram like that shown in Figure 11-1 is used for organization and focus, with the express purpose of uncovering facts and evidence.

Facts

The essential facts that are likely to affect the outcome of the case are **material facts**. Material facts directly relate to an issue in the case. After gaining an understanding of the cause of action and its elements, both primary and secondary, the paralegal begins converting elements into factual terms. Strive to find evidence that will prove facts and thus support substantive legal claims and elements. Do not seek *facts* that prove negligence—instead, seek evidence that proves facts. Proving facts is the goal, and the paralegal should list the elements to be proven in factual terms. To ensure that the investigation remains focused on the particulars of a specific case, tailor the substantive structure of the case to reflect its unique facts.

Matching Elements and Facts

Look again at negligence and its primary element, duty to use reasonable care (one of four primary elements). In Figure 11-1, the reasonable care element is further broken down into subelements, matching the facts of a particular triggering event in a case. In a car accident stemming from problems with antilock brakes, to prove negligence on the part of the automobile manufacturer, the legal team might identify evidence and where it is located by matching the elements to the facts. The conversion of elements to facts may look like the list in Figure 11-2.

Matching elements and facts can be less complicated when subelements are not needed. Consider a negligence case in which the action is against an individual accused of driving drunk and causing an injury. The new conversion might look like the chart in Figure 11-3.

In this second example, each element of negligence has been attached to a factual event, and there is no need to break down the primary elements. As

Figure 11-2
Conversion of case facts into a visual breakdown of legal elements

Element	Fact
1. Duty to test	Investigate the manufacturer's testing procedures for these vans. They are responsible for testing the safety of their product.
2. Duty to warn	The manufacturer has a duty to warn customers, at the time of purchase, of potential dangers. The manufacturer's literature on antilock brakes should provide evidence regarding this subelement.
3. Duty to comply	The manufacturer has a duty to comply with safety regulations set by the government and with industry standards. This can be investigated by gathering materials from regulating agencies.
4. Duty to design and manufacture	There is an inherent responsibility of the manufacturer to design and manufacture a vehicle that meets industry standards and that does not jeopardize the safety of consumers. This is done through quality control and other measures.
5. Duty to train	The manufacturer is obligated to train the car dealers to use the brakes so that they in turn will be able to train customers.
6. Notice	The manufacturer is obligated to provide adequate notice to consumers regarding safety defects or potential problems.

Figure 11-3
Conversion of a less complicated fact scenario into a breakdown of legal elements

Element	Fact
1. Reasonable care	Reasonableness need not be proven when someone exceeds the speed limit.
2. Breach of duty	The drunk driver breached her duty, as a licensed driver, to operate her car at the legal limit when she drove her car while under the influence of alcohol. She had a duty to protect others from this unwarranted risk.
3. Causation	The drunk driver was the proximate cause of the accident; while under the influence of alcohol, she carelessly drove her vehicle over the speed limit, thus causing the accident.
4. Damages	Damages are the death of the plaintiff; the serious injuries of the plaintiff's children; those sustained by the physical body of the vehicle; medical expenses; and emotional distress to the family.

these two fact examples show, some cases present greater challenges than others in matching factual happenings to elements. Finding evidence that answers the needs of some subelements may require more investigation. When a case presents special or complicated challenges in finding facts to support elements, it is helpful to add two new categories to the action/elements diagram: "sources of evidence" and "tools." A general method of charting an evidence search would now look like the example in Figure 11-4.

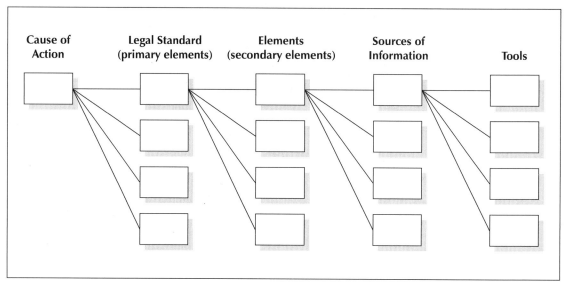

Figure 11-4   Detailed action/elements visual tool for a complex case

Sources of Evidence and Tools

Sources of evidence are sources of items or testimony believed to provide support for the primary and/or secondary elements in the case. Consider again the first accident scenario involving antilock brakes. The paralegal focuses on subelement 1, the "duty to test." In so doing, she develops a list of potential sources of evidence and the tools she will use to obtain the evidence. The charts shown in Figures 11-5 and 11-6 are samples of such lists. When creating this portion of the action/elements breakdown chart, the paralegal remembers that evidence tends to build from itself. For instance, if correspondence pertaining to the testing of antilock brakes is located during document production, common sense says that testing results and surveys must be somewhere. Using a common-sense approach in an evidence search is critical.

Finally, there are five causes of action whose elements all paralegals should know. Figure 11-7 outlines those actions and elements. A paralegal must take time to understand each of these and learn what evidence should be searched for when attempting to prove them.

Figure 11-5
Specific breakdown of evidence to support a single legal element

DUTY TO TEST	
Sources of evidence	**Tools**
Premarket testing materials	Interrogatories, Requests for production
Clinical testing materials	Requests for production
Study records	Requests for production
Correspondence regarding testing and adverse accidents	Requests for production
Postmarket analysis	Interrogatories, Requests for production

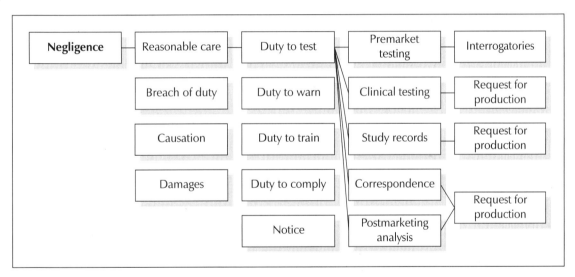

Figure 11-6 Fully detailed breakdown for one specific legal element

ASSESSING DAMAGES

Damages are "[m]onetary compensation that may be recovered in court by someone who has suffered injury or loss to person, to property, or to rights through an unlawful act or omission of another." When a person's legal rights have been violated, she may seek recovery of the damages incurred through civil litigation. The litigation process provides a means for determining the person's rights, to what extent she was damaged, and the nature of the damages; it also specifies a remedy for the loss.

Figure 11-7
The five most
common causes of
action and their
elements

Cause of Action	Primary Elements
Breach of contract	Prove there is a contract by meeting these standards: 1. Both parties are legally competent to enter into contract 2. A valid offer and acceptance resulted in a meeting of the parties' minds concerning the subject of the contract 3. An exchange of legal consideration occurred 4. The contract has a lawful purpose.
Negligence	1. Duty to use reasonable care 2. Breach of duty 3. Causation 4. Damages
Fraud (Misrepresentation)	1. A representation must be made 2. The representation must be false 3. The misrepresentation must be related to a past or present fact 4. The misrepresentation must be material to the contract or transaction 5. The representer must know the representation is false, or must assert the representation as if true without knowing if it is 6. The representer must intend to have another person act on the misrepresentation 7. The other person must justifiably act on the misrepresentation 8. The other person must suffer damage because of his or her reliance on the misrepresentation.
Assault	1. The victim must experience apprehension of an immediate battery 2. The defendant must have an intent to cause harm or make the victim fearful.
Battery	1. Proof of contact 2. The contact must have been made without the actual or implied consent of the victim 3. The contact must be intentional.

Compensatory Damages

In civil litigation, the most common remedy issued by the court is an award of **compensatory damages**. Compensatory damages literally compensate the injured party for whatever injuries were sustained, and nothing more. Compensatory damages are also known as **actual damages**. The judgment debtor (defendant), in the case of actual damages, replaces what has been damaged or "makes good" on costs incurred as the result of an injury or loss of property or rights.

Two factors are considered when a court is determining reimbursement via compensatory damages. First, the court decides if the damages sought compensate the money losses (pecuniary losses) of the plaintiff which are the result of the defendant's wrongdoing. Second, future losses that will occur as a direct result of the defendant's wrong are determined by the trier of fact. Compensatory damages are not limited to an actual loss of time or money, but may include losses for "bodily pain and suffering, permanent disfigurement, disabilities or loss [of] health, injury to character and reputation, and, in most states, wounded feelings and mental anguish."[1] When considering bodily harm and emotional distress, the court may award damages without proof of pecuniary loss. However, any other compensatory damages must generally have a money value and/or be capable of an estimation of money value.[2]

Punitive Damages

Courts use a second category of damages, in conjunction with actual damages, when issuing judgments. These are known as **punitive damages** or, in some jurisdictions, **exemplary damages**. Punitive damages are assessed based on the enormity of the defendant's misconduct and are awarded to the plaintiff over and above the amount awarded in compensatory damages. An award of punitive damages may be made when a wrong committed was aggravated by circumstances of violence, oppression, malice, fraud, or wanton and wicked conduct by the defendant.[3] In most states, the view is that punitive damages punish the defendant for the wrongful act.[4] It is quite common for a plaintiff to seek more than one type of damage recovery in a case.

When a defendant seeks to cross-claim or counterclaim in an action, she may also seek an award of damages. These damages may be punitive in nature, but are directed toward the plaintiff.

Evaluating Damages

Damages, damage, and **injury** are often used interchangeably in the civil suit, but the paralegal should be aware that there is a distinction among these terms. *Injury* is the illegal invasion of a legal right; *damage* is the ruin, harm, or impairment that results from the injury; and *damages* are the recompense or compensation awarded for the injury and/or loss suffered.

In some instances, there are damages without a legally cognizable injury. This is called ***damnum absque injuria***, a Latin term applied when a lawful act causes injury. An injury that is not legally recognized occurs when the act that causes the injury is not a violation of a legal right; therefore, there is no means of recovery. All recovery by an injured party must be based on a legal wrong. An example of *damnum absque injuria* is the depreciation of property values in a neighborhood based on the siting of a large hospital in the neighborhood, if the hospital has complied with all applicable zoning, nuisance, and miscellaneous standards. The decrease in property values and inconvenience to the residents is *damnum absque injuria:* the injury the residents suffer, though monetary, is not legally cognizable and therefore there is no available recovery.

When the paralegal considers what evidence or information to research in a case, she must keep in mind the requirements for proving damages. To become skilled at uncovering evidence to support damage claims, the paralegal must gain an understanding of damage categories.

General and Special Damages

General Damages   **General damages** are the immediate or necessary result of a wrong and are traceable to the wrongful act.[5] These damages are the direct, natural, logical, and necessary consequence of the injury. Common sense and experience often provide adequate knowledge of an act that creates general damages. For instance, a client, in the initial interview, explains that she was hurt in a car accident when the brakes in her car failed, and that new brakes were installed on the car twenty minutes before the accident; general damages will likely be sought against the mechanic who installed the brakes. The rationale for general damages centers on the practical recognition that certain conduct or behavior will result in harm. General damages are not justified when it is not likely or practically foreseeable that a wrong done will cause harm. General damages are closely related to **special damages**, and in some cases are intertwined.

Special Damages   Special damages arise from the unique circumstances of a case. These specific damages are the "actual" result of the injury but not the "necessary" result of the injury.[6] The attorney is required to plead these damages individually and add them to the general damages. Therefore, special damages are not implied by law, but they must be a proximate result of the wrong done. Such damages are directly traceable to the defendant's failure to fulfill the obligations imposed upon her by law. The types of damages in this category are always unique to the case itself.

EXAMPLE

A contractor is hired to build a new staircase. After two weeks, a structure to support the staircase has been built and the stairs are placed on the structure. After the contractor completes this phase, she never returns. The contractor has now breached the contract to build the stairs and the owner has incurred damages. The general or actual damages include the cost of having the staircase completed by another contractor. When the new contractor begins working on the project, she finds that the staircase was not built square and that the steps are uneven; the entire staircase has to be rebuilt. Special damages have now been incurred. The special damages are the natural result of the injury but not the necessary result of the general damages.

Comparing General and Special Damages   The distinguishable difference between special and general damages is seen when pleadings are drafted and filed in a case. General damages need not be specifically pleaded, because the defendant should expect that those damages have been incurred as a result of the happening or event (e.g., the breaching of a contract). What is required of the lawyer for the recovery of general damages is simply a statement of jurisdiction, a statement of the facts upon which she relies for proof of the damages, and a demand for relief.[7] In contrast, federal procedure requires that special damages be "specifically stated" in the complaint.[8]

Liquidated Damages

Some contract cases deal with a particular form of damages, called **liquidated damages**. This means that the parties in a suit have agreed on the amount of money to be awarded if and when a breach of contract occurs. This agreement is made at the time the parties enter into the contract. A liquidated damages provision is an estimate, made by the parties at the time of the agreement, of the extent of injury that would be sustained if a breach occurred. Liquidated damages provisions are helpful in situations in which determination of actual damages may be very difficult. It is believed that liquidated damages also encourage all parties in a contract to perform, as agreed, to avoid the previously agreed-upon penalty. This is commonly seen in building contracts. When a contractor and a business enter into an agreement for the construction of a new facility, the contract typically provides for a completion date. If the contractor does not finish the building in the allotted time, the contractor is liable to the business for a certain amount of money for each day of delay in completion (per diem). This liquidated damage amount covers the cost of renting business space while the contractor completes the structure, or can compensate for other pecuniary losses the business may incur. Generally, these contract provisions make allowances for unforeseen problems that will hinder the contractor's ability to finish the project on time (such as natural disasters).

Categories of Damages

There are sixteen general categories of damages (see Figure 11-8). Each defines a particular injury or loss by the complainant.

The paralegal needs a working knowledge of damages so that she can distinguish what types of evidence support the cause of action and elements, and what types of evidence support the damages. She also needs a practical awareness of evidence and evidence types to complete this portion of the investigation process.

Figure 11-8
Definitions of the
most commonly
litigated damages

Damages	Definition
Actual damages	Real, substantial, and just damages; the amount awarded to a complainant in compensation for actual loss or injury.
Compensatory damages	Another term for actual damages.
Consequential damages	Damage, loss, or injury that does not follow directly and immediately from the act of the party, but from some special circumstances that are not ordinarily predictable.
Direct damages	Damages that follow immediately upon the act done.
Double (or treble) damages	A grant of actual damages that is multiplied by two (or three) (allowed only when statutorily permitted).
Excessive damages	Damages awarded by a jury that are grossly more than the amount warranted by law on the facts and circumstances of the case; unreasonable or outrageous damages.
Punitive damages	Damages awarded to the plaintiff over and above compensation for property loss or injury; used when the wrong committed was aggravated by bad conduct on the part of the defendant. These damages are intended to punish the defendant and deter similar conduct by others.
General damages	Damages accruing from a wrong, complained of because they are the immediate, direct, and proximate result of the injury.
Inadequate damages	Damages that would not compensate the parties or place them in the position in which they formerly stood.
Liquidated damages	Damages ascertained by the judgment in an action; or a specific sum of money expressly stipulated by the parties to a bond or other contract as the amount of damages to be recovered by either party for breach of the agreement.

Figure 11-8
(continued)

Damages	Definition
Nominal damages	A trifling sum awarded to a plaintiff in an action in which there is no substantial loss or injury to be compensated, as legal recognition of a technical invasion of rights or breach of the defendant's duty. Also used in cases in which, although there has been real injury, the plaintiff's evidence entirely fails to show its amount.
Pecuniary damages	Damages that can be estimated and compensated by money.
Permanent damages	Damages awarded on a theory that the injury is fixed and will always remain.
Remote damages	Damages arising from an unusual and unexpected result, which is reasonably unanticipatable, from an accidental or unusual combination of circumstances—a result over which the negligent party had no control.
Special damages	Damages that are the actual, but not the necessary, result of the injury complained of, and which in fact followed as a natural and proximate consequence in the particular case (by reason of special circumstances or conditions).
Substantial damages	Damages that are considerable in amount and are intended as real compensation for a real injury (as opposed to nominal damages).

AFFIRMATIVE AND REBUTTAL EVIDENCE

When thinking in terms of evidence alone, the most important purpose of the investigation is to find persuasive or affirmative evidence to support the client's story. **Affirmative evidence** supports, in a positive way, the legal team's cause of action, elements, and/or story. The legal team also searches for **rebuttal evidence**, which is used to refute the opposing party's story or evidence. Learning to distinguish between these two broad categories of evidence enables the paralegal to separate evidence into useful classifications. Once evidence is qualified as affirmative or rebuttal, it is broken into subcategories.

Subcategories of Affirmative and Rebuttal Evidence

To persuade a trier of fact that certain events in a case happened in a specific manner, each side will present evidence and witness testimony on details supporting that side's theory. Each party uses both affirmative and rebuttal evidence to describe the events in the case, with the basic goal of being the most persuasive in telling the story. Therefore, affirmative and rebuttal evidence is classified into subcategories, to help the team focus and create a more persuasive argument. The four types of affirmative and rebuttal evidence are:

1. *Before-and-after evidence.* Details occurring before and after the substantive or triggering event fall into this category. The objective of using this evidence is to encourage the trier of fact (judge or jury) to believe that critical events occurred in the manner described by the party presenting the evidence.

2. *Explanatory evidence.* Explanatory evidence is offered to the trier of fact in an effort to explain why the critical event(s) happened as presented. When using this evidence, a party is focusing on a particular motive or reason that allegedly created the critical event in dispute.

3. *Credibility evidence.* Credibility evidence concerns the witness who tells the story, and goes to the believability of what she is saying.

4. *Emotional evidence.* Emotional evidence focuses on the subjective aspects of a witness's testimony. This type of evidence may engage a jury's moral conscience and is to some degree psychological in nature.[9]

It is not uncommon to find that a piece of evidence fits into more than one subcategory. The four types of evidence represent general categories for all stories told, regardless of the story's legal status.

EXAMPLE

A child tells her mother that she was sent to the principal's office for fighting and was subsequently suspended from school. The mother's first response may be to assess the credibility of the witness, in this case the daughter. Based on the child's past, the mother will either decide that there must be more to the story, or that the child is guilty as charged (if so, the mother may impose a penalty for the bad behavior). Assume that the mother, who knows that the child is generally mild-mannered, feels that her daughter would not intentionally harm another student. The child is now asked to present her side of the story. While telling her story, she provides before-and-after evidence, explanatory evidence, and emotional evidence: she says that the fight broke out after the other student involved insulted her sister and pushed her. Tearfully she explains her desire to defend her sister's honor. After the fight, she tried to apologize to the other student, but the student again shoved her aside.

All four subcategories of evidence in a breakdown of this story:

1. The mother hears *credibility evidence* as the daughter lays out the bare facts of the event. When there is no history between the trier of fact and the claimant, foundational evidence would be given as credibility evidence. This may include details of the party's character, when applicable and admissible.

2. With affirmative acceptance of the credibility evidence, the daughter offers *before-and-after evidence* by explaining what started the fight and what happened afterward when she attempted to apologize to the other student. There is *affirmative* before-and-after evidence in these statements, as the daughter presents her justification for the fight; and *rebuttal* evidence in her statement that the other student started the fight. The daughter is attempting to persuade the mother to infer a duty to defend the sister under these circumstances.

3. *Explanatory evidence* is incorporated in the before-and-after evidence and in the fact that the daughter had a particular motive. The daughter's story creates a good-guy/bad-guy scenario.

4. Finally, the daughter provides a needed dose of *emotional evidence.* She is attempting to persuade her mother that she did the right thing by defending her sister and demonstrating her love for her sister. This recounting (and its credibility) is influenced by her tears, voice inflection, and body language.

This simplistic example demonstrates the overlap of the four types of affirmative and rebuttal evidence. Each piece of the story offered by the daughter would be countered with a rebuttal from the other student who, in turn, would offer affirmative evidence of her own.

Evidence Investigation

After the development of the affirmative and rebuttal fact scenarios, in this example and in real cases, comes the initiation of evidence investigation. The descriptions of the events, presented as affirmative and rebuttal evidence, dictate what will be searched for in the investigation. Once a legal team has a story with all the elements of the cause of action, and a rebuttal story to refute the opponent, they use the two stories as a starting place for searching out physical evidence and witness testimony.

Hypothesis   The creation of a **hypothesis** connects the affirmative evidence to the legal theory. A *hypothesis* is a potential story of what happened and why, which identifies both affirmative and rebuttal evidence, whether physical evidence or witness testimony. Using the hypothesis as a tool, the paralegal begins constructing the best and most persuasive story possible to support the cause of action. In the playground fight example, the cause of action for the daughter might be battery.

With an awareness of the importance of affirmative evidence, the paralegal begins the search for affirmative evidence as early as possible. The strategy for evidence gathering, when working for the defense, is not to concentrate on producing evidence concerned with the burden of proof (affirmative), but on rebuttal. Limiting an investigation to rebuttal will not provide a complete exploration of the facts, though, so the legal team should search for both affirmative and rebuttal evidence, regardless of the team's position in the case.

Evidence Development

To begin the probe of affirmative and rebuttal evidence, the paralegal develops complete stories of the events making up the dispute. Complete stories are possible when all of the relevant events and details known by the witnesses have been gathered, there is an understanding of the action, there is an awareness of the existing evidence, and there is a solid idea about the additional evidence needed. The paralegal looks at all the evidence available.

On the surface, it may appear that the best way to assist the client is to find all of the affirmative evidence possible. This is true but incomplete. If the paralegal neglects to thoroughly investigate information that may harm or diminish the client's story, she may jeopardize the whole case. A conscious decision to ignore harmful evidence may prevent the attorney from offering the best possible representation to the client and may risk his or her ability to provide ethical representation. From a more practical standpoint, no matter how sound the investigation is, it cannot stand up to surprise evidence and witness testimony at trial. Without adequate preparation, the legal team is defenseless against harmful details.

If a paralegal uncovers harmful evidence, the legal team is not obligated to use it at trial, although the team may be required to disclose the evidence under Fed. R. Civ. P. 26(a) and (3). In any event, the team cannot rebut what it does not know about. Realistically, there are some risks involved in investigating negative evidence. In the course of the investigation, a paralegal may uncover details that the other party has overlooked. If this happens in the presence of the opposing counsel or some member of her legal team, they may be alerted to the new evidence. It is also possible that the paralegal could uncover damaging information during an informal witness interview, without the adversary present—but the information derived from this witness may come out later, at the trial or during a deposition. The likelihood of such an occurrence is low, but it is possible. When negative information is not gathered, the attorney and legal team learn of the harmful evidence for the first time at trial, which is never a good time to be confronted with damaging information or evidence. Therefore, give adequate time and attention to negative evidence, to allow preparation and rebuttal.

Affirmative Evidence

The overall use of affirmative evidence is apparent. To affirm something, *you tell it with confidence.* An investigation should begin with the creation of a hypothesis that accommodates the known facts and initiates the identification of affirmative evidence. Go back to the example involving the daughter and her fight at school: the hypothesis is that the other student started the fight. Affirmative evidence to support this hypothesis was included in the story she told her mother, when she explained that the other student pushed her first. Any affirmative evidence requires physical evidence and witness testimony to support it. Affirmative evidence is expanded as the investigation continues, but is usually obvious. The real challenge comes when developing rebuttal evidence.

Rebuttal Evidence

Rebuttal evidence is not as simply created as affirmative evidence. It has a more complex nature. Unlike affirmative evidence, rebuttal evidence is further subdivided beyond the categories of before-and-after, explanatory, credibility, and emotional. There is rebuttal by denial, explanation, and argument. There is rebuttal aimed at the legal team and rebuttal the legal team directs at the adversary. When developing a strategy for rebuttal against an adversary, the paralegal may find a diagram of the three kinds of rebuttal helpful in sorting out the legal team's options (see Figure 11-9).

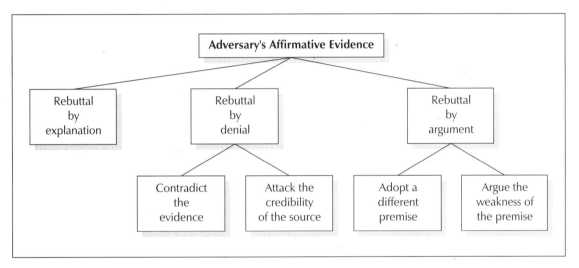

Figure 11-9   Methods of rebutting evidence. (Reprinted with permission from *Fact Investigation from Hypothesis to Proof,* by David A. Binder & Paul Bergman (West, 1984))

Before deciding what type of rebuttal to use, the legal team needs to evaluate the adversary's affirmative evidence. This evaluation identifies both the strengths of the adversary's affirmative evidence and the most effective means of diminishing or detracting from that evidence. What complicates this portion of the strategy is the fact that while the legal team plans its own rebuttal, the opposition is also planning a rebuttal. For the paralegal investigator, this should translate into a heightened awareness of every fact encountered. She should be cautious about omitting details gathered from any interview or during document review. Every detail uncovered may function as a source of evidence, whether it be affirmative or some category of rebuttal.

During the investigation, the paralegal will probably encounter the adversary's rebuttal before any other member of the legal team, because she is deeply involved in the witness interviews and document reviews. This information is most often found during the informal interview of a hostile witness. A hostile witness usually opposes the interviewer or the party the interviewer represents, or knows something that will damage the case or offend the interviewer.

Understanding the value of the hostile witness to the investigation will encourage the paralegal to be patient; a hostile witness commonly provides insight into portions of the opposing party's affirmative story.

Rebuttal by Explanation

Rebuttal by explanation is a powerful tool at trial. This strategy allows disagreement with the adversary's affirmative evidence without questioning the believability of the adversary. The rebutting party admits to the evidence but explains the evidence's shortcomings. After the explanation, the rebutting party offers the court additional evidence that brings the **probative value** of the adversary's evidence into question. *Probative value* describes the weight a piece of evidence carries as it relates to a party's case; it tends to prove (or disprove) an issue (e.g., an eyewitness has more probative value than a collateral witness).

EXAMPLE ——————————————————

Driver A and driver B collide in the center of an intersection. Driver A sues driver B for her injuries and the damage to her car. Driver A claims that she had the right of way at the time of the collision and that driver B negligently ran a red light. An eyewitness claims that she too saw driver B run the red light. At the trial, the attorney for driver B does not dispute the eyewitness testimony, but explains that the witness could not see that driver B was turning right at an intersection that allowed him to do so after stopping.

Counsel for driver B has admitted and explained what the witness saw, without any direct contest. In addition to explaining what the rebutting party believes to be true, the adversary opens the door for the use of circumstantial evidence, to prove implications and allow inferences. Regarding the eyewitness, driver A's counsel is implying that driver B negligently drove into the intersection and thus caused the accident. This implication is what makes the witness's testimony powerful. When counsel for driver B explained the additional circumstances surrounding driver B's behavior, she focused on the inferences to be drawn from the witness's statement, not on the evidence itself, which is the fact that driver B *legally* entered the intersection during the red light.

Rebuttal by explanation is something used every day, in all areas of life; it is in no way unique to legal cases. Most of us develop skill with this technique while going through school and dealing with our parents. Remember the strategy of telling the teacher that your dog ate your homework? The "yeah, but … " strategy serves a variety of purposes and is very effective in the courtroom. What is important for the investigator to remember is that the conscious use of this principle, during critical review of case details, helps locate rebuttal-by-explanation evidence that might otherwise have gone unnoticed. For every story, there is a counter-story that offers a little more explanation; the investigative paralegal is searching for that story.

Rebuttal by Denial

Denial means war. It is very simple: one party sees the evidence as black, the adversary sees the evidence as white. Denial can be approached from two angles:

1. Deny the evidence by contradicting it with opposing evidence or witnesses.

2. Deny the evidence by attacking the credibility of the witness offering the evidence.

To better understand the differences in these approaches, apply them to the car-accident example used previously. The eyewitness claims to have seen driver B run a red light and negligently drive into the intersection. To contradict her statement, the opposing counsel could use one of the following scenarios:

- The eyewitness wears glasses because she has a serious eyesight problem, and her glasses were fogged up at the time of the accident. Therefore, she could not actually see the events.

- Driver B did not run a red light.

Regardless of the type of denial used, the purpose is to find evidence showing that the adversary's evidence is not true. When contradicting evidence, a party is denying that the alleged fact is true; when attacking credibility, a party is indirectly denying the facts.

Rebuttal by Argument

When the investigation fails to find evidence to rebut the adversary's affirmative evidence, the legal team must use rebuttal by argument. However, this form of rebuttal is not as powerful as the others already discussed. Rebuttal by argument is a function the attorney must handle, without much direct involvement of the paralegal; it is commonly used during the closing arguments at trial.

Rebuttal by argument is accomplished by arguing the weakness of the adversary's case and offering alternative explanations for the facts presented by the adversary. What the paralegal can do is offer impressions of the jurors' attitudes toward the evidence already presented by the adversary, which the attorney can use to develop a new direction or premise for the case. Ideally, this new scenario or explanation is accepted by the jury as the more plausible or stronger story. At the least, it is hoped that this new direction will create doubt in the jurors' minds regarding the adversary's current story.

TYPES OF EVIDENCE

The term *evidence* is broadly used to mean something that shows proof. Evidence is anything that helps show or establish the truth or falsity of something; it can be substantive, demonstrative, direct, circumstantial, admissible or inadmissible, material or immaterial. There are broad definitions of usability and then more narrow ones. Requesting that a paralegal student "find the evidence" in a case, or identifying evidence from an academic stance, would be useless without first providing background on general evidence categories. The broad nature of the term *evidence* itself demands that all paralegals understand how evidence is identified and used, rather than simply knowing what it is. Therefore, the paralegal must begin by understanding what a fact is.

Facts

The most broadly used term in investigation is *fact*. A **fact** is a truth; it is something that happened or exists (or at least did exist). Facts are absolutes, but the paralegal should not be fooled into thinking that facts are always clear. If facts were clear, there would be little need for investigation. There are *material facts,* which control or affect an issue in the case, and there are **immaterial** facts, which have no relationship to a case. There are also **ultimate facts**, which may determine a party's legal rights and obligations. For instance, the facts that a driver of a car exceeded the speed limit, and caused an accident, provide evidence to demonstrate the ultimate fact that the driver was negligent in operation of the vehicle. Secondary facts help support the ultimate and material facts.

Collateral Fact   Not all facts discovered from a witness bear on the subject matter being investigated. Some facts are secondary pieces of information that may set the stage for the presentation of primary evidence. Collateral facts are secondary to those that prove the principal issue, and are useful when laying the groundwork to impeach or enhance the credibility of a client or witness. The use of collateral facts is important when forming a hypothesis and telling the story of a case.

EXAMPLE ————————————————————————————————

A product liability case involves a ladder that broke while the client was using it to fix her garage door. During the investigation, the paralegal discovers that a neighbor may have seen the client working on the door and ultimately may have seen her fall and hurt herself. When the paralegal interviews the neighbor, it becomes clear that she saw nothing the day of the accident; however, she owns the same type and brand of ladder as the client and has used it for similar projects. The paralegal asks the neighbor if she has had any trouble with her ladder. The neighbor says she has fallen off the ladder three times in the last six months because it is not very stable and has not been since she bought it. The paralegal has thus uncovered collateral facts that support the foundation of the case, even though they do not directly supply the data initially searched for.

Understanding facts is not as simple as knowing the difference between a primary and a secondary fact. It further requires the paralegal to separate fact from opinion.

Fact and Opinion   Understanding the difference between a fact and an opinion is critical when identifying evidence, though there are times when it is difficult to tell the difference. A *fact* is something that really happened; it has the quality of being real or actual. An **opinion** is a judgment or belief; it is based on a strong impression of something but not on positive knowledge. When interviewing a witness, the difference can sometimes become fuzzy. Witnesses, especially enthusiastic talkers, can confuse beliefs with actual knowledge. The court limits opinion testimony given by lay witnesses.[10] A jury is responsible for drawing conclusions from the facts observed by witnesses, not from the witnesses' opinions; however, there are some important exceptions to this rule.

Opinion Exceptions   Many lawsuits deal with facts that can be supported only by the opinions of witnesses, and the court system allows lay witnesses to testify according to their opinion, provided that the opinion is "rationally based on the perception of the witness and [is] helpful to a clear understanding of the testimony or facts."[11] It would be difficult to provide examples of every situation in which opinion testimony is permitted, but the following example is a good illustration of the need for this exception.

EXAMPLE

A witness saw a person falling down allegedly icy stairs. This witness may not have factual information as to the slipperiness of the stairs when the person fell, but she may be able to provide an opinion based on having observed the plaintiff's difficulty in negotiating the stairs and having found the stairs to be slippery twenty minutes earlier.

The opinion of the witness in the slip-and-fall example is meaningful and thus would normally be permitted. It is valuable to the investigative paralegal to be able to distinguish the difference between testimony based on fact and testimony based on opinion, so that an adequate foundation can be laid to make the opinion admissible. In the slippery stairs example, the paralegal would have erred if she had accepted as fact the witness's opinion that the stairs were slippery when the injured party fell. The condition of the stairs is not a fact; it is inferred from the opinion testimony of the witness.

Every witness statement dealing with a fact issue must be carefully explored so the information can be categorized as fact or opinion. In the stair example, the witness's opinion is valuable and admissible, but it is known that the witness is basing her statement on the condition of the steps twenty minutes before the accident; therefore, the statement is not fact.

Fact/Opinion Comparison   Opinion evidence by a witness, like other evidence, requires a foundation. That foundation is provided when the witness had adequate opportunity to observe the occurrence, condition, or person in question. The following list contrasts some specific facts and opinions.

Fact	*Opinion*
specific color	dark or light
sixty watts	bright or dim
one mile	far or close

After gaining a comprehension of facts, the paralegal begins looking at broad categories of evidence and applications of those categories.

Relevant versus Irrelevant

In a court of law, all parties are obligated to present relevant evidence. **Relevant** evidence is generally **admissible**, unless the law otherwise excludes it.[12] Evidence is relevant if it has "any tendency to make the existence of any fact that is of consequence to the determination of the action more probable or less probable than it would be without the evidence."[13] **Irrelevant** evidence does not relate or apply to the action or any of its elements, and does not prove or disprove any material issue of fact; therefore, it is not admissible at trial. Admissible evidence can be received by a trial court if it aids the trier of fact in deciding a controversy. The Federal Rules of Evidence were created to provide rules about the admissibility of evidence.

The primary purpose of evidence is to prove or disprove a fact. As discussed in the preceding section on affirmative and rebuttal evidence, evidence is also used to develop the most persuasive story possible for the client. The objective of the persuasive story is to educate the jurors and motivate them to apply the law to the evidence and facts so that they may determine the parties' legal rights and obligations. Categories of evidence provide the parties, the attorneys, and the judge with a means of communication and common ground for understanding the uses of evidence. Each category of evidence describes the qualities of the evidence: its meaning, source, character, purpose, and other attributes. Admissibility is not restricted to any individual category of evidence, but is applied as a standard to all. The following broad evidence categories provide the foundation for the fact investigations the paralegal will conduct:

- **Substantive evidence**. Any evidence is considered substantive if a jury is allowed to consider it as support for a verdict. This is a generalized category for evidence that benefits a party's position by proving a fact in issue (as compared to evidence with a narrow purpose, such as the impeachment of a witness).

- **Direct evidence**. Direct evidence is evidence that, if believed, proves the existence of the fact in issue without using any inferences or presumptions. A witness who personally observes a fact or an exhibit in a case establishes that fact directly. A photograph of a bruised body after an assault and battery is direct evidence of the fact that injuries occurred.

- **Circumstantial evidence**. Circumstantial evidence is indirect and is closely tied to common sense. It proves "certain facts in a case from which the jury may infer other connected facts that usually and reasonably follow according to common experience." When presenting circumstantial evidence, a party is providing indirect proof of "something" and depending on inferences to support the existence of the things assumed to be fact. The use of circumstantial evidence relies on deductive reasoning, logic, and common experiences.

- **Impeachment evidence**. **Impeach** means to call into question. Impeachment evidence is used to attack, damage, or diminish the credibility of a witness. When looking for impeachment evidence, a paralegal searches existing deposition testimony, previously documented statements, and even casual conversations the witness may have had. A statement or testimony by a second witness, attesting that the original witness did or did not see, hear, or say something already put into a record in the case, serves as impeachment evidence. Additionally, the paralegal may locate a document that will impeach the witness by contradicting the story (or a part of the story) the witness has already presented. Regardless of the type of impeachment evidence used, the witness's credibility and testimony may be greatly damaged, or at least brought into question in the minds of the judge or jury.

- **Demonstrative evidence**. Demonstrative evidence is tangible and includes any real object related to the case. Ordinarily, demonstrative evidence is used as exhibits at trial; original contracts, car bumpers, and photographs are examples of demonstrative evidence. The jury may be permitted to take the exhibits created from demonstrative evidence into the jury room during deliberation. Exhibits offer a visual explanation and may concern the core issue of the controversy.

- **Testimony**. Testimony is the most common form of evidence. It consists of a statement, oral or written, given under oath or affirmation, and is subject to cross-examination. Generally, a statement not given under these circumstances is not admissible, but it may be allowed under certain conditions and exceptions. Testimony must be based upon the personal knowledge of the witness who is testifying regarding the subject matter.[14] In an automobile accident, skid marks are a fact proving that the accident happened. A witness to the accident may offer testimony as to his observation of the skid marks, and his testimony is evidence of the fact. Fact witnesses are not, however, allowed to give opinions, unless the testimony is rationally based on the witness's perception and would be helpful to the court.[15] The ultimate facts, in this example, are the speed of the car, when the skid marks were made, and the negligence of the driver who made them and caused the accident. The same witness who can testify to the existence of the skid marks *cannot* testify as to his opinion of the speed of the car at the time the skid marks were made. Only expert witnesses are allowed to give opinions on such issues.

- **Expert witnesses**. A person who has special education, training, knowledge, and experience in a specialized subject or field may qualify as an expert witness. **Expert testimony** requires a foundational basis to support the opinion provided by the expert witness; this foundation is provided by the expert's sufficient knowledge, background, and study in the field or subject matter in question.[16] The expert's background and education make her testimony reliable and reasonable.

For example, if a physician is to provide expert testimony and opinion on a subject matter, she must be specifically qualified to do so (e.g., a family practitioner may not offer expert testimony on a specialized neurology issue if she does not have the background or experience to support that opinion).

- **Probative evidence**. Probative evidence tends to prove, or actually does prove, the issue of the case. Probative facts furnish, establish, or contribute toward proof.

SUMMARY

- A cause of action is made up of elements, all of which must be proven with facts and evidence to the satisfaction of the court if the party is to receive a remedy.

- *Damages, damage,* and *injury* are often used interchangeably in litigation. The recovery of damages is a part of the remedy allowed for injury.

- Once investigative needs are outlined, further review of the legal elements will help identify the types of evidence needed to support the affirmative and rebuttal aspects of the case. All evidence will fall into one of these two broad categories.

- Affirmative and rebuttal evidence also falls into one of four more specific categories: before-and-after, explanatory, credibility, and emotional. Evidence in each of these categories may have a further classification, such as direct, circumstantial, or demonstrative.

- Locating and evaluating facts is often difficult. The paralegal must separate primary facts from secondary facts and fact from opinion. She must also understand when witness opinion is acceptable (admissible) and when it is not.

- Identifying evidence is one of the most critical functions of the investigation. An investigative paralegal should have a complete understanding of the classifications of evidence. Without this knowledge, the investigation will lack focus and direction.

- The purpose of identifying evidence is to support the action. An action must be supported by admissible, relevant evidence.

ACTIVITIES

1. Review the antilock brake fact scenario from the "Cause of Action" section early in this chapter. Identify as many classifications of existing and poten-

tial evidence as possible. Describe how you classified each piece of evidence identified.

2. Create a fact scenario involving a breach of contract. Outline that scenario in as much detail as possible, perhaps using an LSD or witness timeline. After creating the story, determine the damages and list them specifically, in a two-column table. Write the type of damage in the left-hand column. In the right-hand column, detail what jurisdictional limits there are on such damages, what part of the damage amount is recoverable and why, and what evidence will be needed to support the claim for such damages.

3. Using the scenario you created in exercise 2, begin identifying evidence by diagramming the action and its elements. Once you have diagrammed breach of contract in terms of cause of action and primary elements, outline the evidence needed to support the elements and where that evidence might come from.

4. Compare your breach-of-contract diagram with the damages table created for your fact scenario. Identify what evidence overlaps between the two. Does the comparison suggest any evidence that was not previously mentioned in either of these investigative tools? Is any of the evidence previously identified no longer relevant? Why or why not?

    Draft an evidence log or chart to manage the search for and gathering of the evidence (refer to Chapter 8 if necessary). On this chart, be creative: label the evidence, its potential location, status, and so on. Refer to the text for more details on evidence specifics. Identify each piece of evidence specifically, as affirmative, rebuttal, material, collateral, negative, substantive, circumstantial, and so on.

5. Return again to the fact scenario created for exercise 2. Identify, by means of some type of organizational tool, the material facts, opinions, and ultimate facts of the case. Base your identification not only on the story but on the evidence as well. Identify the evidence that supports your facts, opinions, and ultimate facts.

CASE STUDY

Sugar v. Black

Susan Sugar has come to your attorney's firm for representation. She is an elderly woman who owns a nursery and landscaping business. Her partner in the business is a much younger man, Robert, who approached Susan with the idea of opening the landscape/nursery business. Robert said that he had no money to offer as start-up capital but that he would provide his specialized expertise and run the operation as his partnership contribu-

tion. Susan agreed to the proposal and established a corporation. She protected herself by holding the majority of stock in the company. Her contract with Robert stated that as Robert became able to pay his portion of the start-up costs and add to the profitability of the company, he too could gain shares of stock.

Over several years, the business grew and was well patronized. However, profits were not as good as Susan had expected. When Susan discussed her concerns with Robert, he explained why the business had not yet shown the profits that Susan had expected; to help reassure Susan, Robert suggested that his wife, Mary, who was an accountant, look over the accounting records and meet with Susan to discuss them. After meeting with Mary, Susan felt that Robert had provided good reasons for expenditures and revenues and believed that better profit was yet to come. After two additional fiscal quarters passed, Susan again became concerned. She arranged for an independent auditor to perform a surprise audit of the books—which resulted in strong evidence of fraudulent activity. Susan decided to hire an attorney because it appeared that Robert had taken company funds and materials for his personal use and was skimming off the top.

Susan brought an action to dissolve the partnership, obtain an accounting, and recover partnership assets. The present action alleges that Robert breached his fiduciary duty, converted partnership property, and committed fraud and conspiracy. These are serious charges and require a tremendous amount of investigation to support them. The other charges, however, are less overwhelming and are the focus of your investigation.

As part of your investigation, do the following:

1. Research the causes of action described here and diagram their elements.

2. Assess the damages.

3. From the story details provided here, outline the affirmative and rebuttal areas. Spend time not only on your rebuttal evidence, but also on the rebuttal Robert's legal team will present.

4. List the facts, ultimate facts, and opinions in the case. Describe what areas of the story are supported by evidence or fact and which are not. For those that are, what evidence will you gather to support them? Where will you find that evidence? Why do you believe it is supportive? Do the same for the areas of the story that you believe are not supported by fact or evidence. What will you do about that?

NOTES

1 22 Am. Jur. 2d *Damages* § 28 (1988).

2 *Id.*

3 22 Am. Jur. 2d *Damages* § 731 (1988).

4 *Id.* §§ 733–735.

5 *Black's Law Dictionary* 391 (6th ed. 1990).

6 *Black's Law Dictionary* 392 (6th ed. 1990).

7 *See* Fed. R. Civ. P. 8(a).

8 *See* Fed. R. Civ. P. 9(g).

9 David Binder & Paul Bergman, *Fact Investigation From Hypothesis to Proof* 14 (West, 1984).

10 *See* Fed. R. Evid. 701.

11 *Id.*

12 Fed. R. Evid. 402.

13 Fed. R. Evid. 401.

14 Fed. R. Evid. 602.

15 *See* Fed. R. Evid. 701.

16 *See* Fed. R. Evid. 702, 704.

12 DEVELOPING AND PRESERVING EVIDENCE

OBJECTIVES   After completing this chapter, you will know:

- A successful investigator creates a hypothesis to support the legal theory and cause of action; this hypothesis drives the investigation and helps the investigator develop evidence.

- Qualifying the claim and identifying potential evidence are the two primary aims when developing evidence.

- Stories are expanded when evidence and discovery are reviewed and evaluated, and new details are uncovered.

- Gaps in the story are uncovered by using common sense.

- All evidence must be protected after it has been gathered.

INTRODUCTION

The process of evidence development is similar to the process a spider uses to spin a web. An investigator spins a story based on (1) the core details of an event provided by the client and (2) inferences created through a hypothesis. He uses the facts of the event or happening, dates, and names to develop the base of the story, and expands it by exploring hypotheses and legal theories. Hypotheses and legal theories lead paralegals and attorneys down some of the many paths toward evidence. Evidence paths were shown in Chapter 11 through diagrams used to identify legal elements and potential evidence.

Once evidence has been developed, it is gathered and stored. Storing evidence requires the paralegal to have a complete understanding of evidence frailties and needs. Special care should be given to all evidence being held for use at trial or deposition.

THE HYPOTHESIS

There are two general categories of hypotheses: factual and explanatory. The **factual hypothesis** is descriptive and provides a narrative of past events, including inferences made to support the legal theory. An **explanatory hypothesis** provides an explanation for the events as they happened and also includes inferences. The explanatory hypothesis is narrower in scope than the descriptive narrative version. Regardless of the type of hypothesis used, the purposes are the same: to lay the foundation for a plausible, favorable story, and to provide a tangible guide to follow when developing evidence. Hypotheses are chosen by how well they support the legal theory and direct the investigation.

The Factual Hypothesis

The factual hypothesis is the most commonly used, because it is descriptive by nature, explains what happened and why, and is built from past events and inferences. These elements activate one or more legal theories. Multiple factual hypotheses, developed early in the investigation, offer the legal team different versions of the same story. Development of the hypothesis serves one basic purpose: to create the most persuasive story possible to trigger one or more legal theories. Legal theories provide a litigator with a cause of action or affirmative defense on which to build a case. The hypothesis supports the legal theory by answering legal questions and providing evidence to support those questions.

EXAMPLE

Your firm's client, a homeowner, is suing a contractor for breach of contract. The plaintiff contracted with the defendant to build and finish an addition to the plaintiff's house. The defendant contractor built the addition but did not put in the carpet. After providing evidence to support the legal elements required to prove that a valid contract existed, the more specific carpet question is addressed. The issue to prove: "Was the carpet installation required by the contract?" (See the accompanying table for this breakdown.)

Legal Theory	Element
Breach of contract	Carpeting (as part of the contract)

The hypothesis, for this sample story, explains why the carpet installation is part of the contract and that it is required to complete the contract.

Without a hypothesis, any legal theory the attorney wishes to use is worthless. The attorney needs a story, supported by facts and evidence, to attach to an action. In terms of the investigation, the hypothesis, once selected, suggests the direction the legal team will take to identify the affirmative and rebuttal evidence.

Multiple Hypotheses

The hypothesis is based on the client's interpretation of the events, but the client is often unable to distinguish what details are relevant. A lack of legal understanding can keep the client from providing all the information needed to create a hypothesis. This necessitates the development of multiple hypotheses, which are important for two reasons:

- They serve the client by ensuring that all possible answers are considered and that research time is not focused on a single solution (that may not work).
- A more thorough investigation is conducted by using multiple hypotheses.

The hypothesis is a method for qualifying a particular legal theory and its cause of action. Using more than one hypothesis can help ensure that sufficient evidence is found to support all legal theories applicable to a case. A solid hypothesis drives an investigation and meets the legal criteria. If the legal team investigates multiple hypotheses, the attorney has the luxury of deciding which legal theory and cause of action to use at trial.

In all cases, the paralegal must consult with the attorney when developing a hypothesis. The attorney is responsible for identifying the hypothesis that will support the best legal theory.

Hypothesis Development

The development of the hypothesis is relatively simple. The client tells a story; a hypothesis is proposed; one or more legal theories are triggered. The hypothesis is reviewed in light of each of the theories and causes of action and the evidentiary proof required for suit. When a hypothesis coincides with any of the legal theory's criteria, a case is born. The strongest hypothesis is selected and the others are set aside. If multiple hypotheses have been developed, one is selected for use and the others are set aside, although never discarded. The "spare" hypotheses may be useful in rebuttal, or may later be applied to the case as additional details are discovered during the course of the investigation.

Common sense and footwork encourage evidence and hypothesis development, yet these two steps may be overlooked by the legal team that focuses on substantive tasks. In many civil litigation matters, the lack of common sense and footwork undermine the investigation and leave the client, law firm, and paralegal at a disadvantage. Consider the *Wilhoff v. Jones* case study as an example of hypothesis and evidence development in relation to common sense and footwork.

CASE STUDY

Wilhoff v. Jones

A law firm in a **no-fault insurance** state is hired to represent an insurance company. (No-fault insurance, used in some states, permits the insured to be reimbursed for damages regardless of who is responsible for the accident.) The insurance company has paid costs incurred by a customer in a car accident. When the insurance company contacts the law firm, its insured, Mr. Jones, has accepted responsibility for the accident; the company has paid for the damages to Mr. Wilhoff's car and his medical bills. Mr. Wilhoff, the plaintiff, now wants to collect on a wage-loss claim in addition to those damages already paid. The client (the defendant insurance company) wants to avoid paying these claims and feels that the plaintiff lacks proof of proximate cause for the wage-loss claim. The company has authorized an investigation and consequently the paralegal is given the file.

To date, it is known that the accident occurred in late December, at night. Both of the drivers were in their early twenties at the time of collision. Though both cars were damaged, both drivers were able to leave the scene in their own vehicles. The plaintiff has complained of neck and back injuries and some medical expenses have been paid by the insurance company. Wilhoff, the plaintiff, did not go to a hospital immediately after the accident. He has, however, sought medical treatment several times since the accident. Wilhoff also claims that he lost his job due to the injuries he suffered in the accident and the time it took to recover from them. He alleges that the long-term complications of the injuries have made it difficult for him to find new employment.

The story web shown in Figure 12-1 uses the accident as the base, along with the central fact that the plaintiff was injured. In this example there is no litigation involving negligence, as this is a no-fault state and defendant Jones acknowledged his responsibility for the accident to the insurance company. In turn, the defendant insurance company has paid the medical claims filed by the plaintiff. These early story details expand the story to show that: (1) the defendant insurance company has compensated the plaintiff for the injury suffered; and (2) the plaintiff is now making a wage-loss claim in connection with the accident. A wage-loss claim seeks recovery beyond actual damages in order to make the plaintiff whole again; it alleges that as a result of the accident, the plaintiff is unable to earn the wages he normally would.

The story now requires a hypothesis and legal theory, because there has been no initial client interview in this case (the actual client is a large company). The

Figure 12-1
The initial story web

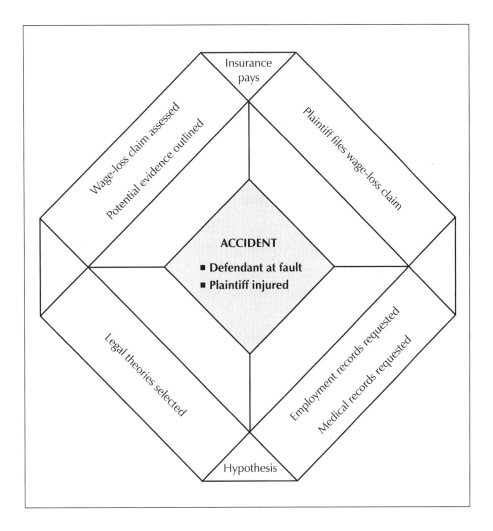

creation of the hypothesis may take longer than usual. When a client is not involved in the triggering event, the paralegal is required to perform informal interviews with witnesses—in this case Mr. Jones—to develop the hypothesis. For the legal theory, the team initially employs the client's suggested theory that Wilhoff lacks proximate cause for the wage-loss claim.

Primary Evidentiary Tasks

After the story's base is created (see Figure 12-1), the paralegal has two primary evidentiary tasks to complete: qualify the wage-loss claim and determine the status of any potential evidence. These tasks break down as follows.

- *Qualifying the claim.* What is the actual value of the wage-loss claim? Has the claim been calculated correctly based on the earning capacity of the plaintiff? This is determined by gathering evidence that shows the plaintiff's earning capacity, such as tax returns, unemployment claims, and personnel files. Once evidence is collected, the paralegal must calculate the plaintiff's potential earnings based on the records obtained, and compare them with the dollar amounts claimed by the plaintiff.

- *Potential evidence.* Can the investigation go further? In *Wilhoff v. Jones,* this is determined by researching what type of employee Wilhoff was, when and why he left each position, and if anything significant happened during his employment. Medical records are gathered and reviewed to determine the legitimacy of his injury claims, and witness interviews are used to uncover credibility and rebuttal evidence.

The paralegal begins developing evidence required for further investigation while qualifying the claim with the information gathered to answer the first questions. For *Wilhoff v. Jones,* assume that the following information is uncovered.

CASE STUDY

Case Details

- Medical records show repeated work-related injuries dating back to Wilhoff's first job. Most, if not all, involved worker's compensation claims. Medical records also show substance abuse treatment.
- Employment records show that Wilhoff was fired from every job and that he received multiple disciplinary reports on several before termination.

- Further investigation, done through informal telephone interviews and review of the medical and employment records, shows a continuous pattern of alcohol-related problems. The alcohol problems appear to have caused his loss of employment.

Based on what has been found, an inference can be made and a hypothesis suggested, that Wilhoff is unable to keep a job because of his reckless behavior. Additional records relating to Wilhoff's lifestyle are now important. Academic records (high school, college, tech school, etc.) should be requested in an attempt to uncover any other alcohol-related problems. At this point in the investigation, it is not clear how Wilhoff's alcohol problems relate to his wage-loss claim, or if they are even relevant; however, the hypothesis suggests that alcohol abuse is the real reason for Wilhoff's lost wages, not his injuries from the car accident. If proven, this hypothesis supports the theory that Wilhoff lacks proof of proximate cause for the wage-loss claim.

To continue review of this case, assume that the following information is discovered after receipt of Wilhoff's academic records.

CASE STUDY

Case Details

Academic records paint a similar picture of alcohol abuse. They describe Wilhoff as a troubled teen placed in a work/study program due to truancy. The work/study program is used to keep high-risk students in school and train them for skilled jobs after graduation. Wilhoff's first job came from this program. He was fired from that job after alcohol-related trouble both at work and after working hours. All of this information now suggests that Wilhoff's police records and driving record should be investigated.

Reviewing the total picture of all evidence gathered to date helps the paralegal expand the story and hypothesis. Consider the following.

CASE STUDY

Evidence Review

- Plaintiff has a medical history of substance abuse. (The legal team hypothesizes that this is why he cannot find or keep employment.)
- Plaintiff has an employment history showing substance abuse. (This may prove that he was not employable because of alcohol dependency.)
- Plaintiff has an academic history showing substance abuse and work-related trouble. (This evidence supports the hypothesis that Wilhoff has an ongoing problem with alcohol.)
- Plaintiff has credibility issues that are directly tied to his past history with alcohol. (This helps the case if the hypothesis is proven.)

- Substance abuse, at this point in the investigation, may not be relevant to the wage-loss claim. Substance abuse itself is not allowed as a defense because it is not related to the car accident; the accident occurred in a no-fault state (this depends on state law; see Am. Jur. 2d *Automobile Insurance* at 31, 34). However, substance abuse may be used as foundational evidence (rebuttal/credibility) regarding plaintiff's employability at the time of the accident and thereafter.

The evidence developed damages the plaintiff's credibility with regard to obtaining employment, and questions Wilhoff's ability to hold a job. The paralegal must continue searching for relevant evidence that will **mitigate** or negate Wilhoff's claim, thus supporting the theory. *Mitigation* is the process of decreasing the amount of damages caused by the offense or injury (wage loss).

EXPANDING STORIES

As the hypothesis continues to develop and evidence is uncovered, the paralegal expands the stories of both plaintiff and defendant by reevaluating the evidence and uncovering new evidence, eventually completing the story.

Reevaluating Evidence to Support the Hypothesis

With a better understanding of what to look for, reevaluation of the employment records and interrogatory answers is required; thus, the hypothesis is researched. Assume that the following is discovered during the review.

CASE STUDY

Case Details

In the interrogatory answers, the paralegal notices that the start and end dates for each employer vary from the dates in the actual employment records. In addition, each employment application lists a different start and end date for previous employment. None of the dates exactly matches the plaintiff's claims. This information requires more subsequent investigation and is given to the attorney for use as impeachment evidence at Wilhoff's deposition. Any type of impeachment evidence is critical.

To investigate the inconsistencies found in the job applications, the employers or agents of the employers must be interviewed. (Refer to Chapter 6 for information on investigative interviews.) Through the investigative interviews, the following information is discovered.

CASE STUDY

Case Details

The plaintiff was fired from his last job (Castle Construction) two days before this accident occurred, and thus suffered no lost wages. It is also possible that he filed for unemployment benefits against Castle Construction sometime after the accident. This is the first piece of direct, relevant evidence developed that supports the hypothesis and theory.

With all of the data uncovered regarding Wilhoff's past, additional documents must be requested from the police department and the motor vehicle department in an effort to find more evidence relating to Wilhoff's character and past experiences. Assume that the following information is found in police records.

CASE STUDY

Case Details

Wilhoff has an arrest record, and on at least two occasions he was arrested for domestic violence. The domestic violence charges obviously are not relevant to the car accident, but the date of the last arrest and what happened during the arrest are, because the arrest occurred two weeks after the car accident. This report states that Wilhoff, while intoxicated, lifted and threw heavy furniture during an assault and battery of his girlfriend. The report also states that three policemen were needed to detain him and mace was used to bring him under control. This information brings into question the seriousness of Wilhoff's accident-related injuries. When asked in a deposition, or in court, if he suffered injuries severe enough to prohibit him from working, Wilhoff will have difficulty saying yes, because of the activity recorded in the arrest record.

Uncovering Additional Evidence

Expanding stories can be difficult; it requires brainstorming, creative thinking, and uncovering additional details. In *Wilhoff v. Jones,* the hypothesis was expanded and details uncovered each time new information was found. As discussed in Chapter 11, evidence builds on itself, and the continued search for evidence ensures a thorough, complete investigation.

As details are uncovered, the paralegal must be willing to adapt his hypothesis and make assumptions about the direction the evidence is going. This was done on several occasions in *Wilhoff v. Jones.* There will be times when assumptions regarding the facts are wrong—but there will also be times when the assumptions are right. The investigation requires some risk-taking by the investigator.

Another review of the plaintiff's answers to interrogatories, materials received through authorizations, and data gained from interviews and reports is warranted to reevaluate the usefulness of the hypothesis and its applicability to the theory.

CASE STUDY

Evidence Review

- Plaintiff has substance abuse issues that will damage his credibility (impeachment).
- Plaintiff may have been lying about the degree of his injuries.
- There are discrepancies in employment dates between plaintiff's applications and his interrogatory answers.

The story is now several layers deep, but it continues to challenge the investigator to find additional ties between the plaintiff and his possible intention to defraud the insurance company. Figure 12-2 shows the newest layers of the story web.

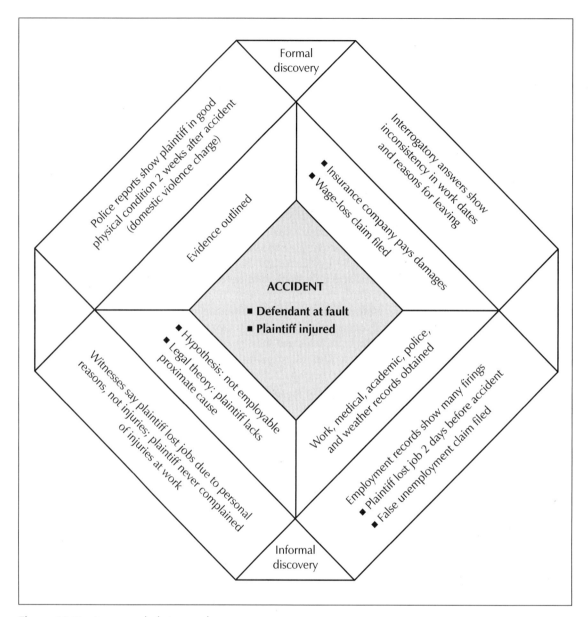

Figure 12-2 An expanded story web

Developing the Story

The story for *Wilhoff v. Jones* has become increasingly more complex. The base has been established; records have been obtained and used to corroborate evidence, qualifying (or in this case disqualifying) the plaintiff; the hypothesis is in development. What, if anything, is missing? Assume that the following happens.

CASE STUDY

Case Details

In yet another review of the interrogatory answers, the paralegal notices that Wilhoff claims to have filed for unemployment and received some benefits. Wilhoff's most recent employer also mentioned an unemployment claim. The paralegal calls the unemployment office to check this information.

During a phone interview with the unemployment office, an employee talks freely about Wilhoff and his claim. The employee knows Wilhoff personally and, without much explanation as to why the information is needed, offers a great deal of data on Wilhoff. The employee provides exact details on the amount of money paid to Wilhoff and the employment dates reported to the office. He tells the paralegal that Wilhoff is a troubled young man, and also admits to helping Wilhoff fill out these forms. Claim numbers for the unemployment filings are obtained. In the records, Wilhoff claims to have worked for his last employer three months longer than he actually did. Clearly, he has made a false representation to the unemployment office to receive additional benefits. This one interview provides information to prove that Wilhoff lied in the civil suit about his dates of employment and wages earned.

Developing evidence and gathering records (like those in the unemployment office) may be difficult, but it must be done so that the legal team can offer direct proof for the hypothesis and theory.

☑ **PRACTICAL TIP**   A subpoena is required to obtain copies of unemployment claims.

Ethical Consideration   Attorneys make all decisions relating to the depth of and time spent on an investigation, as well as making all substantive legal decisions. This fundamental rule must not be broken. Paralegals cannot practice law, and careful consideration should be given to all tasks performed during the investigation to avoid risking the unauthorized practice of law.

Completing the Story

The investigation has now provided evidence to support the theory and show that the wage-loss claim is at least deeply flawed and perhaps totally invalid. Witnesses have been located and informally interviewed, documents supporting the defense have been obtained, and the plaintiff's credibility has been damaged. This was a successful investigation. Take a last look at what was discovered.

CASE STUDY

Evidence Review

- Plaintiff has substance abuse problems (credibility evidence).

- Plaintiff was repeatedly fired from jobs (foundational evidence).

- Plaintiff lost his last job two days before the accident (direct, relevant evidence).
- Plaintiff is not employable because of alcohol-related problems, not accident-related injuries (proven through employment records and interviews with past employers).

- Plaintiff has credibility issues:
  - Discrepancies in employment dates.
  - Physical status at the time of his arrest for domestic violence (domestic violence itself is not relevant or admissible).

Consider the outcome of this case if the paralegal had investigated only the first evidentiary criteria: qualifying the wage-loss claim and the correctness of its calculation.

COMMON SENSE AND EVIDENCE

Common sense is a learned skill for which organization is required. Organization allows an investigator to find holes in the stories or in the logic employed during the investigation. The organized development and collection of evidence requires the use of charts, memos, and other organizational tools, as well as practical judgment.

When ideas and evidence are placed in a graph or chart, finding inconsistencies in logic or the hypothesis becomes easier. Common sense is critical to an investigation as a measure of a story's worth; by now the paralegal should understand the importance of evaluating the case story and the adversary's version of the story. *Common sense* is defined as sound practical judgment. It is considered to be the natural discernment of persons in general. Common sense permits the paralegal investigator to use all of his life experiences to evaluate evidence, witnesses, and the various stories. This insight expands not only the investigation but also the hypothesis.

Uncovering Gaps

Gaps discovered during a common-sense review of evidence and the parties' stories helps generate ideas and strategies during the investigation. A hole in the hypothesis or fact scenario shows where missing evidence may be identified; once that evidence is located, the story is either supported or damaged. If evidence cannot be found to fill a gap in the story, logic, or hypothesis, the investigation strategy may have to be changed. An example in the *Wilhoff v. Jones* case is the discovery of the plaintiff's repeated job losses. Originally the plaintiff claimed that he was unable to maintain or find new employment because of the injuries he suffered in the car accident. Through a review of his employment history, it became apparent that Wilhoff had had trouble maintaining employment well before being injured. Logically, this brings his story of employability into question. Common sense says that one must be employable to suffer a wage loss.

In *Wilhoff v. Jones,* repeated review of the documents and discovery answers consistently led to new and more valuable evidence. Common sense dictated each discovery and continually prompted the investigation. Links between evidence can be overlooked if the paralegal does not use common sense and practical knowledge when evaluating it.

Team Approach

Common sense requires paralegals to work with each other and the attorney(s) to help discover the connections and relationships between events and information. The technique of brainstorming is particularly helpful in investigation. Teamwork is of great help when attempting to obtain documents or materials the opposing party may not want located, and repeatedly working through case scenarios improves and sharpens the use of common sense in the investigation. Review the common-sense links found in the *Wilhoff v. Jones* case, shown in Figure 12-3.

A basic outline of the common-sense approach used in this case shows how logic and patience build a defense. This structure allows constant reevaluation of information and is of great value to the story. In comparison, some parts of

Figure 12-3

Common-sense flowchart of events in *Wilhoff v. Jones*

the investigation story die after common-sense review. When dead ends show up, an outline provides a visual reminder that every angle has been investigated.

Once the evidence has been developed to support the hypothesis, it is gathered and stored. The paralegal is responsible for the care and management of the evidence and for knowing and understanding the various methods of preserving evidence.

PRESERVING EVIDENCE

There is no single, universally applicable method for preserving evidence, but the paralegal must nevertheless be proficient in safeguarding evidence during an investigation. As discussed in Chapter 10, physical evidence must be placed in a secure location free from theft, fire, and other destructive elements. Unfortunately, not all evidence is physical. Witnesses and their testimony also require care and preservation. Each distinct type of evidence requires an ever-expanding knowledge of safeguarding techniques.

Physical Evidence

A wide variety of evidence characteristics influence preservation and methods used for storage of physical evidence. Photographs require more care in storage than contracts, unless the only copy of the original contract is on microfiche. Damaged car bumpers may have to be carefully photographed if the vehicle is to be repaired and driven again, or if the bumper is useless and will be sold for scrap. Accident scenes also have to be preserved, so carefully timed photography may be required to ensure that a jury during trial sees the same accident scene (e.g., railroad tracks or roadway) that the parties saw on the day of the accident. No matter what kind of demonstrative or physical evidence is being dealt with, some method of preservation must be used to ensure the integrity of the evidence in relation to the time and place of its origin. Figure 12-4 details the specific preservation problems that certain types of evidence may present.

Testimony

Witnesses and their testimony must be carefully guarded and preserved. Initial interviews can offer a great deal of information, but stories can change over time, and witnesses may disappear or become uncooperative. These unfortunate facts of life mean that the investigator must preserve witnesses' statements. In a deposition or during courtroom testimony, a formal record of the witness's statement is made. In the informal investigative interview, the paralegal must create the record of what was said. Note taking and tape recording are two methods of preserving a witness's statement.

☑ **PRACTICAL TIP**   The witness must be told when a tape recorder is used during an interview.

Evidence	Problem	Safe Storage
Photographs	Heat-sensitive, light-sensitive, water-sensitive, touch-sensitive.	Specialized vault, air/light/heat controlled. Place prints in protective plastic (check with a photographer for appropriate kinds); negatives stay in a protective folder.
Maps	Paper dries with time, also yellows and fades. Ink may smudge, run, fade. Paper tears and people write on public maps found in the recorder's office.	Request certified copies when applicable, copy the certified copy for the investigation, and place the certified copy in a fireproof vault.
Machinery/Equipment	Badly damaged machinery is often totaled by the insurance company and sold to a salvage yard; there it is destroyed. When machinery is not totaled, additional accidents can occur if an owner continues using it. This may change or destroy the original condition of the machine at the time of the accident.	Immediately take photographs and video of the machine. Secure both of the visual images in the manner described for photographs. If possible, impound the machinery until trial or deposition. If it is to be sold to a salvage company, seek an order from the court to prohibit destruction of the machinery until the trial is completed.
Cars/Trucks/Trains/Airplanes	Similar to those for machinery and equipment. Commonly, a moving vehicle may be driven or used again directly after the accident. This can destroy the visual integrity of the evidence. Airplanes will seldom be useable after a crash, but the physical airplane will be impounded by the FAA, and will require that agency's cooperation to be seen.	Photograph the entire vehicle and collect any broken parts left at the scene. Photograph any skid marks. Store all collected evidence using the best method described in this text.
Objects of Product Liability Suits (toasters, ladders, garbage cans, toys, etc.)	The item or product may be destroyed by fire, breakage, or other occurrence related to the triggering event. Those items not completely destroyed at the time of the event may be used again, causing additional damage to the item or to another person. This may create a problem in using the evidence at trial, as it could be involved in two separate actions.	Collect any and all parts of the item the first time you come into contact with it, unless it is held by the police or a third party. Photograph the item in its location at the time of the incident. Collect an undamaged replica of the item for later use. Store the item in an appropriate safe or storage facility and label it as evidence so no one else uses the item.

Figure 12-4   Evidence preservation methods

Evidence	Problem	Safe Storage
Accident Scenes	Accident scenes have the potential to change very quickly. At intersections or train crossings, trees, shrubs, rocks, bumps, and other physical features can be swiftly removed or changed after a serious accident, or they may grow or be cut back. When this happens, the accident scene may never be accurately re-created for the judge or jury.	Take photographs of the scene from as many angles as possible. Take the photographs at different times of day. Photograph all trees, shrubs, curbs, stop lights, signs, houses near the scene, and conditions that may show additional factors in the accident. Use inferential reasoning at the scene to determine what aspects of the accident may be critical to the jury and photograph or preserve them using the best method possible. Measure the distance of such things as the stop light to the center of the intersection, the height of bushes or trees, the distance one can see down the railroad tracks, and any other applicable distances.
Documents	Documents come in so many varieties that no one list of the problems experienced with them can suffice. The most basic problem is flammability and human destruction. If the documents are originals, there are no others! Handle all documents as if they were the only source of evidence in the case.	Gather original documents, number them, copy them, index them, and store them immediately in a fireproof location. Do not punch holes in original or certified copies of documents and never mark on them. Always use work copies of the documents for the investigation. Separate "smoking guns" and privileged documents early and identify them as such in a generalized index. Place the "special" documents in a separate but equally secure fireproof safe.
Microfilm	Images can fade over time; they can easily be torn or damaged in the viewer.	Copy the information onto paper and store the film in a dry, temperature-controlled, fireproof vault. Secure a safe paper copy of the film in a fireproof vault and work from a second copy of the document.

Figure 12-4 (continued)

Evidence	Problem	Safe Storage
Public Records	These can be lost, checked out, marked on, torn, stolen, and in some rare cases altered.	*Always* request certified copies unless specifically instructed otherwise. If possible, review the source material personally before accepting the copies, to verify that you have all the material available. Make working copies of the documents and store the certified copies in a fireproof vault. Once the documents are certified, do not mark or alter them in any way.
Private Records	These are usually sensitive and require discreet use. Not all of the material will be useable, but all of it should be protected.	Gather, number, copy, index, and store the originals in a fireproof safe. If the material is sensitive, mark it as such so that no unauthorized person can view the documents. Use work copies of the applicable material for investigative activities.

Figure 12-4   (*continued*)

Formal Statements   Whether or not a formal statement is being collected, an investigator must take notes during an interview, and an overview of the witness's feelings, recollections, and details is required. Notes are used to draft an affidavit of the story (formal statement). After reading the affidavit to verify its accuracy, the witness signs the statement; if specific details were omitted or recorded incorrectly in the affidavit, the witness makes corrections right on the draft. The paralegal can depend on the witness for accuracy when drafting a formal statement.

Informal Statements   The paralegal's notes are the only record of the conversation during an informal interview, and these notes are used to guide the investigation. The following are useful guidelines for taking notes while interviewing:

- Guide the witness with carefully planned questions. By doing so, the interviewer regulates the amount of information received and controls the speed of responses.
- To increase accuracy in note taking and to make a record of the interview, use a physical diagram or drawing to manage the witness.

EXAMPLE —————————————————————————————————

Jim is interviewing Roger, a witness to a car accident. Jim is confused about the seating of the passengers in the cars. Jim draws a diagram of the cars to assist and memorialize Roger's recall of where the passengers were in the cars at the time he saw the accident and again when he pulled them out of the cars. In addition, Jim needs to take notes of Roger's responses to his questions while the diagram is being filled out.

Jim: Roger, did you notice where the passengers were sitting in the blue car as the accident happened? How about for the red car?

Roger: Yes, I saw where all of the people were as the accident happened.

Jim: Would you please mark on this diagram where the passengers were just as the accident occurred, the way you remember them?

Roger: [Writes and draws on the diagram.]

Jim: What did you see before the accident happened?

Roger: [Explains all the details he can remember about the minutes before the accident, while he continues work on the diagram.]

In this example, Jim, the interviewer, has managed a difficult portion of the conversation by guiding Roger with questions and an activity. While Roger diagrams the seating of the passengers, he explains what he saw before the accident, and Jim is able to take careful notes and help Roger refresh his memory. As the interview continues, Jim uses the diagram created during this questioning to keep Roger focused; this also allows more opportunities for Jim to take notes.

When a witness's recorded statement or affidavit is complete, it should be protected like any other documentary evidence. Notes from an informal interview should be copied and stored with other investigative materials.

SUMMARY

- The way to develop a successful story and hypothesis is to:
  - Gather the core details of the event or happening and use them as the base.
  - Collect the applicable records in the case and use them to begin developing a hypothesis.
  - Identify the legal theory and the elements required to prove the theory.
  - Use common sense when reviewing the hypothesis created and the evidence to support it.
  - Manage the documents, details, and evidence with integrity, care, and wisdom.
- The hypothesis is a practical tool for uncovering evidence that supports the legal theory and cause of action; the purpose of developing evidence is to prove the hypothesis and legal elements.

- To conduct the most complete investigation possible, thoroughly research both of the primary evidentiary tasks.
- Reevaluation is one of the most productive and useful tools in expanding stories and developing evidence.
- Preserving evidence is the responsibility of the paralegal. He should strive to learn and understand all new methods of and technology for ensuring the safety of each type of evidence.

ACTIVITIES

1. Challenge yourself to find stories in newspapers, magazines, or on television that provide enough material for you to build a defense or prosecution based on what you are told. How would you go about investigating the case? Practice expanding stories and communicating in specific detail and in general terms. Enjoy this task—it can be fun and productive.

2. Explain the standard methods of handling evidence. What problems do you perceive in using these standard methods? How would you handle those problems?

3. Explain the difference between the factual hypothesis and the explanatory hypothesis. In your explanation, clarify why and when you would use a factual hypothesis and why and when you would use an explanatory hypothesis.

4. Look again at the Jim and Joan Klosty case at the end of Chapter 7. Based on the facts given there, develop two or more hypotheses. Be prepared to select one of the hypotheses and defend it based on the facts presented.

5. You have now been assigned to this case as part of the legal team for the Klostys. Draft a set of questions for use during any number of investigative interviews you will use to find evidence in this case. Use the investigative Five Ws described in Chapter 6 to draft the questions. Explain why you selected the questions you did, what you expect to find based on those questions, and how the anticipated answers will satisfy your hypothesis.

6. Draft a memorandum to the attorney concerning the interviews you have conducted with some of the neighbors in the Klostys' block. Detail how the information gathered will influence your hypothesis and your search for evidence.

7. At the conclusion of this assignment, list the areas of evidence gathering that you think will be difficult. What specifically are the difficulties? What are your concerns about developing a hypothesis and supporting it? Be as specific as possible about the things that are causing you problems and why. Be prepared to discuss your feelings.

CASE STUDY

Powers v. Clauster

Review the details of the following case study, entitled *Powers v. Clauster,* and compile a list of potential hypotheses. Identify evidence sources you will research to support one or more of your hypotheses. Describe the type of evidence you hope to find and how you will preserve it.

Powers v. Clauster

This is a new file from ABC Insurance Company (a regular client of your law firm) involving a collision between a tractor and a Pontiac Grand Am. It appears from the police report that Sam Howland was driving a farm tractor owned by Clauster Farms on Highway 98 near the intersection of County Road 111. The ABC insured, Riley Powers, was in the process of passing the tractor when the tractor made a left turn at the intersection and struck the rear of the Powers vehicle. ABC paid Powers $1,533.06 for property damages. This amount plus Powers' $250 deductible makes a total claim of $1,783.06.

This is a difficult liability case and recovery for ABC may be difficult. The goal is to prove that Clauster Farms and Sam Howland are responsible for the damages incurred by Powers.

13 ANALYZING EVIDENCE

OBJECTIVES   After completing this chapter, you will know:

- There are eleven articles in the Federal Rules of Evidence and all are used to promote truth and fairness. Many states have adopted similar codes, which the paralegal must apply to the investigation.

- Exclusionary rules were created to prevent the court from receiving certain evidence under some circumstances.

- Evidence analysis depends on circumstantial evidence and inductive reasoning.

INTRODUCTION

The primary objective of evidence analysis is to assess existing evidence and identify missing evidence. This is done by separating the evidence into fundamental parts and applying those parts to the legal elements. During review of the physical evidence and testimony, the paralegal relies on the Federal Rules of Evidence and/or applicable state rules of evidence to determine the admissibility of the evidence. By analyzing evidence, the investigator can determine its usefulness in relation to the jury's ability to discern the truth of a matter based on the evidence presented to it.

FEDERAL RULES OF EVIDENCE

Eleven specific functions, qualifications, and categories of evidence make up the Federal Rules of Evidence (FRE or Fed. R. Evid.). These eleven sections cover the following:

1. General provisions
2. Judicial notice
3. Presumptions in civil actions and proceedings
4. Relevancy and its limits
5. Privileges
6. Witnesses
7. Opinions and expert testimony
8. Hearsay
9. Authentication and identifications
10. Contents of writings, recordings, and photographs
11. Miscellaneous rules.

The Federal Rules of Evidence were enacted by Congress in 1975[1] for the purpose of promoting truth and fairness, in practical terms. According to Rule 102: "These rules shall be construed to secure fairness in administration, elimination of unjustifiable expense and delay, and promotion of growth and development of the law of evidence to the end that the truth may be ascertained and proceedings justly determined."

The Federal Rules of Evidence apply to civil and criminal judicial proceedings in the federal court system,[2] but many states have adopted similar rules, which help promote uniformity in the laws and procedures nationwide. The paralegal must review her state's rules and apply them appropriately to evidence analysis. The Federal Rules of Evidence, as originally written, were based on common law and on evidence rules in existence at the time.[3] When a piece of evidence is believed to be inadmissible, the party challenging the evidence must present an objection to the court. Such an objection to evidence must be made in a timely manner; if the opposing party fails to do so, she generally waives the objection.[4]

EXCLUSION OF EVIDENCE

The purpose of rules that exclude evidence is to preclude a court from receiving evidence offered by a party under special circumstances. Most exclusionary rules were drafted to ensure that a jury's verdict is based on evidence that is true, factual, probative, and nonprejudicial. The Federal Rules of Evidence, and similar state rules, provide a framework of admissibility for attorneys and the court. Judges use their discretion when applying these rules, and once a judge has acted within his discretion based on the exclusionary rules, he will not be reversed unless there has been an abuse of discretion.

Categories of Rules Excluding Evidence

The following is a brief description of the exclusionary rules. The terms listed are not all-inclusive, but represent general areas of concern.

1. The witness is **incompetent** or is disqualified from testifying because he:

   a. has not taken the oath or affirmation

   b. lacks knowledge about the matter

   c. cannot qualify as an expert.

2. The testimony lacks probative value and is therefore **irrelevant**.

3. The testimony is **hearsay** because, for example, it is based not upon what the witness said, but rather upon what someone told the witness. Or perhaps the testimony or documents contain unsworn statements that are not subject to cross-examination.[5]

4. The testimony would require the disclosure of privileged communications or privileged records. The privilege must be duly asserted or it is waived. The exclusion of privileged communications applies to both oral and written communications. Matters to which a privilege may apply, depending on state law, include:

   a. communications between lawyer and client

   b. communications between husband and wife during their marriage

   c. communications between physician and patient about the patient's medical condition, and the physician's treatment records

   d. communications between a person and his priest or minister for spiritual guidance.[6]

5. The evidence lacks **foundation**. Before a witness may testify about a fact, it must be shown that the witness was able to make reasonably reliable observations concerning the fact. If the witness is to testify as an expert, it must be shown that he has adequate training and experience to render expert opinions concerning the subject matter.

6. Testimony is inadmissible because a statute forbids the court to allow the evidence. A legislature or other rule-making body may establish a policy against the use of certain evidence.

RULES OF EVIDENCE

General Provisions—Article I

Fed. R. Evid. 103 gives the court direction on evidence rulings. When an attorney believes the court has erred in excluding evidence, she may make an **offer of proof** outside the presence of the jury. The benefit of the offer of proof lies in the court record: when the testimony of a witness or the statement of the attorney is made during the offer of proof, it becomes a court record and can be used during any subsequent appeal (Fed. R. Evid. 103(a)(2)).

Judicial Notice—Article II

A trial judge may take **judicial notice** of certain facts, after which those facts are binding upon the parties and the jury (that is, they may not be contested). Fed. R. Evid. 201 sets the boundaries for using and understanding judicial notice. Article II governs only **adjudicated facts**, which are facts that have been judicially noticed. The kind of facts considered to be judicially noticed are defined in 201(b).

Rule: Fed. R. Evid. 201(b)

A judicially noticed fact must be one not subject to reasonable dispute in that it is either (1) generally known within the territorial jurisdiction of the trial court or (2) capable of accurate and ready determination by resort to sources whose accuracy cannot reasonably be questioned.

By taking judicial notice of a fact, a judge establishes the truth of the fact without either party presenting evidence to support it. (Examples are the determination that there are twelve inches in one foot, or that Christmas Day is December 25th.) In addition, the court may also take judicial notice of scientific facts. (Examples are time zones for particular sections of the country, or the temperature at which water boils in a specific area of the country). Within the boundaries of Rule 201, the court may take judicial notice of facts with or without a request by the parties, or may conduct a hearing in the absence of the jury, to determine the status of a fact and whether to take judicial notice of it. In civil court, the jury must accept judicially noticed facts as conclusive.

Presumptions—Article III

Article III of the Federal Rules of Evidence deals with **presumptions** in civil actions and proceedings. According to Article III, some facts are established, at trial, as presumptions of law. Presumptions are not binding upon the parties or the jury, as is the case with judicially noticed facts. A *presumption* is an assumption of fact that a rule of law requires to be assumed from another fact or group of facts that have been established. A presumption is distinguished from an inference: a judge or jury may or may not infer that something is true, whereas a presumption *requires* an inference to be drawn. When reaching a verdict, the jury may or may not find for a presumed fact.

Common presumptions of civil law, which vary from jurisdiction to jurisdiction, include:

- Involving death, the law presumes that a decedent has not committed suicide
- Involving railroad accidents, the law presumes that the railroad company acted negligently and caused the accident, unless proven otherwise.

It is crucial to remember that each state enacts its own presumptions; not all fall under the rule of the federal government. Some presumptions have been created by the courts, as a function in common law; others have been created by statute.

Relevancy—Article IV

All evidence is required to be relevant if it is to be admitted by the court. Relevancy requires evidence to be material and possess probative value. Article IV deals with relevancy and its limits, and Rule 401 defines relevant evidence.

Rule: Fed. R. Evid. 401

[E]vidence having any tendency to make the existence of any fact that is of consequence to the determination of the action more probable or less probable than it would be without the evidence.

EXAMPLE

Materiality depends on the weight evidence carries on the issues in the case. Consider the *Wilhoff v. Jones* case from Chapter 12. The defendant, Mr. Jones, accepted responsibility for an automobile accident in which Mr. Wilhoff was injured, even though the accident occurred in a no-fault state. Jones's insurance company paid for Mr. Wilhoff's immediate and long-term injuries and for the damage to his car. When Wilhoff filed suit to collect wages lost due to his injuries, the insurance company questioned the validity of the claim. Relevant evidence was needed for the legal team to show that Wilhoff lacked proof that the accident was the proximate of his lack of employment. The severity of the accident, Wilhoff's injuries, Wilhoff's employment history, his character, and many other topics are relevant to prove Wilhoff lacked proximate cause. Before initiation of the wage-loss claim, however, none of these categories of evidence was relevant.

Privileges—Article V

Originally, Article V of the Federal Rules of Evidence proposed nine categories of privileges, including lawyer-client, doctor-patient, husband-wife, clergy-penitent, and others. The draft also provided that the federal court system would recognize only those privileges set forth in the rules. The House of Representatives' Judiciary Committee amended the proposed rule to eliminate all specific rules of privilege, and replaced them with a general rule, Rule 501.

Rule 501 states that privileges are governed by common-law principles and that when state law supplies a rule of decision, such state rule will determine the existence of a privilege.

The rationale behind the new provision is that federal law should not supersede state law in substantive areas. When considering the new rule, the committee was concerned that civil litigators would be encouraged to "shop around" for a forum favorable to their privilege issues before presenting their case. Therefore, the legislators bound the federal courts to apply individual state privilege laws to actions, thereby removing any incentive for forum shopping.[7]

Witnesses—Article VI

Article VI focuses on the competency of witnesses.

Rule: Fed. R. Evid. 601

Every person is competent to be a witness except as otherwise provided in these rules. However, in civil actions and proceedings, with respect to an element of a claim or defense as to which State law supplies the rule of decision, the competency of the witness shall be determined in accordance with State law.

Topics concerning witnesses include personal knowledge, the oath or affirmation of the witness, interpreters, a judge as a witness, a juror as a witness, impeachment, character and conduct, religion, manner of interrogation, refreshing the witness's memory, prior statements, and exclusion of witnesses.[8]

Knowing and understanding the rules of Article VI are critical to the investigative paralegal, as she dedicates a large portion of the investigation to witnesses, their statements, and their value. The paralegal must guard against violating or overlooking rules governing witnesses.

Rule 612   While preparing a witness for deposition or trial testimony the paralegal often helps refresh the witness's memory.

Rule: Fed. R. Evid. 612

"[I]f a witness uses a writing to refresh memory for the purpose of testifying, either—

    (1) while testifying, or
    (2) before testifying, if the court in its discretion determines it is necessary in the interests of justice,

an adverse party is entitled to have the writing produced at the hearing, to inspect it, to cross-examine the witness thereon, and to introduce in evidence those portions which relate to the testimony of the witness … .

It is critical for the paralegal to understand the parameters set by this rule, to avoid costly errors.

Cross-examination is perhaps the most critical aspect of this rule, because privileged material used to refresh a witness's memory forfeits protection under this rule. An error under Rule 612 may cost a legal team valuable evidence.

Expert Witnesses—Article VII

Expert testimony (also called **expert opinion testimony**) is frequently used in all forms of litigation. Because this specialized testimony is so common, Article VII was created to address its unique requirements. Expert opinion requires a foundation to establish the sufficiency of the witness's background and knowledge of a subject matter.

According to Rule 702, an expert may be used when "scientific, technical, or other specialized knowledge will assist the trier of fact to understand the evidence or to determine a fact in issue." The rule allows expert testimony by saying: "a witness qualified as an expert by knowledge, skill, experience, training, or education, may testify thereto in the form of an opinion or otherwise."

Rules 701–706 establish a basis for using experts and their testimony, set limits on their ability to qualify as experts, and allow opinion testimony.

Rule: Fed. R. Evid. 703

"[T]he facts or data in the particular case upon which an expert bases an opinion or inference may be those perceived by or made known to the expert at or before the hearing … ."

Rule 704 goes one step further and allows expert testimony (and in some cases lay testimony) that deals with the ultimate issue of the case.

Hearsay—Article VIII

Hearsay is defined in Fed. R. Evid. 801(c) as "[a] statement, other than one made by the declarant while testifying at the trial or hearing, offered in evidence to prove the truth of the matter asserted."

Cross-examination is the focal point of the hearsay rule, and is believed to be the most effective method of exposing imperfections in a witness's perception, memory, or narration of fundamental facts. If a witness were allowed to present hearsay evidence, opposing counsel would be denied the opportunity to cross-examine the source. In addition, the jury cannot evaluate the demeanor and quality of the "real" witness who holds personal knowledge of the event in question; therefore, hearsay is not admissible except as provided for under Rules 802 through 806.

Rules 801 and 806 define the terms involved in hearsay and the hearsay rule itself.

Rule: Fed. R. Evid. 801

Definitions

The following definitions apply under this article:

(a) Statement. A "statement" is (1) an oral or written assertion or (2) nonverbal conduct of a person, if it is intended by the person as an assertion.

(b) Declarant. A "declarant" is a person who makes a statement.

(c) Hearsay. "Hearsay" is a statement, other than one made by the declarant while testifying at the trial or hearing, offered in evidence to prove the truth of the matter asserted.

(d) Statements Which Are Not Hearsay. A statement is not hearsay if—

(1) Prior Statement by Witness. The declarant testifies at the trial or hearing and is subject to cross-examination concerning the statement, and the statement is (A) inconsistent with the declarant's testimony, and was given under oath subject to the penalty of perjury at a trial, hearing, or other proceeding, or in a deposition, or (B) consistent with the declarant's testimony and is offered to rebut an express or implied charge against the declarant of recent fabrication or improper influence or motive, or (C) one of identification of a person made after perceiving the person; or

(2) Admission by Party-Opponent. The statement is offered against a party and is (A) the party's own statement, in either an individual or a representative capacity or (B) a statement of which the party has manifested an adoption or belief in its truth, or (C) a statement by a person authorized by the party to make a statement concerning the subject, or (D) a statement by the party's agent or servant concerning a matter within the scope of the agency or employment, made during the existence of the relationship, or (E) a statement by a coconspirator of a party during the course and in furtherance of the conspiracy. ...

Rule: Fed. R. Evid. 802

Hearsay Rule

Hearsay is not admissible except as provided by these rules or by other rules prescribed by the Supreme Court pursuant to statutory authority or by Act of Congress.

Rule: Fed. R. Evid. 803

Hearsay Exceptions; Availability of Declarant Immaterial

The following are not excluded by the hearsay rule, even though the declarant is available as a witness:

(1) Present sense impression. A statement describing or explaining an event or condition made while the declarant was perceiving the event or condition, or immediately thereafter.

(2) Excited utterance. A statement relating to a startling event or condition made while the declarant was under the stress of excitement caused by the event or condition.

(3) Then existing mental, emotional, or physical condition. A statement of the declarant's then existing state of mind, emotion, sensation, or physical condition (such as intent, plan, motive, design, mental feeling, pain, and bodily health), but not including a statement of memory or belief to prove the fact remembered or believed unless it relates to the execution, revocation, identification, or terms of declarant's will.

(4) **Statements for purposes of medical diagnosis or treatment.** Statements made for purposes of medical diagnosis or treatment and describing medical history, or past or present symptoms, pain, or sensations, or the inception or general character of the cause or external source thereof insofar as reasonably pertinent to diagnosis or treatment.

(5) **Recorded recollection.** A memorandum or record concerning a matter about which a witness once had knowledge but now has insufficient recollection to enable the witness to testify fully and accurately, shown to have been made or adopted by the witness when the matter was fresh in the witness's memory and to reflect that knowledge correctly. If admitted, the memorandum or record may be read into evidence but may not itself be received as an exhibit unless offered by an adverse party.

(6) **Records of regularly conducted activity.** A memorandum, report, record, or data compilation, in any form, of acts, events, conditions, opinions, or diagnoses, made at or near the time by, or from information transmitted by, a person with knowledge, if kept in the course of a regularly conducted business activity, and if it was the regular practice of that business activity to make the memorandum, report, record, or data compilation, all as shown by the testimony of the custodian or other qualified witness, unless the source of information or the method or circumstances of preparation indicate lack of trustworthiness. The term "business" as used in this paragraph includes business, institution, association, profession, occupation, and calling of every kind, whether or not conducted for profit.

(7) **Absence of entry in records kept in accordance with the provisions of paragraph (6).** Evidence that a matter is not included in the memoranda, reports, records, or data compilations, in any form, kept in accordance with the provisions of paragraph (6), to prove the nonoccurrence or nonexistence of the matter, if the matter was of a kind of which a memorandum, report, record, or data compilation was regularly made and preserved, unless the sources of information or other circumstances indicate lack of trustworthiness.

(8) **Public records and reports.** Records, reports, statements, or data compilations, in any form, of public offices or agencies, setting forth (A) the activities of the office or agency, or (B) matters observed pursuant to duty imposed by law as to which matters there was a duty to report, excluding, however, in criminal cases matters observed by police officers and other law enforcement personnel, or (C) in civil actions and proceedings and against the Government in criminal cases, factual findings resulting from an investigation made pursuant to authority granted by law, unless the sources of information or other circumstances indicate lack of trustworthiness.

(9) **Records of vital statistics.** Records or data compilations, in any form, of births, fetal deaths, deaths, or marriages, if the report thereof was made to a public office pursuant to requirements of law.

(10) **Absence of public record or entry.** To prove the absence of a record, report, statement, or data compilation, in any form, or the nonoccurrence or nonexistence of a matter of which a record, report, statement, or data

compilation, in any form, was regularly made and preserved by a public office or agency, evidence in the form of a certification in accordance with Rule 902, or testimony, that diligent search failed to disclose the record, report, statement, or data compilation, or entry.

(11) **Records of religious organizations.** Statements of births, marriages, divorces, deaths, legitimacy, ancestry, relationship by blood or marriage, or other similar facts of personal or family history, contained in a regularly kept record of a religious organization.

(12) **Marriage, baptismal, and similar certificates.** Statements of fact contained in a certificate that the maker performed a marriage or other ceremony or administered a sacrament, made by a clergyman, public official, or other person authorized by the rules or practices of a religious organization or by law to perform the act certified, and purporting to have been issued at the time of the act or within a reasonable time thereafter.

(13) **Family records.** Statements of fact concerning personal or family history contained in family Bibles, genealogies, charts, engravings on rings, inscriptions on family portraits, engravings on urns, crypts, or tombstones, or the like.

(14) **Records of documents affecting an interest in property.** The record of a document purporting to establish or affect an interest in property, as proof of the content of the original recorded document and its execution and delivery by each person by whom it purports to have been executed, if the record is a record of a public office and an applicable statute authorizes the recording of documents of that kind in that office.

(15) **Statements in documents affecting an interest in property.** A statement contained in a document purporting to establish or affect an interest in property if the matter stated was relevant to the purpose of the document, unless dealings with the property since the document was made have been inconsistent with the truth of the statement or the purport of the document.

(16) **Statements in ancient documents.** Statements in a document in existence twenty years or more the authenticity of which is established.

(17) **Market reports, commercial publications.** Market quotations, tabulations, lists, directories, or other published compilations, generally used and relied upon by the public or by persons in particular occupations.

(18) **Learned treatises.** To the extent called to the attention of an expert witness upon cross-examination or relied upon by the expert witness in direct examination, statements contained in published treatises, periodicals, or pamphlets on a subject of history, medicine, or other science or art, established as a reliable authority by the testimony or admission of the witness or by other expert testimony or by judicial notice. If admitted, the statements may be read into evidence but may not be received as exhibits.

(19) **Reputation concerning personal or family history.** Reputation among members of a person's family by blood, adoption, or marriage, or among a person's associates, or in the community, concerning a person's birth, adoption, marriage, divorce, death, legitimacy, relationship

by blood, adoption, or marriage, ancestry, or other similar fact of personal or family history.

(20) Reputation concerning boundaries or general history. Reputation in a community, arising before the controversy, as to boundaries of or customs affecting lands in the community, and reputation as to events of general history important to the community or State or nation in which located.

(21) Reputation as to character. Reputation of a person's character among associates or in the community.

(22) Judgment of previous conviction. Evidence of a final judgment, entered after a trial or upon a plea of guilty (but not upon a plea of nolo contendere), adjudging a person guilty of crime punishable by death or imprisonment in excess of one year, to prove any fact essential to sustain the judgment, but not including, when offered by the Government in a criminal prosecution for purposes other than impeachment, judgments against persons other than the accused. The pendency of an appeal may be shown but does not affect admissibility.

(23) Judgment as to personal, family, or general history, or boundaries. Judgments as proof of matters of personal, family or general history, or boundaries, essential to the judgment, if the same would be provable by evidence of reputation.

Rule: Fed. R. Evid. 804

Hearsay Exceptions; Declarant Unavailable

(a) Definition of unavailability. "Unavailability as a witness" includes situations in which the declarant—

(1) is exempted by ruling of the court on the ground of privilege from testifying concerning the subject matter of the declarant's statement; or

(2) persists in refusing to testify concerning the subject matter of the declarant's statement despite an order of the court to do so; or

(3) testifies to a lack of memory of the subject matter of the declarant's statement; or

(4) is unable to be present or to testify at the hearing because of death or then existing physical or mental illness or infirmity; or

(5) is absent from the hearing and the proponent of a statement has been unable to procure the declarant's attendance (or in the case of a hearsay exception under subdivision (b)(2), (3), or (4), the declarant's attendance or testimony) by process or other reasonable means.

A declarant is not unavailable as a witness if exemption, refusal, claim of lack of memory, inability, or absence is due to the procurement or wrongdoing of the proponent of a statement for the purpose of preventing the witness from attending or testifying.

(b) Hearsay exceptions. The following are not excluded by the hearsay rule if the declarant is unavailable as a witness:

(1) Former testimony. Testimony given as a witness at another hearing of the same or a different proceeding, or in a deposition taken in compliance with law in the course of the same or another proceeding, if the party against whom the testimony is now offered, or, in a civil action or proceeding, a predecessor in interest, had an opportunity and similar motive to develop the testimony by direct, cross, or redirect examination.

(2) **Statement under belief of impending death.** In a prosecution for homicide or in a civil action or proceeding, a statement made by a declarant while believing that the declarant's death was imminent, concerning the cause or circumstances of what the declarant believed to be impending death.

(3) **Statement against interest.** A statement which was at the time of its making so far contrary to the declarant's pecuniary or proprietary interest, or so far tended to subject the declarant to civil or criminal liability, or to render invalid a claim by the declarant against another, that a reasonable person in the declarant's position would not have made the statement unless believing it to be true. A statement tending to expose the declarant to criminal liability and offered to exculpate the accused is not admissible unless corroborating circumstances clearly indicate the trustworthiness of the statement.

(4) **Statement of personal or family history.** (A) A statement concerning the declarant's own birth, adoption, marriage, divorce, legitimacy, relationship by blood, adoption, or marriage, ancestry, or other similar fact of personal or family history, even though declarant had no means of acquiring personal knowledge of the matter stated; or (B) a statement concerning the foregoing matters, and death also, of another person, if the declarant was related to the other by blood, adoption, or marriage or was so intimately associated with the other's family as to be likely to have accurate information concerning the matter declared.

* * *

(6) **Forfeiture by wrongdoing.** A statement offered against a party that has engaged or acquiesced in wrongdoing that was intended to, and did, procure the unavailability of the declarant as a witness.

Rule: Fed. R. Evid. 805

Hearsay with Hearsay
Hearsay included within hearsay is not excluded under the hearsay rule if each part of the combined statements conforms with an exception to the hearsay rule provided in these rules.

Rule: Fed. R. Evid. 806

Attacking and Supporting Credibility of Declarant
When a hearsay statement, or a statement defined in Rule 801(d)(2)(C), (D), or (E), has been admitted in evidence, the credibility of the declarant may be attacked, and if attacked may be supported, by any evidence which would be admissible for those purposes if declarant had testified as a witness. Evidence of a statement or conduct by the declarant at any time, inconsistent

with the declarant's hearsay statement, is not subject to any requirement that the declarant may have been afforded an opportunity to deny or explain. If the party against whom a hearsay statement has been admitted calls the declarant as a witness, the party is entitled to examine the declarant on the statement as if under cross-examination.

Rule: Fed. R. Evid. 807

Residual Exception

A statement not specifically covered by Rule 803 or 804, but having equivalent circumstantial guarantees of trustworthiness, is not excluded by the hearsay rule, if the court determines that (A) the statement is offered as evidence of a material fact; (B) the statement is more probative on the point for which it is offered than any other evidence which the proponent can procure through reasonable efforts; and (C) the general purposes of these rules and the interests of justice will best be served by admission of the statement into evidence. However, a statement may not be admitted under this exception unless the proponent of it makes known to the adverse party sufficiently in advance of the trial or hearing to provide the adverse party with a fair opportunity to prepare to meet it, the proponent's intention to offer the statement and the particulars of it, including the name and address of the declarant.

Authentication and Identifications—Article IX

Article IX provides guidelines and limits for authenticating evidence: Rule 901 gives illustrations of how evidence may be authenticated and Rule 902 identifies evidence that is self-authenticated.

Rule 901   Illustrations of such methods of authentication under Rule 901 include:

- Testimony of witness with knowledge
- Nonexpert opinion on handwriting
- Comparison by trier of fact or expert witness
- Distinctive characteristics and the like
- Voice identification
- Telephone conversations
- Public records or reports
- Ancient documents or data compilations
- Process or system
- Methods provided by statute or rule.

Rule 902   In Fed. R. Evid. 902, the following types of evidence are recognized as self-authenticating; that is, the rule does not require the party presenting the evidence to offer extrinsic (additional or outside) evidence to support it.

- Domestic public documents under seal
- Domestic public documents not under seal

- Foreign public documents
- Certified copies of public records
- Official publications
- Newspapers and periodicals
- Trade inscriptions and the like
- Acknowledged documents
- Commercial paper and related documents
- Presumptions under Acts of Congress.

As the investigative paralegal gathers evidence, she should categorize it according to Rules 901 and 902 and focus attention on evidence that requires additional investigation and support. Consider again the *Wilhoff v. Jones* case.

EXAMPLE ——

All of the medical and employment records, along with the unemployment records from the state, fall under Fed. R. Evid. 901 and are not admissible without further qualification. The hypothesis and theory were supported by records and witness testimony proving that Wilhoff was unemployable due to personal characteristics rather than injuries sustained in the automobile accident. The allegation that Wilhoff was not injured as severely as he claimed was supported by evidence that required authentication under Rule 901, and the documentary evidence used must be supported by the personal knowledge of past employers and testimony from the police officers who arrested Wilhoff during a domestic violence call. Some records will be certified by the custodians or makers to authenticate them, others will be authenticated by witness testimony.

Contents of Writings, Recordings, and Photographs—Article X

The Federal Rules of Evidence discuss the admissibility of the often voluminous and cumbersome documents produced during the investigation and at trial. Rule 1001 defines terms related to documents, including writings, recordings, photographs, originals, and duplicates. Rule 1002 describes the "**best evidence rule**."

Rule: Fed. R. Evid. 1002

To prove the content of a writing, recording, or photograph, the original writing, recording, or photograph is required, except as otherwise provided in these rules or by Act of Congress.

Nevertheless, when the authenticity of a duplicate is not in doubt, and no unfairness would result, the rules allow the use of duplicates. Thus, most of the time, an original will not be required.[9]

Original Evidence   When original evidence is required, some judges set standards for its condition.

EXAMPLE

A plaintiff is seeking $500,000 in a breach-of-contract case. At the time of trial, plaintiff's counsel introduces into evidence the original contract. Upon review of the document, the judge notices that there are holes punched in the contract and that many sections of the contract have been highlighted. When questioned about the condition of the evidence, plaintiff's counsel states that a three-hole punch was used on the document so that it could be placed in a trial notebook, and that the highlighting was done during review of the contract. Plaintiff's counsel thus admits to altering the original integrity of the document. Occasionally, a judge will not accept original evidence that has been altered in such a way. The original integrity of a document must always be protected; copies should be made of all evidence for trial notebooks and investigations to ensure the admissibility of original documents during trial.

If an original is not useable, because it has been damaged or lost, Fed. R. Evid. 1003 allows the use of copies. When using a duplicate original, an **affidavit of authenticity** may be required. This affidavit, which is completed by a credible witness such as the attorney or a records custodian, states that the original is not available and that the duplicate is a true and correct copy of the original.

When thousands of documents are produced in a case, Fed. R. Evid. 1006 provides relief for both parties.

Rule: Fed. R. Evid. 1006

[T]he contents of voluminous writings, recordings, or photographs which cannot conveniently be examined in court may be presented in the form of a chart, summary, or calculation. The originals, or duplicates, shall be made available for examination or copying, or both, by other parties at a reasonable time and place. The court may order that they be produced in court.

Work Product   Lists, charts, and summaries prepared under Fed. R. Evid. 1006 are not considered to fall under the attorney work-product privilege. Thus, they should be prepared in a manner that does not compromise the producing party. A more detailed index or summary may be prepared for the legal team's use during the investigation, which does not have to be produced. Documents containing important information that are considered to be investigative tools should be marked as such, and indexes should reflect the privilege claimed and nothing more. Indexes and/or summaries dealing with "special" documents (i.e., privileged documents) should be kept separate from the original documents. A list of the originals provided to the opposing party should state only the privilege asserted for any documents not produced.

ANALYZING EVIDENCE

Investigation and evidence analysis are a process of reasoning, requiring the paralegal to break down the process into specific objectives. The primary objective of evidence analysis is to review existing evidence and determine what potential evidence is missing. Begin the examination by looking at three types of evidence: (1) the client's statement, (2) witness interviews, and (3) the factual components of the existing evidence.

EXAMPLE ───────────────────────────────────

Consider the methods used to analyze and locate potential evidence in *Wilhoff v. Jones*. Initially, the investigative paralegal reviewed the data from the defendants (the insurance company and Mr. Jones), witness reports, and police reports. She analyzed each category individually and as a whole; this analysis showed that Wilhoff probably was injured in the accident, but nothing provided adequate information as to the extent of his injuries. The initial analysis led to a search of Wilhoff's medical records (to qualify the extent of the injuries), which led to employment records (demonstrating that he could not hold a job), which led to the discovery of alcohol problems (credibility issues and inability to hold a job), which led to past worker's compensation claims (more credibility problems and evidence proving that Wilhoff could not prove proximate cause). The analysis also led to the development of a useable hypothesis that supported the legal theory and cause of action.

Potential Evidence

The development of potential evidence is a building process, because each piece of evidence can expand the investigation and prove the cause of action or defense. As seen in *Wilhoff v. Jones,* not all evidence is admissible or relevant, but it may help the investigation nevertheless. For instance, Wilhoff was driving his car without a license on the night of the accident. This fact, by itself, is of limited use, yet it instigated questions regarding Wilhoff's past criminal record and credibility. Those questions in turn pointed the paralegal toward relevant and material evidence, which helped prove that Wilhoff lacked proximate cause for a wage-loss claim.

Circumstantial Evidence   The paralegal depends on circumstantial evidence to initiate the analysis, because "the proof of certain facts ... infer[s] other connected facts that usually and reasonably follow according to common experience." The inferential principle is the basis for the entire investigation, and the hypothesis is based on the investigator's ability to use **inductive reasoning** and circumstantial evidence.

Inductive Reasoning   Inductive reasoning is a logical process of reasoning, based on inferences about particular facts or details of a story.[10]

EXAMPLE ───────────────────────────────────

While investigating a product liability case, the paralegal may infer that other consumers have suffered injury or property damage from the manufacturer's defective product. The inference is based on a logical assumption—that the defect caused one injury, so it probably caused others—and may be substantiated by circumstantial evidence, such as information from a retailer that many of the same product item have been returned damaged. An analysis of other evidence, the client's story, witness reports, and existing evidence can be conducted to find connections to the idea that others have also been injured, which helps to narrow the investigation and find evidence to support the cause of action.

To help expedite this process of connecting inferences and evidence, the paralegal may use an analysis chart.

The Analysis Chart

An analysis has the best chance of success when evidence is charted. Within a chart, evidence is placed in five basic categories that have already been determined, and require no additional or repetitive work:

1. Chronology
2. Client's existing affirmative evidence
3. Adversary's existing affirmative evidence
4. Client's potential affirmative evidence
5. Client's potential rebuttal evidence.

Each piece of evidence is evaluated based on its status (i.e., relevant, demonstrative, circumstantial, probative value, and origination) and authentication, and then placed in one of the five categories. Some evidence may fit into more than one category.

Category #1 The chronology section provides an overview of the entire case and evidence collected to support both positions, and gives perspective.

Categories #2 and #3 Section 2 lists the client's existing affirmative evidence, and is based on substantive legal issues. For instance, if the case involves a contract dispute, the client's copy of the contract will be obtained and entered. The same is done with the adversary's affirmative evidence in section 3.

☑ **PRACTICAL TIP** List the legal issue at the top of the chart or graph and itemize the evidence according to the elements it will support. See Figure 13-1.

Categories #4 and #5 The final two sections consist of the client's *potential* affirmative and rebuttal evidence. These categories are based on legal issues and their elements, but are expanded to include collateral evidence and circumstantial evidence that will be used to build and support the hypothesis.

Use of this type of charting system helps the paralegal make inferences and connect them to existing evidence. It should be used whenever necessary to expedite the investigation and enhance its efficiency.

Figure 13-1
Evidence analysis chart: Client's existing affirmative evidence broken down by legal elements

Breach of Contract	Source of Evidence
Element #1 Both parties are legally competent to enter into a contract.	Testimony of business associates or employees as to age, mental capacity, financial sophistication. Documents exemplifying previous business relationships. Age-related documents such as birth certificates, etc. Partnership or corporate records authorizing a person to act on behalf of a business or partnership.
Element #2 A valid offer and acceptance were made between the parties.	Client's copy of the contract. Testimony of one or both parties or witnesses to the negotiating and signing of the contract. Opposing party's copy of the contract.
Element #3 An exchange of legal consideration has occurred.	Cashed checks, real estate filings, or other monetary-related documents. Testimony of witnesses, including banking personnel, family members, business associates, or employees.
Element #4 Compliance with special statutes has occurred.	**Statute of Frauds**—a state statute requiring that certain contracts must be in writing to be enforceable.
Element #5 Proof that the breach occurred.	

SUMMARY

- The Federal Rules of Evidence set rules for determining the admissibility of evidence in federal court proceedings.
- Eleven topical categories are covered in the FRE, including such subjects as judicial notice, presumptions, relevancy, and witnesses.
- The FRE contain provisions limiting the admissibility of relevant evidence in such areas as incompetence, hearsay, and foundation.
- Evidence analysis allows the paralegal to evaluate the existing evidence and apply it to the hypothesis. By charting the evidence, she can find connections between existing evidence and missing evidence.

ACTIVITIES

1. Refer to the example given on page 334 of Chapter 15. Which rules of evidence will influence this interview and the documents produced thereafter? How will you apply the rules? Are there any issues of witness competency? How will you handle any evidence produced as a result of this interview? Be specific.

2. A successful investigation and hypothesis are based on an investigator's ability to use inferential reasoning. Explain how inferential reasoning works and what investigative tools are used to determine the probative value of certain evidence.

CASE STUDY

Emery v. Hall

Review the details of the case entitled *Emery v. Hall* and complete the following:

1. Analyze the evidence that is known to date, using the strategies and techniques described in Chapters 11–13.

2. Detail any potential evidence you may need and where you might obtain it.

3. How will you preserve the evidence? Be specific, addressing any special concerns about particular items of evidence.

4. Identify any rules from the FRE that will apply to using or entering each piece of evidence at trial or deposition.

5. For the witness, what evidence will you use or try to gather to support her testimony?

6. Analyze the circumstantial evidence in the case, using it to determine your progress, uncover new and missing evidence, and encourage inductive reasoning.

Emery v. Hall

This case involves a woman in her early thirties (Colleen Emery) who was babysitting for a friend (Karen Metcalf) in Good Haven, Montana. Emery was caring for Metcalf's son on a winter night in February 1990. At 11:00 P.M. she left Metcalf's four-plex and headed for the parking lot. When she got to the parking lot, she fell and hurt her knee. Emery was accompanied that night by her husband, who subsequently took her to the emergency room and St. Joseph's Hospital. Since the fall, Emery has undergone extensive medical treatment for back injuries. She claims that her injuries were caused by the fall.

Your law firm is defending the action. You note that she did not complain of back problems until eight months after the fall. Her only complaint prior to October 1990 was that her knee hurt. The medical records have been obtained and summarized. Employment records have also been gathered. Weather reports have been obtained from the National Weather Service and local newspapers. There are four witnesses in the case: (1) Emery's husband, (2) Metcalf, (3) Mary Lenox (a renter in the four-plex), and (4) Emery herself. All the witnesses except Emery and her husband have been interviewed.

To date, Emery has incurred $47,511.86 in medical bills for back surgery and follow-up care. She claims that the owner of the four-plex, Marge Hall, is responsible for these bills and future medical expenses incurred as a result of the fall. Emery claims that the parking lot had not been cleared after a heavy snowfall prior to her fall. She also alleges that the parking lot was slippery and poorly lit, all of which contributed to her fall. The following information and evidence has been gathered to support your team's defense against Emery's claim:

- Emery's medical records show a preexisting medical condition regarding her back. According to the records, Emery has suffered back pain for years due to obesity.
- Employment records show that Emery has left several jobs during the last eight years. In the exit paperwork, the employers claim that Emery left due to poor physical health.
- The intake report at the hospital makes no mention of back pain or injury after the fall.
- Interviews with Ms. Metcalf were unproductive, as she is hostile.

- The interview with Mary Lenox produced the following details:
  - Lenox was asked to move out of the four-plex by Marge Hall shortly after the fall happened. She does not have a good relationship with Hall.
  - Lenox claims that the property was poorly maintained and that Hall cleared the snow out of the parking lot and off the sidewalk only when she felt like it.
  - Lenox lived in apartment 2-B (upstairs, above Metcalf) for one year, September to September.
  - The parking lot was gravel, square in shape, and held two cars at a time.
  - Lenox never slipped in the parking lot or on the sidewalk while she lived there.
  - Lenox claims Hall came into her apartment while she was not home on more than one occasion.
- Weather reports for the week of the accident show mild snow accumulation. No more than two inches fell two days prior to Emery's accident and no snow was recorded on the day of the fall. Temperatures were in the mid-twenties. No fog or precipitation impeded visibility on the night of the fall.

NOTES

[1] Pub. L. No. 93-595, § 1, 88 Stat. 1926 (1975).

[2] Fed. R. Evid. 1101(b).

[3] See P. Rothstein, *Evidence in a Nutshell: State and Federal Rules* 1–2 (1997).

[4] Fed. R. Evid. 103(a)(1).

[5] Fed. R. Evid. 801, 802.

[6] Fed. R. Evid. 501 and applicable state law.

[7] Fed. R. Evid. 501 advisory notes.

[8] Fed. R. Evid. 601–615.

[9] Fed. R. Evid. 1003.

[10] Based on *New Webster's Dictionary of the English Language, College Edition* 770 (Consolidated Book Publishers, 1975).

14

LOCATING WITNESSES

OBJECTIVES   After completing this chapter, you will know:

- What steps to take to plan the witness search.
- How to conduct the witness search, including identifying and locating the witnesses; using public, private, and Internet sources; managing the search; and observing the ethical boundaries of the search.
- How to evaluate the search using common sense and the facts.
- How to locate expert witnesses via the Internet and other sources.

INTRODUCTION

Witnesses hold some of the most critical evidence in a lawsuit: evidence that provides a jury with answers that physical evidence cannot and answers "why" questions. Unfortunately, many witnesses are not immediately known or available to the legal team. When they are missing, the paralegal must identify and locate them by creating a plan for the search.

Planning the search for witnesses is done based on the paralegal's personal preferences, skill level, and past experience. Not all persons are comfortable canvassing neighborhoods or blindly calling strangers, so other methods may be used, such as interviewing the client and reviewing physical evidence. Following a few basic procedures will help plan a search for witnesses:

- *Identifying unknown witnesses.* Witnesses are identified by interviewing the client and reviewing existing physical evidence. Reviewing the evidence also helps educate the paralegal on the legal issues and subject matter, preparing him for witness interviews and connecting the facts to the witnesses.

- *Use a variety of public, private, and printed materials and the Internet to locate witnesses.* The paralegal should familiarize himself with all possible resources available to locate the identified witnesses, including the public, private, and printed materials listed in Chapter 9. (A discussion on Internet sources appears later in this chapter.) Charting or listing witnesses and resources assists the paralegal in tracking successes and failures during the search. Management of the search helps avoid repeating search activities.

- *Observe ethical boundaries.* Before contacting any persons for information, the paralegal should review ethical obligations, to ensure a professional search that will not jeopardize the admissibility of evidence.

- *Strategize the search.* The paralegal should carefully strategize his search by knowing who he wants to find and why. His method(s) will depend on personal style and preferences, but should include use of visual guides to details and leads as they develop.

CONDUCTING THE SEARCH

Begin the search by categorizing the witnesses, who will fall into one of two categories:

- Identified witnesses—those who have been specifically named by one of the parties or in a document or piece of physical evidence.

- Unknown witnesses—those who have not been specifically identified by the legal team.

Identifying Witnesses

To work efficiently, it is critical to identify unknown witnesses before searching for identified but missing witnesses. This strategy saves time and effort and is the best use of billable time. Searching for unidentified witnesses requires a thorough examination of the existing documentation and physical evidence, along with a review of all client interviews.

The paralegal identifies witnesses by fully understanding the background of the client, the events prior to the triggering event, the triggering event, and the events following the triggering event. Using the base information from the client and any details provided by the opposing party, the stage is set for witness identification. What the paralegal does next determines how many additional witnesses are located.

Interviewing the Client   Use the logical sequence diagram and proximate probability, in conjunction with the client's data, to identify witnesses. Consider the injured renter in the Chapter 10 case study.

EXAMPLE

The injured renter allegedly slipped and fell on the steps of her apartment building when leaving for work one morning. Shortly after she fell, another tenant found her lying on the steps. No other witness was present. During the initial client interview, an outline of the fall (LSD) is drafted. The paralegal notes as many potential witnesses as his imagination allows while hearing the story. He employs the proximate probability theory, while listening, as a means of identifying witnesses. At the conclusion of the interview, a list of possible witnesses is drafted. The client is then given a copy of the list to review, and identifies any additional witnesses or deletes any witnesses as necessary.

Using this scenario, a potential witness outline will include the persons listed in Figure 14-1, all of whom were found through proximate probability. Once a potential witness outline is drafted, there are endless opportunities to uncover new witnesses by contacting the persons identified in the outline.

All physical evidence, including documents gathered from the client and any other sources, is reviewed. Based on the review, the paralegal may add police personnel, ambulance staff, hospital staff, insurance adjusters, neighbors, family members, or other persons to a potential witness list.

The Witness List   The construction of a witness list is much like building a pyramid. A broad base is used to start construction, and as information is uncovered the list is narrowed until the "best" witnesses are identified. As the list narrows, general categories of potential witnesses are replaced with specific names of witnesses in the case. See Figure 14-2. After completing the witness list, the paralegal must begin looking for the physical location of the witness.

Locating Witnesses

Any witness who is identified by the client, or by physical or testimony evidence, is usually known by name. Locating these witnesses is expedited simply because their names are known. All witnesses in the "identified" category are listed in an organizational chart (see Figure 14-3) and held until all **general-category witnesses** have been identified. The general-category witness

Figure 14-1
Potential witness
outline

Potential Witness	Connection to Case
1. Other tenants	Any other person who would have used the stairs on which the injured renter fell that morning; tenants who use those same stairs regularly.
2. Visitors to the complex	Any person who was visiting a tenant in the building where the fall occurred, on the night and/or morning of the fall, or within one week of the fall.
3. City/county/state/private workers (postal carriers, garbage workers, electric company workers, etc.)	Any person who would have been in the area on the morning of the fall (possibly repairing damage from the inclement weather); any person who regularly works in or around the apartment complex and more specifically the building where the fall occurred.
4. Past tenants	Anyone who has experience with the client or the injured renter prior to the triggering event.
5. Employees of client	Any employees of the client who regularly work on snow or ice removal.
6. Renter's co-workers	Any co-worker of the injured renter who may offer a better understanding of the renter's injuries and motivations.

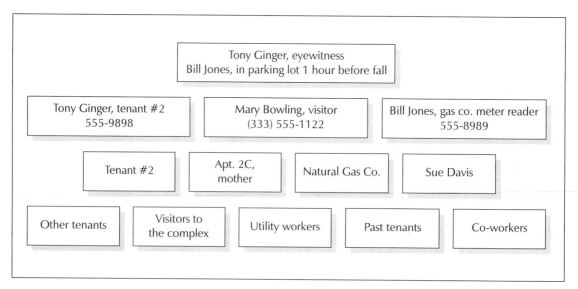

Figure 14-2   Witness pyramid

Figure 14-3
Potential witness
organizational
chart

POTENTIAL WITNESS LIST

Identified Witnesses	Status	General-Category Witnesses	Status
Tenant #2, Tony Ginger	Eyewitness, Apt. 2B 555-9898		
		Mother of tenant in Apt. #2C	No name yet; need to contact tenant, Zach Bowling
Co-worker, Sue Davis	Works with plaintiff at XYZ Company; no personal data		
		Natural Gas Company employee	No name as of 1/96; contact at Gas Company is Scott Schmidt

is originally identified through proximate probability and is known only by general description, such as a utility worker or neighbor. The general-category witness remains nameless until the paralegal personally identifies him or her.

Once a thorough list of witnesses is compiled, the paralegal can begin physically locating the witnesses. General-category witnesses are the most challenging to find, and thus receive first priority.

General-Category Witnesses   Locating witnesses is a challenging and time-consuming task that begins by focusing on those identified only by general category.

EXAMPLE ——————————————————————————————————

It is believed that a utility worker for the gas company was in the parking lot of the apartment complex one hour before the renter slipped and fell. This unknown witness may provide proof of the client's claim that there were no slipping hazards on the steps or in the parking lot at the time the renter fell.

———

A two-tiered process is used in attempting to locate a general-category witness. The first step consists of contacting the **general-category identifier**, in this case the gas company that employs the potential witness. A general-category identifier is a person or entity that has the closest contact with the witness and therefore can aid in identifying and locating him or her. Be aware, however, that personnel departments (whether of private businesses or public companies) will seldom identify employees over the phone without adequate reason. When communicating with a company, be prepared to offer as much detail as possible to the contact person about the inquiry, and explain the need to know the witness's identity. Personnel staff are trained to guard the privacy of employees. Therefore, to receive the data desired, it may be necessary to personally go to the company and ask for help; a written request for the information may be required, if such information can be obtained at all.

By having an employee called as a witness, the company's use of the employee may be compromised, as participating in an investigation and testifying at trial requires time away from work. Refrain from offering too many details to the contact person regarding the witness's responsibility to testify; a forewarned contact may create a barrier in identifying the witness or may simply refuse to help. Preconceived ideas regarding commitments for the witness may influence both the employer's and the witness's cooperation.

If the contact at the general-category identifier does not produce the name of the witness, the paralegal must move to the second step of the process, which is to canvass the location where the triggering event occurred. If the general-category witness is not known to work for a specific company, the paralegal must look for other or different types of general-category identifiers.

EXAMPLE

The paralegal is told that an unknown person was in the parking lot at the time the renter fell, but it is not known who the person is or why he was in the parking lot. The paralegal must look for a source to identify this witness (general-category identifier). Canvassing of the neighbors may reveal who had a visitor on the morning of the fall, and thus uncover the identity of the witness. Identifying all persons who had visitors on the morning of the fall may lead to specific tenants and the witness.

Using Public and Private Resources

The Telephone   The most accessible and inexpensive resource for a missing-witness search is the telephone. Always use this resource first. As noted in Chapter 10, telephone and city directories for every major city in the country can be found at the local library.

Here are some basic rules for telephone canvassing:

- Practice to obtain a well-modulated and pleasing telephone voice.
- Always treat the party you are calling with extreme politeness.
- Speak slowly and quietly.
- Time each call carefully. Never call people at home or at the office late in the afternoon, as this disrupts the closing of normal daily routines. (Businesspersons are winding down for the day and persons working at home are preparing for the return of their families.)
- Identify yourself at the beginning of the phone conversation.

- Never contact someone via a collect call.

- Prepare for the call by thoroughly understanding the details of the case and the need for the witness. Also be very familiar with all the current information that has been obtained on the witness's background.

The Postmaster   When a physical address has been obtained, the paralegal can forward mail to the address for verification, marking the envelope, "Address Correction Requested."

When no physical location for the witness has been identified, the paralegal may make an address request to the local postmaster; this ensures that an accurate address is obtained and keeps the search private. It is often necessary to avoid alerting the witness to the fact that he is being sought; reluctant or hostile witnesses may disappear again.

The postmaster is a prime resource for locating physical addresses. Fees for such searches vary from state to state and are normally inexpensive; however, it takes time to request and receive information from the postmaster. The postmaster can provide forwarding addresses, post office box information, and previous addresses for fees ranging from free to about $5.00, with timelines from one week to a month. Do not use the postmaster for immediate searches, as longer time lags are possible.

When a P.O. box number is provided for the witness, use the county clerk's office to research the plat maps, block books, or other physical boundaries of the zip code area. Then narrow the search by using a city directory or by canvassing the area.

Other General Sources   Depending on the value and nature of the witness's testimony, the paralegal may use other resources from the public sources discussed in Chapter 10 to locate the witness.

☑ **PRACTICAL TIP**   Information found in voter registration records, plaintiff and defendant indices, marriage and divorce records, and records of professional organizations, alumni associations, and utility companies are especially helpful. When a witness does an unintentional skip (that is, when a cooperative, missing witness does not know that she is needed), the paralegal may seek the assistance of the motor vehicle department and research driver's license records. If the witness is intentionally avoiding the legal team (intentional skip), the paralegal may be forced to become more aggressive, contacting neighbors or business associates or researching real estate sales and transfers.

Ethical Consideration   Clients are concerned about and acutely conscious of money being spent during an investigation, including billable time. Therefore, consult the attorney each time a new search is necessary, to avoid billing time not recoverable from the client. All decisions involving a client's costs must be the attorneys', as they work in a fiduciary capacity for the client.

Using the Internet

For most investigators, the Internet has become a primary tool for finding witnesses. To use the Internet for locating phone numbers and addresses, consider the following suggestions:

- Select a search engine.
  - Yahoo: http://www.yahoo.com (people search)
  - Excite: http://www.excite.com/Reference/people.html
- In the search engine, look for a "People Finder" or the equivalent. Each engine will have a different name for its service and a different method of gathering information on the missing person. In general, all engines ask for:
  - First, middle, and last names of the person
  - City, county, state of residence (if known)
  - Telephone number, e-mail address (if known).
- Wild-card searches are an option in all engines. Most searches use some form of a wild-card search if no information is placed in the city, county, state, or telephone number categories.
- To use reverse telephone number listings, try the GTE SuperPages: http://superpages.gte.net/ and select a detailed search.

Links to related sources and directories are commonly made while performing searches, but there are too many possibilities to list here. Create a search engine log or chart that lists all directories, shortcuts, and data found while searching for witnesses. This will expedite future searches.

Because the circumstances of civil litigation vary, it is impossible to give examples of all the uses for public and private resources in the search for a missing witness. Each search must include creativity, organization, and time to locate the missing witness.

⚊≣ MANAGING THE SEARCH

Organization is instrumental in locating witnesses. It is very common for the paralegal to enlist the help of other members of the legal team, or other paralegals, to aid in the search for missing witnesses. When additional persons become involved in a search, information may be duplicated, overlooked, or lost, so create a search flowchart to avoid confusion and needless repetition (see Figure 14-4).

The data at the top of the chart provides the researcher with critical details that are frequently needed, including the witness's date of birth, Social Security number, and last known address. It is imperative that organizational charts and diagrams be created to manage information on the witnesses (and client) in every case. It is also helpful to attach a witness chart to the cover of a file designated for witnesses.

WITNESS LOCATING CHART

Case Name _____   Lead Paralegal_____

Case Number_____

Witness Category _____   Date of Birth_____

Witness Name_____   Social Sec. #_____

Last Known Address _____   Driver's License # _____

Last Known Phone # _____   Spouse Name _____

Occupation _____

Source Researched	Status of Search	Date of Search	Follow-Up Date	Paralegal Doing the Search
1.				
2.				
3.				
4.				

Figure 14-4   Organizational chart for locating witnesses

Develop a strategy for managing all witness charts and graphs, such as using a three-ring binder to track witnesses and materials relating to them. This binder should be clearly labeled and a memorandum regarding its existence placed in the case general file. This binder helps guide the search and provides details on the witnesses' backgrounds.

KNOWING THE BOUNDARIES

A conscientious paralegal always stays abreast of his ethical responsibilities. The task of searching for witnesses is unique and requires the paralegal to use methods of motivating people to help. When dealing with family members or friends of a person who has intentionally skipped, a paralegal is often faced with a situation that requires honesty.

EXAMPLE

During the search for a missing evidence witness, a paralegal phones the father of the witness. He explains to the father that he is looking for the son; the father asks why. The paralegal would certainly get more information from the father if he lied and said he was an old high school buddy who simply wanted to arrange to meet his friend on his next visit home. However, it is ethically imperative that the paralegal accurately and truthfully identify himself when asked. Of course, the father will probably offer very little help as to the son's whereabouts once he understands who the paralegal is and what he wants. Nevertheless, ethical constraints demand that the paralegal be honest.

The paralegal must become proficient in interviewing and questioning. When required to divulge his identity early in a conversation, he must do so in a calm, nonthreatening manner. Perfecting interviewing skills is the key to success in these situations. As easy and effective as it may be to lie about one's identity and the reason for contacting a person, it is not ethical.

Aside from honesty, there are several other guidelines the paralegal must follow to avoid overstepping ethical boundaries:

- Always identify yourself when asked.
- Never threaten someone with legal action for not cooperating.
- Never use illegal methods to obtain information.
- Always behave in a courteous, professional manner.
- Never offer confidential or privileged information to someone in an attempt to entice him or her into speaking.
- Never express legal opinions or advice.
- Always treat any information received as private and confidential.

Violation of ethical obligations may result in professional sanctions for the attorney and loss of employment for the paralegal. Improper information gathering is usually discovered by opposing counsel during the course of the investigation, and may threaten the entire case, in addition to jeopardizing use of the data. Tainted evidence or information may be excluded by the court.

EVALUATING THE SEARCH

Throughout the process of searching for a witness, the paralegal must evaluate the search by: (1) initial impressions, (2) bare facts, and (3) the potential for continuing the search. Each of these questions can be answered by gathering and recording the information drafted during the search, and reviewing it with the attorney and other members of the legal team.

Initial Impressions

Always leave space on any charts or graphs for personal impressions. For instance, when contacting a records custodian, friend, or employer, the paralegal should record his feelings about the interview, the interviewee, and the information garnered; he should also note common-sense thoughts and intuitions. Those impressions help direct future searches and spur new ideas. When the paralegal has finally located the witness, the feelings and impressions recorded during the search will dictate both the manner in which the witness will be approached and interviewed and the way the legal team prepares for interviews and depositions with the witness.

EXAMPLE

The paralegal is assigned to a case involving a missing witness who is a well-respected dog trainer. Her expertise with dogs and personal experiences with the opposing party are critical to the case. As the paralegal conducts the search, he discovers that several people close to the witness are willing to talk with him about the witness but are not willing to reveal her current whereabouts. The witness herself has told these secondary sources that she is afraid of the opposing party in the case and therefore does not want to be directly involved.

After several interviews with the secondary sources, the paralegal reviews the results of his search. He has not uncovered any solid information on the witness's location, so he reviews his initial impressions. Those impressions tell him that the witness very much wants to talk, but is inhibited by fear; her fear stems from the opposing party's violent nature. He also feels that the secondary sources want to help; their cooperation makes him believe that all the contacts are motivated to "do the right thing."

A better understanding of the problems in the search, including the reason the witness is hiding and the loyalty of the secondary sources, gives the paralegal a new direction for the search: the secondary sources themselves. He develops a plan to appeal to the sources' desire for justice and to empathize with the witness's fear, in the hope that this will motivate the sources to offer enough useable information to locate the witness.

The information considered useable, in this example, includes background details on the witness's expertise and personal life. By creating a rapport with the sources, the paralegal finds out that the witness is married, that the marriage occurred since the triggering event, that she has moved, that she still trains dogs, and what her hobbies are. He also uncovers more specific details on the frightening activities of the opposing party. This information allows the paralegal to better understand the witness and bridge any barriers in the search.

Making notes on all impressions is critical. For example, during a meeting with a secondary source, the paralegal's feeling that the source is dishonest or uninterested in helping him find the witness is important. Such an insight will offer a clearer understanding of the personality and behavior of both the missing witness and the secondary source.

The Bare Facts: Is There Potential to Continue?

The most obvious task in evaluating a search is to assess the information gathered to date. Consider again the example involving the dog trainer.

EXAMPLE

At the conclusion of the interviews with the secondary sources, the paralegal has determined the following information:
- The trainer handles field retrievers exclusively.
- The trainer is in her late twenties.
- She was married during the later part of 1998.

- The trainer also enjoys reading and subscribes to many professional periodicals on dog training.
- The trainer has contributed articles to at least one of these specialized periodicals.
- The trainer is frightened of the opposing party because he violently abused several of his dogs and she witnessed the abuse.
- The opposing party is believed to have threatened her.
- The trainer's extended family still lives in the general area.

After a review of the bare facts, the paralegal must decide if he has begun to gather information that will lead to the witness. In this case, the answer is a definite yes.

EXAMPLE

It has been discovered that the trainer deals with field retrievers only and that she contributes to and subscribes to periodicals on the subject. It has also been discovered that the witness was recently married. Secondary sources have also said that the witness's extended family still lives in the area. Each of these associations will direct the search for the witness:

- Research all periodicals dealing with field retrievers and the training of field retrievers.
- Contact the staff of each of those periodicals and determine when and if the witness contributed to the magazine.
- Ask the editors of the magazines that the witness has written for if they have a current or past address and phone number for the witness.
- Use current or past addresses and phone numbers to track the witness and contact her.
- Research the marriage licenses in the county where she lived during 1998 to locate her new name and that of her new husband.
- Contact the motor vehicle department to check for a change of name and address on the witness's driver's license.
- Contact the family living in the area and begin new secondary source interviews if the witness has not been located.

If, at the conclusion of reviewing and acting on the bare facts, the paralegal is still unable to locate the witness, he should again review the facts and his initial impressions. Once that is completed, he must either discontinue the search or hire a private detective or skiptracer.

LOCATING EXPERT WITNESSES USING THE INTERNET

Locating expert witnesses can be easy when using the Internet and a variety of other public sources of information. It can also be difficult if the search is conducted without a plan and understanding of the type of expert desired. For instance, when searching for a mechanical engineer, the paralegal first must determine if there are any special requirements for the expert, such as unique skills or education; if location is a problem (whether in terms of time or money); or if demographics will negatively influence the expert's testimony in any way. Once the search field has been narrowed, the paralegal may begin the search by looking at Web sites for publications, professional organizations, private institutions, public or private corporations, or universities or colleges. Consider all of the following Internet sites and other services. (Please note that Web sites change and close often; at the printing of this text, the following sites were available.)

- Martindale-Hubbell: http://www.martindale.com
- On any search engine, search for specific universities, colleges, or technical schools.
- Legal/Accounting: http://www.users.cloud9.net then select a personal home page, as shown in the parenthetical example (http://www.users.cloud9.net/~kvivian/html/legal_accounting_web.html)
- Technical Assistance Bureau: http://www.intr.net/tab
- Technical Advisory Services for Attorneys: http://www.tasanet.com
- Medical Literature Research: http://www.medoptionslegal.com
- Internet Public Library: http://ipl.sils.umich.edu
- The Cosmetic, Toiletry, and Fragrance Association: http://www.ctfa.org/
- Engineering and Safety Service: http://www.safetyengineers.com/
- Municipal Code Corporation: http://www.municode.com or infor@mail.municode.com

The following sources are not found on the Internet, but offer a variety of options in locating expert witnesses.

- Electronic Text Retrieval Systems, Inc.: 1-800-910-0910 or 303-247-1482
- Libraries Unlimited: info@librarium.com
- Library of Congress: lc.web.loc.gov or 202-707-6100
- National Association of Boards of Pharmacy: 847-698-6227 or 847-698-0124
- National Committee for Clinical Laboratory Standards (NCCLS): 610-525-2435
- National Fire Protection Association (NFPA): http://www.nfpa.org or 800-344-3555.

SUMMARY

- To plan the search for witnesses, identify the witnesses and public and private resources for the search. Draft organizational tools to manage the data. Consider and respect ethical boundaries.

- The search is conducted by first seeking out general-category witnesses, and then by identifying the physical locations of all witnesses.
- The investigator evaluates the search by noting and reviewing his personal impressions and the facts of the case.
- Experts are found after carefully evaluating the needs of the case and skills of the expert. Using the Internet or other public and private companies expedites the search for experts.

ACTIVITIES

1. Discuss with a reference desk librarian the options you have in locating an expert witness to deal with a mechanical failure in a log flume ride at an amusement park. List in detail the variety of resources you may use to locate such an individual.

2. When identifying witnesses, which category of witness do you believe should be searched for first? Why?

3. Refer to Figure 14-1. Select a potential general-category witness from this list. Describe in detail how you will attempt to locate the witness. Include in your answer all organizational tools you will use to manage the search; name the general-category identifiers you will contact and explain how you chose those identifiers. Also, outline the questions you will ask the identifier and the witness. What problems do you anticipate in the interviews? Finally, list the resources you will use to find this person.

CASE STUDIES

Wilson v. Sonic

Review the following case details and draft a potential witness outline. Explain why you chose the witnesses you did and what resources you will use to find the physical location of those witnesses.

Case Details

Mr. Wilson was visiting friends in Yuma, Arizona, on November 8, 1998. He stayed overnight at the Americana Hotel. He and his wife went to dinner at a nearby Holiday Inn and then returned to their hotel room and played cards until 1:00 A.M. Around 2:00 A.M., Wilson received a phone call from the police asking him if he knew that his car had been stolen. Apparently, sometime around 1:00 A.M., Mr. Sonic stole Wilson's car by breaking a window and using a screwdriver to start the car. Someone reported the vehicle traveling at a high rate of speed near the Holiday Inn. The police tried to stop Sonic, but Sonic evaded them. During the subsequent chase, he drove through a trailer park, over speed bumps, and through a plowed field; ultimately, he hit a large rock that blew out the right front tire.

The car, quite a bit the worse for wear, was taken to the police station. The next day Wilson contacted his insurance agent and arranged for the car to be towed from the police garage to an Oldsmobile dealer's garage. The stolen car was a 1997 Oldsmobile with just over 22,000 miles on it.

Wilson was told that Sonic was eighteen years old and had a blood alcohol level of .10 at the time of the incident. In a criminal trial, Sonic was jailed for sixty days and ordered to pay restitution to Wilson. After serving his sentence, Sonic left the county jail and was never seen again. Wilson is now suing Sonic in civil court for the money owed to him.

Swan v. Madison

Review the following case details and then complete the following assignments:

1. Begin tracking down the missing boyfriend.
2. Name the people you will interview to find the boyfriend.
3. Name any resources you will use to find the boyfriend.
4. Create a witness locating chart for the boyfriend. Explain how you will obtain the information needed for the chart.
5. Are there any ethical considerations in this search? If so, what are they specifically?
6. How long do you anticipate it will take to find the boyfriend? Explain your answer.

Case Details

On January 27, 1998, William Swan and his daughter, Amanda, were looking at mobile homes to buy. The two had been looking for a home they could share, to accommodate William's failing health. Two days earlier, on January 25, 1998, Amanda had spoken with Mrs. Bret Hollingsworth, who owned and managed a trailer park in Center City. Hollingsworth explained that she and her husband lived on the property and were responsible for the upkeep and management of the community property within the park. She also said they owned several of the trailers and currently had one for rental or sale. The Swans decided to look at the trailer on January 27.

At 10:00 A.M. on January 27th, Amanda set out to drive herself, her father, and her boyfriend, Mike Timberland, to the trailer park. The trailer park was located exactly fifteen miles from their apartment in the neighboring community of St. Charles. Amanda claims that the weather conditions were bad that morning, but because they desperately needed to find a new home, they decided to go to the trailer park anyway. She estimates it took her forty-five minutes to get to the trailer park, due to snow and blowing conditions, and she claims to have driven very slowly.

Upon arriving at the trailer park, the Swans and Mr. Timberland found their way to trailer #15 and then to the Hollingsworth trailer. Mrs. Hollingsworth answered the door when they knocked. Amanda introduced herself and asked to be taken to see the trailer; Mrs. Hollingsworth said she would page her husband, who was out on the property removing snow and ice, to meet them at the trailer. She was caring for their three small children and could not leave.

Approximately fifteen minutes later, Mr. Hollingsworth arrived at trailer #15 and walked up the driveway to the trailer. He cautioned the Swans that the drive, though shoveled, was slick due to underlying ice. He asked that they wait in their car until he opened the door and made a safe path for them. Mr. Swan either did not hear the warning or did not care about the warning, and started walking up the drive to the trailer anyway. His daughter and her boyfriend were right behind him. A few feet up the drive, Mr. Swan fell and injured his ankle. The Swans are suing the Hollingsworths for the injuries, claiming that Hollingsworth was negligent in his care of the property.

Your firm has been hired by the Hollingsworths' insurance company to investigate the validity of the claim. The only witness who has not been interviewed is Amanda Swan's now ex-boyfriend, Mike Timberland. It is believed that he knows what the conditions were really like that day and what the truth is regarding the injuries and the Swans' motives. Timberland has not seen Amanda for at least six months.

Huggem v. Tuttle Railroad

Review the case study entitled *Huggem v. Tuttle Railroad,* introduced in Chapter 5, and then complete the following assignments. You are to find one or more expert witnesses to support Tuttle Railroad's position in this case. Each expert should be a real person either located in your immediate community or active on a national level. For each expert:

1. Name the expert and his or her field of specialization; provide his or her curriculum vita.

2. Create a list of all the experts you originally located before selecting those listed in question 1.

3. Explain how you determined the need for the expert selected and why you chose that expert.

4. Specifically describe the steps you used to find the expert, and detail your first conversation with the expert.

5. Draft a personal detail chart for each expert named.

6. Explain how long it took you to:
   a. determine the type of expert you needed
   b. research the experts in that field
   c. interview the experts
   d. select the single expert you finally chose.

7. List and describe the resources you used to find the expert(s).

15
THE COLLECTION INVESTIGATION

<u>OBJECTIVES</u> After completing this chapter, you will know:

- What tools are used to begin the collection investigation and why they are used.

- How assets are discovered and in what order certain discovery tools are used to find assets.

- Why the garnishment, sheriff's sale, liens, and attachments are the most commonly used methods for collecting assets, and how they are used.

- The Fair Debt Collection Practices Act applies to both attorney and paralegal in regard to judgment collection; several sections of the act focus on paralegal responsibilities.

INTRODUCTION

The collection investigation is a function in and of itself, though it is practical to apply many of the principles and techniques discussed thus far to the collection task. The paralegal specializing in this field will find that collection strategies vary greatly from those used in prejudgment investigations. This chapter covers the basic functions and procedures for managing and conducting a specialized postjudgment (collection) investigation, and tries to prepare the paralegal to be quick-thinking and aggressive.

BEGINNING THE COLLECTION INVESTIGATION

The paralegal begins the collection investigation by reviewing the judgment (the amount of money to be recovered) and all asset details uncovered during the prejudgment investigation. These are found in the interrogatories and deposition transcripts of the **judgment debtor**, the person who lost the civil trial and has had a judgment levied against her. A **judgment creditor** is the party who won the judgment against the judgment debtor.

Using the Judgment

There are two reasons for reviewing the judgment. First, the paralegal determines the amount of the judgment and begins calculating interest for the future collection of moneys. Postjudgment interest is calculated at a **per diem** rate dictated by state statute (*per diem* is Latin for daily). Interest on the judgment begins to run from the date the judgment is entered, and may be calculated as in the following example.

EXAMPLE

A—Judgment amount × interest rate = _____
B—Total of A divided by 365 (days per year) = _____
C—Total of B × number of days since date of judgment = _____
    A judgment for $1,000 at 10% interest after 200 days is worth $1,054.79:
        A—$1,000 × .10 = 100
        B—$100 divided by 365 = $0.273
        C—$0.273 × 200 days = $54.79

Interest must be calculated anew each time a collection tool is used, such as **garnishment** or the sheriff's sale. All prejudgment interest must be included in the amount petitioned before the court at the conclusion of the trial, along with costs. Interest rates for postjudgment moneys are set by state statute, and the paralegal must stay informed on expediting the recovery of a judgment.

Second, the paralegal uses the judgment amount to begin strategizing her search for assets and satisfying the judgment.

EXAMPLE ————————————————————————————————————

In a case with a judgment for $1,500, the paralegal plans to recover the moneys by using tools that are low in cost and quick to use, because the judgment amount is considered minimal. For instance, she may garnish the judgment debtor's wages or bank account.

When the judgment amount is substantial, the paralegal needs a long-term plan for executing on the judgment debtor's assets, including real property, liquid assets, and any third-party assets due and owing the judgment debtor. (A more detailed discussion of these strategies is found later in this chapter.)

Using Prejudgment Formal Discovery

After assessing the judgment and interest rates, the paralegal reviews the formal discovery gathered during the prejudgment phase of the case, to help determine what options are available for recovery. During formal discovery, the legal team will lay the groundwork for the collection investigation by incorporating questions in the interrogatories and deposition about assets the judgment debtor possesses and where those assets are located.

EXAMPLE ————————————————————————————————————

While drafting questions for the deposition, the attorney includes a series of queries regarding the deponent's current employment (location of employer, name of supervisor, years on the job, skills, full- or part-time status, income level, etc.), Social Security number, driver's license number, telephone number, spouse's name, spouse's occupation, and spouse's place of employment. In certain cases, it is also legitimate to ask the deponent to explain any other litigation she is or has been involved in, including existing judgments.

The purpose of these questions is simple. By identifying the deponent's occupation and current employment, the paralegal is able to garnish wages, or locate the judgment debtor in his new job if he moves in an attempt to avoid paying the judgment. Identifying property owned by the judgment debtor allows the paralegal to prepare a lien on the property, if state law permits such an attachment. Information on a spouse is useful if state law allows attachment of joint property or assets. It is also helpful to know the spouse's occupation and background if the judgment debtor flees the jurisdiction of the court to avoid paying the judgment. Tracking a deadbeat judgment debtor is easier if the legal team has adequate information on the debtor's spouse.

After the initial review of the judgment and formal discovery are completed, the paralegal will have an outline of the judgment debtor's finances and employment. The information gleaned from this data aids in determining if the judgment can be satisfied by garnishing wages or placing a lien on property, or if satisfaction will require complex methods.

☑ **PRACTICAL TIP**   A few states do not allow garnishment of wages. The paralegal should check with her supervising attorney and consult the state rules before considering garnishment of wages.

Requesting Payment from the Judgment Debtor

Before taking any aggressive steps to collect a judgment, the paralegal should contact the judgment debtor and attempt to collect the money personally. Begin this process by writing the judgment debtor a letter requesting the amount due and owing, and enclosing a copy of the judgment. The debtor should already have received a copy of the judgment from the clerk of the court, but it is good procedure to enclose a copy with a demand for payment. Also, include a paragraph stating that the law firm will seek alternative methods of collecting the judgment should the debtor ignore this demand.

If, after ten working days, the judgment debtor has not responded to the request for payment, attempt to contact her by phone. Start by calling during the day, then in the evening. If it is not possible to reach her at home, attempt to contact her at work.

☑ **PRACTICAL TIP**   Use extreme caution when contacting a judgment debtor at work. For that matter, be careful when contacting the judgment debtor at any time. The paralegal may inadvertently violate some of the many statutes and regulations designed to protect debtors from harassment. Many of these laws apply specifically to law firms collecting judgments. See the section in this chapter entitled "The Fair Debt Collection Practices Act."

Once the judgment debtor has been personally contacted, explain to her that the firm is attempting to collect on the judgment, and that she has options for paying the debt. For instance, she may make one lump-sum payment, or she may set up scheduled payments (if the client has agreed to these terms). If scheduled payments are agreed to, the debtor should be required to sign a payment schedule, make the first payment, and provide the law firm with financial information, including the name and account numbers for all banking accounts; the amount of money she earns (ask for copies of pay stubs); title information on any vehicles and sporting equipment (boats, motorcycles, jet skis, snowmobiles, airplanes, etc.); and details on any guns, antiques, or other valuables she may own. It should be made clear to the debtor that the firm is serious about collecting the debt, which is why all this information is necessary. If the debtor resists setting up payments or providing the information, remind her that collection attempts will begin with or without her cooperation; however, resort to this form of motivation as a last effort. In some states, the collection of assets may not begin until a specific amount of time (e.g., thirty days) has passed from the date the judgment was entered (check state rules for specific time frames for execution on judgments). During that period, the paralegal should be searching for assets and working with the debtor.

In many cases, the judgment debtor is not cooperative and the paralegal will have to collect the judgment without cooperation, even if this magnifies the debtor's feeling that the judgment was issued unfairly. Whatever the situation is, the paralegal must move quickly from the demand-for-payment stage to executing on the judgment. Once the debtor is aware that the legal team is seeking her assets, she may swiftly move or hide assets.

Protecting Existing Assets

Guard against losing existing assets by doing the following:

- File an **abstract of judgment**, or other appropriate form, in the county office that holds real estate records for the county in which the debtor lives and where it is believed that she owns property.

- Acquire at least two or three certified copies of the judgment, holding them in the file for future use. The copies can be used in various ways, including collection of foreign judgments and **sheriff's sales**, and can be kept until needed. A *sheriff's sale* is, literally, a sale of real estate and other property, carried out by the sheriff under a decree from the court. The sheriff's sale may also be called an **execution sale** or a **judicial sale**. By requesting the certified copies early in the collection investigation, the paralegal assures that quick action can follow once recoverable property or assets are located.

- Prepare all the paperwork needed for a garnishment or **writ of execution** ahead of time. A writ of execution is an order of the court to enforce a court's judgment.

- Organize all the judgment debtor's data, including place of employment, banking statistics, and other asset details, to expedite the investigation and execution.

Use all these sources to quickly and efficiently identify and attach the debtor's assets to satisfy the judgment.

The paralegal does not always have a great deal of asset information at the onset of the collection investigation, so she must become proficient at locating and attaching assets without the cooperation of the judgment debtor.

DISCOVERING ASSETS

When collecting a judgment, the paralegal is required to have a practical knowledge of state and federal laws and processes, including:

- How and when to use postjudgment creditors' remedies
- The procedures and workings of the local sheriff's office
- Federal bankruptcy rules and provisions
- How and when to use subpoenas and court orders

- How to liquidate assets
- How to use the many relationships inside and outside the judicial system
- How to research public and private records.

Time is of the essence when searching for assets and executing on a judgment—the longer a judgment goes uncollected, the less likely it is to be collected.

Public and private records, and the material gathered during the prejudgment investigation, are used to continue the collection investigation. The paralegal will contact a variety of public and private agencies to gather data on the judgment debtor's past and present debts, banking and spending habits, employment history, and ownership of real property or other assets. She can use the proximate probability strategy and personal life experience to help uncover the debtor's assets by making inferences about the debtor, the debtor's lifestyle, and his assets. Sometimes the best allies in the search for assets are other persons or companies also trying to collect against the debtor. Be as open about the search as possible when talking with these persons, but do not sabotage your investigation by offering too much detail.

Example

While researching a debtor's bank account, the paralegal contacts another creditor who is believed to be looking for the same debtor. During her conversation with the collector, the paralegal asks if she has any back account information on the debtor. The collector says that she has some unverified information about an account with a large national bank; she names the bank and the city where the bank is located, and gives the approximate date the account was opened, but she does not ask if the paralegal knows anything about the account. The conversation then moves to another topic and the paralegal shares some information about the debtor's physical address.

The key in this example is that the paralegal has a bank account number for the bank named by the collector, in the same city, and during the same time frame. She did not share this bank account information, because that could directly threaten her ability to execute on the account. She did, however, offer other useable information to the collector in return.

Debtor's Examination

In many states, the discovery of assets begins by conducting a debtor's examination (called a *postjudgment deposition* in some states). This deposition occurs immediately after the thirty-day (or other specified) waiting period, during which review of the prejudgment formal discovery has occurred. Many judgment debtors are fully aware of this part of the collection process and are reluctant to cooperate in the debtor's examination.

Most, if not all, states have some method for deposing the judgment debtor, so always check local rules for specifics. Generally, the creditor may ask, under oath, about the judgment debtor's assets, liabilities, cash flow, and tax returns. A subpoena and subpoena duces tecum may be used to compel the debtor to produce tax returns and banking statements, and the legal team uses a notice to take deposition to inform the judgment debtor of the time and location of the deposition. Service of the subpoena and notice are perfected according to applicable rules of procedure.

At this stage in the discovery of assets, some states do not require the creditor to show cause for wanting to talk to the debtor. In other jurisdictions, the legal team may have to request a writ of execution for property believed to be attachable, send the sheriff to retrieve the property, learn that there is no property, and *then* ask to speak with the debtor about assets. If the debtor does not respond to the subpoena, she may not be penalized for missing the postjudgment deposition until the court is shown just cause and proof that the judgment creditor cannot find assets by its own efforts. Any supplemental proceeding, such as an order to compel, requires the filing of the unsatisfied writ of execution and personal service of the order compelling the debtor to attend the subsequent deposition. The sheriff's office serves this order.

The attorney, or in some states the paralegal, conducts the postjudgment deposition, asking only questions that pertain to the discovery of assets. The paralegal must depend on her pre- and postjudgment investigations to determine what questions will best direct the legal team toward useable money and property. However, she should always ask for general data, including:

- Social Security number
- Driver's license number
- Addresses, telephone numbers, and previous states lived in
- Employers, both past and current
- Spouses, both former and current.

As the deposition continues, narrow questions are used to search for specific data, including:

- Bank accounts
- Loan payments to be made to the debtor by third parties
- Earnings.

Order for Disclosure

To minimize costs, the legal team may seek an order for disclosure rather than a postjudgment deposition. Many states' rules allow the judgment creditor to request the district court to order the debtor to provide the creditor with information regarding her assets (including the location, nature, and identity of those assets). Usually, though, the judgment must have been docketed for a certain period of time before the disclosure is useable.

In states that allow orders of disclosure, the judgment creditor mails a completed request for order for disclosure, with the required filing fee, to the court administrator. The order for disclosure and a financial disclosure form are then mailed to the judgment debtor by the court administrator. The debtor has a number of days, usually ten, to complete the forms and return them to the creditor or her counsel. Failure to return the completed form may trigger contempt-of-court proceedings. The paralegal may be expected to monitor the court's forwarding of the documents to the debtor and the debtor's return of documents to the creditor. The court, though functioning as efficiently as possible, does not always have the staff to promptly follow up on delinquent answers, so it is the legal team's job. A reliable tickler system will help manage this and all other collection investigation procedures.

Postjudgment Interrogatories

Closely related to the disclosure statement are postjudgment interrogatories. Under Rules 69 and 33 of the Federal Rules of Civil Procedure, the legal team is allowed to draft interrogatories for the judgment debtor. The debtor must answer promptly and under oath. The interrogatories may be served on the debtor by mail or personal service; the paralegal should carefully determine which method is most beneficial to the client. Failure to answer the interrogatories within thirty days of the date of service may subject the debtor to an order to compel discovery.[1] If the debtor still fails to comply with the order, he may be found in contempt of court. In many states, the contempt-of-court ruling is followed by issuance of a bench warrant for the debtor, which may not be very effective. Commonly, a bench warrant is executed only when an officer of the law comes into contact with the debtor under unrelated circumstances, such as a traffic stop. If she learns of the bench warrant during the stop, she arrests the debtor. In reality, though, few arrests actually occur in response to bench warrants.

Additional Methods of Discovering Assets

All the remaining methods for unearthing a debtor's assets require aggressive footwork and creative thinking. To gather information, the paralegal must use credit reports (when she has access to them); public and private agencies, offices, and records; and persons who know the judgment debtor.

Credit Reports Many law firms specializing in collection practice subscribe to one or more credit reporting services. The paralegal may use these reports to identify fellow creditors, which may be contacted for information on the debtor. If the paralegal does not have immediate access to a credit reporting service, she may utilize any contacts the client may have, hire a skiptracer, or even ask a collection firm in town to run a report for a fee. The following is a list of the various national credit reporting services:

CSC Credit Services
Consumer Assistance Center
P.O. Box 674405
Houston, TX 77667
(800) 759-5979

Equifax
One East 22d Street, #520
Lombard, IL 60148
(800) 685-1111

TRW Credit Data Division
Consumer Relations
2051 Killebrew Drive
Bloomington, MN 55425
(800) 422-4879

Dun & Bradstreet Information Services
Small Business Services
Three Sylvan Way
Parsippany, NJ 07054
(201) 605-6000 or (800) 552-3867

Trans Union Corporation
Consumer Information
2780 Snelling Avenue
Roseville, MN 55113
(612) 639-0007

NACM North Central Corporation
1201 Marquette Avenue
Minneapolis, MN 55403
(612) 341-9600

Secretary of State's Office   The secretary of state's office is a good source of information for corporate debtors and debtors involved in partnerships or other business ventures. Generally, articles of incorporation, UCC filings, amendments to filed documents, assumed name applications, and other useful documentation are attainable from the secretary of state. See Appendix A for more details on each state's secretary of state division.

Conclusion   Overall, the paralegal can use any of the many sources discussed in Chapter 9 of this text to locate information on the judgment debtor's finances and assets. Once discovered, assets must be reviewed for exemption.

Exempt Property

Critical to the paralegal's success in collecting a judgment is her ability to identify **exempt property** or money; that is, property or money excused or released from collection. As a rule, there are both federal and state exemptions that may apply to debtor property. The paralegal should review state regulations, particularly those covering real and personal property and usury, before executing on a judgment. Usury laws deal with the charging of interest rates. Ordinarily, the federal law deals with bankruptcy. Exemptions are set out in the federal bankruptcy code[2] and in state and nonbankruptcy federal law. The specific bankruptcy and nonbankruptcy exemptions vary in scope and dollar amount, and each should be consulted individually by the legal team for the jurisdiction in which the judgment will be executed. The following is a listing of the property commonly considered exempt, in both bankruptcy and nonbankruptcy provisions, from seizure and sale to satisfy a judgment:

- homestead
- family Bible, library, and musical instruments
- burial plot
- motor vehicle
- household furnishings, household goods, wearing apparel, appliances and books
- jewelry

- implements, professional books, office furniture, tools, and library
- farm machinery and implements
- unmatured life insurance contract
- loan valued or accrued dividend under an unmatured life insurance contract
- health aids
- earnings
- Social Security benefits, unemployment compensation, local public assistance benefits
- veteran's benefits
- disability, illness, or unemployment benefits
- alimony, support, or maintenance
- stock bonus, pension, profit-sharing, or similar benefits
- award under a crime victim's reparation law
- payment on account of wrongful death
- payments to beneficiaries under life insurance policies
- payment on account of personal bodily injury.

Other than property or money directly involved in a bankruptcy proceeding, the paralegal must be aware of the following exemptions:

- Social Security payments (42 U.S.C. § 407)
- Veteran's benefits (38 U.S.C. § 5301)
- Railroad Retirement Act annuities and pensions (45 U.S.C. § 231m)
- Civil Service retirement benefits (5 U.S.C. § 8346)

There may be other federal and state exemptions as well.

The paralegal and supervising attorney should review all active exemptions on the state and federal level before moving forward in an attachment or seizure process, to avoid violating any laws protecting debtors. Then draft a list of the judgment debtor's available property to keep the legal team organized and informed of all collectable assets.

RECOVERY OF ASSETS

There are a variety of methods available to recover a judgment debtor's assets, such as garnishment, the sheriff's sale, and liens or attachments.

Garnishments

A garnishment is a statutory proceeding that authorizes a judgment creditor to enforce a money judgment against the judgment debtor through a third party, the **garnishee**.[3] The garnishment is not a proceeding in itself; rather, it depends on the commencement of an action for a money judgment. Types of garnishments include:

- Garnishments for wages
- Garnishments involving financial institutions (savings accounts, checking accounts)
- Garnishments involving moneys owed to the debtor by a third party for some other service or good.

The primary objective is to reach out to the garnishee for money or property owned or controlled by her and due to the judgment debtor. In this process, the garnishee has two major duties: (1) to retain the assets and (2) to disclose the assets. To initiate the garnishment:

- The judgment creditor files a petition or affidavit for garnishment with the court, to initiate issuance of a writ of garnishment, and then serves the writ on the third party.
- The third party discloses the assets, retains them, and reports to the court what is available.
- The judgment creditor levies the garnished property with a writ of execution and obtains a court order or consent from the debtor to release the property.

In some states a garnishment for wages will run consecutively for sixty to ninety days. The garnishee regularly forwards moneys to the court that are due to the debtor each pay period; the money from the garnishment is then forwarded to the creditor. In these cases, the paralegal must carefully track all payments, accruing interest, and dates for renewing the garnishment, until the judgment is satisfied.

When the paralegal is attempting to acquire assets in a bank account, she petitions for the garnishment and serves the writ of garnishment on the bank or financial institution. When service is perfected, the institution freezes the account, reports the amount available, and forwards the money to the court for disbursement to the judgment creditor. This same procedure is used for garnishments to contractors or other third parties who owe money to the judgment debtor.

EXAMPLE

There is a judgment against Mary Wiggins. The paralegal learns that Mary is receiving money outside of her regular full-time job, from a painting contractor with whom she works on weekends. After determining who the contractor is, the paralegal prepares a garnishment and serves it on the contractor. For each service Mary performs for the contractor, the contractor is obligated to forward Mary's payment to the court for the life of the garnishment.

This example demonstrates why the paralegal must be keenly aware of all places a judgment debtor may receive money or goods, so that she can obtain the assets and satisfy the judgment.

The use of garnishments can quickly and inexpensively satisfy a judgment, but the paralegal must know that some moneys and goods are not collectable under the garnishment. Garnishment exemptions vary from state to state, but the following are commonly not collectable:

- Any judgment in favor of the debtor against the garnishee if the property is liable on a levy. In other words, a garnishment cannot be honored if the property in question is already under levy by someone else.
- Any debt relating to a negotiable instrument (so as to avoid multiple liability for the negotiable instrument).
- Any indebtedness due to the debtor with a cumulative value of less than $10.
- Any disposable earning or indebtedness exempt under state or federal law.
- Any indebtedness owed to the debtor from a bank or savings institution.
- Personal property exempt to a certain dollar amount as set by each state.
- Farm exemptions (vary in dollar amount by state statute).
- Business exemptions (vary in dollar amount by state statute).
- Exempt insurance benefits (varies by state).
- A manufactured home.
- Commonly, one motor vehicle.
- Accrued interest (varies by state).
- Employee benefits.

In addition to the money and property recoverable from the garnishment, the paralegal can use a sheriff's sale to help satisfy a judgment. Writs of garnishment and orders for sheriff's sales can be executed at the same time, which motivates the debtor to satisfy the remainder of the judgment herself to avoid losing additional assets.

Sheriff's Sale

Through a writ of execution, the paralegal can request the sheriff to make an immediate levy upon certain property of the judgment debtor. This method is effective yet challenging, as the paralegal must know there is property to be seized, must know where it is, and must provide a description of it to the court and the sheriff.

EXAMPLE

While trying to collect a judgment, an investigator makes a random check of the debtor's residence by driving by. On that day, she notices the debtor parking a new speedboat in a neighbor's garage and then going home. Before the garage door is closed, the investigator gets the license plate on the boat. She then returns to the office and begins checking public records regarding the title on the boat. She quickly learns that the boat was newly purchased by the debtor and believes that the debtor is attempting to hide the boat. She files a writ of execution and promptly delivers it to the sheriff for execution. The sheriff is obligated to swiftly seize the property and sell it.

Limitations of the Sheriff's Sale   Although the sheriff's sale is a powerful tool, it has some limitations:

- The sheriff is only obligated to execute on one writ at a time, for one judgment debtor, and writs are served on a first-come, first-served basis. If many creditors are chasing a single debtor, timing is everything.

- It is important to give the sheriff as complete a description as possible of the property, so as to avoid the collection of incorrect items. It is a good idea to follow the sheriff to the location and encourage her to note any other valuable property located at the home, business, or other place where the current seizure is occurring, so that future seizures may be planned. The sheriff is responsible for an immediate levy of the property and it is reasonable to remind her of that duty.

- No force may be used to execute the writ, so plan ahead for a time when the least amount of resistance will occur. The paralegal must work with the sheriff to ensure a successful operation, and planning ahead is important for a smooth seizure. At the conclusion of the execution, the officer must return the writ with a full inventory of all property levied.

- Commonly, the sheriff will attempt to execute a writ three times. In some states and counties, the sheriff can attempt execution several times, as there are fewer time demands on her. In most venues, though, the sheriff has limited time available to continue attempting to execute the same writ unsuccessfully. The paralegal should fully investigate the property and the location of the property before sending the sheriff to execute on the writ.

- A writ is good for 180 days in most jurisdictions. Again, timing is everything, and the paralegal must manage the service and execution of the writ to ensure success.

Proceeds of the Sale   Once property is seized, it must be sold. In some states the sale of the property actually occurs on the courthouse steps. In other jurisdictions, the sale is held in alternative locations. Proceeds of the sale are disbursed very specifically, for the protection of all parties involved:

1. The cost of the sale is covered, including the price of service and the cost of the writ.

2. The creditor is paid the full amount of the judgment if there is enough money to cover it in full.

3. The debtor is given any extra money from the sale.

Normal protocol (in most states) requires the judgment creditor to post a bond for the goods seized, to protect the debtor from any unnecessary losses in the process of executing the writ.

The process of writ of execution and sheriff's sale are actually more complex than it initially appears, because the judgment creditor wants to satisfy the judgment without the expense of issuing and serving multiple writs. Some sales yield little or no reward. It is believed that seizing large items of valuable property early in the collection process will motivate the judgment debtor to sell property of her own choosing to satisfy the judgment. Use the sale as a motivator by explaining to the debtor that a writ of execution may actually diminish her liquid cash, and that paying off the judgment in whatever way she deems proper will be a cleaner and quicker method of satisfying the judgment.

Liens and Attachments

One of the most common liens in civil litigation is the **mechanic's lien**, which was created by law to secure payment for services rendered and/or materials furnished when improving the real property of another. The term is derived from the practice of using tradespeople, but presently may refer to all professionals, ranging from engineers to suppliers to attorneys to contractors. The purpose of the mechanic's lien is to force persons who receive the benefit of another's services to pay for those services, or share the value added to the improvements as a result of those services.

To file a mechanic's lien, a claimant typically must satisfy two general conditions. The first condition requires the party filing to have made an improvement on the property of the debtor; the second requires the claimant to have consent from the owner to perform the improvement. There are many distinctions in state law regarding consent, so the paralegal should consult her state's statutes.

After qualifying to file a lien, the claimant must understand who and what property can be subject to the lien. Ordinarily, the term *owner* is much broader in scope and meaning than the layman's interpretation, and may include:

- Holders of equitable interests
- Tenants in common (*tenancy in common* is when two or more persons own a collective interest in a holding or property)
- Mortgagees in possession of a legal or equitable title
- Holders of a leasehold interest.

The Mechanic's Lien and the Collection Investigation

Essentially, the mechanic's lien is used in two ways. First, the lien may be used for a client who has a justifiable monetary dispute regarding services rendered and who has come to the law firm for representation. During the course of the initial client interview, the legal team may determine that the client would best be served by filing a mechanic's lien against the delinquent party, thereby minimizing the client's out-of-pocket expense in collecting the money. Once the paralegal has filed the lien, the client is charged a minimal fee for the preparation and filing time. Thereafter, the client is responsible for monitoring the lien and refiling it before it expires.

A different use of the mechanic's lien is as a research tool against the judgment debtor. When a paralegal is searching for assets of a particular judgment debtor, she may find motor vehicles, jet skis, boats, investment property, or other such items for attachment. Before the paralegal can attach such assets, though, she must verify that they are free and clear of other liens or encumbrances, such as mechanic's liens. Once the lien check is completed, the paralegal may either execute on the property or notify the attorney that another creditor is also acting against the judgment debtor. Because the mechanic's lien functions on a priority ("first-come, first-served") basis, the judgment creditor may decide to buy out the holder of the lien and execute on the property.

Whatever use the paralegal makes of the mechanic's lien, she will find it to be a useful and powerful tool.

There are a variety of statutory liens that the paralegal may use in addition to the mechanic's lien. Special interest creditors often use statutory liens to try to gain priority over or leverage against rival security interest lien holders, such as mortgage companies. All paralegals working in collection law should familiarize themselves with the variety of liens available and check state statutes to clarify how they function in relation to Uniform Commercial Code filings, security interests, and filings with the secretary of state's office.

Attachments: A Prejudgment Remedy

An attachment is placed at the initiation of the suit. It ensures that a defendant will not sell or transfer title or property before, during, or immediately after the lawsuit in an effort to avoid paying the judgment. It is critical for the paralegal, especially the collection paralegal, to understand the power of attachment and use it whenever necessary. All prejudgment activities, such as the attachment, greatly influence the success of the postjudgment investigation and collection of the judgment. She must consider the postjudgment aspects of the case during each phase of the investigation and maneuver to attach and locate assets.

Conclusion

Successful postjudgment recovery requires the paralegal to use sound judgment and quick thinking, and to have good communication with the supervising attorney. All decisions regarding attachments and liens must be made by the attorney, but a skilled paralegal can provide quality information about assets, their location, and their value. Paralegals must understand the Fair Debt Collection Practices Act and other legislation that monitors and controls the collection of money.

THE FAIR DEBT COLLECTION PRACTICES ACT

The Fair Debt Collection Practices Act (FDCPA)[4] was first passed in 1978 to help curb abuse against debtors by collection agencies, but it was not until 1986 that the FDCPA provision exempting lawyers and their agents was removed.[5]

In 1995, the United States Supreme Court held that the FDCPA "applies to attorneys who 'regularly' engage in consumer-debt-collection activity, even when that activity consists of litigation."[6]

According to the FDCPA, *debt collector* is defined as "any person who uses any instrumentality of interstate commerce or the mails in any business the principal purpose of which is the collection of any debts, or who regularly collects or attempts to collect, directly or indirectly, debts owed or due or asserted to be owed or due another ... ."[7] This definition essentially describes all of the postjudgment work of the paralegal, those working in a collection practice, and all prejudgment work. Do not be misled by the term "regularly collects": the courts have not consistently defined in their rulings how much debt collection constitutes "regularly," so any collection work should be considered potentially subject to the FDCPA standards.[8]

Communication

Communication under the FDCPA is defined as "[t]he conveying of information regarding a debt directly or indirectly to any person through any medium."[9] Therefore, each letter sent to the debtor, including the request for payment ten days after the judgment, is considered communication and is strictly regulated by the FDCPA.

The paralegal must understand that the activities of postjudgment collection (demand for payment) are very different from those of prejudgment collection (demand for payment, payment stipulations), although either type of communication may be subject to the FDCPA guidelines. Consider the comparison.

EXAMPLE

Prejudgment Communication: The paralegal sends a demand for payment to the debtor. The written notice gives the name of the creditor and the amount owed. In addition, the paralegal attempts to contact the debtor by phone. A series of written and oral communications may follow before a lawsuit is initiated or the debt is paid. Therefore, the collection paralegal has many more opportunities to violate the FDCPA rules than the postjudgment paralegal.

Postjudgment Communication: The activities of postjudgment collection include sending a written demand for payment, along with a copy of the judgment. However, the paralegal doing postjudgment work attempts to locate and execute on assets at the same time. If improper communication with the debtor occurred early in the process, any use of the assets becomes questionable, as the debtor's rights may have been violated.

Regardless of the paralegal's role, the FDCPA requires her to know the guidelines for collecting money and executing on judgments. The workings of the FDCPA, from a paralegal's perspective, primarily focus on the second and third most troubling areas; namely, validation of the debt and notification of the debtor.

Validation of the Debt and Notification of the Debtor

A substantial amount of litigation has been brought regarding the validation of debts. The FDCPA describes the role of the debt collector regarding validation and notification in 15 U.S.C. § 1692g. Essentially, this section says that the debtor must be given notice within five days after the first communication (probably a phone call in prejudgment cases, or a copy of the judgment in postjudgment matters) to validate the debt. In one obvious sense, it is good practice to give such notice during any first communication; however, it is prudent to follow these guidelines and send a validation notice as well. In addition to stating the amount of the debt and the name of the creditor, the validation must contain a notice saying:

> Unless you notify this office within 30 days after receiving this notice that you dispute the legitimacy of the debt or any portion thereof, this office will assume this debt is valid. If you notify this office in writing within 30 days from receiving this notice disputing the debt, this office will either: 1) obtain verification of the debt; or 2) obtain a copy of a judgment and mail you a copy of such judgment or verification. In addition, if requested from this office in writing within 30 days after receiving this notice, this office will provide you with the name and address of the original creditor, if different from the current creditor.[10]

15 U.S.C. § 1692g(a) requires all notices also to include the following information:

- The amount of the debt
- The name of the creditor to whom the debt is owed
- A statement saying that unless the consumer, within thirty days after receipt of the notice, disputes the validity of the debt or any portion thereof, the debt will be assumed to be valid by the collector
- A statement saying that if the consumer notifies the collector in writing within the thirty-day period that the debt (or any portion of the debt) is disputed, the collector will obtain a verification of the debt or a copy of the judgment against the consumer and will mail such items to the consumer
- A statement saying that upon the consumer's written request, within the thirty-day period, the collector will provide the consumer with the name and address of the original creditor if different from the current creditor.

An important fact to remember about the FDCPA, whether the debt is pre- or postjudgment, is that all collection must stop during the thirty-day grace period. This includes holding any mechanic's liens, executing on garnishments, and attaching to property. Not waiting through the grace period can greatly jeopardize the attorney and the client; the debtor may actually seek action against the attorney for monetary damages should any form of execution occur before the end of thirty days.

SUMMARY

- The collection investigation initially relies on the information found in the judgment and on details uncovered in the prejudgment investigation.
- The debtor's assets are found by using the debtor's examination, orders for disclosure, postjudgment interrogatories, credit reports, and the secretary of state's office. Exempt property that may not be executed on is identified through state and federal law.
- Assets are recovered by first contacting the debtor and giving her an opportunity to pay the debt. If the debtor does not cooperate, garnishments, sheriff's sales, liens, and attachments may be used to satisfy the judgment.
- Request payment from the debtor immediately and follow the guidelines set out in the Fair Debt Collection Practices Act for validating and notifying the debtor.

ACTIVITIES

1. Obtain a copy of the Fair Debt Collection Practices Act. (*See* 15 U.S.C. §§ 1692–1692o). Review §§ 1692b, "Acquisition of location information"; 1692c, "Communication in connection with debt collection"; and 1692k, "Civil liability." What does each of these sections say specifically to the paralegal about collecting both prejudgment and postjudgment debt?

2. Contact your local sheriff's office and interview the sheriff regarding the county's procedures for a sheriff's sale. Outline your findings.

3. Review your local rules concerning debtor's examinations and/or debtor's disclosure statements. Follow up your research by contacting a collection firm in your area and interviewing a paralegal who regularly handles collection cases. What did you learn about collecting judgments in your immediate jurisdiction?

4. Explain how the Fair Debt Collection Practices Act applies to you. What parts of the act will you look to specifically when planning your strategy to collect against a judgment debtor? Research your state laws and regulations relating to collection law and compare the federal act to your state law. Is your state debtor-friendly or not? How do you know?

5. Calculate the per-diem interest owed by a judgment debtor when the judgment amount is $11,235, the interest rate is 7.25 per annum, and the current life of the judgment is 6 years, 4 months, and 13 days. In arriving at your total, factor in the length of the judgment.

CASE STUDY

General Business File

Go to your local library and find the Yellow Pages for any other city in your state (the city must be located in another county). Select a business that uses heavy or expensive equipment.

1. Call the secretary of state's office requesting information on the business. Specifically ask for:

   - The status of the company (corporation, partnership, etc.).
   - The name of the registered agent and owner of the company.
   - Any UCC filings against the equipment.
   - The company's standing with the secretary of state.

2. Contact the appropriate state office and check for mechanic's liens on any of the equipment. Then contact the state and county to check for any judgments against the business or its owner.

3. After you have completed these tasks manually, repeat them using the Internet. Did you find conflicting information? If so, which method provided more accurate and up-to-date information?

4. Check with the motor vehicle department about title to any motorized equipment, if that is what you are concentrating on.

5. Draft a memorandum on the business, and specifically identify all information that would allow your firm to collect on a judgment against the business.

NOTES

1 Fed. R. Civ. P. 37.
2 11 U.S.C. § 522(d).
3 6 Am. Jur. 2d *Attachment & Garnishment* § 2 (1963).
4 15 U.S.C. §§ 1692–1692o (1994, as amended).
5 *Heintz v. Jenkins,* 115 S. Ct. 1489, 1491 (1995).
6 *Id.* at 1493.
7 15 U.S.C. § 1692a(6).
8 *Mertes v. Devitt,* 734 F. Supp. 872 (W.D. Wis. 1990); *Stojanovski v. Strobl & Manoogian, P.C.,* 783 F. Supp. 319 (E.D. Mich. 1992).
9 15 U.S.C. § 1692a(2).
10 *See* 15 U.S.C. § 1692g.

APPENDIX A

Public Information Sources

☑ **PRACTICAL TIP**   When attempting to contact the Secretary of State, Department of Transportation, or Department of Motor Vehicles, call early in the morning. Phoning early and constantly enhances your chances of success in reaching the appropriate office.

ALABAMA

Secretary of State
State Capital
Montgomery, AL 36104
(334) 242-7200

State Capital: Montgomery

Department of Public Safety
Driver's License Division
500 Dexter Avenue
Montgomery, AL 36104-3718

ALASKA

Secretary of State
Corporations
State Capital
Juneau, AK 99801-1182
(907) 465-2521

State Capital: Juneau

Department of Public Safety
Driver's License Division
Box 2719
Juneau, AK 99801

ARIZONA

Secretary of State
Chairman
Corporation Commission
State Capital
Phoenix, AZ 85007
(602) 542-4285

State Capital: Phoenix

Superintendent—Division of Motor
    Vehicles
Arizona Highway Department
1801 W. Jefferson
Phoenix, AZ 85007-3224

ARKANSAS

Secretary of State
State Capital
Little Rock, AR 72201-1095
(501) 682-1010

State Capital: Little Rock

Motor Vehicle Division
Department of Revenue
Little Rock, AR 72201
(501) 682-7076

CALIFORNIA

Secretary of State
State Capital
Sacramento, CA 95818
(916) 657-5448 Filing Department
(916) 654-7960 Name Division
(916) 657-3537 Officers Listings
(916) 653-7315 General

State Capital: Sacramento

Department of Motor Vehicles
Division of Driver's Licenses
Sacramento, CA 95818
(916) 657-6555

COLORADO

Secretary of State
Department of State
State Capital
Denver, CO 80203
(303) 894-2251

State Capital: Denver

Colorado Department of Revenue
Motor Vehicle Division
Denver, CO 80214
(303) 937-9507

CONNECTICUT

Secretary of State
State Capital
30 Trinity Street
Hartford, CT 06106-1629
(860) 509-6000

State Capital: Hartford

Department of Motor Vehicles
State Office Building
60 State Street
Hartford, CT 06161
(860) 566-4710

DELAWARE

Secretary of State
State Capital
Dover, DE 19901
1-800-464-4357 (in state)
1-800-273-9500 (out of state)

State Capital: Dover

Motor Vehicle Commissioner
State Highway Department
Kent County
Dover, DE 19901
(302) 856-2571

DISTRICT OF COLUMBIA

Secretary of State
Recorder of Deeds
Corporation Files
Washington, D.C.
(202) 727-6306

Department of Motor Vehicles
Government of District of Columbia
Washington, D.C.
(202) 727-6680

FLORIDA

Secretary of State
State Capital
Tallahassee, FL 32399
(850) 414-5500

State Capital: Tallahassee

Florida Department of Public Safety
Driver Record Information
Tallahassee, FL 32399-0621
(850) 487-4303

GEORGIA

Secretary of State
Corporation Clerk
214 State Capital
Atlanta, GA 30334-1600
(404) 656-2817

State Capital: Atlanta

Department of Public Safety
Driver's License Division
959 E. Confederate Avenue SE
Atlanta, GA 30316-2531
(404) 624-7478

HAWAII

Secretary of State
Corporate Law Registrar
Department of Treasury & Regulation
State Capital
Honolulu, HI 96814

State Capital: Honolulu

Honolulu Police Department
Bethel & Merchant Streets
Honolulu, HI 96814
(808) 58061

IDAHO

Secretary of State
State Capital
700 W. Jefferson
Boise, ID 83720-0001
(208) 334-2300

State Capital: Boise

Department of Law Enforcement
Driver's License Bureau
7200 Barrister Drive
Boise, ID 83704
(208) 377-6658

ILLINOIS

Secretary of State
Chief Clerk
Office of Secretary of State
State Capital
Springfield, IL 62706
(217) 789-4162

State Capital: Springfield

Driver's License Division
Office of Secretary of State
Springfield, IL 62706

INDIANA

Secretary of State
State Capital
Indianapolis, IN 46204
(317) 232-6531

State Capital: Indianapolis

Commissioner
Bureau of Motor Vehicles
Indianapolis, IN 46204
(317) 233-6000

IOWA

Secretary of State
Corporations
Hoover Building
Des Moines, IA 50319
(515) 281-5204

State Capital: Des Moines

Director—Driver's License Division
Department of Public Safety
Des Moines, IA 50319
(515) 281-3211

KANSAS

Secretary of State
State Capital Building
Topeka, KS 66612
(785) 296-2236

State Capital: Topeka

Supervisor—Driver's License Division
Motor Vehicle Department
915 S.W. Harrison, Rm. 100
Topeka, KS 66612-1505
(785) 295-3671

KENTUCKY

Secretary of State
State Capital
Frankfort, KY 40601
(502) 564-7130

State Capital: Frankfort

Department of Public Safety
Division of Driver Licensing
Frankfort, KY 40601

LOUISIANA

Secretary of State
State Capital
Baton Rouge, LA 70804-0401
(504) 925-4707

State Capital: Baton Rouge

Department of Public Safety
P.O. Drawer 1271
Driver's License Division
Baton Rouge, LA 70821-1271
(504) 926-2590

MAINE

Secretary of State
Supervisor, Corporation Division
Office of Secretary of State
State Capital
Augusta, ME 04333-0029
(207) 287-3676

State Capital: Augusta

Department of State
Motor Vehicle Division
Augusta, ME 04333-0029

MARYLAND

Secretary of State
Director, Department of Assess
    and Tax
State Capital
Baltimore, MD 21401
(410) 974-5522

State Capital: Annapolis

Commissioner—Department of Motor
    Vehicles
Baltimore, MD 21401
(410) 768-7000

MASSACHUSETTS

Secretary of State
Commissioner, Department
    of Corporations & Taxation
1 Ashburton Place
Boston, MA 02108
(617) 727-7750

State Capital: Boston

Registry of Motor Vehicles
100 Huntington Avenue
Boston, MA 02116
(617) 351-4500

MICHIGAN

Secretary of State
Commissioner, Corporations &
    Securities
State Capital
Lansing, MI
(517) 334-8305

State Capital: Lansing

Deputy Director
Division of Driver & Vehicle Services
Michigan Department of State
Mutual Building, Capital Avenue
Lansing, MI
(517) 322-1460

MINNESOTA

Secretary of State
Director, Corporation Division
State Capital
St. Paul, MN 55155-1299
(612) 296-2803

State Capital: St. Paul

Minnesota Department of Highways
Driver's License Office
St. Paul, MN 55155
(612) 296-6911

MISSISSIPPI

Secretary of State
State Capital
Jackson, MS 39205-0136
(601) 359-1350

State Capital: Jackson

Motor Vehicle Department
State of Mississippi
Jackson, MS 39205
(601) 987-1274

MISSOURI

Secretary of State
Corporation Counsel
State Capital
600 W. Main
Jefferson City, MO 65101-1532
(573) 751-4936

State Capital: Jefferson City

Department of Revenue
Operators & Chauffeurs
License Registration
301 W. High
Jefferson City, MO 65101
(573) 751-4509

MONTANA

Secretary of State
Corporation Clerk
Rm. 225
State Capital
Helena, MT 59601
(406) 444-2034

State Capital: Helena

Montana Highway Patrol
Drivers Examination Section
2550 Prospect Avenue
Helena, MT 59601-9726
(406) 444-7000

NEBRASKA

Secretary of State
Corporate Division
State Capital
Lincoln, NE 68528
(402) 471-4097

State Capital: Lincoln

Drivers License Bureau
500 W. "O" Street
Lincoln State Capital Building
Lincoln, NE 68528-1524
(402) 471-2823

NEVADA

Secretary of State
Capital Complex
Carson City, NV 89701
(702) 687-5203

State Capital: Carson City

Department of Motor Vehicles
Drivers License Division
555 Wright Way
Carson City, NV 89701-5224
(702) 687-5368

NEW HAMPSHIRE

Secretary of State
State House
Concord, NH 03301-4989
(603) 271-3242

State Capital: Concord

Commissioner—Motor Vehicle Department
State House Annex
Concord, NH 03305-0002
(603) 271-2251

NEW JERSEY

Secretary of State
State Capital
315 W. State
Trenton, NJ 08618-5703
(609) 984-1900

State Capital: Trenton

Division of Motor Vehicles
Department of Law & Public Safety
20 W. State
Trenton, NJ 08608-1206
(609) 292-6500

NEW MEXICO
State Capital: Santa Fe

Secretary of State
Chairman, Corporations Commission
State Capital
Santa Fe, NM 87501-2749
(505) 827-3600

Bureau of Revenue
Driver Services Department
P.O. Box 1686
Santa Fe, NM 87504-1686
(505) 827-2518

NEW YORK
State Capital: Albany

Secretary of State
Chief, Division of Corporations
41 State Street
State Capital
Albany, NY 12207
(518) 474-2121

Bureau of Motor Vehicles
Driver's License Records
Albany, NY 12207
(518) 267-9800

NORTH CAROLINA
State Capital: Raleigh

Secretary of State
State Capital
Raleigh, NC 27603
(919) 733-4161

Director
Driver's License Division
Department of Motor Vehicles
Raleigh, NC 27697
(919) 715-7000

NORTH DAKOTA
State Capital: Bismarck

Secretary of State
State Capital
600 E. Boulevard Avenue
Bismarck, ND 58505-0660
(701) 328-2900

Director—Safety Responsibility Division
Capital Building
State Highway Department
Bismarck, ND 58505
(701) 328-2455

OHIO
State Capital: Columbus

Secretary of State
State Capital
Columbus, OH 43215
(614) 221-7691

Chief—Records Division
Bureau of Motor Vehicles
275 S. 4th Street
Columbus, OH 43215-5245
(614) 221-4531

OKLAHOMA
State Capital: Oklahoma City

Secretary of State
101 State Capital Building
2300 Lincoln Blvd.
Oklahoma City, OK 73105-4805
(405) 521-2011

Department of Public Safety
Motor Vehicle Division
Oklahoma City, OK 73105
(405) 232-1261

OREGON
State Capital: Salem

Secretary of State
Corporation Department
State Capital
Salem, OR 97310-1334
(503) 986-1500

Director
Department of Motor Vehicles
Driver's License Division
Salem, OR 97310
(503) 945-5000

PENNSYLVANIA
State Capital: Harrisburg

Secretary of State
Director, Corporations Bureau
Department of State
State Capital
Harrisburg, PA 17120
(717) 787-1057

Director of Motor Vehicles
Department of Revenue
Harrisburg, PA 17120
1-800-442-1368

RHODE ISLAND
State Capital: Providence

Secretary of State
State Capital
Providence, RI
(401) 277-2357

Highway Safety Department
Providence, RI
(401) 521-7100

SOUTH CAROLINA
State Capital: Columbia

Secretary of State
Corporations
Brown Building
Columbia, SC
(803) 734-2158

State Highway Department
Columbia, SC
1-800-442-1368

SOUTH DAKOTA
State Capital: Pierre

Secretary of State
State Capital
Pierre, SD
(605) 773-3537

Department of Motor Vehicles
Commerce & Regulation
Office of Secretary of State
Pierre, SD
(605) 773-6883

TENNESSEE
State Capital: Nashville

Secretary of State
State Capital
Nashville, TN
(615) 741-2816

Director of Driver's License
Department of Safety
Cordell Hull Building
Nashville, TN
(615) 741-2101

TEXAS
State Capital: Austin

Secretary of State
State Capital
Austin, TX 78711
(512) 463-5701

License Issuance & Driver Records
Texas Department of Public Safety
Austin, TX 78711
(512) 465-5471

UTAH   State Capital: Salt Lake City

Secretary of State   Driver's License Division
State Capital   Department of Public Safety
Salt Lake City, UT 84114-1103   Salt Lake City, UT 84114
(801) 530-4849   (801) 965-4437

VERMONT   State Capital: Montpelier

Secretary of State   State of Vermont
State Capital   Motor Vehicle Department
Montpelier, VT   Montpelier, VT
(802) 828-2363

VIRGINIA   State Capital: Richmond

Secretary of The Commonwealth   Director—Bureau of Operators Licenses
Richmond, VA   Division of Motor Vehicles
(804) 786-2441   Richmond, VA
                                            (804) 367-0538

WASHINGTON   State Capital: Olympia

Secretary of State   Department of Licenses
State Capital   Drivers License Division
Lexington Building   Olympia, WA 98504
P.O. Box 40220   (360) 902-3900
Olympia, WA 98504-0220
(360) 753-7121

WEST VIRGINIA   State Capital: Charleston

Secretary of State   Commissioner—Department of Motor
Capital Complex   Vehicles
Charleston, WV   State Office Building
(304) 558-6000   Charleston, WV
                                            (304) 558-3900

WISCONSIN   State Capital: Madison

Secretary of State   Motor Vehicle Department
Supervisor of Incorporations   4802 Sheboygan Avenue
State Capital   Madison, WI 53702-0002
30 W. Mifflin Street   (608) 266-2353
Madison, WI 53703
(608) 256-4411

WYOMING   State Capital: Cheyenne

Secretary of State   Department of Motor Vehicles
State Capital   Wyoming Department of Revenue
Cheyenne, WY   Cheyenne, WY
(307) 777-7378   (307) 777-4810

APPENDIX B
Sample Forms

CONTENTS

1. Accident Report

ACCIDENT FACT SHEET	
Client Personal Data	Age, Date of Birth
Client Name	Home Phone
Address	Work Phone
City, State, Zip	Social Security No.
Place of Employment	Time Lost from Work
Job Description	
Date/Time of Accident	
Location of Accident	
Bodily Injuries	
Name and Cost of Ambulance	
Name and Address of Hospital	
Names of Treating Physicians, including Physical Therapist	
Client Insurance Information	
Insurance Company	Phone Number
Address	Contact Person
Owner of Motor Vehicle	Claim/File No.
Defendant Insurance Information	
Insurance Company	Phone Number
Address	Contact Person
Owner of Motor Vehicle	Claim/File No.
Insured	
Accident Description _____	

(blank ruled lines)

2. Accumulative Time Chart

Month	January			February			March			April		
Day	Bil.	Non.	Tot.	Bil.	Non.	Tot.	Bil.	Non.	Tot.	Bil.	Non.	Tot.
1												
2												
3												
4												
5												
6												
7												
8												
9												
10												
11												
12												
13												
14												
15												
16												
17												
18												
19												
20												
21												
22												
23												
24												
25												
26												
27												
28												
29												
30												
31												

3.   Case Rapid Reference Tickler Sheet

RAPID REFERENCE TICKLER SHEET

Case No. _____

_____   Court:

vs.   _____

_____

Date of Occurrence: _____

Client:
    Name _____
    Address _____
    Phone Nos. _____

Plaintiff Attorney:
    Name _____
    Address _____
    Phone Nos. _____

Co-Defendant Attorney:
    Name _____
    Address _____
    Phone Nos. _____

Insurance Carrier (if applicable):
    Claims Representative _____
    Address _____
    Phone Nos. _____

Claim No.: _____
DOC: _____
Claimant: _____
Insured: _____

4. Case Status Sheet

CASE STATUS SHEET

Case No. _____

Plaintiff _____

Defendant(s) _____

Handling Attorney _____   Assoc. _____

County _____

File No. _____

Status Report _____   _____   _____

Type of Case _____

Insured _____

Date of Incident (DOI) _____

		Alleged	Amount Plead
DAMAGES:	Punitive	_____	_____
	Exemplary	_____	_____
	Medical		
	—past	_____	_____
	—future	_____	_____
	Lost Wages		
	—past	_____	_____
	—future	_____	_____
	Atty fee	_____	_____
	Mental Anguish		
	—past	_____	_____
	—future	_____	_____
	Pain & Suffering	_____	_____
	Loss of Consortium	_____	_____
	Prejudgment interest	_____	_____

TRIAL SETTING

Peer Reviews:	Dr. _____	Date _____	Report _____
	Dr. _____	Date _____	Report _____
	Dr. _____	Date _____	Report _____

Pleadings:	Original Petition	Answer	Co-Def. Answer
	1._____	_____	_____
	2._____	_____	_____
	Amended Petitions		
	1._____	_____	_____
	2._____	_____	_____

5. Client Profile Sheet

CLIENT PROFILE SHEET

Client Name: _____

Date of Accident: _____

Date of Statute of Limitations: _____

Date of Initial Interview: _____

CLIENT INFORMATION

Address: _____

_____

Telephone Numbers: _____
    (work/home & others)

Date of Birth: _____

Date of Death: _____

Date of Marriage: _____ Name of Spouse: _____

Date of any divorces & name of spouse: _____

Social Security numbers:

Client: _____

Spouse: _____

Ex-Spouse: _____

Driver's license number: _____

States in which currently holds or previously held a driver's license:

_____

List all living relatives; their addresses, phone numbers, and places of employment (including spouse, children, stepchildren, parents, stepparents, grandparents, and any others that are applicable):

_____

_____

_____

_____

_____

_____

_____

_____

_____

Client Profile Sheet (continued)

Education:
List all schools attended; include dates of attendance and degrees earned.

_____
_____
_____
_____
_____

Armed Services:
List any and all service in the U.S. armed forces; include dates of enlistment, superior officer, bases stationed at and their addresses, and status of dismissal.

_____
_____
_____
_____
_____

History of Residence:
List the locations of residence for the last ten years, including: address; phone number; status of ownership; length of time lived at the residence; name, address, and phone number of landlord, if applicable.

_____
_____
_____
_____
_____

Work Experience:
List all employers for past ten years, including: name of employer; employer's address, phone number; names of supervisors; dates of employment; positions held; reasons for leaving; names, addresses, and phone numbers of employees who can be used as references.

_____
_____
_____
_____
_____
_____

Special Skills:
List all the special skills the client possesses in relation to his/her occupation or hobbies.

_____
_____
_____

Client Profile Sheet (*continued*)

Fact Witnesses:
1. Name: _____
    Address: _____
    Telephone number: _____
    Place of employment: _____
    Occupation: _____
    Interviewed (yes/no):_____   Date interviewed: _____
    Ranking in case: _____
    Status: _____
    Credibility issues: _____

2. Name: _____
    Address: _____
    Telephone number: _____
    Place of employment: _____
    Occupation: _____
    Interviewed (yes/no):_____   Date interviewed: _____
    Ranking in case: _____
    Status: _____
    Credibility issues: _____

3. Name: _____
    Address: _____
    Telephone number: _____
    Place of employment: _____
    Occupation: _____
    Interviewed (yes/no):_____   Date interviewed: _____
    Ranking in case: _____
    Status: _____
    Credibility issues: _____

4. Name: _____
    Address: _____
    Telephone number: _____
    Place of employment: _____
    Occupation: _____
    Interviewed (yes/no):_____   Date interviewed: _____
    Ranking in case: _____
    Status: _____
    Credibility issues: _____

Client's Credibility Issues:

_____
_____
_____

Client Profile Sheet (*continued*)

For personal injury cases, list all medical providers here. Include the names of the doctors; their addresses and phone numbers; dates they treated the client; clinics and hospitals the doctors are associated with; whether medical records have been gathered, reviewed, and summarized; special treatment; need for experts.

_____

_____

_____

_____

_____

_____

_____

_____

_____

6. Detailed Witness List

DETAILED WITNESS LIST

Case Name: _____ Court: _____

Case Number: _____ Trial Date: _____

Name	Address and Phone Number	Deposition given (yes/no) Date	Evidence to be introduced by witness	Subpoena needed (yes/no) Date issued Date served	Date and time witness to testify Length estimated for testimony
1.					
2.					
3.					

7. Employment and Medical Record Log
(adaptable to either employment or medical records production)

EMPLOYMENT/MEDICAL RECORDS LOG

Case Name: _____   Date of Loss: _____
Case Number: _____   Updated On: _____
Court: _____   Trial Date: _____

Employer Physician/ Facility	Employment dates Treatment dates	Requested by authorization (A) or by subpoena (S)	Date received	Summarized or computerized	Comments
1.					
2.					
3.					
4.					
5.					

8. Flow Chart—Time Management

FLOW CHART—WEEKLY

Paralegal's Name: _____   Date: _____
Billing Number: _____

Days Hours	Monday	Tuesday	Wednesday	Thursday	Friday	Saturday
1st						
2nd						
3rd						
4th						
5th						
6th						
7th						

Comments: _____
_____
_____

Total Billable: _____   Total Nonbillable: _____

9. Formal Discovery Checklist

DISCOVERY CHECKLIST

_____ 1. Prepare appropriate interrogatories.

_____ 2. Prepare appropriate request for production of documents and request for admissions.

_____ 3. Obtain authorizations for:

    ____ a. Medical records   ____ d. Social Security records/
    ____ b. IRS records   Disability records
    ____ c. Employment records   ____ e. Other (specify)

_____ 4. Order records.

_____ 5. Calendar response dates.

_____ 6. Research for:

    ____ a. News articles   ____ d. Weather reports
    ____ b. Medical literature   ____ e. Police reports
    ____ c. Legal memoranda   ____ f. Other (specify)

_____ 7. Research warranties and representations, stated or implied.

_____ 8. Get lab testing as needed.

_____ 9. Obtain expert witnesses:

    ____ a. Medical—doctor   ____ d. Engineer/design
    ____ b. Medical—nurse   ____ e. Other (specify)
    ____ c. Economic

_____ 10. Evaluate and summarize discovery responses.

_____ 11. Chronology/summary of records.

_____ 12. Status report to client:

    ____ a. 30 days   ____ d. 120 days
    ____ b. 60 days   ____ e. Other (specify)
    ____ c. 90 days

_____ 13. Determine witnesses.

_____ 14. Schedule depositions.

_____ 15. Summarize depositions:

    ____ a. Page/line   ____ c. Outline
_____   ____ b. Keyword/name   ____ d. Narrative

_____ 16. Produce materials promised during depositions.

_____ 17. Independent medical examination, as needed.

_____ 18. Summarize employment history.

_____ 19. Summarize income records.

_____ 20. Summarize damages.

10. General Timetable/Conversion for Individual Cases

Case Name	Days	Court/calendar	Authority	Serve/file
Complaint				
Response				
Trial Date				
Motions				
Discovery				
Demand				
Motions to Compel				
Motion for Protective Order				
Subpoenas				
Subpoenas Issued/ Served/Filed				
Opposition to Motions				
Reply to Oppositions				
Proof of Service				
Pretrial Activities				
Trial Notebook				
IME				
IME deposition				
Other				

11. General Witness Information Sheet

GENERAL WITNESS INFORMATION SHEET

Client Names & Matter: _____ File No.: _____

Responsible Atty: _____ Date: _____

Name of Witness: _____

Aliases, if any: _____ U.S. Citizen: Y___   N___

Current Home Address: _____

Telephone/Contact Numbers: _____

Past Addresses: _____

_____

Sex: ___   Race: _____   Age: ____

Current Marriage Status: Single ___   Married ___   Separated ___   Divorced ___   Widowed ___

Name of Spouse: _____ Number of Former Marriages ___

No. Children: _____

Names & Ages of Children (include natural and adopted children):

1. _____

2. _____

3. _____

4. _____

Current Employer (name and address):_____

_____

Job Title: _____

Supervisor:_____

From: _____   To: _____

Education (give name & address of school):

High School: _____ From _____ To _____ Degree _____

College: _____ From _____ To _____ Degree _____

Technical: _____ From _____ To _____ Degree _____

Other:_____ From _____ To _____ Degree _____

Capacity in Lawsuit:

Witness for: Plaintiff ___   Defendant ___   Type: Expert ___   Personal ___   Eye ___

Have you ever been a party or a witness in a court suit: Y ___   N ___

If so, when? _____

Where?_____

Brief description of suit: _____

_____

12. Informational Statement (Pleading)

STATE OF _____   IN THE DISTRICT COURT
                                         CIVIL DIVISION

COUNTY OF _____   _____ JUDICIAL DISTRICT

_____,
                Plaintiff

VS

_____,   INFORMATIONAL STATEMENT
                Defendant.

1. All parties have been served with process.

2. All parties have not joined in the filing of this form.

3. Brief description of the case: _____

   _____

   _____

4. It is estimated that discovery specified below can be completed within _____ months from the date of this form. (Check all that apply, and supply estimates where indicated.)

   a. Factual depositions   Y___ N___   Est. time _____

   b. Medical experts   Y___ N___   Est. time _____

   c. Experts for discovery   Y___ N___   Est. time _____

5. Assignment as an _____ expedited _____ standard _____ complex case is requested. (If not standard case assignment, include brief statement setting forth the reasons for the request.)

6. The dates and deadlines specified below are suggested.

   a. _____ Deadline for joining additional parties.

   b   _____ Deadline for bringing nondispositive motions.

   c. _____ Deadline for bringing dispositive motions.

   d. _____ Deadline for submitting _____ to the court [specify the issue].

   e. _____ Deadline for completing independent physical examination pursuant to [state law here].

   f. _____ Date for formal discovery conference pursuant to [state law here].

   g. _____ Date for pretrial conference pursuant to [state law here].

   h. _____ Date for scheduling conference.

   I. _____ Date for submitting of a joint statement of the case pursuant to [state law here].

   j. _____ Trial date.

   k. _____ Deadline for filing proposed instructions, verdicts, findings of fact, witness list, exhibit list.

   l. _____ Other. _____

Informational Statement (*continued*)

7. Estimated trial time: _____

8. A jury trial is: ___ waived by consent of _____
                          ___ requested by plaintiff

9. *A. MEETING:*

   ____ Counsel for the parties met on _____ to discuss case management issues.

   ____ Counsel for the parties have not yet met. Defendant has a summary judgment motion pending. Counsel respectfully requests that consideration of alternate dispute resolution be deferred until after a ruling on the summary judgment motion.

   B. ADR PROCESS (check one):

   ____ Counsel agree that ADR is appropriate and choose the following:

      ____ Mediation
      ____ arbitration (nonbinding)
      ____ Med-Arb
      ____ early neutral evaluation
      ____ moderated settlement conference
      ____ mini-trial
      ____ summary jury trial
      ____ consensual special magistrate
      ____ impartial factfinder
      ____ other [describe] _____

   ____ Counsel agree that ADR is appropriate but request that the court select the process.

   ____ Counsel agree that ADR is NOT appropriate because:

      ____ the case implicates the federal or state constitution.
      ____ other [describe with particularity] _____
      _____

   C. PROVIDER (check one):

   ____ The parties have selected the following ADR neutral: _____.

   ____ The parties cannot agree on an ADR neutral and request the court to appoint one.

   ____ The parties agree to select an ADR neutral on or before _____.

10. Please list any additional information that might be helpful to the court when scheduling this letter.

Dated:_____

Signature line: _____

13. Interrogatory Timetable

INTERROGATORY TIMETABLE				
Discovery	**Days**	**Calendar**	**Authority**	**Serve/File**
With complaint				
Answers due				
Before trial				
Answers due: Discovery cutoff				
Extra if mailed				
Demand if not adequate				
Motion to compel				
Motion for protective order				
Notice of motion				
Extra if mailed				
Extra if mailed to out-of-state address				
Extra if mailed to out-of-country address				
Opposition to motion				
Reply to opposition				
Proof of service				
Meet-and-confer statement				
Motions cutoff before trial				
Other				

14. Request for Admissions Timetable

REQUEST FOR ADMISSIONS TIMETABLE				
Discovery	**Days**	**Calendar**	**Authority**	**Serve/File**
After complaint				
Response due				
Before trial				
Response due: Discovery cutoff				
Extra if mailed				
Extra if mailed out of state				
Demand if not adequate				
Notice that requests have been deemed admitted				
Motion for protective order				
Notice of motion				
Extra if mailed				
Extra if mailed out of state				
Opposition to motion				
Reply to opposition				
Proof of service				
Meet-and-confer statement				
Motions cutoff before trial				
Other				

15.   Request for Change of Address or Boxholder, Information Needed for Service of Legal Process

Postmaster   Date _____

_____
City, State, Zip Code

Request for Change of Address or Boxholder
Information Needed for Service of Legal Process

Please furnish the new address or the name and street address (if a boxholder) for the following:

Name: _____

Address: _____

NOTE: The name and last known address are required for change-of-address information. The name, if known, and Post Office box address are required for boxholder information.

The following information is provided in accordance with 39 C.F.R. § 265.6(d)(6)(U). There is no fee for providing boxholder information. The fee for providing change-of-address information is waived in accordance with 39 C.F.R. § 265.6(d)(1) and (2) and corresponding Administrative Support Manual § 352.44a and b.

1. Capacity of request (e.g., process server, attorney, party representing himself): _____
   _____

2. Statute or regulation that empowers me to serve process (not required when requester is an attorney or a party acting pro se—except a corporation acting pro se must cite statute):
   _____
   _____

3. The names of all known parties to the litigation: _____
   _____

4. The court in which the case has been or will be heard: _____
   _____

5. The docket or other identifying number if one has been issued: _____
   _____

6. The capacity in which this individual is to be served (e.g., defendant or witness): _____
   _____

WARNING

THE SUBMISSION OF FALSE INFORMATION TO OBTAIN AND USE CHANGE-OF-ADDRESS INFORMATION OR BOXHOLDER INFORMATION FOR ANY PURPOSE OTHER THAN THE SERVICE OF LEGAL PROCESS IN CONNECTION WITH ACTUAL OR PROSPECTIVE LITIGATION, OR TO AVOID PAYMENT OF THE FEE FOR CHANGE-OF-ADDRESS INFORMATION, COULD RESULT IN CRIMINAL PENALTIES INCLUDING A FINE OF UP TO $10,000 OR IMPRISONMENT OF NOT MORE THAN 5 YEARS, OR BOTH (18 U.S.C. § 1001).

Request for Change of Address or Boxholder (*continued*)

I certify that the above information is true and that the address information is true and that the address information is needed and will be used solely for service of legal process in connection with actual or prospective litigation.

_____   _____
Signature   Address

_____   _____
Printed Name   City, State, Zip Code

FOR POST OFFICE USE ONLY
___ No change of address order on file.
___ Not known at address given.
___ Moved, left no forwarding address.
___ No such address.

NEW ADDRESS OR BOXHOLDER'S POSTMARK
NAME AND STREET ADDRESS

_____
_____
_____

16. To-Do List

Case Name & Case Number	Atty & L.A.	Description Comments	Assigned	Due	Done

17. Witness Questionnaire

WITNESS QUESTIONNAIRE

1. When did the accident occur? _____

2. Where did the accident occur? _____
   _____

3. What is your complete name and address? _____
   _____

4. What is your telephone number? _____

5. What is your occupation and who is your employer?_____
   _____

6. What were you doing when the accident occurred? _____
   _____

7. Did you really see the accident happen? _____

8. What did you observe?_____
   _____
   _____

9. How fast do you think the two cars were going?_____
   _____

10. Did either vehicle run a red traffic light or stop sign? _____
    _____

11. Did either vehicle fail to yield the right of way? _____
    _____

12. Was either vehicle traveling on the wrong side of the street? _____
    _____

13. Did either vehicle make an unsafe lane change? _____
    _____

14. Did either vehicle use directional signals? _____
    _____

15. Did either vehicle have its headlights on? _____
    _____

16. Was there any construction in the area?_____

17. Was either driver trying to avoid some sort of obstacle?_____
    _____

18. Do you think either driver was under the influence of drugs or liquor at the time of the
    accident? _____
    _____

APPENDIX C
Anatomy

CONTENTS

INTRODUCTION

Anatomy is a descriptive science that depends on specialized terminology to describe body structures. Because all lawsuits deal with damages, and because many times damages include pain and suffering or injury claims, each section in this appendix outlines basic anatomy terms and principles used to evaluate medical records and damages. The concepts explained here provide a foundation for summarizing medical, dental, chiropractic, and ambulance (emergency care) records.

SECTION 1   GENERAL ANATOMY I

The human body consists of four basic structural and functional levels: cells, tissues, organs, and systems.

Cells: The basic structural and functional unit of any living organism; *cytology* is the study of cells.

Tissue: An aggregate of similar cells and materials that perform specific functions. The four types of tissues are epithelial (skin), connective, muscle, and nervous.

Organ: An aggregate of tissues that performs particular functions. Examples of organs are the heart, lung, kidney, ovary, and brain.

System: A number of different organs that work together in performing a general function.[1]

Besides these basics, the human body is divided into regions and cavities (see Figures A-1 and A-2). Most of the organs in the body are contained in one of the body cavities, which are protected, confined, and supported. The main cavities are:

1. *Posterior* (back/dorsal) body cavity
2. *Anterior* (front/ventral) body cavity.

The anterior cavity contains multiple subcavities: the best known are the abdominopelvic and the thoracic. The abdominopelvic cavity is located in the abdominal and pelvic regions; the thoracic is located in the chest area; the dorsal cavity contains the cranial, brain, and spinal cavities.

For a basic introduction to anatomy, you need to know the basic *planes* of the body. These terms are used by doctors and pathologists to refer to the structural arrangement of the human body or body parts, and to signify direction. The three most common planes are midsagittal, coronal, and transverse (see Figure A-3).

Midsagittal: The plane that passes lengthwise through the midline of the body, dividing it into right and left halves. A sagittal (lengthwise) or parasagittal (partial lengthwise) plane also extends vertically; however, it is not along the midline of the body.

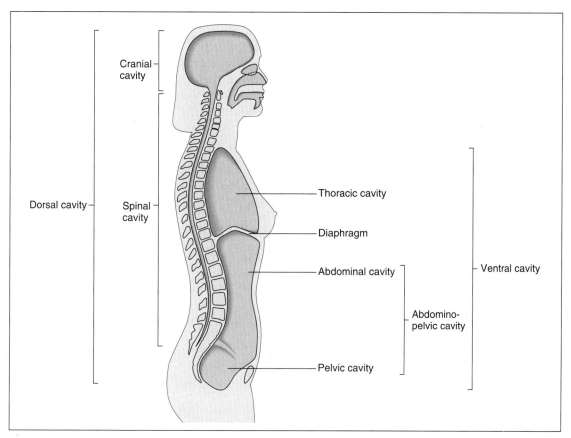

Figure A-1 Major body cavities

Figure A-2
The nine regions
of the abdominal
area

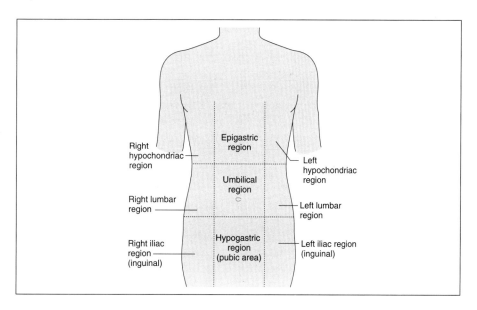

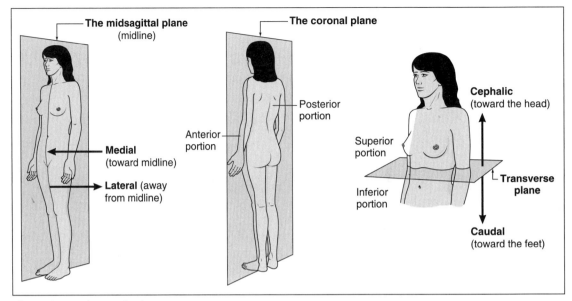

Figure A-3   Planes of reference

Coronal: A frontal plane that passes lengthwise and divides the body into front (anterior) and back (posterior) portions.

Transverse: Also called a horizontal or cross-sectional plane; divides the body into superior (upper) and inferior (lower) portions.

SECTION 2   GENERAL ANATOMY II

As discussed, anatomy is a descriptive science that uses terms to describe body parts and locations from an anatomical position, which correlates to the relationships between body parts. The *anatomical position* is the position of the body when it is standing erect, feet are parallel to one another and flat on the floor, eyes are directed forward, and the arms are at the sides of the body *with the palms of the hands turned forward.* This is very important to remember when determining specific directions. Directional terms are used to locate and relate the structures, surfaces, and regions of the body, based on the anatomical position (see Figures A-4 to A-6). For instance, when looking at the body in the anatomical position, the hand is inferior to the shoulder.

Self-Test

1. Your tonsils are _____ to your teeth.

2. Your buttock is _____ to your navel, but is _____ to your feet.

3. Your thumb is _____ in relation to your little finger.

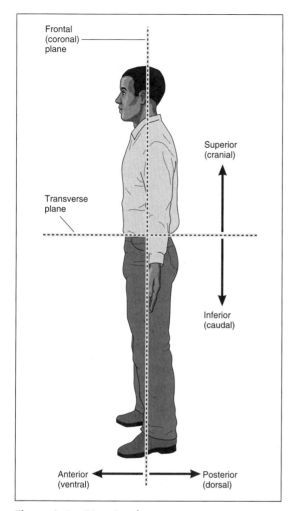

Figure A-4 Directional terms

Figure A-5 Directional terms

Figure A-6
Table of directional terms

Term	Definition	Example
Superior	Toward the top (toward the head)	The elbow is superior to the hand.
Inferior (caudal)	Toward the bottom (away from the head)	The legs are inferior to the trunk of the body.
Anterior (ventral)	Front side	The navel is located on the anterior surface of the body.
Posterior (dorsal)	Backside	The tailbone is posterior to the pelvis.

Figure A-6
(continued)

Term	Definition	Example
Medial	Toward the midline of the body	The little finger is medial to the thumb.
Lateral	Toward the side of the body	The ears are located on the lateral portion of the body.
Internal (deep)	Away from the surface of the body	The tongue is internal to the jaw.
External	Toward the surface of the body	Skin is external.
Proximal	Toward the main mass of the body	The knee is proximal to the foot.
Distal	Away from the main mass of the body	The hand is distal to the elbow.
Parietal	Relates to the body walls	The parietal pleura line the thoracic cavity.
Visceral	Relating to internal organs	The lung is covered with a thin membrane called the visceral pleura.

SECTION 3   BONES I

The skeletal system is divided into two groups, the axial skeleton and the appendicular skeleton. Each contains separate bone structures.

Axial skeleton: Consists of the skull, vertebral column, and the rib cage.

Appendicular skeleton: Consists of the girdles and appendages of the body, such as the hip and pelvic region, and arms and legs.

Section 3 focuses on the axial skeleton. To make learning easier, remember that most of the bones discussed in this section can be palpated (felt or touched through the skin). It is also important to understand which bones make up both the axial and the appendicular skeletons.

Bones are classified into categories (see Figure A-7):

1. Long bones, like the leg (femur) and upper arm (humerus).
2. Short bones, like the kneecap (patella).
3. Flat bones, like the ribs.
4. Irregular bones, like the facial bones and vertebrae.

Understanding bone classifications is important because different types of bones fracture in different ways, and when reviewing medical records the paralegal may be better able to understand certain injuries when she knows something about the bones involved. A detailed discussion on fractures appears in Section 4.

The axial skeleton is divided into the skull, vertebral column, and the ribs (see Figure A-8).

Figure A-7
Bone shapes

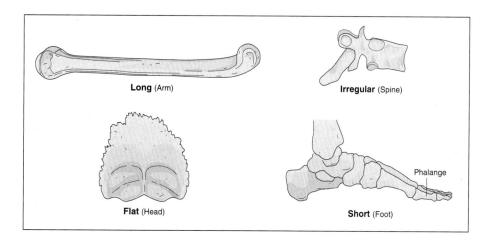

Long (Arm)

Irregular (Spine)

Flat (Head)

Short (Foot)

Phalange

Figure A-8 Side view of the human skeleton

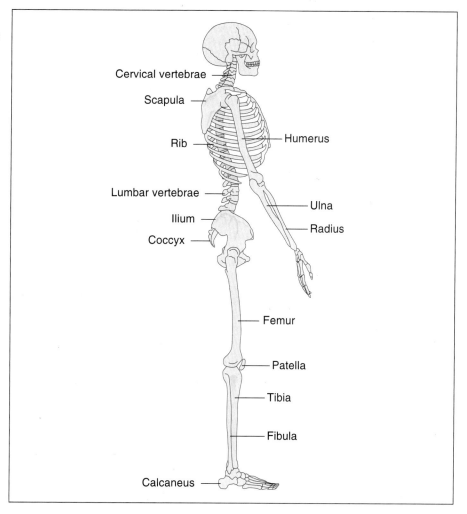

Cervical vertebrae

Scapula

Rib

Humerus

Lumbar vertebrae

Ulna

Ilium

Radius

Coccyx

Femur

Patella

Tibia

Fibula

Calcaneus

Skull   Eight separate bones make up the skull or cranium, which encloses the brain (see Figure A-9). Cranial bones are referred to in medical records as they relate to head trauma, disease, and long-term headache regions resulting from injuries like whiplash (see Figure A-10). These eight bones are:

1. *Frontal* (1 total): This is located in the front of the head and is known as the forehead.
2. *Parietal* (2 total): These are located on the top of the head (or crown); there is one on each side, right and left.
3. *Temporal* (2 total): These small, flat bones are located at the temples; there is one on each side of the head, right and left.
4. *Occipital* (1 total): This singular bone constitutes the back of the head; it is the most common area for headaches after whiplash.
5. *Sphenoid* (1 total): This singular bone is long and runs behind the eyes.
6. *Ethmoid* (1 total): This bone is part of the bones and cartilage that form the nasal septum, which is part of the nose.

There are fourteen bones in the face. The major ones are:

Mandible: Jaw

Maxilla: Top bone of the jaw (actually part of the skull), located above the teeth and extending from the left zygomatic to the right zygomatic bone.

Zygomatic: Cheek bone

Temporomandibular joint: The joint bringing together the upper and lower jaws; located below the temple.

Figure A-9
Human skull

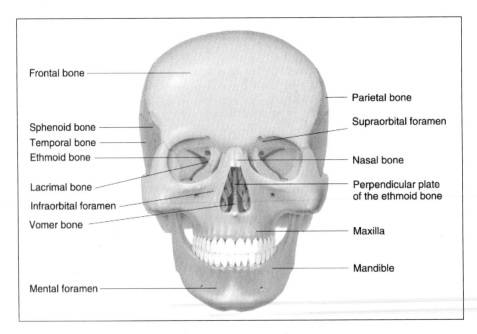

Frontal bone

Parietal bone

Supraorbital foramen

Sphenoid bone
Temporal bone
Ethmoid bone

Nasal bone

Lacrimal bone

Perpendicular plate
of the ethmoid bone

Infraorbital foramen

Vomer bone

Maxilla

Mandible

Mental foramen

Figure A-10
Side view of the
human skull

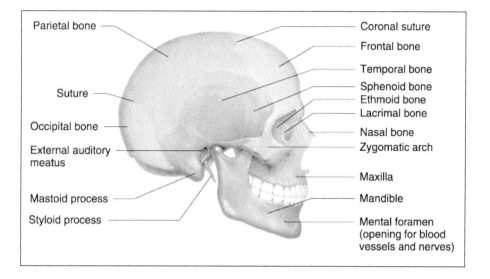

Vertebral Column The vertebral column is divided into five groups, each consisting of a varied number of vertebrae (see Figure A-11). These divisions are:

1. *Cervical vertebrae* (7 total): Located at the top of the spine; connect the head to the neck.

2. *Thoracic vertebrae* (12 total): Located from the C-7 or last cervical vertebra to the L-1, or first lumbar vertebra; constitutes the upper back.

3. *Lumbar vertebrae* (5 total): Located in the lower back and extending from the T-12 or last thoracic vertebra to the tailbone.

4. *Sacrum vertebrae* (5 total fused vertebrae): Large section of bone located above the tailbone.

5. *Coccyx vertebrae* (4 total fused vertebrae): Constitute the tailbone.

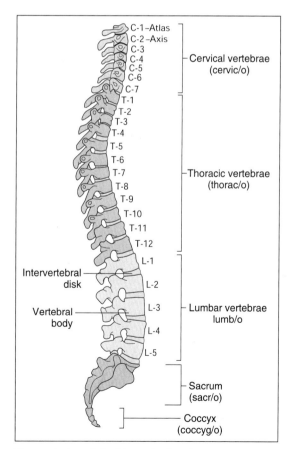

Figure A-11 Spinal (vertebral) column

Rib Cage   The rib cage consists of twelve total ribs (see Figure A-12), which are broken down into categories:

Ribs 1–7:   Known as "true" ribs; located at the top of the rib cage.

Ribs 8–10:   Known as the "false" ribs; found in the midsection of the rib cage.

Ribs 11–12:   Known as the "floating" ribs.

All twelve ribs connect to the spine posteriorly, but vary in their connection anteriorly. In the front, the true ribs connect directly to the sternum. The false ribs connect indirectly to the sternum by means of cartilage, and the remaining floating ribs are not attached to the sternum.

As a whole, the rib cage consists of many more components than ribs. Ribs are made of costal cartilage; *costal notches* are the locations where the true ribs attach to the sternum on the anterior portion of the body. The *clavicular notch* is where the collar bones attach to the sternum. *Intercostal spaces* are the openings between the ribs, and the *xiphoid process* is a taillike structure at the bottom of the sternum. This piece of the sternum is the most likely to be injured during cardiopulmonary resuscitation (CPR); trainers instruct students of first aid to feel for the bottom of the sternum, or xiphoid process, and then move up before compressing the chest.

Common names for bones in the axial skeleton are:

Cervical: neck bone

Coccyx: tailbone

Vertebrae column: backbone or spine

Sternum: breastbone

Frontal: forehead

Mandible: jawbone

Zygomatic: cheekbone

Figure A-12
Rib cage

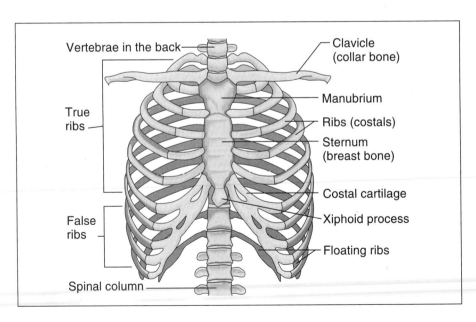

SECTION 4   BONES II

Section 3 discussed the axial skeleton, which includes the skull, spine, and rib cage. This section discusses the appendicular skeleton, which includes girdles and appendages of the body. Because so many lawsuits revolve around broken bones, particularly those of the appendicular skeleton, common fractures of the appendages (arms and legs) are also covered here.

The appendicular skeleton is made up of 126 bones and includes the upper extremities, lower extremities, and shoulder (or pectoral) and pelvic girdles. See Figures A-13A, A-13B, and A-14 to A-16.

There are four categories of appendages in the human body: the arms, the legs, the feet, and the hands. Each is made up of different bones and joints. These bones and joints are commonly injured in falling and motor vehicle accidents. The most common appendage terminology is listed in Figure A-17.

There are two girdles in the body, the pectoral girdle and the pelvic girdle.

Pectoral girdle: Two scapulae (shoulder blades located on the back, connecting to the shoulder). Two clavicles (collar bones).

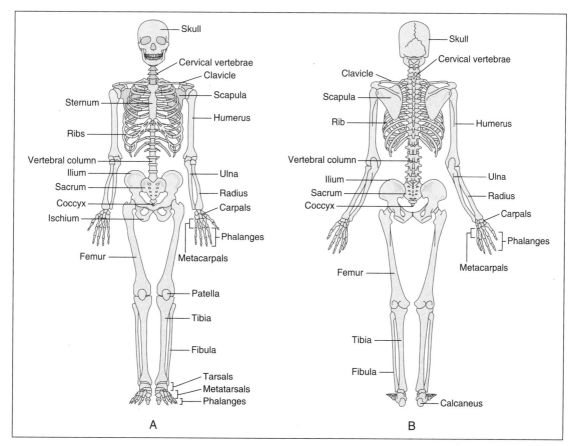

Figure A-13   (A) Anterior view of appendicular skeleton; (B) Posterior view of appendicular skeleton

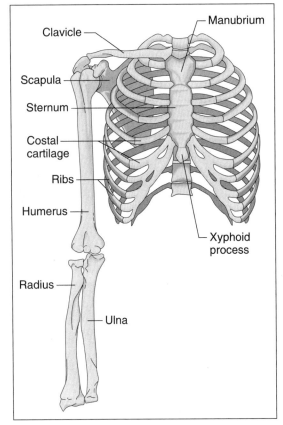

Figure A-14 Anterior view of ribs, shoulder, and arm

The pectoral girdle is not a complete girdle, as it has only an anterior attachment to the axial skeleton. The primary function of the pectoral girdle is to provide attachment of the many muscles that move the upper extremities.

> **Pelvic girdle:** Two hip bones (os coxae), joined by the pubic bone in the front and the sacrum or lower portion of the spine in the back.

The pelvic girdle and its ligaments support the weight of the body from the vertebral column, and support and protect the lower viscera, which are the soft organs of the body.[2]

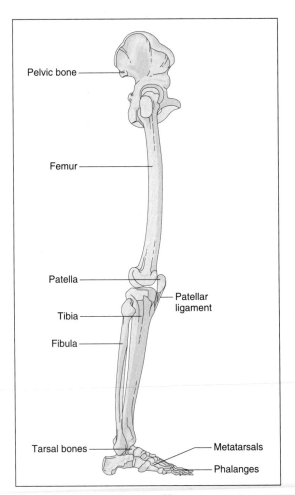

Figure A-16 Lateral view of lower extremity

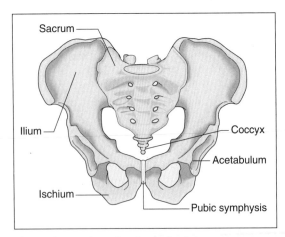

Figure A-15 Anterior view of pelvis

Anatomical name of bone	Common name of bone and location
Humerus	Upper arm
Ulna	Smaller bone of the forearm, located at the medial aspect of the forearm (see anatomical position, little finger side)
Radius	Larger bone of the forearm, located at the distal aspect of the forearm (see the anatomical position, thumb side)
Epicondyles	Elbow
Carpals	Bones above the wrist leading to the hand
Metacarpals	Bones of the hand
Phalanges	Finger bones
Femur	Thigh bone
Patella	Knee
Tibia	Larger shin bone, located at the medial aspect of the lower leg
Fibula	Smaller of the two shin bones, located at the distal aspect of the lower leg
Calcaneus	Heel bone
Lateral malleolus	Outer portion of the ankle
Medial malleolus	Inside of the ankle bone
Talus	Top bone of the ankle
Tarsals	Bones leading from the ankle to the foot bones
Metatarsals	Foot bones
Phalanges	Toe bones

Figure A-17 Appendage terminology

Fractures Injuries from bone fractures are common and can occur at any age. The degree of a fracture can range from a minor crack in the surface of the bone (fissure) to a complete break. Fractures are caused by unusual impact, compression, sudden injury, or by constant or prolonged straining of the bone (known as a *stress fracture*).

There are three categories of broken bones (see Figure A-18):

1. *Simple* (closed): Under-the-skin fracture.
2. *Compound* (open): When the broken bone protrudes out of the skin.
3. *Displaced:* When bones are forced from their normally aligned position and a fracture occurs.

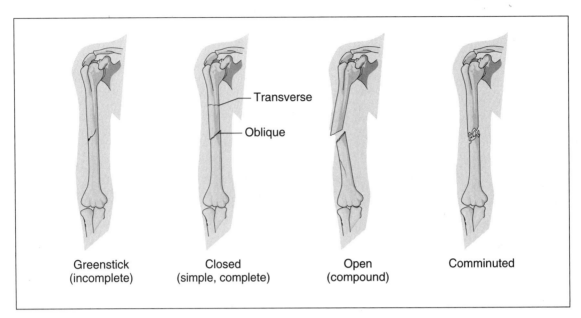

Transverse

Oblique

| Greenstick (incomplete) | Closed (simple, complete) | Open (compound) | Comminuted |

Figure A-18   Types of bone fractures

Because the appendages (namely, arms and legs) constitute the majority of the appendicular skeleton, the paralegal can expect to review medical records dealing with a variety of injuries to the appendicular skeleton. Figure A-19 lists the five most common fractures.

Fracture type	Explanation
Transverse fracture	A break straight across the width of the bone. These are usually stable fractures.
Spiral fracture	A fracture that runs diagonally across the shaft or long portion of the bone leaving a jagged edge. A sharp twist causes this break.
Comminuted fracture	A crushing or shattering of the bone. It is common in motor vehicle accidents and is caused by a powerful direct impact.
Greenstick fracture	A fracture that occurs in a long bone, when the bone bends, cracking only on one side. This is common in young children. The greenstick fracture heals well.
Colles's fracture	A fracture that occurs at the tip of the radius and occasionally at the tip of the ulna. This happens during a fall when a person reaches down to catch himself or herself with a flexed wrist.

Figure A-19   Most common bone fractures

Self-Test Using the figures in this section and other sections dealing with bones, answer the following questions.

1. Name the heel bone. _____

2. Identify the bone of the upper arm. _____

3. Who will most likely suffer a Colles's fracture, and why?_____

    _____

4. The tibia is what direction (use the correct anatomical term) from the fibula? _____

5. What is the difference between a metatarsal and a metacarpal? _____

    _____

SECTION 5 MUSCLES I

The human body is largely made up of muscle tissue. The more than 600 skeletal muscles account for about half of the body's weight. These muscles work together with the bones to provide power that enables the body to move under conscious and voluntary control. There are three specific muscle types:

1. Striated skeletal muscle
2. Involuntary/smooth muscle
3. Cardiac muscle.

All of the muscles in these three categories have the ability to contract, relax, respond to stimuli, and return to their original shape and size. Involuntary muscles handle the unconscious routines of the body and are always at work, doing things like keeping eyes focused and propelling food through the stomach. Cardiac muscle is located in the heart and is specialized, with branching interconnections. Skeletal muscle usually attaches to one end of a bone, stretches across a joint, and attaches to another bone. When the muscle contracts, it moves one bone while the other remains fairly stable. Muscles that accomplish movement are *synergistic;* muscles acting in opposition to each other are called *antagonists.* Due to the large number of muscles in the body, this section addresses only anterior (front) skeletal muscles in the upper and lower extremities.

Skeletal muscles are voluntary; one chooses to contract and relax them. All of the muscles in the limbs and trunk of the human body are kept partially contracted, to give them tone, by a steady impulse received by the nerves of the spinal cord. When, or if, a muscle loses its nerve supply, it will shrink to approximately two-thirds of its bulk within months. Many diseases damage both the nervous system and the muscular system, resulting in decreased muscular performance.

Muscles are more commonly injured than they are diseased. Fortunately, muscles are capable of self-repair. If a portion of a muscle is destroyed, the remaining portion will grow larger and stronger to compensate. Figure A-20 lists the major anterior skeletal muscles.

Figure A-20

Major anterior skeletal muscles

Muscle	Description
Deltoid	Shoulder
Triceps	Upper arm, medial to shoulder, attaches to the humerus
Biceps	Midline, center of the upper arm, running along the humerus
Internal oblique	Inner band of stomach muscle that runs left to right
External oblique	Outer layer of stomach muscle that runs from the back around and down the front of the body to the pubic bone
Pectoralis major	Greater chest muscle
Quadriceps femoris	Greater thigh muscle on the anterior, midline of the femur (thigh)
Tibialis anterior	Distal calf muscle, located distal to the tibia
Gracilis	Inner thigh muscle

Muscles make movement possible and are used to hold the body erect. The three types of muscle tissue perform various functions, including movement of the body (skeletal), movement of internal organs (smooth), and movement of the heart (cardiac). Because the paralegal will rarely be expected to review individual muscle fibers, her understanding of tissue types is relevant only with regard to recognizing their unique differences. The concentration of this and all sections dealing with muscles is to help locate specific muscles of the body in relationship to the anatomical position and applicability of muscle movement. Figures A-21 through A-24 provide a visual portrait of the major anterior muscles.

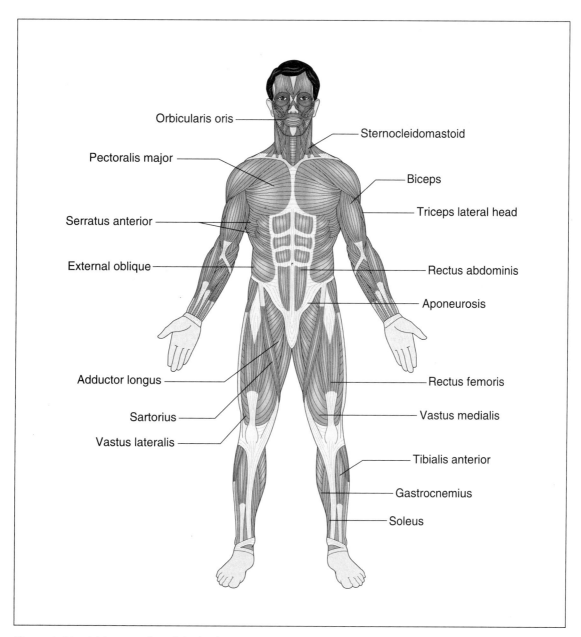

Orbicularis oris

Pectoralis major

Serratus anterior

External oblique

Adductor longus

Sartorius

Vastus lateralis

Sternocleidomastoid

Biceps

Triceps lateral head

Rectus abdominis

Aponeurosis

Rectus femoris

Vastus medialis

Tibialis anterior

Gastrocnemius

Soleus

Figure A-21   Major muscles of the body, anterior view

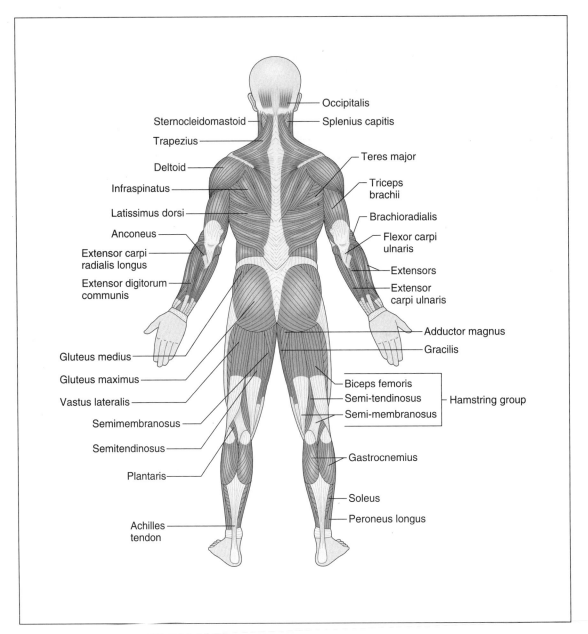

Figure A-22   Major muscles of the body, posterior view

Figure A-23
Triceps and biceps

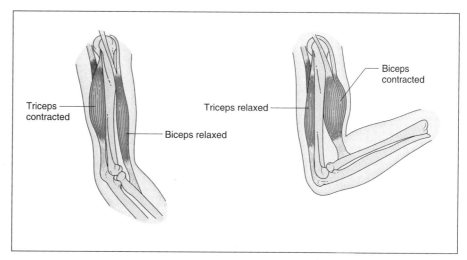

Figure A-24
Muscles of the
lower extremity

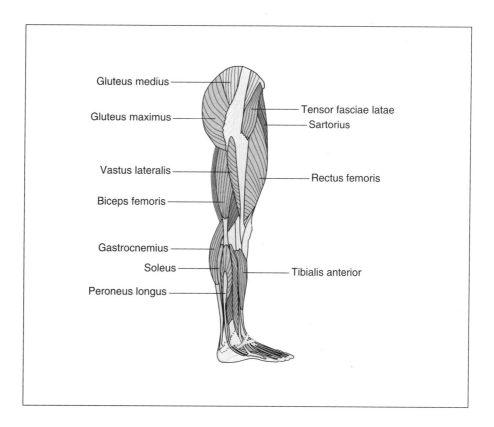

ANATOMY REVIEW SECTIONS 1–5

Answer the following questions regarding the material presented in the first five sections of this appendix.

Labeling

Label the following items on Figure A-25.

1. Zygomatic bone
2. Ulna
3. Talus
4. Tibia
5. False ribs

6. Patella
7. Location of the deltoid muscle
8. Location of the gracilis muscle
9. Location of the triceps muscle
10. The most superior point in the body

Figure A-25

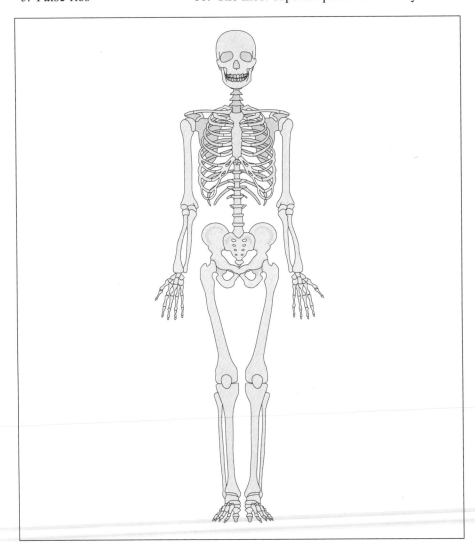

Definitions
Write a brief definition of each term.

1. Organ _____

   _____

2. Midsagittal _____

   _____

3. Distal _____

   _____

4. Visceral _____

   _____

5. Anterior _____

   _____

6. Long bone _____

   _____

7. Axial skeleton _____

   _____

8. Mandible _____

   _____

9. Vertebral column _____

   _____

10. Epicondyles _____

    _____

11. Greenstick fracture _____

    _____

12. Abdominopelvic cavity _____

    _____

Short Answer
Fill in the blanks with the correct word, term, or phrase.

1. The head is _____ to the feet.

2. The anatomical position means the person is standing _____

   _____.

3. There are _____ [number] bones in the skull.

4. Flat bones are usually bones like the _____.

5. The lumbar vertebrae follow the _____ vertebrae when moving inferiorly on the spine.

6. There are _____ [number] lumbar vertebrae.

7. Ribs numbered _____ are considered floating because _____

   _____.

8. The two girdles in the human body are _____ and

   _____.

9. Compound fractures are sometimes gruesome because _____

_____ .

10. After slamming into the steering wheel of her car, the victim suffered severe bruising of the muscles of her stomach, also known as the _____

_____ .

▬ᴵ SECTION 6   MUSCLES II

Muscle appearance differs greatly throughout the body, from the massive triangular muscles running up the top of the spine to the slender cable-like muscles extending into the hand. Muscle shape determines strength for contraction and influences specific functions. The most powerful muscles run along the spine; they maintain posture and provide strength for lifting and pushing. Muscles of the neck and upper back provide the strength needed for complex movement and support the head, keeping it upright. The upper back muscles, attached to the winglike scapulae, stabilize the shoulder, which is the most mobile joint in the body.

The muscles of the neck and back are susceptible to many injuries commonly seen in litigation, including those related to car accidents, slip-and-fall accidents, and stress. Figure A-26 is a short list of commonly injured back and neck muscles, some of which may experience spasm from whiplash injuries or stress. Because there are so many muscles in the back and neck, only the most visible and commonly damaged are noted here.

Figure A-26
Commonly injured muscles of the back and neck

Name of Muscle	Description
Trapezius	Triangular muscle running up the thoracic and cervical spine to the neck and across to a point on the shoulder. The widest portion of the muscle attaches to the spine. This is the outermost muscle of the upper back.
Latissimus dorsi	Muscle running from the thoracic spine across and under the armpit.
Teres major	Muscle coming from under the deltoid (shoulder) muscle to the spine and under the trapezius muscle.
Rhomboideus minor	Slim muscle connected to the cervical spine region, running over and under the trapezius muscle.
Sternocleidomastoid	Front neck muscle attaching at the sternum (top of the rib cage), and clavicle (collar bone) in the front of the neck, and bottom of the muscle; coming down from the mastoid process of the skull (jaw). This muscle is responsible for the turning of the head and neck.
Occipital	Muscle on the occipital bone of the head (back of the head).

The majority of muscle injuries are strains or tears. A muscle strain causes a moderate amount of damage to muscle fibers, limited bleeding inside the muscle, tenderness, swelling, painful spasms, and visible bruising afterward. Strains may be caused by repetitive motion, as in carpal tunnel syndrome. A more severe damage is called a *muscle tear,* which causes extensive bleeding, pain, and swelling, and may even cause a blood clot.

SECTION 7 MUSCLES III

Of the 600-plus muscles in the body, a large number are found in the face, as humans have well-developed facial musculature. The muscles of the face (see Figure A-27) allow complex facial expressions, most of which provide social communication; one conveys a large number of unspoken messages by using the muscles of the face. Facial muscles are highly complex because they attach within the skin, allowing movement and a change in appearance. Repair of such muscles can be very difficult. Figure A-28 lists some major facial muscles and their functions.

Muscles of Mastication (Chewing) Four pairs of muscles are responsible for chewing, including biting and grinding:

1. *Masseter:* used for elevating the mandible (jaw).
2. *Lateral pterygoid:* used for protracting (lengthening) the mandible.

Figure A-27
Head and neck muscles controlling facial expression and mastication

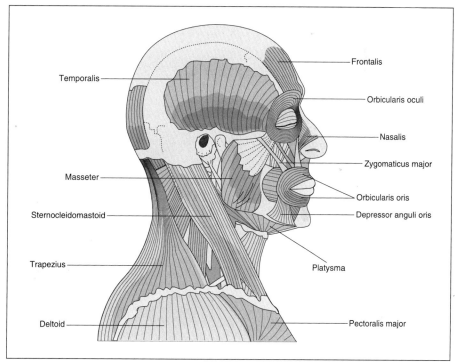

Figure A-28
Facial muscles and functions

Muscle	Function
Buccinator	Cheek muscle used for compressing the cheek
Corrugator	Draws the eyebrow to the midline
Epicranis	Wrinkles the forehead and moves the scalp
Zypomaticus	Elevates the corner of the mouth (smile)
Triangularis	Depresses the corner of the mouth (sad)
Risorius	Draws angle of the mouth laterally (laugh)
Obicularis oculi	Closes the eyes
Obicularis oris	Closes and purses the lips

    3. *Medial pterygoid:* used to elevate and move the mandible laterally.

    4. *Temporalis:* used for elevating the mandible.

Eye Muscles   The muscles that control eye movement are shown in Figure A-29.

Figure A-29
Eye muscles

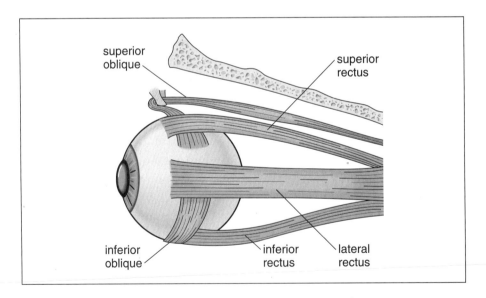

SECTION 8   NERVES I

The brain and its many connecting pathways constitute the nervous system (see Figures A-30 and A-31), which is specialized for the perception of and response to events of the internal and external body. The nervous system, along with the endocrine system, regulates the functions of other body systems, and it

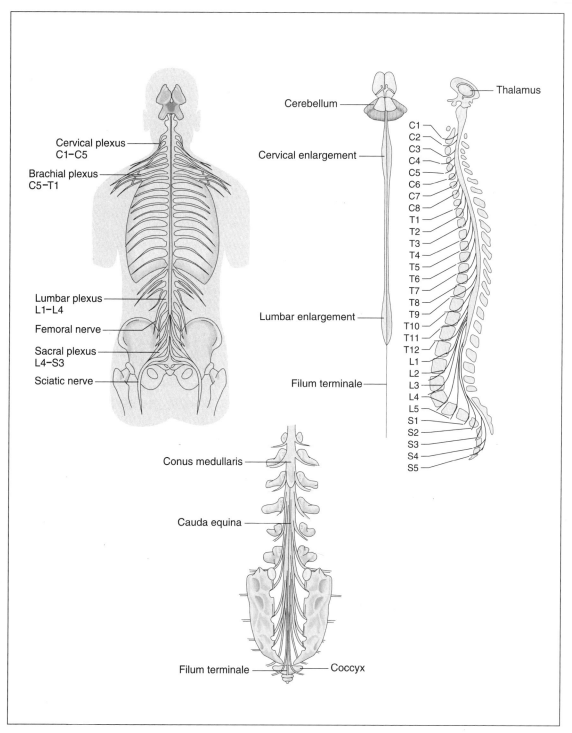

Cerebellum

Thalamus

Cervical plexus
C1–C5

Brachial plexus
C5–T1

Cervical enlargement

Lumbar plexus
L1–L4

Femoral nerve

Sacral plexus
L4–S3

Sciatic nerve

Lumbar enlargement

Filum terminale

Conus medullaris

Cauda equina

Filum terminale

Coccyx

C1
C2
C3
C4
C5
C6
C7
C8
T1
T2
T3
T4
T5
T6
T7
T8
T9
T10
T11
T12
L1
L2
L3
L4
L5
S1
S2
S3
S4
S5

Figure A-30   Structural organization of the central and peripheral nervous systems

Name	Location	Function
Cervical plexus	C1–C4	Supplies motor movement to muscles of neck and shoulders and receives messages from these areas. **Phrenic nerve** is part of this group and stimulates the diaphragm.
Brachial plexus	C5–C8, T1	Supplies motor movement to shoulder, wrist, and hand and receives messages from these areas. **Radial nerve** is part of this group and stimulates the wrist and hand.
Lumbar plexus	T12, L1–L4	Supplies motor movement to buttocks, anterior leg, and thighs and receives messages from these areas. **Femoral nerve** is part of this group and stimulates the hip and leg.
Sacral plexus	L4–L5, S1–S2	Supplies motor movement to posterior of leg and thighs and receives messages from these areas. **Sciatic nerve** is the largest nerve in the body and is part of this group. It passes through the gluteus maximus and down the back of the thigh and leg. It extends the hip and flexes the knee.

Figure A-31 The ANS controls the involuntary actions of the body; these are examples of the major body systems affected.

is the most complex of all. The following terms are a few of the more common words used in medical records relating to the nervous system.

Nerve: A cordlike structure comprising a collection of nerve fibers that convey an impulse; visible to the naked eye on x-rays.

CNS: Central nervous system; includes the brain and spinal cord.

ANS: Autonomic nervous system; the functional subdivision of the entire nervous system.

PNS: Peripheral nervous system; includes the cranial nerves arising from the brain and spine.

Ulnar nerve: Medial, lower arm nerve running along the ulna.

Radial nerve: Distal, lower arm nerve running along the radius.

Infraorbital nerve: The nerve lying under or on the floor of the orbit of the eye.

Greater occipital nerve: The nerve running along the back of the head from the crown of the head.

Femoral nerve: The nerve of the femur.

Buccal nerve: The nerve of the cheek.

The nervous system is controlled by the brain, which is the center of the entire system and coordinates and manages all bodily functions and activities. If the brain dies, the body dies.

The major structures of the nervous system are the brain, spinal cord, nerves, and the sensory organs. Because the nervous system is so complex, it is divided into subsystems, separating specific functions into specific systems. Those systems are the CNS, PNS, and ANS (see Figures A-32 and A-33).

Figure A-32
Cranial nerve composition and function

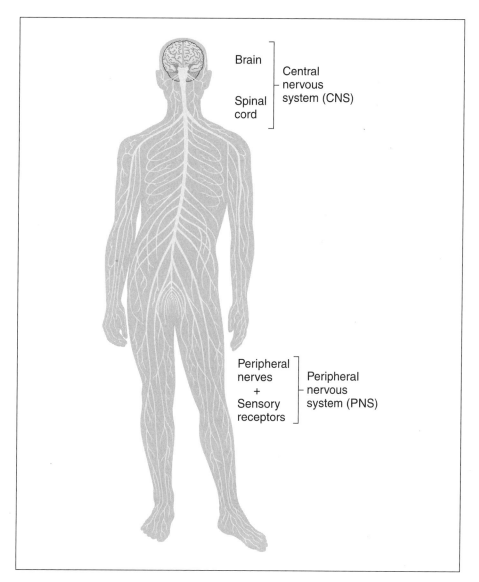

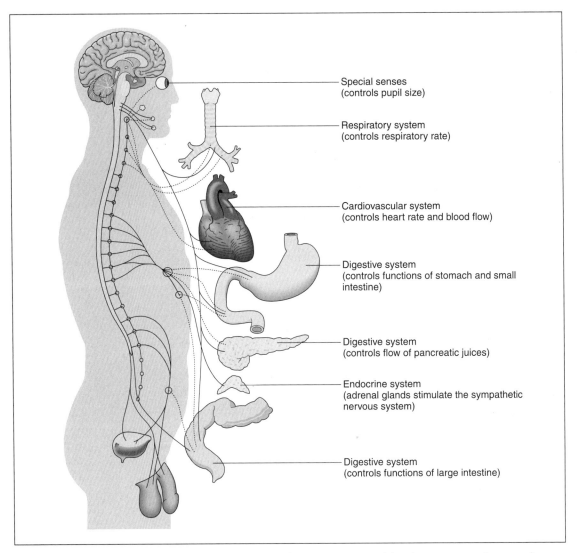

Figure A-33   The spinal cord and nerves. Most spinal nerves are named for the corresponding vertebrae.

⚖ SECTION 9   NERVES II

There are twelve pairs of cranial nerves, which come out of the inferior surface of the brain and pass through the opening of the skull (known as the foramen) into the head, neck, and torso. The cranial nerves are part of the PNS; are classified as either motor nerves, sensory nerves, or both; and are extremely fragile. Figure A-34 lists the cranial nerves, their classifications, and their functions.

Neurological damage that accompanies many head injuries can affect one or more of the cranial nerves, with symptoms of damage varying according to the nerve injured. The paralegal should understand which cranial nerves affect

Name/Cranial Nerve #	Composition (M = Motor S = Sensory)	Function
I. Olfactory	S	Smell
II. Optic	S	Sight
III. Oculomotor	MS	Eye movement, focusing, pupil changes, muscle sense
IV. Trochlear	MS	Sensory and motor function to the superior oblique (angular muscles of the eyes)
V. Trigeminal	MS	Conveys sensation from the head
VI. Abduceans	MS	Sensory and motor function to the lateral rectus (several straight muscles of the eye)
VII. Facial	MS	Small sensory division—taste for anterior two-thirds of the tongue. Large motor division—muscles of facial expression
VIII. Vestibulocochlear	S	Posture and hearing
IX. Glossopharyngeal	MS	Muscles for swallowing and taste for the posterior third of the tongue
X. Vagus	MS	A major component of the ANS; controls visceral muscle movement
XI. Accessory	M	Swallowing and head movement
XII. Hypoglossal	M	Speech and swallowing

Figure A-34 Spinal nerve plexes

which movements (as listed in Figure A-34), to increase his ability to evaluate medical records. Two examples of nerve damage are:

- No sensation of sweet tastes on the tip of the tongue indicates injury to cranial nerve VII or facial nerve IX (glossopharyngeal).
- Difficulty swallowing indicates injury to cranial nerve IX (glossopharyngeal) or nerve XI (accessory).

Most nerve injury cases will relate to the PNS and one or more cranial nerves. For instance, a whiplash injury may cause the brain to hit the back of the skull and damage the vagus and accessory nerves. Damage to these nerves may cause difficulty in visceral muscle movement, relating to muscles like the heart, intestine, and stomach (vagus nerve) or large muscle movement in facial expression (facial nerve). The PNS is especially important when assessing damages during an interview with a client who has suffered a head injury and is experiencing difficulty in using any of the muscles connected to one of the cranial nerves.

SECTION 10   ORGANS AND BODY SYSTEMS

The tissues and organs of the body are arranged into systems (see Figure A-35), with each system performing a specific function (see Figure A-36). Each of the organ systems relates to a specific organ and its function, such as respiratory, nervous, digestive, and circulatory. An *organ* is a relatively independent part of the body that performs a special function or functions; major organs include the lungs, brain, stomach, and kidney.

Figure A-35
The human body as organs and systems

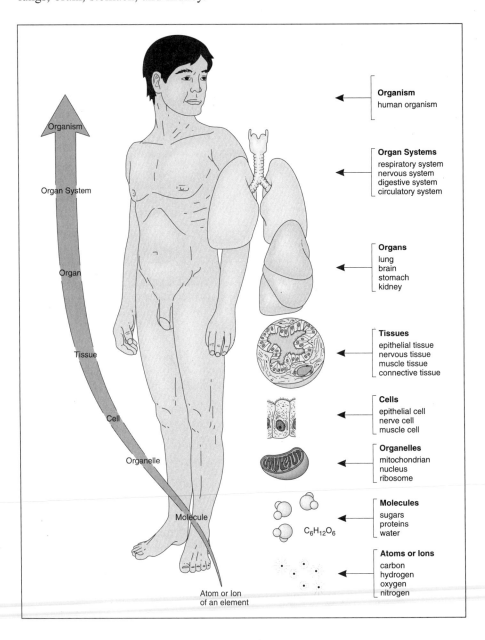

System	System Functions	Organs
Skeletal	Gives shape to body; protects delicate parts of body; provides space for attaching muscles; is instrumental in forming blood; stores minerals.	Skull, Spinal column, Ribs and Sternum, Shoulder Girdle, Upper and Lower Extremities, Pelvic Girdle.
Muscular	Determines posture; produces body heat; provides for movement.	Striated Voluntary Muscles—Skeletal Striated Involuntary—Cardiac Smooth—Nonstriated.
Digestive	Prepares food for absorption and use by body cells through modification of chemical and physical states.	Mouth (salivary glands, teeth, tongue), Pharynx, Esophagus, Stomach, Intestines, Liver, Gallbladder, Pancreas.
Respiratory	Acquires oxygen; rids body of carbon dioxide.	Nose, Pharynx, Larynx, Trachea, Bronchi, Lungs.
Circulatory	Carries oxygen and nourishment to cells of body; carries waste from cells; body defense.	Heart, Arteries, Veins, Capillaries, Lymphatic Vessels, Lymph Nodes, Spleen.
Excretory	Removes waste products of metabolism from body.	Skin, Lungs, Kidneys, Bladder, Ureters, Urethra.
Nervous	Communicates; controls body activity; coordinates body activity.	Brain, Nerves, Spinal Cord, Ganglia.
Endocrine	Manufactures hormones to regulate organ activity.	Glands (ductless): Pituitary, Thyroid, Parathyroid, Pancreas, Adrenal, Gonads (ovaries, testes).
Reproductive	Reproduces human beings.	*Male* *Female* Testes Ovaries Scrotum Fallopian tubes Epididymis Uterus Vas deferens Vagina Seminal vesicles Bartholin glands Ejaculatory duct External genitals Prostate gland (vulva) Cowper's gland Breasts Penis (mammary Urethra glands)
Integumentary	Helps regulate body temperature, establishes a barrier between the body and environment; eliminates waste; synthesizes Vitamin D; contains receptors for temperature, pressure, and pain.	Epidermis, Dermis, Sweat Glands, Oil Glands.

Figure A-36 The ten body systems

A *tissue* is collection or layer of specialized cells that link together to perform a specific function. The human body contains:

- Nervous tissue.
- Muscle tissue.
- Connective tissue, which holds the organs of the body in place and binds the body parts together (bones and cartilage are connective tissue, as is fat).
- Epithelial tissue (more commonly called skin), which is divided into two general categories—epithelium (outer layer of skin covering the external surfaces) and endothelium (lining the internal organs and blood vessels).

Histology is the study of tissue.

SECTION 11   DISEASES

The two main categories of diseases are:

1. *Infectious diseases,* caused by pathogenic organisms (bacteria and viruses). Viruses are remarkably small infectious agents that grow once they have invaded living cells. Examples of infectious diseases include mumps, chickenpox, rabies, herpes, and strep throat.

2. *Communicable diseases* (contagious diseases), caused by the transmission of a contaminant from one person to another or from contact with a contaminated object.

There are also diseases of genetic origin, not caused by microorganisms, including Alzheimer's disease and glaucoma. Most common diseases encountered in civil litigation are related to an injury, the stress of an injury, or emotional stress relating to the cause of action (see Figure A-37). The paralegal will also encounter medical specialists of many kinds; several are listed in Figure A-38.

Disease	Description
Asthma	Common in smokers and in urban or industrialized areas, as are other lung diseases. Respiratory problems are now becoming a focal issue in civil litigation. Asthma involves wheezing and breathlessness. It varies in intensity and is caused by the constriction of airways. Allergic asthma often develops in childhood and may be accompanied by eczema (a skin condition). Lung function tests are used to confirm asthma and skin and blood tests are used to identify the triggering substances.
Bronchitis	Recurring acute bronchitis may be caused by a virus or bacterium; however, smoking and chemical irritants are the most common cause. In the beginning the patient suffers from a cough during the damp, cold months, but eventually the cough continues all year through. Symptoms include hoarseness and breathlessness.

Figure A-37   Common diseases

Disease	Description
Emphysema	With this incurable respiratory disease, the alveoli, which are tiny air sacs that fill the lungs, are overstretched and rupture. Most people afflicted with emphysema are heavy, long-term smokers. However, there is a rare inherited enzyme deficiency risk factor.
Epilepsy	The cause of epilepsy is often unknown. It can be related to brain conditions like a tumor or abscess; or it can be initiated by a head injury, stroke, or chemical imbalance. One in 200 persons is affected by the repeated seizures of this disease. During a seizure the victim may become unconscious and make twitching movements for as long as several minutes. Seizures vary in severity.
Gastritis	An inflammation of the stomach lining; it is very painful. Causes include irritation from alcohol, nonsteroidal anti-inflammatory drugs, and smoking tobacco. Recent medical research discovered that the *Helicobacter pylori* bacterium is another cause (particularly of ulcers). This disease may appear suddenly or develop slowly. Symptoms include nausea, upper abdominal pain, and indigestion.
Hepatitis	Hepatitis or liver inflammation is commonly caused by a viral infection. This is especially true with hepatitis A. Viral hepatitis is acute and short-lived. Chronic strains of the disease (B or C) can lead to cirrhosis and increased risk of liver cancer.
Inflammatory bowel disease	Includes ulcerative colitis and Crohn's disease. Both of these conditions result in chronic intestinal inflammation. Fever, chills, diarrhea, constipation, pain, and rectal bleeding are symptoms. The condition may be caused by the immune system attacking the body's own tissues and it may be genetically predisposed in families. It is not uncommon to see this problem in persons suffering from high levels of stress.
Irritable colon syndrome	Irritable colon syndrome may affect up to 40% of the population; however, few people seek medical treatment for the problem. This chronic condition results from a disturbance of muscular movement within the large intestine. Symptoms include constipation and diarrhea, gas, bloating, and abdominal pain and can be aggravated by anxiety.
Migraine	Migraine headaches are a continual problem for 10% of the population. There are many forms of migraines, many of which include symptoms of pain, dizziness, and visual disturbances. Sometimes the victim even experiences nausea and vomiting. Complicated migraines may cause disturbance of brain function. Symptoms of this condition are linked to changes in the diameter of blood vessels.
Peptic ulcer	Smoking, stress, alcohol, and family history all contribute to the development of peptic ulcers. The primary symptom is recurring upper abdominal pain, relieved by eating or ingesting antacids.

Figure A-37   (*continued*)

Disease	Description
Pneumonia	The development of pneumonia begins when the bronchioles and alveolar tissue become inflamed. Early symptoms include chills, fever, sweating, joint and muscle pain, and headache. Chest pain, coughing, and breathlessness may also occur. Pneumonia usually results from a viral or bacterial infection and may be related to a separate ongoing respiratory or immune system condition.

Figure A-37   *(continued)*

Medical Specialties	Definition
Bariatrics (*bar*-ee-**AT**-ricks)	The study of obesity, its causes, prevention, and treatment.
Cardiologist (*kar*-dee-**OL**-uh-jist)	A specialist in the diagnosis and treatment of abnormalities, diseases, and disorders of the heart.
Chiropractor (**KYE**-roh-*prack*-tor)	A person who holds a Doctor of Chiropractic degree, also known as a D.C.; specializes in manipulating the spine to treat disorders and misalignments of the spine.
Endocrinologist (*en*-doh-krih-**NOL**-uh-jist)	A specialist in the diagnosis and treatment of diseases or malfunctions of the glands of internal secretion.
Gastroenterologist (*gas*-troh-*en*-ter-**OL**-uh-jist)	A specialist in the diagnosis and treatment of disorders and diseases of the stomach and intestines.
Hematologist (*hem*-uh-**TOL**-uh-jist)	A specialist in the diagnosis and treatment of disorders and diseases of the blood.
Internist	A specialist in the field of internal organs.
Neurologist (new-**ROL**-uh-jist)	A specialist in the diagnosis and treatment of disorders and diseases of the nervous system.
Urologist (you-**ROL**-uh-jist)	A specialist in the diagnosis and treatment of disorders and diseases of the female urinary system and the male genitourinary system.

Figure A-38   Medical specialties

SELF-TEST

Section One

Using Figure A-39, match each of the following to the appropriate body location or part.

1. Coronal plane
2. Mandible
3. Talus
4. Phalanges
5. Radius
6. Deltoid muscle
7. Gracilis muscle
8. Trapezius muscle
9. Occipital muscle
10. Buccinator muscle

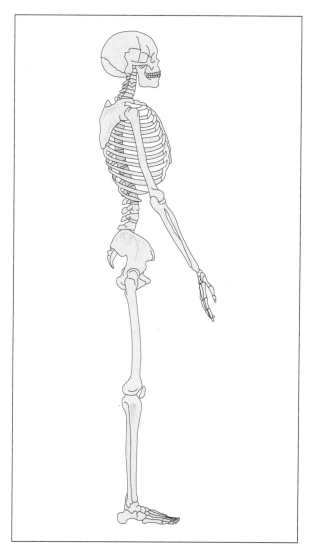

Figure A-39

Section Two

Interpret the following medical record. Explain as much of the report as you understand. Once you have summarized the report, define the terms printed in bold within it. Review your answers against this appendix to locate any missing or incorrect information.

After informed consent was obtained, the patient was taken to the Operating Room and placed **supine** on the operating table, where general anesthesia was induced without difficulty. A well-padded tourniquet was placed about the **proximal** right thigh and the right **lower extremity** was prepped and draped in a sterile fashion. One gram of Ancef was given intravenously and a foam wedge was placed beneath the right lower extremity to provide for internal rotation of the limb. After a brief period of limb elevation, the tourniquet was inflated to 30 mmHg for the 57-minute procedure. Longitudinal incision was made over the **lateral** aspect of the ankle over the subcutaneous margin of the **fibula**. Blunt dissection then continued to the lateral fibular cortex. The **fracture** was identified and fracture hematoma evacuated. Soft tissue was cleared from the fracture site and the fracture was reduced with the aid of bone-holding clamps. A 3.5 mm A-O cortical screw was placed in a lag fashion to hold the fracture in a reduced position and a 6-hole $\frac{1}{3}$ tubular plate was then bent appropriately and applied to the lateral fibular cortex with 3.5 mm cortical screws. Intraoperative mortise and lateral view radiographs were taken which showed anatomic reduction of the fracture and the ankle mortise. One screw was slightly long and this was adjusted. The wound was then irrigated and closed with #2-O Vicryl in the subcutaneous tissues and staples used to close the skin. A sterile dressing was applied to the wound and a bulky Robert Jones dressing reinforced with plaster splints was applied to the leg. The patient was transferred to the Recovery Room in good condition, having tolerated the procedure well. No complications were noted.

Section Three
Describe the difference between the axial and appendicular skeletons.

_____

_____

_____

_____

Section Four
Label the vertebrae on Figure A-40.

Section Five
Define the following terms.

1. Histology _____

_____

2. Posterior_____

_____

3. Colles's fracture _____

_____

4. Spiral fracture _____

_____

5. Lateral malleolus_____

_____

Figure A-40

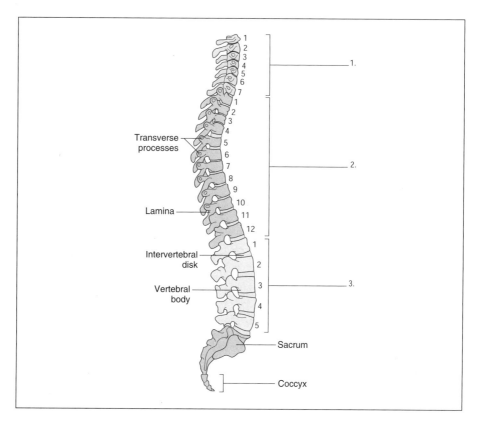

Transverse processes

Lamina

Intervertebral disk

Vertebral body

Sacrum

Coccyx

6. Pectoral girdle _____

   _____

7. Radial nerve _____

   _____

8. CNS _____

   _____

9. Transverse plane _____

   _____

SECTION 12 MEDICAL TERMINOLOGY I

Medical language is formed by joining word parts. There are three different types of word parts:

Prefix: This portion of the word usually, but not always, describes the location, time, number, or status of something. Example: *pre* or *post.*

Combining form: This usually, but not always, signifies a specific body part. Example: *cardio* (cardiac) or *neuro* (neurological).

Suffix: This usually, but not always, indicates the condition, disorder, disease, or procedure associated with the other "root" words. Example: *itis* (inflammation) or *ectomy* (surgical removal).

Figure A-41 is a table of some of the most common word parts used in medical terminology.

Prefix	Combining form	Suffix
AN (away from, negative, without)	ARTH/O (joint)	AC (pertaining to) [cardi**ac**]
AB (away from) [**ab**normal]	CARDI/O (heart, cardiac)	AL (pertaining to) [ren**al**]
AD (toward or in the direction of) [**ad**duction]	CYAN (bluish)	EAL (pertaining to) [esophag**eal**]
DYS (difficult, painful, bad) [**dys**function]	ERYTH/O (red)	IC (pertaining to) [gast**ric**]
EU (well, easy, good)	LEUK/O (white)	OUS (pertaining to) [cutane**ous**]
HYPER (over, above, increased)	MELAN/O (black)	ECTOMY (surgical removal) [cyst**ectomy**]
HYPO (below, under, decreased)	MY/O (muscle)	MEGALY (large or enlarged) [acro**megaly**]
INTER (between, among)	MYEL/O (bone marrow, spinal cord)	OLOGY (the study of) [hist**ology**]
INTRA (within, inside)	NEUR/O (nerve)	OTOMY (cutting into or a surgical incision) [lapar**otomy**]
PRE (before)	OSTE/O (bone)	OSIS (disease or abnormal condition) [nec**rosis**]
PERI (around, surrounding)	POLI/O (gray)	PLASTY (surgical repair) [rhino**plasty**]
POLY (many)		SCOPY (to see or a visual examination)
POST (after)		MIA/IA (condition) [leuke**mia**]
OLIG/O (few, scant, little)		
SUB (under, less, below)		
Super or SUPRA (above, excessive, beyond)		

Figure A-41   Common word parts for medical terminology

SECTION 13 MEDICAL TERMINOLOGY II

Figure A-42 lists the most common medical terms as they relate to one another and apply to all aspects of medicine. Follow the table in order to understand the way the terms relate to one another.

Term	Definition
Diagnosis	The determination of the nature of a cause of disease.
Differential diagnosis	The attempt to determine which of several possible diseases may be producing symptoms.
Prognosis	A forecast or prediction of the probable process and/or outcome of a disorder.
Sign	Evidence of a disease (such as a fever) that can be observed by the patient and others. A sign is objective, as others can evaluate it.
Symptom	A subjective indicator of a condition or problem (such as a headache or pain) that can be evaluated only by the patient.
Syndrome	The set of signs and symptoms that happen together as part of a disease process.
Acute	A disease or symptom that occurs quickly at the beginning of the illness, is severe, and has a relatively short duration.
Chronic	A symptom or disease that lasts for a long time.
Remission	The partial or complete disappearance of symptoms of a chronic or malignant disease. Usually temporary.
Endemic	The ongoing presence of a particular disease with a group of people, population, or geographic location.
Epidemic	A sudden, widespread outbreak of a particular disease in a geographic location and the population inhabiting that location.
Pandemic	The worldwide occurrence of a disease, or the occurrence of a disease over a large geographical area.

Figure A-42 Common medical terms

Terms of pharmacology are often used in civil litigation and require an understanding of basic prescription and over-the-counter drugs. A *prescription drug* is a medicine legally purchased only with a prescription from an appropriately licensed doctor or dentist. An *over-the-counter drug* is widely available to the public. Figure A-43 is a table of the most important terms relating to prescription drugs.

Figure A-43
Common terms relating
to prescription drug use

Instruction	Meaning
a.c.	Before meals
ad lib.	As desired
b.i.d.	Twice a day
c	with
NPO	Nothing by mouth
p.c.	After meals
p.r.n.	As needed
p.o.	By mouth
q.d.	Every day
q.h.	Every hour
q.i.d.	Four times a day
t.i.d.	three times a day

⚖ ANSWER KEY

Page 380:

1. Your tonsils are <u>internal or posterior</u> to your teeth.

2. Your buttock is <u>inferior</u> to your navel, but is <u>superior</u> to your feet.

3. Your thumb is <u>distal</u> in relation to your little finger.

Page 391:

1. Name the heel bone. <u>calcaneus</u>

2. Identify the bone of the upper arm. <u>humerus</u>

3. Who will most likely suffer a Colles's fracture, and why? <u>All persons; these fractures commonly occur when people slip and fall and use their arms to catch themselves.</u>

4. The tibia is what direction (use the correct anatomical term) from the fibula? <u>anterior</u>

5. What is the difference between a metatarsal and a metacarpal? <u>The metatarsal is a toe bone and the metacarpal is a finger bone.</u>

Page 396–398:

All labeling and definitions can be identified as correct or not by consulting the many figures presented in this text.

Short Answer:

1. The head is <u>superior</u> to the feet.
2. The anatomical position means the person is standing <u>facing forward, with the palms of the hands forward</u>.
3. There are <u>eight</u> bones in the skull.
4. Flat bones are usually bones like the <u>ribs</u>.
5. The lumbar vertebrae follow the <u>thoracic</u> vertebrae when moving inferiorly on the spine.
6. There are <u>five</u> lumbar vertebrae.
7. Ribs numbered 11–12 are considered floating because <u>they are not attached to the sternum</u>.
8. The two girdles in the human body are <u>the pectoral girdle</u> and <u>the pelvic girdle</u>.
9. Compound fractures are sometimes gruesome because <u>the bone comes through the skin</u>.
10. After slamming into the steering wheel of her car, the victim suffered severe bruising of the muscles of her stomach, also known as the <u>abdominals</u>.

Page 411–413:

All labeling can be identified as correct or not by consulting the various figures throughout this appendix.

The terms to be defined, both in the sample medical record and in straight definition questions, can be identified as correct or not by consulting the material in this appendix.

--- **NOTES** ---

1 Information in this section is based on Ann Senisi Scott and Elizabeth Fong, *Body Structures & Functions* 9th ed. (Delmar Publishers, 1998).

2 *Id.*

BIBLIOGRAPHY

Andrews, K. "Legal Interviewing & Information Discovery." 7 *Legal Assistant Today* 36, 40 (July/August 1990).

Ashley, B. "Constructing the Case." Seminar materials (Lambert & Boeder, Wayzato, MN).

Baker, J. *Traffic-Accident Investigation Manual* (Northwestern University Traffic Institute, 1979).

"Bank's liability, under state law, for disclosing financial information concerning depositor or customer." 81 A.L.R.4th 378 (1990).

Barge, J. "Is Technology Taking Away Paralegal Jobs?: Or simply making it necessary for paralegals to move beyond word processing?" 13 *Legal Assistant Today* 5 (May/June 1996).

Binder, David, and Paul Bergman. *Fact Investigation* (West, 1984).

Binder, David, and S. Price. *Legal Interviewing and Counseling* (West, 1977).

Blanchard, R. *Litigation and Trial Practice for the Legal Paraprofessional* (West, 1982).

Breslauer, S., D. Crosby, and S. Easter. *Document Organization, Management and Production* (Professional Education Systems, Inc., 1988).

Brookes, D., C. Evans, R. Leiter, and B. Roper. "The Best Legal Software for Paralegals." 13 *Legal Assistant Today* 5 (May/June 1996).

Cherban, John T. *Interviewing in Depth: The Interactive-Relational Approach* (Sage, 1996).

Cohn, S. "Beyond the 'Chinese Wall.' " 13 *Legal Assistant Today* 1 (November/December 1995).

"Damages" 22 Am. Jur. 2d 32–57, 62–67, 664–65, 672–77, 742–45, 754–57, 782–89, 794–809, 816–37, 870–73 (1988).

"Defamation: Privilege Accorded State or Local Governmental Administrative Records Relating to Private Individual Member of Public." 40 A.L.R.4th 318 (1990).

Dillion, J. T. *The Practice of Questioning* (Routledge, 1990).

"Discovery and Disclosure." *Reference Manual on Scientific Evidence: Management of Expert Evidence* (_____, 19__).

"Dockets and Calendars." 75 Am. Jur. 2d 286–89 (1976).

Dohrenwend, Barbara Snell. "Some Effects of Open and Closed Questions on Respondent's Answers." 24 *Human Organizations* 175–84 (1964).

Dohrenwend, Barbara Snell, and Stephen Richardson. "A Use for Leading Questions in Research Interviewing." 23 *Human Organizations* 76–77 (1964).

Downs, Cal. W., G. Paul Smeyak, and Ernest Martin. *Professional Interviewing* (Harper & Row, 1980).

Ehrick, A. *Medical Terminology for Health Professionals.* 3d ed. (Delmar, 1997).

Eyers, P. "ABCs of Databases: Full-text or abstract—it depends what you're looking for." 14 *Legal Assistant Today* 1 (September/October 1996).

Gair, H. "Selecting and Preparing Expert Witnesses." 2 Am. Jur. *Trials* 585–667 (1964 & Supp. 1998).

Gallup, George. "The Quintamensional Plan of Question Design." 11 *Public Opinion Quarterly* 384–93 (1947).

Gorden, Raymond L. *Interviewing Strategy, Technique, and Tactics.* 4th ed. (Dorsey Press, 1980).

Gross, I. "Locating and Interviewing Witnesses." 2 Am. Jur. *Trials* 264–65 (1964).

Gross, I. "Locating Public Records." 2 Am. Jur. *Trials* 414 (1987).

Gulbis, V. "Construction and Application, Under State Law, of Doctrine of 'Executive Privilege.' " 10 A.L.R.4th 355 (1990).

Herman, R. "Stop ... Look ... Listen: Interviewing and Choosing Clients." *Trial* 48 (June 1995).

Hunt, S. "The Case Reference Manual: A valuable key to information management." 13 *Legal Assistant Today* 3 (January/February 1996).

Hunt, S. "Curtain Call: Selecting and Preparing Exhibits for Trial." 13 *Legal Assistant Today* 1 (September/October 1995).

Hunt, S. "Precision, Consistency and Thoroughness: The Art of Inputting Documents." 14 *Legal Assistant Today* 1 (September/October 1996).

"The Initial Conference." *Reference Manual on Scientific Evidence: Management of Expert Evidence* (_____, 19__).

"Investigations and Surveillance, Shadowing and Trailing, as Violation of Right of Privacy." 13 A.L.R.3d 1025 (1990).

"Judgments." 46 Am. Jur. 2d 372–99, 406–13, 418–27, 436–51, 452–73, 476–79, 486–89, 494–99, 502–05, 512–45, 552–53, 654–57, 678–87, 716–19, 730–33, 748–57 (1994).

Klein, R. "Winning Cases with Body Language: Moving Toward Courtroom Success." *Trial* 82 (July 1995).

Krivonos, Paul D., and Mark L. Knapp. "Initiating Communication: What Do You Say When You Say Hello?" 26 *Central States Speech Journal* 115–25 (1975).

Lang, D. "Emotions: How to Read Body Language." 110 *Ladies Home Journal* 67 (No. 67, June 1993).

Leiter, R. "The Art of On-line Factual Discovery: Going beyond traditional legal research." 13 *Legal Assistant Today* 1 (September/October 1995).

Lewis, M. "Feelings: Body Language, How to Tell What Others Are Really Thinking." 36 *New Choices* 95 (October 1996).

Littlejohn, Stephen W. *Theories of Human Communication.* 2d ed. (Wadsworth, 1996).

Lynton, Jonathan. *Ballentine's Legal Dictionary and Thesaurus* (Delmar 1995).

Magarick, P. "Investigating the Civil Case: General Principles." 1 Am. Jur. *Trials* 361 (1987).

Marvel, C. "Telephone Company's Liability for Disclosure of Number or Address of Subscriber Holding Unlisted Number." 1 A.L.R.4th 218 (1990).

Miro, A. "Ten Thousand Documents ... and Counting: The mechanics of project control and database design." 13 *Legal Assistant Today* 4 (March/April 1996).

National Association of Legal Assistants. *Code of Ethics and Professional Responsibility* (1990).

Orlik, D. *Ethics for the Legal Assistant.* 3d ed. (Marlen Hill Publishing, 1994).

Payne, Stanley L. *The Art of Asking Questions* (Princeton University Press, 1951).

"Privacy." 62A Am. Jur. 2d 672-829 (1990 & Supp. 1998).

"Records and Recording Laws." 66 Am. Jur. 2d 342–455 (1973 & Supp. 1998).

Statsky, William. *Introduction to Paralegalism: Perspectives, Problems, and Skills.* 2d ed. (West, 1982).

Statsky, William. *West's Legal Thesaurus/ Dictionary* (West, 1985).

Stearn, G. "Dealing with Difficult Clients: And what to do about them." 13 *Legal Assistant Today* 4 (March/April 1996).

Stewart, Charles, and William Cash, Jr. *Interviewing Principles & Practices.* 8th ed. (McGraw-Hill, 1997).

Thorp, E. "How to Locate Elusive Witnesses." 8 *Legal Assistant Today* 60, 64 (November/December 1990).

"Trial." 75 Am. Jur. 2d 232–77, 544–77 (1991 & Supp. 1998).

"The Unauthorized Practice of Law." 8 *Journal of Paralegal Education and Practice* 22 (1991).

Van De Graaff, K. *Human Anatomy.* 3d ed. (Wm. C. Brown Publishers, 1988).

Williams, J. "Regulation of Private Detectives, Private Investigators, and Security Agencies." 86 A.L.R.3d 691 (1990).

Williams-Morton, Jean. *Interviewer Approaches* (Darmouth, 1993).

"Witnesses." 81 Am. Jur. 2d 96–101, 176–205, 274–75, 476–87, 622–37, 706–17, 820–23, 840–55 (1992 & Supp. 1998).

Zalewski, D. *Paralegal Discovery* (Cross, 1987).

GLOSSARY

abstract (database) A document management system that requires all documents to be reviewed and abstracted into preselected categories or fields, such as topics, dates, names, and type of documents. All documents are reviewed, numbered, and abstracted, and the information correlating to the document is then entered into the database system.

abstract of judgment A summary of the court's judgment used in postjudgment collections work.

active listening The process of receiving a person's oral communication and feeding it back (rebounding it) by using reflective statements that reflect what has been said.

actual damages Compensatory damages for actual loss or injury; damages in satisfaction of, or in recompense for, loss or injury actually sustained; all damages other than punitive or exemplary damages. *See* compensatory damages.

adjudicated facts Facts (in dispute before an administrative agency) about the parties, their activities, business, and property. Adjudicated facts usually answer the questions of who did what, where, when, how, why, and with what motive and intent.

admissible Pertaining to that which can be allowed because it is relevant or pertinent to the matter at hand and should be considered … . Whether it is true or false will be determined separately.

affidavit of authenticity A sworn statement made by the holder or owner of records or documents, attesting to the originality and authentication of the documents.

affidavit of registration A sworn statement issued by the secretary of state's office (in some states) verifying that a particular company or entity is registered for business in that state.

affirmative evidence Evidence that supports a party's position in a case.

affirmative feedback Positively rebounding or reflecting information being provided by a witness or client during an interview.

agency records Official documents or recording of a public agency, whether state or federal, that are required to be produced to the public.

assessment rolls A listing of property information, both secured and unsecured, that outlines the name and address of the property owner, interest in the property, improvements, leaseholds, and the like. Some assessment rolls are closed because of confidentiality requirements.

authorization Empowerment; power given to another party in a litigated matter to gather personal, private, or confidential records (e.g., medical records, employment records, Social Security records).

backtracking A memory stimulation method used when interviewing witnesses or the client. The witness is asked to regress through the events of a certain period of time, in sequence, to recall missing details of a story.

balancing method The method used by judges to determine whether information in a private record will be released; this process allows the judge to balance the benefit of releasing the information against the potential harm it may do.

bankers box A long, narrow cardboard box that resembles a single file-cabinet drawer, used to store documents in law firms and other businesses.

Bates stamp A numerical code applied manually to documents and pleadings produced in litigation. In this system, the numbering sequence is generally six digits deep and can be prefaced by alpha characters when needed. The numbering is commonly found in the lower right-hand corner of the document.

best evidence rule   A rule of evidence requiring that a party produce the most reliable proof of a fact that is available. For example, if a painting is available as evidence, a photograph of the painting will not always be adequate.

bipolar question   A question designed to elicit a yes or no response.

block books (plats)   Large books that contain a map of every block, the size of the numbered or lettered parcels or lots, and the name of the person to whom taxes are assessed in a given urban area. Through block book, the names of adjacent streets in a given area are obtainable.

boilerplate language   Standard language in legal documents that is identical in documents of a like nature; language often used in documents having a definite meaning in the same context without variation (two thirds of the deed is boilerplate). Uniform language, stereotyped language, accepted language, conventional language, standardized language, customary language, stock language.

case checklist   An organizational tool used to categorize and itemize a paralegal's case load.

cause of action   The fact or facts that give a person a right to judicial redress or relief against another; a legally acceptable reason for suing. May also be called *right of action, claim for relief, ground for relief.*

certificate of existence   An official record, provided by some secretaries of state's offices, that proves a corporation is in good standing. The certificate attests that a corporation has not been dissolved or suspended, and that its existence is not impaired.

certificate of good standing   A written assurance from the secretary of state's office, attesting that the corporation's payment of fees to the office is current.

certification   A formal assertion, usually in writing, of some fact … .

circumstantial evidence   Evidence of certain facts in a case from which the jury may infer other connected facts that usually and reasonably follow according to common experience.

closed question   Question that is restrictive by nature and asks for a specific piece of information; it allows the respondent to supply a variety of answers, but only in an interviewer-determined range. Closed questions vary in degree: some are only moderately closed, whereas others are very narrow in scope.

collateral evidence   Secondary evidence used to support primary or material evidence (e.g., weather reports are collateral evidence if they create a visual picture of the conditions influencing a triggering event).

common-ground technique   An interviewing technique used to identify commonalties between the paralegal/interviewer and the witness or client.

compensatory damages   Damages that will compensate the injured party for the injury sustained and nothing more. Damages that will make good or replace the loss caused by the wrong or injury. Includes out-of-pocket expenses, pain and suffering.

confidential   Pertaining to that which is done in confidence with the expectation of privacy.

counterclaim   A cause of action or claim asserted by one or more defendants against one or more plaintiffs in the same action.

credibility witness   A witness who saw, heard, or experienced something personally, relating to the believability of another witness, client, or party in the lawsuit, or relating to a specific piece of real evidence.

curriculum vita   A résumé (commonly used for expert witnesses).

damages   Monetary compensation that may be recovered in court by someone who has suffered injury or loss to person, to property, or to rights through an unlawful act or omission of another.

damnum absque injuria   A loss that does not give rise to an action for damages against the person causing it.

demonstrative evidence Evidence addressed directly to the senses apart from the testimony of witnesses; real evidence … .

deposition log An organizational tool used to manage the paralegal's deposition schedule for a particular case.

deposition timetable An adaptable organizational tool used to track the completion of tasks required for the conducting of a deposition. For instance, the chart will include if and when a subpoena was issued, served, and filed with the court.

direct evidence Evidence that, if believed, proves the existence of the fact in issue without using any inferences or presumptions; testimony from a witness who actually saw, heard, or touched the matter in question.

directive interview An interviewing style used when the interviewer intends to control the purpose, subject matter, formality, and/or pace of the interview. Closed and sometimes leading questions are used to draw out and direct specific answers from the interviewee.

docket A list or calendar of cases to be tried at a specified term of the court.

element A constituent part … .

event Something that happens; an occurrence.

evidence Any kind of proof (e.g., testimony, writings, demonstrations) offered to establish the existence or nonexistence of a fact in dispute.

evidence witness One who personally saw or perceived information relating to a specific piece of real evidence.

execution sale A sale of a debtor's property under the authority of a writ of execution by a sheriff or other ministerial officer. *See also* sheriff's sale.

exemplary damages Punitive damages; increased damages awarded to the plaintiff over and above what will compensate for his or her property loss, where the wrong was aggravated by circumstances of violence, oppression, malice, fraud, or wanton conduct of the defendant.

exempt property Property or money excused or released from collection; real or personal property freed from a duty.

expert testimony The opinion evidence of a person who possesses special skill or knowledge in some science, profession, or business that is not common to the average person.

expert witness A person who by reason of education or specialized experience possesses superior knowledge on a subject about which persons of no particular training are incapable of forming an accurate opinion or deducing correct conclusions.

explanatory hypothesis A hypothesis that provides an explanation of the events surrounding a triggering event and includes inferences in the explanation.

expunge To erase or eliminate.

fact That which is ascertained by the senses or by the testimony of witnesses describing what they perceived; an actual thing, event, action, circumstance, or phenomenon, affair, episode.

factual hypothesis A descriptive story; a potential story of the triggering event explaining what happened and why. The story is built based on inferences, past events, and information gathered from the client.

fear factor One of three elements making up the *silence factor;* the fear factor inhibits an interviewee from providing full details during an interview. The fear factor must be identified and dealt with if the interviewer is to uncover the information the witness holds.

Federal Register A daily publication that prints federal agency regulations and other legal documents of the executive branch, thereby making them available to the public. It includes proposed changes in rules, regulations, and standards on which the public is invited to submit commentary before final adoption.

feedback probe A probe or question that encourages the respondent to provide a better or more complete response when he or she refuses to answer a primary question, offers an irrelevant response to a primary question, or provides an incomplete response to a primary question. May be in the form of a restatement, a reflection, or a mirror.

fields   Topics or data headings that identify predetermined portions of a document to be entered into the computer. Examples include document date, document topic, and document author.

filtering question   A question that focuses on a respondent's knowledge of a topic by first defining the words in the question. When using this type of question, the interviewer "filters" out or identifies respondents' varying levels of knowledge on the subject matter at hand.

formal interview   A style of interviewing conducted during a preplanned meeting, which is commonly held in the law office. The interviewer sets the tone of the interview in a manner that implies a serious, and sometimes even rigid, nature.

foundation   … Basis or support … .

Freedom of Information Act (FOIA)   A federal statute making information held by federal agencies available to the public unless it falls within one or more categories, specified in the statute, that are exempt from public disclosure.

full-text database   A document management system that provides for full inputting of all documents. Every word of every document is input into the system, commonly with a scanner.

garnishee   A person against whom the process of garnishment is issued; a person who has property of the judgment debtor that is being reached or attached (garnished) by another.

garnishment   A statutory proceeding whereby a person's property or credits in the possession or under the control of another are applied to the former's debt to a third person; the satisfaction of an indebtedness out of property or credits of the debtor in the possession or owed by another … .

general-category identifier   The connecting component (company, neighbor, spouse) that provides information as to a general-category witness's identity.

general-category witness   A witness known only in a general capacity, rather than by name. Eventually the unnamed witness will be identified through a general-category identifier.

general damages   Damages accruing from a wrong, complained of because they are the immediate, direct, and proximate result of the injury. *See* compensatory damages.

hearsay   Testimony in court of a statement made by another out of court when the statement is being offered to assert the truth of the matter in the statement. The value of such a statement depends on the credibility of the out-of-court asserter, and admissibility is limited.

hostile witness   A witness who has an adverse relationship to a party in a lawsuit; a witness who manifests so much hostility or prejudice under examination that he or she can be treated as though called by the other side.

hypothesis   An assumption or theory to be proven or disproved.

immaterial   *See* irrelevant.

impeach   To attack; to accuse; to challenge the credibility of.

impeachment evidence   Evidence used to attack or diminish the credibility of a witness or party.

in camera   In private with the judge; in chambers; without spectators.

incompetent   Without ability, legal qualification, or fitness …

inductive reasoning   The act, process, or result of an instance of reasoning from a specific piece of data, from the particulars to the general. In investigation, this means drawing a logical conclusion from a specific detail or fact.

informal interview   An interviewing style used primarily by the paralegal as part of the informal investigation. This style is commonly employed while interviewing witnesses at the scene of a triggering event; with a witness who has agreed to speak with the paralegal but subsequently becomes hostile; when a witness is tentative about speaking; or when full details of the triggering event have not been gathered.

informational probe   Allows the interviewer to get additional information and/or explanations from the respondent; frequently begin with, "Tell me more about," or "Explain your point regarding _____ further."

injury   Any wrong or damage done to another; an invasion of a legally protected interest of another … .

interview   An interactional communication process that occurs between two persons, one of whom has a deliberate purpose for the meeting. The interview is identified by its nature, the asking and answering of questions.

interview guide   An organizational tool used for nonscheduled informal interviews. Its purpose tool is to identify the general goals of the interview and the relevant and/or adequate responses required from the interviewee.

interview outline   An organizational tool used by an interviewer to guide him or her through any interview, whether formal or informal. The outline focuses on certain topics and questions, but is neither rigid like the interview schedule nor loosely structured like the interview guide; it is a flexible and adaptable tool.

interview schedule   An organizational tool used to manage a formal interview. The schedule is designed to be rigid, outlining exact questions to be asked, how the questions will be asked, and the type and degree of answer expected. Such a tool may be used in a deposition.

investigative interview   A specific interview type that focuses on gathering information and details from witnesses.

investigative outline   An organizational tool that helps generate topics for specific inquiries instead of focusing on the recording of information. The outline functions as a guide during the investigation.

irrelevant   Not relating or applicable to the matter in issue; not tending to prove or disprove any issue of fact involved in the case.

judgment creditor   A person in whose favor a money judgment is entered or who becomes entitled to enforce it.

judgment debtor   A person who has yet to satisfy a judgment that has been rendered against him or her.

judicial notice   The recognition of certain facts (usually matters of common knowledge) that a court may take into consideration without requiring evidence to be introduced to establish the facts.

judicial sale   A sale based on a decree of a court directing the sale. *See also* sheriff's sale.

jurisdictional timetable   An organizational chart used for quick reference to the state, local, or federal authority having jurisdictional control over a case. For instance, Fed. R. Civ. P. 30 applies to depositions in federal court cases, but it is common practice to follow local authority for depositions in state court cases; therefore, the local rule is included in the timetable.

lay witness   A nonprofessional person who has no particular expertise in a specific topic area.

lead-in question   A type of question used as an introduction to a following, topically relevant question. It is not related to any of the objectives of the interview or subject matter, but rather sets the stage for respondents to provide the most accurate responses.

leading question   Question that suggests, implicitly or explicitly, the answer expected or desired. Because of the nature of such questions, the respondent commonly finds it easier (or tempting) to give the answer he or she thinks is desired rather than a genuine or honest response.

liquidated damages   The amount of the damages has been stipulated by the parties or has been ascertained by a judgment.

loaded question   The most extreme type of leading question; often appears to offer the respondent only a bipolar option for response and virtually dictates the "correct" answer. The use of loaded questions requires skill and careful planning.

logical sequence diagram (LSD)   The organizational product of the logical sequence procedure; a chart-style timeline that outlines the client's story of the triggering event.

logical sequence procedure   An investigative procedure used to understand the client's version of a triggering event and the evidence and witnesses that will influence the story.

manual tickler system   An organizational tool used to manage various litigation events and tasks; a calendar system using 3×5 index cards and color codes.

master document index   A record of the general number groupings used in any document production and the subsequent management of those documents. The numbering system identifies documents both produced and received; the master document index shows who produced what documents and any special circumstances relating to the documents.

material fact   An influencing fact; a fact that induced the action or inaction; an essential fact; a fact likely to affect the result.

mechanic's lien   A security interest (in the nature of a mortgage) created by law on real property and the improvements thereon to secure those persons who have furnished labor or materials for the erection of structures or for the making of improvements on the real property.

micro-expression   An unconscious facial posture that appears briefly and is quickly removed; a signal that the interviewee is trying to hide a feeling.

mirror probe   Probe that summarizes the answers on a specific topic; used to help the interviewer ensure that she or he has understood a series of answers correctly.

mitigate   To render less painful or severe.

mitigating circumstances   Circumstances surrounding the commission of an act, which in fairness can be considered as extenuating or reducing the severity or degree of moral culpability of the act, but do not serve to excuse or justify it.

name index   A public-record reference tool, compiled by a county or city, that lists property by owner's name. Name indexes are usually revised annually and provide access to information in assessment rolls, block books, sale books, and county maps, all of which serve as cross-references to each other.

no-fault insurance   A type of automobile insurance in which each person's own insurance company pays for injury or damages up to a certain limit regardless of whether its insured was actually at fault.

nondirective interview   An interviewing style that allows the interviewee to control the purpose, subject matter, formality, or pace of the interview. Open-ended and neutral questions are used to maximize the interviewee's responses.

nudging probe   A simple and brief statement or question, often used in conjunction with a *silent probe,* that urges the respondent to elaborate on or continue an answer to a primary question.

objective question   Question that focuses on observable events, such as actions and statements; on physical surroundings; and on the dress and manner of persons.

offer of proof   Telling the court what evidence a party proposes to present in order to obtain a ruling on admissibility.

open question   Broad question that often directs the respondent to focus on nothing more than a topic; allows the respondent to freely determine how much and what kind of information to provide.

opinion   ... 2. A belief or conclusion not proven by complete or positive knowledge by appearing to the witness to be true, based on his or her own ideas and thinking ... .

parroting   The act of restating what has been said by the respondent in a way that is perceived to be negative or mocking.

per diem interest By the day; an allowance or amount of so much interest charge per day.

personal data notebook A tool created to manage information source lists, such as phone numbers of commonly contacted courthouse personnel, and research data. Its purpose is to allow the paralegal to log and record valuable data as his or her career progresses, and to avoid repeating research unnecessarily.

physical evidence *See* real evidence.

presumptions An assumption of fact that a rule of law requires to be assumed from another fact or group of facts that have been established … .

primary question Question that introduces a topic or new subject within a topic; stands alone when taken out of the interview context.

privileged Protected from forced disclosure by virtue of a special relationship.

probative evidence Evidence that furnishes, establishes, or contributes toward proof.

probative value Tending to prove an issue; carrying a quality of proof.

proximate probability A creative investigation theory used as a tool to make assumptions and inferences as to probable witnesses or evidence in a case. Proximate probability is used with timelines and the logical sequence procedure.

public record Record that a governmental unit is required by law to keep or that it finds necessary to keep to discharge its duties imposed by law.

punitive damages *See* exemplary damages.

real evidence Evidence furnished by things themselves on view or inspection, as opposed to a description of them from the testimony of a witness.

reasonable person standard A measure of what a fictitious person of ordinary prudence would do or not do under the circumstances.

rebuttal evidence Evidence given to explain, counteract, or disprove facts given in evidence by the other side.

record (n.) A written account of some act or event (e.g., court records); … [t]he available facts (e.g., employment record).

reflective probe Probing question that repeats ("reflects") the answer received; acts to check the interviewer's accuracy in recording and understanding the information given.

relevant Applying to the matter in question; having a logical tendency to prove or disprove a material fact; having the tendency of making the existence of a fact more probable or less probable than it would otherwise be … .

restatement probe A tool used when the respondent does not completely answer a primary question or fails to answer the primary question at all. The restatement probe simply restates the original primary question, but uses voice inflection or a slight rephrasing of the question to emphasize the information requested.

sale books Regarding researching the sale of property, records used to record the name of the purchaser, the subject of a particular sale, and the date of recordation of the instrument of conveyance. These books are maintained by location of the property, not by purchaser's name.

secondary question Question that probes the respondent for more detail than a primary question does; a follow-up question.

secured rolls A part of a county's assessment rolls that are generally open to the public and available in the county assessor's office upon request. The secured roll catalogues property on which the assessed taxes constitute liens.

sheriff's sale A sale of real property carried out by the sheriff under a court order (writ of execution or other court decree).

silence factor A characteristic of the interviewee that inhibits him or her from fully disclosing all the information he or she may know regarding a specific subject matter or topic. Often the interviewer will be alerted to a silence factor by nonverbal communication or simply by the interviewee's hesitancy to discuss a topic.

silent probe   Using nonverbal communication, encourages the respondent to complete an answer or respond when hesitant to answer a primary question based on the subject matter of the question. Often used in conjunction with *nudging probes.*

special damages   Damages that are peculiar to the particular plaintiff; damages that are the natural, but not the necessary, result of the injury complained of.

Statute of Frauds   [Doctrine, embodied in some state statutes, holding that n]o suit or action shall be maintained on certain classes of contracts or engagements unless there shall be a note or memorandum thereof in writing, signed by the party to be charged or by his or her authorized agent.

street index   A public-record reference tool, compiled by a county or city, that lists property by street name.

subjective question   Question that focuses on the respondent's thoughts and feelings, and his or her inferences about others' thoughts and feelings.

subrogation   The substitution of a third party in place of a party having a claim, demand, or right against another party.

substantive evidence   Such evidence that a reasonable mind might accept as adequate to support a conclusion.

survey interview   An type of interview used in many fields, including research, law, politics, medicine, and others. Its purpose is to establish a solid base of fact from which to draw conclusions, make inferences, and determine any future courses of action.

sweeping probe   Question that seeks any information the respondent may have that has not already been given; commonly used during the closing of an interview. (Example: "Have I missed anything that you can think of?")

testimony   Evidence given by a competent witness under oath or affirmation.

tickler system   A memorandum or reference work maintained to jog memories about happenings and events.

topic   Deals with a particular subject matter involved in an investigation. A topic is distinguished from an *event* when creating questions for a story outline. Questions created for a topical probe seek information relating specific times when the object of the subject matter occurred (e.g., the filing of unemployment claims: unemployment records are the topic, the dates of filing of the claims are the events).

translator's affidavit   A written or printed declaration or statement of facts, created by or signed by a translator who is assisting in a legal interview, made voluntarily and confirmed under oath; a sworn statement or declaration under oath.

ultimate facts   Facts essential to a cause of action or a defense; the facts on which the ultimate decision rests.

unsecured rolls   A part of a county's assessment rolls that are generally open to the public and available in the county assessor's office upon request. The unsecured rolls list personal property that is not taxed and therefore has no formal liens against it.

wandering   An interviewing term used to describe an interviewee's attempt to avoid a specific topic or subject matter by diverting the interview to a new direction or going off on tangents. Wandering is not always negative, as it may lead to new and undisclosed details; however, if wandering is used as a means of hiding information, the interviewer must confront and redirect the interviewee in a tactful manner.

witness report   An investigative tool used to document the data obtained from a witness during an interview.

writ of execution   The process of carrying into effect the decisions in a decree or judgment; a court officer, e.g., sheriff, is commanded to take the property of the losing litigant in order to satisfy the judgment debt.

INDEX